Humanistic Management, Organisation, and Aesthetics

The book is the first worldwide publication of a complex theory of management aesthetics in humanistic management based on the aesthetics and arts approach allowing for a complete and systemic understanding of the management art and art management phenomena. The methodology is based on the critical literature review and empirical research applying qualitative, quantitative, and autoethnographic approaches. The main goal of this monograph is to create a holistic model that organises the issues of management aesthetics and shows the interdependence of the components of this model. The role of this model should be to perform a central function for a complete and systemic understanding of the phenomenon of management aesthetics, as well as to perform the function of a field based on which analysis of individual issues in the area of management aesthetics is conducted. The critical component of this holistic model is Maria Gołaszewska's theory of the aesthetic situation. Two theses of the book are the following: (1) the theory of aesthetics and artistic practice have the potential to enrich the theory and practice of management with qualitative components through deep immersion in the world of values; and (2) management theory and practice have the potential to enrich the theory of aesthetics and artistic practice with efficiency components.

Michał Szostak is Associate Professor of Management and Head of the Institute for Management Research at Collegium Civitas in Warsaw, scientifically focused on humanistic management and management aesthetics. He conducts extensive teaching activities on academic levels in Polish, Czech, Slovak, and Lithuanian universities. He is Doctor of Musical Arts in organ performance and plays dozens of recitals worldwide annually. He is a business practitioner in top management positions in capital groups in an international environment in the commercial and industrial sectors.

Humanistic Management

Series Editors: Michael Pirson, Erica Steckler, David Wasieleski, Benito Teehankee, Ricardo Aguado and Ernestina Giudici

Humanistic Management draws together the concepts of social business, sustainability, social entrepreneurship, business ethics, conscious capitalism and cooperative capitalism to present a new humanistically based research paradigm. This new paradigm challenges the prevailing neo-liberal 'economistic' approach that dominates twentieth-century management theory and practice, and instead emphasises the need to protect human dignity and wellbeing as well as economic drivers.

Humanistic Management and Sustainable Tourism
Human, Social and Environmental Challenges
Edited by Maria Della Lucia and Ernestina Giudici

Humanistic Tourism
Values, Norms and Dignity
Edited by Maria Della Lucia and Ernestina Giudici

Humanistic Management in Latin America
Edited by Consuelo A. García-de-la-Torre, Osmar Arandia and Mario Vázquez-Maguirre

Alternative Theories of the Firm
Edited by Michael Pirson, David M. Wasieleski and Erica L. Steckler

Love and Organization
Lessons of Love for Human Dignity, Leadership and Motivation
Edited by Michael Pirson

Humanistic Management, Organisation, and Aesthetics
Art of Management and Management of Art
Michał Szostak

For more information about this series, please visit www.routledge.com/Humanistic-Management

Humanistic Management, Organisation, and Aesthetics

Art of Management and Management of Art

Michał Szostak

Routledge
Taylor & Francis Group
NEW YORK AND LONDON

First published 2024
by Routledge
605 Third Avenue, New York, NY 10158

and by Routledge
4 Park Square, Milton Park, Abingdon, Oxon, OX14 4RN

Routledge is an imprint of the Taylor & Francis Group, an informa business

ISBN: 978-1-032-59985-4 (hbk)
ISBN: 978-1-032-60195-3 (pbk)
ISBN: 978-1-003-45802-9 (ebk)

DOI: 10.4324/9781003458029

Typeset in Times New Roman
by Apex CoVantage, LLC

Contents

Figures

Tables

Introduction

Research procedure course

I have undertaken the described research procedure for several years, simultaneously exploring the theory of management and art and gaining practical experience in both fields. Along with the increase in competences in these areas, I became gradually convinced of the many similarities between management and artistic practices. The analysis of literature in the field of management, aesthetics, and art convinced me that in all these areas, there are more or less similar concepts that are analysed by researchers fragmentarily – only based on their discipline, without mutual references. Initially, out of respect for the lines of research developed by generations, defined by the framework of individual fields and disciplines, I tried to keep the usual patterns of analysis and reasoning. Then, however, I began to notice numerous limitations resulting from the arbitrary and somehow artificial division of human activity into these fields and disciplines of scientific cognition in the areas of management and art. Yes, I understood the need to use research methods and tools adequate to particular areas; however, I could not ignore the fact that an individual, while carrying out his activity (managerial and artistic – these two areas were and are the essence of my considerations), treats himself and his environment holistically. He does not consider whether, in a given circumstance, he is more of a manager in terms of art or more of an artist in terms of management and organisation – he is an artist-manager. Then, during the analysis of sporadic literature in the field of management aesthetics, a sense of selectivity and fragmentation of the research was born in me. Yes, the problems raised concerned management treatment from an aesthetic (sometimes also an artistic) perspective. Still, I did not find a transparent model that would convince me that we are dealing with interdisciplinarity, resulting in synergy, and added value for both management and art sciences. It was the crucial point of developing the research model that was the spine for empirical exploration results analysis and conclusion drawing.

The course of the research procedure is graphically presented in Figure 0.1.

DOI: 10.4324/9781003458029-1

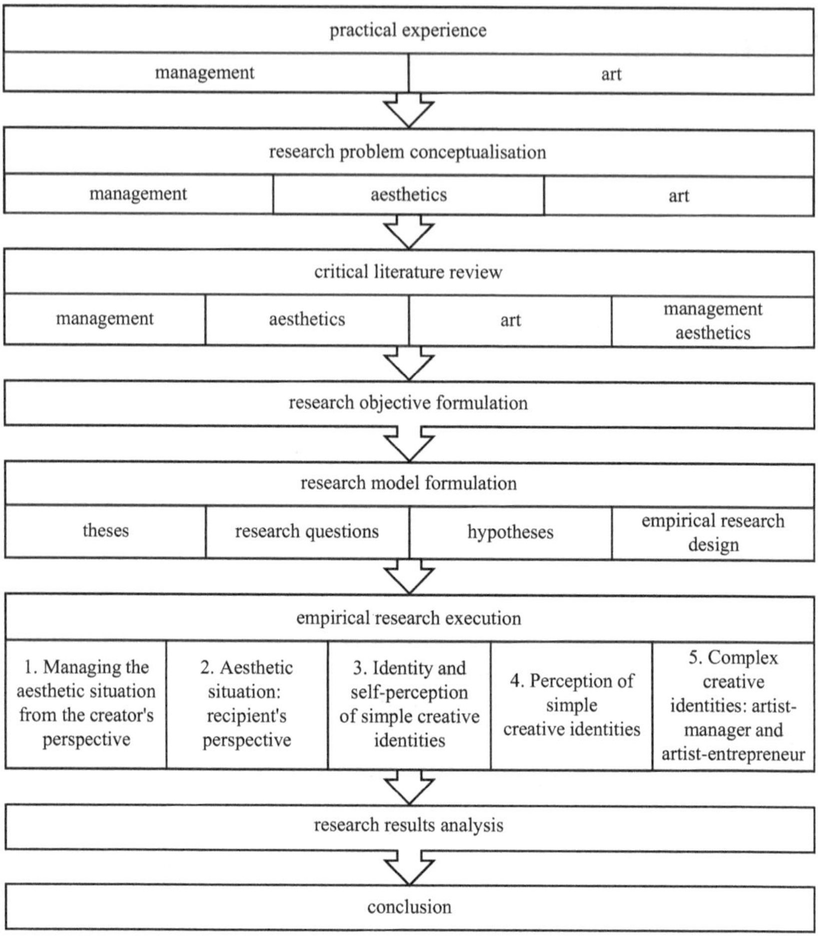

Figure 0.1 Research procedure course

Source: Author's own elaboration

Contexts, research gap, and research problem

Nature and culture are two components that constitute the concept of humanity inseparably. Since nature, i.e., the world of wild powers, and culture, i.e., the world of human creations, are constantly evolving, catalysing, and complementing each other, it is challenging to define a clear line separating these two areas. Management, belonging to the world of culture, helps to order and organise the human environment (nature and culture). In turn, art belonging to the world of culture also helps to release emotions (catharsis), dynamises a person's inner life, and inspires (Tatarkiewicz, 2015, pp. 24, 380). This ordering function of management and the creative function of art determine the commonly perceived opposition of the two fields. However, only delving into the essence of management and the essence of artistic creativity allows us to discover many common sources of these two areas – for example, creativity. Life, based on repetition and copying, would be monotonous and ossified if it was not for the factor of creativity, which both managers and art creators desire. On this basis, it can be concluded that the seemingly opposite fields of management and art can complement and inspire each other.

Management is constantly evolving: from the 19th-century engineering approach, characterised by treating organisational reality as a system of soulless elements that had to be ordered like a non-jamming machine (a metaphor of the organisation as a machine); through the 20th-century managerial efficiency in achieving economic goals, which is a transposition of an engineering approach but dominated by the market factor; to humanistic management, which has been developing in recent decades. The trend of humanistic management, which is the dominant theoretical approach of this work, is aimed at creating sustainable human well-being (Kociatkiewicz & Kostera, 2013). In turn, this lasting human well-being in the spirit of humanism consists primarily of: (1) unconditional respect for dignity, individuality, and protection against exploitation of every human being; (2) ethical reflection relating to the universal value, which is good, which is an integral part of business decisions; and (3) implementing this ethical reflection into the actual conduct of the organisation in the spirit of reconciling intentions with actions. These three dimensions of humanistic governance promote human development through economic activities that are conducive to life and add value to society as a whole (Melé, 2016). Analysing the evolution of the essence of management, it can be said that in management sciences, it has only recently been understood that life has a more profound value, and technical ordering and market optics should be treated as methods of achieving goals by organisations and not goals in themselves. Therefore, a natural consequence will be the marriage of humanistic management with aesthetics, which – focused on the universal values of truth and beauty and art, accumulating the most abstractly advanced products of humanity – is the quintessence and emanation of humanity.

Another key that complements the essence of this work is the phenomenon of the aestheticisation of reality, which uses para-artistic structures to describe phenomena occurring in the real world. However, this attitude is not about searching for aesthetic values in the whole of reality or beautifying it, but about making an intellectual effort to broaden the perception of phenomena with additional dimensions (Ossowski, 1949, pp. 239–269; Welsch, 2005). Aestheticisation of reality, by its very nature, is somewhat subjective than objective, while – as with any methodological activity, even in the field of metaphysics – concepts can arise that will be objectively universal. Aestheticisation of reality should therefore be treated parallel to the strictly scientific understanding of reality without seeking the superiority of any of the optics (Gołaszewska, 1984a, pp. 183–233). On this basis, the aestheticisation of management – understood as the perception of managerial activity (both by the managers themselves and by employees, but also by management researchers) through the use of para-artistic structures – appears as an innovative direction in relation to the technocratic approach focused only on economic efficiency in achieving goals. This novelty of the aestheticisation of management draws attention to empirically intangible – but no less critical – metaphysical issues in the form of, e.g., motives and sources of inspiration in managerial activity, "good taste" seen through the prism of truth, and the beauty of managerial activity manifested, for example, in its "non-kitschiness".

The issue of identity should also be introduced into these considerations because it determines the individual's approach to the actions taken, and these, in turn, can be implemented in various ways. More precisely, it is about creative identity resulting in creative results of undertaken projects while considering certain circumstances and constraints. After all, we know that the exact circumstances in which people with different identities find themselves do not guarantee the same fruitful results. Research on creative identities in the world of management and the world of art has even allowed defining of the complex creative identities of artists-managers and artists-entrepreneurs (Szostak & Sułkowski, 2020, 2021a, 2021c), and the holders of these identities, using paradoxical thinking that catalyses identity tensions and combines seemingly contradictory optics, develop their creativity and the creativity of the organisations they manage in an above-average way (DeFillippi et al., 2007; Szostak & Sułkowski, 2021b).

The problem of demarcation, i.e., setting the boundaries separating management sciences from other sciences, shows two perspectives: (1) management as a separate and independent science, and (2) management as a synthetic science, drawing only from the achievements of other fields (Sułkowski, 2007; Sułkowski & Lenart-Gansiniec, 2021, pp. 60–64). It is difficult to ignore the term *management* as an art. It is not about emphasising the mystical element in this highly pragmatic field, but rather about the "learnability" of broadly understood managerial skills and their conscious management. Scientific fields and disciplines are autonomous and have their concepts, laws, and methods; however, the benefits of observing analogies and the results of interdisciplinary research should not be underestimated. In technical, natural, or even economic sciences, the amount of assimilated scientific and instrumental knowledge translates proportionally into practical knowledge (Ainsworth et al., 2020; Liu et al., 2017; Sereenonchai & Arunrat, 2020). On the other hand, there is no such unambiguous correlation in management: exploring the management theory does not have to go hand in hand with being an effective manager. On the contrary, often people with too extensive theoretical knowledge are not able to make a complex decision with limited time for analysis and under the influence of a stressful situation, while people with little knowledge in the field of management but, e.g., endowed with charisma are often excellent management practitioners who accomplish their goals efficiently (Chen & Hitt, 2021; Isaksen & Nilsson, 2013). The same analogy can be drawn in the field of art: theoretical knowledge and technical skills (virtuosity) do not have to go hand in hand with artistry and creativity, and vice versa – individuals without the support of extensive theories of art or highly developed virtuosity can, thanks to their artistry and creativity, achieve creative heights beyond the range of possibilities of the former (Dahlhaus, 2007; Szostak, 2020, 2021b, 2021a).

The *research gap*, which this work intends to define and preliminarily develop, is an area common to the theory of aesthetics and artistic performance practice, as well as the theory and practice of management. This gap at the epistemological level can be defined as follows:

1. in the literature on the aesthetics of management, there is no holistic model that would organise the previously analytically presented problems of management aesthetics; there are a number of texts on selected topics in the field of management aesthetics, but they are loosely related and do not have a common backbone in the form of a holistic model ordering all these considerations;
2. in the literature on the field of management, there is an evident shortage of publications dealing with the problem of management aesthetics; while in recent years, individual studies on humanistic management, which is the theoretical basis for management aesthetics, have begun to appear, the issues of management aesthetics are discussed very rarely, in a selective and fragmentary way;
3. in the literature on the aesthetics of management, terms from the field of art and aesthetics are used freely and not always in line with their proper meaning; it is necessary to organise terminology in terms of concepts (including virtuosity, artistry, and creativity) in the spirit of aesthetics based on management; the correct use of concepts – mainly based on abstraction and metaphysics – has an ordering dimension and facilitates the perception of the phenomena to which the concepts used to refer;
4. lack of application of the theory of aesthetics, e.g., in terms of sources of creative activity, types of creative personalities, the role of motives for creative activity, or the role of inspiration in creative activity based on management theory;
5. lack of application of issues related to artistic performance practice, e.g., in the field of improvisation and creativity based on management theory and practice;
6. lack of studies indicating the role of the manager's identity in management activities; in addition to the appropriate scope of theoretical knowledge, practical knowledge, and experience, identity has a crucial impact on managerial effectiveness;

7. lack of analysis of undesirable phenomena in management practice relating to universal values, which can be defined as organisational kitsch and analysed with the use of aesthetic tools;
8. lack of studies on ignorance towards the aestheticisation of management; understanding and analysing the phenomenon of ignorance is the key to the process of eliminating barriers to the dissemination of the aestheticisation of management;
9. in the management field literature, no publications are devoted to the essence of holistic art management.[1]

A *vulnerability at the empirical level* can be defined as follows:

1. lack of research analysing the quality of the aesthetic situation and differences in the quality of the aesthetic situation from the perspective of the creator understood as the manager of the aesthetic situation;
2. lack of research analysing the quality of the aesthetic situation and differences in the quality of the aesthetic situation from the perspective of the recipient of art, whose reception process is shaped by the artist – understood as the manager of the aesthetic situation – employing a work of art;
3. lack of comparative research in the field of simple creative identities (artist, creator, manager, leader, and entrepreneur) and the mutual influence of the identity of the manager and the identity of the artist;
4. lack of research analysing the complex creative identities of artists-managers and artists-entrepreneurs and the implications of the results for the theory and practice of management.

These gaps led to the determination of the research problem, which is based on the phenomenon of synergy and interconnections of elements of reality. It is creating a holistic model ordering the issues of management aesthetics based on the aesthetic situation theory.

Own experiences in art and management *inspired* the topics to be tackled. More than 20 years of professional work in management and musical arts, preceded by education in both areas, allowed me to deeply internalise the issues of both areas and the possibility of their conceptualisation – in terms of differences, similarities, and mutual complementation. An equally important motive for taking up this work's subject was the sense of internal disagreement with the (anti)aesthetics of management practices used by many managers and numerous organisations. Being at least slightly sensitive to the quality of the surrounding world, it is difficult to be indifferent to often dehumanising managerial and organisational activities that prefer particularism and inbreeding to a special mission that management should have, which consists in improving reality. At every step and every level of reality – from big politics, through complex organisations, to small enterprises – there are noticeable phenomena that contradict the idea of humanism, manifesting themselves in torrents of impertinence and behaviour that can be collectively referred to as "lack of taste". It seems that the aestheticisation of the management process, an essential component of every organisation, could be an effective remedy for this kind of illness.

Objectives, theses, research questions, hypotheses

The main goal of this monograph is to create a holistic model that organises the issues of management aesthetics and shows the interdependence of the elements of this model. The role of this model should be to perform a central function for a complete and systemic understanding of the phenomenon of management aesthetics, as well as to perform the function of a field based on which analysis of individual issues in the area of management aesthetics is conducted. The critical component of this holistic model is Maria Gołaszewska's theory of the aesthetic situation (Gołaszewska, 1984b), which is an application of the axiological situation theory (Gołaszewska, 1986b, pp. 23–38) based on the achievements of Roman Ingarden's phenomenology (Ingarden, 1970, 1981). The theory proposed by Gołaszewska is fundamental, universal, and systemic. Its fundamentality manifests itself in considering all the problems and phenomena belonging to the consideration of aesthetics, which is unique in the world literature in the field of aesthetics, which abounds in an analytical and fragmentary approach. The universality of Gołaszewska's theory consists in its adequacy both for the consideration of holistic problems of aesthetics, as well as for specific problems, the placement of which in the diagram of this theory only shows their full significance. On the other hand, the systemic nature of the theory draws attention to the interconnections between its elements and the consequences of modifying each element affecting the remaining elements (Ostrowicki, 1997).[2]

Specific goals of this work, which are an extension of the main goal and filling the indicated research gaps, are:

1. application of the aesthetic situation theory based on management theory as a meta-model for management aesthetics; this meta-model will organise the previously analytically presented problems of management aesthetics, constituting the backbone of all considerations in the field of management aesthetics;
2. filling the gap in the field of management literature in terms of the lack of publications addressing the problem of management aesthetics holistically and systemically;
3. terminological ordering in terms of concepts (including virtuosity, artistry, and creativity) in the spirit of management aesthetics so that the correct use of concepts related to abstraction and metaphysics organises and facilitates the perception of the phenomena of management aesthetics;

4. application of the theory of aesthetics in terms of sources of creative activity, types of creative personalities, the role of motives for creative activity and the role of inspiration in creative activity based on management theory; this step will bring a novelty to the theory and practice of management;
5. application of issues related to artistic performance practice, e.g., in the field of improvisation and creativity based on management theory and practice; improvisation, as a phenomenon closely related and commonly used in creative artistic practice, will bring a novelty to the theory and practice of management;
6. developing the issue of the role of the manager's identity – as one of many creative personalities – in management activity;
7. defining undesirable phenomena in management practice related to the lack of universal values as organisational kitsch and their analysis with the use of aesthetic tools;
8. developing the phenomenon of ignorance towards the aestheticisation of management so that the understanding and analysis of the phenomenon of ignorance support the process of removing barriers to the dissemination of aestheticisation of management;
9. development of a methodology and implementation of research analysing the quality of the aesthetic situation and differences in the quality of the aesthetic situation from the perspective of the artist understood as the manager of the aesthetic situation;
10. development of a methodology and implementation of research analysing the quality of the aesthetic situation and differences in the quality of the aesthetic situation from the perspective of the recipient of art, whose reception process is shaped by the artist – understood as the manager of the aesthetic situation – through a work of art;
11. development of methodology and implementation of comparative research in the field of simple creative identities (artist, creator, manager, leader, and entrepreneur) and the mutual impact of the identity of the manager and the identity of the artist;
12. development of a methodology and implementation of research analysing the complex creative identities of artists-managers and artists-entrepreneurs and the implications of the results for the theory and practice of management;
13. application of the conceptual and cognitive apparatus from the discipline of management in the theory of artistic creativity and aesthetics, thus filling the gap in the management literature in the field of publications devoted to the essence of holistic art management.

The theses of the work are:

1. *The aesthetics theory and artistic practice have the potential to enrich the theory and practice of management with qualitative components through deep immersion in the world of values;*

2. *Management theory and practice have the potential to enrich the theory of aesthetics and artistic practice with efficiency components.*[3]

In order to structure the whole consideration, the following research questions were formulated, the answers to which will be sought in the relevant chapters:

1. Can management draw from art and art from management? (Chapters 1–3).
2. To what extent can management draw from art, and to what extent can art draw from management? (Chapters 1–3).
3. Can aestheticisation bring added value to management in the theoretical and practical dimensions? (Chapters 1–3).
4. Can aestheticisation change the perception of management? (Chapters 1–3).
5. Can aestheticisation be – next to ethics and corporate social responsibility – an additional qualitative dimension drawing attention to the issues of universal values in management? (Chapters 1–3, 6).
6. What characterises virtuosity, artistry, and creativity in managerial activity? (Chapter 3).
7. What role does identity play in an individual's artistic, managerial, and entrepreneurial activity? (Chapter 4).
8. How do forced virtualisation and digitisation affect the quality of the creative process, and how does it affect the quality of the reception process in the case of each art discipline? (Chapter 5).
9. What are the common denominators of art and management? (Chapter 5).
10. What perspectives does artistic improvisation bring to management? (Chapter 5).
11. Can ignorance and kitsch in management, based on dialectics, help in understanding the essence and meaning of the aestheticisation of management? (Chapter 6).
12. How to counteract ignorance regarding the aestheticisation of management? (Chapter 6).

In turn, based on these research questions, the following working hypotheses were formulated (the number of the hypothesis corresponds to the number of the research question; if more than one hypothesis resulted from one question, letter division was used):

1. A. The art factor is no less important in effective management than the science factor.
   B. The management factor is important in fruitful artistic activity.
2. A. Management can derive added value from the arts.
   B. Art can derive added value from management.
3. Aestheticisation can bring added value to management both in the theoretical and practical dimensions.

4. Aestheticisation can change the perception of the management process.
5. Aestheticisation can be – apart from ethics and corporate social responsibility – an additional quality dimension in management (Chapters 1–3, 6).
6. Virtuosity, artistry, and creativity in managerial activity are the essential competencies of a manager from the point of view of the aestheticisation of management.
7. A. The role of individual identity is essential for the success of the creative activities of an artist, manager, and entrepreneur.
   B. The majority of society does not see the difference between creativity and artistry.
   C. The social perception of the creator and manager has much in common.
8. A. Forced virtualisation and digitisation affect the quality of the creative process within the aesthetic situation.
   B. The impact of forced virtualisation and digitisation on the quality of the creative process is different for each art discipline.
   C. Forced virtualisation and digitisation affect the quality of the reception process within the aesthetic situation.
   D. The impact of forced virtualisation and digitisation on the quality of the reception process is different for each art discipline.
   E. Forced virtualisation and digitisation determine the necessity of changes in the process of managing the aesthetic situation (in terms of the creative process and the reception process) in a different way for each art discipline.
9. A. Art and management have common denominators, and their analysis and mutual references add value to each of these areas.
   B. Motives for undertaking creative activity may broaden the perspective of motives for undertaking managerial activity.
10. Artistic improvisation brings a number of essential issues to management.
11. A. The theory of aesthetic kitsch can be successfully applied in management.
    B. Ignorance and kitsch in management can, based on dialectics, help in understanding the essence and meaning of the aestheticisation of management.
    C. Understanding the essence of ignorance is crucial in eliminating ignorance concerning the aestheticisation of management.
12. Counteracting ignorance towards the aestheticisation of management requires knowledge of the aestheticisation of management and examples of its practical application.

Methodology and research model

The *research methods* used in this work are a critical review of the literature supported by the technique of its qualitative analysis, qualitative research (as the dominant method of verifying the theoretical considerations), quantitative research (mainly to show the possibility of their application in the field of theoretical considerations), and autoethnography (as a complement to the whole). The methodological strategy in the spirit of a systemic approach based on the developed research model is characterised by an interdisciplinary and multi-paradigm approach, considering achievements in aesthetics and management. The research model, which is the fundamental tool of the system approach, is presented in a graphic form in Figure 0.2. Due to its complex and multidimensional structure, it has also been developed in tabular form (Table 0.1), which contains theses, research questions, and hypotheses and indicates the methods used at the various stages of the work.

A critical review of the literature concerned primarily two areas: (1) aesthetics, in terms of the possibility of adapting aesthetic theories in management sciences; and (2) management, in terms of identifying areas for which aestheticisation can be a significant added value. As a supplement to the cognitive gaps in the essential threads of the considerations, the literature in the fields of philosophy, psychology, sociology, and pedagogy was also analysed to a limited extent. The primary language of the analysed publications was English; individual key publications in Polish, German, and French were also analysed. The qualitative analysis of the literature was based primarily on monographs with an established position in the field of aesthetics (Dahlhaus, 2007; Gołaszewska, 1967, 1984a, 1984b, 1986a, 2001, 2005; Ingarden, 1981; Levinson, 2003; Ossowski, 1949; Wilkoszewska, 2007), management (Drucker, 2006b, 2006a, 2009; Griffin, 2005; Kotler & Keller, 2016; Koźmiński, 2005; Koźmiński & Piotrowski, 1999; Mintzberg, 2012; Porter, 1980) and management aesthetics (Biehl-Missal, 2011; Guillet de Monthoux, 2004; Kostera, 2014, 2019; Kostera & Woźniak, 2022; Linstead & Höpfl, 2000; Minahan, 2020; Strati, 1999), as well as on analyses of research results published in the form of scientific articles, which were accessed by exploring the scientific databases of EBSCO, Google Scholar, JSTOR, Mendeley, Scopus, and Web of Science.

In addition to the analysis of the results of secondary research published in the literature, many primary studies were carried out for this work, the aim of which was to fill both the methodological and cognitive gaps in the literature on the subject and to enable the continuity of reasoning and inference for this work. The primary research conducted concerned: (1) the perspective of the creator of individual art disciplines (as defined by the manager of the aesthetic situation) in terms of the aesthetic situation taking place in the traditional and virtual form (qualitative research); (2) perspectives of the recipient of particular art disciplines in terms of the aesthetic situation taking place in the traditional and digital form (quantitative research); (3) identity and self-perception of simple creative personalities (qualitative research); (4) perception of simple creative identities (quantitative research); and (5) identity and self-perception of complex creative personalities of artists-managers and artists-entrepreneurs (qualitative research). At this point, it should be noted that the actions taken in the field of quantitative research were intended not to represent the phenomena studied in reality, but only to serve as a goal for the use of quantitative methods in the study of mysterious phenomena in the area of

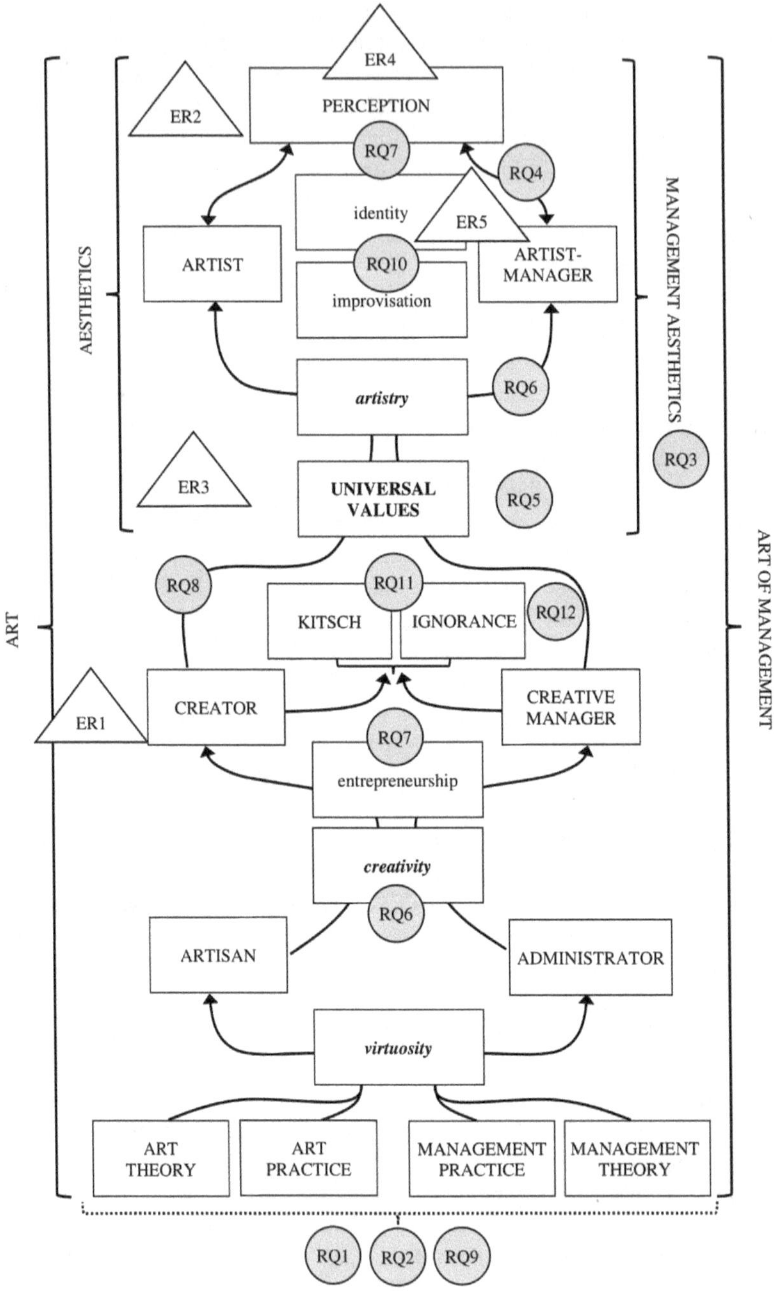

Figure 0.2 Research model[4]

Source: Author's own elaboration

Table 0.1 Research model

Argument	*Research question*	*Hypothesis*	*Method*	*Chapter(s)*
T1. The theory of aesthetics and artistic practice has the potential to enrich the theory and practice of management with qualitative components through deep immersion in the world of values.	1. Can management draw from art and art from management?	H1A. The art factor is no less important in effective management than the science factor. H2B. The management factor is essential in fruitful artistic activity.	Literature analysis	1–3
	2. To what extent can management draw from art, and to what extent can art draw from management?	H2A. Management can derive added value from the arts. H2B. Art can derive added value from management.	1. literature analysis; 2. autoethnography	1–3
	3. Can aestheticisation bring added value to management in the theoretical and practical dimensions?	H3. Aestheticisation can bring added value to management both in the theoretical and practical dimensions.	1. literature analysis; 2. autoethnography	1–3
	4. Can aestheticisation change the perception of management?	H4. Aestheticisation can change the perception of the management process.	1. literature analysis; 2. empirical study	1–3
	5. Can aestheticisation be – next to ethics and corporate social responsibility – an additional qualitative dimension drawing attention to the issues of universal values in management?	H5. Aestheticisation can be – next to ethics and corporate social responsibility – an additional qualitative dimension in management.	1. literature analysis; 2. autoethnography	1–3, 6

(*Continued*)

Table 0.1 (Continued)

Argument	*Research question*	*Hypothesis*	*Method*	*Chapter(s)*
	7. What role does identity play in an individual's artistic, managerial, and entrepreneurial activity?	H7A. The role of individual identity is essential for the success of the creative activities of an artist, manager, and entrepreneur. H7B. Most people do not see the difference between creativity and artistry. H7C. The social perception of the creator and the manager have a lot in common.	1. literature analysis; 2. autoethnography; 3. empirical research	4
	9. What are the common denominators of art and management?	H9A. Art and management have common denominators, and their analysis and mutual references add value to each of these areas. H9B. The motives for undertaking creative activity may broaden the scope of the motives for undertaking managerial activity.	1. literature analysis; 2. autoethnography	5
	10. What perspectives does artistic improvisation bring to management?	H10. Artistic improvisation brings a number of important issues to management.	1. literature analysis; 2. autoethnography	5
	11. Can ignorance and kitsch in management, based on dialectics, help in understanding the essence and meaning of the aestheticisation of management?	H11A. The theory of aesthetic kitsch can be successfully applied in management. H11B. Ignorance and kitsch in management can, based on dialectics, help understand the essence and meaning of the aestheticisation of management.	1. literature analysis; 2. autoethnography	6

		H11C. Understanding the essence of ignorance is crucial in eliminating ignorance concerning the aestheticisation of management.		
	12. How to counteract ignorance regarding the aestheticisation of management?	H12. Counteracting ignorance towards the aestheticisation of management requires knowledge of the aestheticisation of management and examples of its practical application.	literature analysis	6
T2. The theory and practice of management have the potential to enrich the theory of aesthetics and artistic practice with efficiency components	6. What characterises virtuosity, artistry, and creativity in managerial activity?	H6. Virtuosity, artistry, and creativity in managerial activity are the basic competencies of a manager from the point of view of the aestheticisation of management.	1. literature analysis; 2. autoethnography	3
	8. How do forced virtualisation and digitisation affect the quality of the creative process, and how does it affect the quality of the reception process in the case of each art discipline?	H8A. Forced virtualisation and digitisation affect the quality of the creative process within the aesthetic situation. H8B. The impact of forced virtualisation and digitisation on the quality of the creative process is different for each art discipline.	1. literature analysis; 2. autoethnography; 3. empirical research	5

(Continued)

Table 0.1 (Continued)

Argument	*Research question*	*Hypothesis*	*Method*	*Chapter(s)*
		H8C. Forced virtualisation and digitisation affect the quality of the collection process within the aesthetic situation. H8D. The impact of forced virtualisation and digitisation on the quality of the reception process is different for each art discipline. H8E. Forced virtualisation and digitisation determine the necessity of changes in the process of managing the aesthetic situation (in terms of the creative process and the reception process) in a different way for each art discipline.		
	9. What are the common denominators of art and management?	H9A. Art and management have common denominators, and their analysis and mutual references add value to each of these areas. H9B. The motives for undertaking creative activity may broaden the scope of the motives for undertaking managerial activity.	1. literature analysis; 2. autoethnography	5

Source: Author's own elaboration

management aesthetics and the development of detailed methodologies for undertaking extensive quantitative research. Due to the potential unrepresentativeness of the results of quantitative research undertaken on small samples, detailed results have been published in separate articles. At the same time, in this monograph, only the author's methodological layer and an outline of general conclusions are presented that can be obtained from carrying out representative quantitative research. A detailed description of the research methods used in the individual empirical studies is discussed in the remainder of this section.

Inference in terms of secondary and primary research results was based mainly on the synthesis of results and was conducted with awareness, rigour, systematics, pluralism, and methodological triangulation. The methods used in the qualitative and quantitative research were repeatable according to the canon and can be repeated to verify the results obtained or extend the conclusions.

A robust research method for this work was also autoethnography, based on my own experience: over 20 years as a musical artist (an instrumentalist performing dozens of solo recitals around the world a year), several years of experience as a manager operating at the level of management boards of companies operating in an international environment, and several years of experience as a researcher of this interdisciplinary area. Autoethnography, however, was a secondary method concerning the aforementioned methods, constituting a source of thoughts filling the substantive content of the backbone of considerations shaped by a thorough analysis of the literature on the subject.

Research methodology 1: managing the aesthetic situation from the artist's perspective

In order to explain the changes in the nature of the creative process depending on the form of presenting the work (live/traditional or digital/virtual) from the creator's perspective, the study used the method of exploratory research. The qualitative study was conducted in the form of structured in-depth formal interviews with key informants in the researched field, i.e., people who are active in the arts. The choice of such a methodology seems to be the most appropriate for the pilot nature of the study. The selection of the research sample was justified by the availability of people from different countries and cultures who carry out creative activities in various fields and their openness to participate in such research. The study was designed to examine representatives of all artistic disciplines. Within each discipline,

a. *Music arts* (instrumental/vocal concerts, oratorios):

   i. composer
   ii. performer (instrumentalist, vocalist, conductor)
   iii. other (sound director, etc.)

b. *Performing arts* (theatre, opera, ballet, dance, pantomime, performance):

   i. actor
   ii. director
   iii. screenwriter
   iv. other

c. *Literary arts* (prose, fiction/non-fiction, drama, poetry):

   i. editor
   ii. translator
   iii. writer
   iv. other

d. *Audiovisual arts* (film, clip, video game):

   i. actor
   ii. director
   iii. editor
   iv. screenwriter
   v. other

e. *Visual arts* (painting, drawing, photography, sculpture, ceramics, architecture, comics, design, fashion):

   i. creator (painter, photographer, sculptor, architect, fashion designer, etc.)
   ii. other

Sixty-four creators were asked to participate in the study; eventually, 34 of them took part in the project. The original idea to study representatives of all art disciplines was not implemented due to the difficulties in gathering the optimal number of participants from each discipline. Finally, answers allowing for conclusions were collected in the field of musical arts (n = 19, 55.9%), literary arts (n = 3, 8.9%) and visual arts (n = 12, 35.2%). Respondents came from the following countries: Bulgaria, Chile, the Czech Republic, France, Germany, Nigeria, Poland, Ukraine, the United Kingdom, and the United States. The interviews were conducted over five months, from April to August 2022, in person or virtually depending on the interviewees' preferences. The majority of the research sample came from Poland (n = 17, 50%), two participants each from Bulgaria, the Czech Republic, and Ukraine (5.8% each), and one person each from Chile, Nigeria, Germany, Turkey, the United Kingdom, Vietnam, and Italy (2.9% each). In addition, one person indicated their nationality as European ("I do not have a strict national identity; if I had to choose, it would be Ashkenazi-Jewish"), and another person as Jewish-Russian-American. Most of the respondents were men (n = 25, 73.5%). Due to the pilot nature of this study, no effort was made to balance participants' gender, age, or length of artistic experience. The impact of these elements on the research results was fully understood, but the results were analysed to obtain at least a general picture of the examined problems. Data analysis was performed using NVivo software.

Interviews with Polish respondents were conducted in the Polish language, while interviews with other respondents were conducted in English, and answers were recorded. Then they were written down to standardise the analysis and inference process, and the answers obtained from the English-language interviews were translated into Polish. Description of the research sample – in terms of: (1) represented field of art; (2) gender; (3) year of birth; (4) year of commencement of artistic activity (number of years of artistic activity); (5) determination of whether the artistic activity is performed as primary, additional, or one of many forms of professional activity; (6) artistic education; (7) non-artistic education; and (8) declared nationality – is presented in Table 0.2.

The interview questionnaire was divided into parts (AF), and within each part, the participants answered the following 53 detailed questions based on five-point Likert scales to clarify the classification of answers.[5] The questionnaire was placed as an appendix to this monograph.

The conclusions from the study were used in subsection 2.3.2 in Chapter 2 and subsection 5.4.1 in Chapter 5.

Research methodology 2: aesthetic situation; viewer's perspective

Analogous to the analysed perspective of the creator towards the virtualisation of the aesthetic situation significantly accelerated by the COVID-19 pandemic, the viewer's perspective was also examined in the same circumstances. However, in this case, it was about getting to know the opinions of recipients of individual art disciplines on the process of perceiving a work of art in traditional and virtual forms of the aesthetic situation. In other words, an answer was sought to the question of how forced virtualisation and digitisation affect the quality of the artwork receiving process.

Initially, secondary research was undertaken in terms of literature and data review. The literature review was based on a qualitative selection of publications in the EBSCO, Google Scholar, JSTOR, Mendeley, and Scopus scientific databases, especially from recent years (2017–2023). The methodological approach to the literature review was based on an interdisciplinary and multi-paradigm tactic considering publications in the fields of aesthetic theory, reception studies, information visualisation, human-computer interaction, digital arts, and management. The literature review was conducted using the NVivo Pro software.

For this study, the arts were divided into five distinct fields:

1. musical arts (instrumental/vocal concerts, oratorios);
2. performance/stage arts (dance, ballet, opera, theatre, pantomime, performance);
3. literary arts (prose, fiction/non-fiction, drama, poetry);
4. audiovisual arts (film, clip, video game);
5. visual arts (painting, drawing, photography, sculpture, ceramics, architecture, comics, design, fashion).

Table 0.2 Managing the aesthetic situation from the creator's perspective: a description of the research sample

Code	*Sex*	*Year of birth*	*Artistic experience (in years)*	*Artistic activity as a basic, additional, or one of many forms of professional activity*	*Artistic education*	*Non-artistic education*	*Nationality (national identification)*
MUS01	F	1967	39	one of many	postgraduate music studies	Master of Pedagogy	Poland
MUS02	M	1983	17	additional	private lessons	Doctor of Chemistry	Czech Republic
MUS03	M	1961	46	additional	private lessons	Doctor of Physics	Germany
MUS04	F	1978	37	primary	Master of Musical Arts, instrumentalist	Doctor of Chemistry	United Kingdom
MUS05	M	1991	12	primary	Doctor of Musical Arts, instrumentalist	postgraduate studies in management	Poland
MUS06	M	1991	22	additional	first-degree music school	lack	Poland
MUS07	M	1999	9	primary	lack	medium	Poland
MUS08	M	1993	13	primary	Master of Musical Arts	postgraduate studies: (1) sound production, (2) music pedagogy	Poland
MUS09	M	1998	16	primary	Master of Musical Arts	lack	Bulgaria
MUS10	M	1954	43	primary	Master of Musical Arts, conducting	Master in Theology, Linguistic Studies	United States
MUS11	M	1984	33	primary	Master of Science	bachelor's degree	France
MUS12	M	2000	6	primary	second-degree music school	lack	Poland
MUS13	M	1964	44	one of many	Master of Pedagogy	medium	Poland
MUS14	M	1978	14	additional	private lessons	lack	Bulgaria
MUS15	F	1977	4	additional	private lessons	Bachelor of Psychology	Jewish-Russian-American
MUS16	M	1971	41	primary	second-degree music school	lack	Nigeria

MUS17	F	1970	34	primary	second-degree music school	Master of Musicology	Czech Republic
MUS18	M	1993	7	additional	private lessons	Master of Music Pedagogy	Chile
MUS19	M	1980	25	one of many	Doctor of Musical Arts, instrumentalist	Associate Professor of Management	Poland
LIT1	M	1974	23	additional	lack	Master of Political Sociology	Europe ("I do not have a strict national identity")
LIT2	F	1976	17	additional	Doctor of Linguistics, translator	postgraduate studies: finance, linguistics, pedagogy	Ukraine
LIT3	F	1963	23	additional	Doctor of Literature	Master of Art History	Italy
VIA01	M	1983	25	primary	Doctor of Arts, painting, Master in Art History	lack	Poland
VIA02	K	1964	30	one of many	Doctor of Arts, painting	Master of Polish Studies	Poland
VIA03	M	1983	25	primary	Doctor of Arts, painting	MSc	Poland
VIA04	K	1999	3	primary	Master of Arts, Painting	lack	Vietnam
VIA05	M	2000	10	additional	lack	Bachelor of Management (in progress)	Turkey
VIA06	M	1990	18	additional	lack	MSc	Poland
VIA07	F	1976	26	one of many	Doctor of Arts	MSc	Poland
VIA08	M	1985	22	one of many	Doctor of Arts	blockchain postgraduate studies: business, law, technology	Poland
VIA09	M	1995	2	additional	lack	Master of Cybersecurity	Ukraine
VIA10	M	1985	18	one of many	Doctor of Arts	lack	Poland
VIA11	M	1984	14	additional	Doctor of Arts	lack	Poland
VIA12	M	1995	6	additional	lack	Master of Physical Education	Poland

Source: Author's own elaboration

The assumption was that the quality of audience participation in each type of art should be analysed using criteria that are understandable to the audience but also applicable to each type of art simultaneously. After reviewing the literature, ten factors were identified for this purpose:

1. satisfaction (Guo et al., 2020; Jarrier & Bourgeon-Renault, 2019; Quattrini et al., 2020; Zollo et al., 2021),
2. pleasure (Dunne-Howrie, 2020),
3. engagement (Dube & İnce, 2019; Quattrini et al., 2020; Sosnowska, 2015; Wu et al., 2017),
4. the possibility of experiencing catharsis (Craig et al., 2020; Lee, 2011; Phillips, 2000),
5. contact with the artwork itself (Habelsberger & Bhansing, 2021),
6. contact with the creator himself (Wu et al., 2017),
7. the comfort of participation (Guidry, 2014),
8. possibilities of shaping the aesthetic experience (Jackson, 2017; Park & Lim, 2015),
9. own motivation to participate (Hobbs & Tuzel, 2017; Pianzola et al., 2021),
10. easiness of participation (Dunne-Howrie, 2020; Fancourt et al., 2020).

In the next step, quantitative research was conducted based on a survey. This step aimed to assess the quality of audience participation in each art type analysed based on ten criteria selected after a literature review. Moreover, this step aimed to extract meaningful results about possibly different artistic activities and to describe which are coherent and similar. Data analysis was performed using IBM SPSS and MS Excel; however, no complex statistics were performed due to the small sample size ($n = 221$).

The quantitative study was carried out from 1 May to 17 December 2021 – i.e., within 230 calendar days – using the Survio tool available only in digital form. The link to the survey was distributed on social media through direct requests and official announcements, e.g., from the university. The survey, prepared only in English and containing 71 questions, was divided into six segments. The first five segments covered each type of art. All questions were closed-ended; respondents could only choose prepared answers. When evaluating the level of factor quality, the respondents used a 5-point Likert scale: very low (−2), rather low (−1), neutral (0), rather high (+1), and very high (+2). The sixth segment of the survey contained questions categorising respondents.

A total of 777 visits resulted in 221 (28.4%) responses from survey participants. Most participants (63.8%) spent 5 to 30 minutes answering all the questions. The characteristics of the research sample are as follows. Respondents, among whom men constituted 55.2% and women 44.8%, represented 38 countries from different continents (in descending order): 37.2% from Poland, 11.2% from the United States, 7.4% from Ukraine, 7.4% from Finland, 3.7% from

Germany, 3.7% from India, 2.7% from Turkey, 2.7% from the United Kingdom; the other countries represented less than 2.2% (i.e., four or fewer participants). In addition, most respondents (60.1%) graduated from bachelor's, master's, or engineering studies programmes; 28.2% had a doctorate, habilitation, or professorship; 9.4% graduated from a technical school or high school; and 2.3% from a primary or lower secondary school.

The study's conclusions are described in subsection 5.4.2 in Chapter 5.

Research methodology 3: identity and self-perception of simple creative personalities

In order to clarify the exact nature of the identity problem of simple creative personalities of artists and managers, the method of exploratory research was used. The qualitative research was conducted in the form of structured in-depth formal interviews with key informants in the researched field: people who are or have been both artists and managers in their professional lives. The respondents came from an international environment – Bulgaria, Nigeria, Poland, Ukraine, the United Kingdom, and the United States – and the interviews were conducted in February and March 2020. The chosen methodology was the most appropriate for the pilot nature of the study. The research sample was not limited to people holding both roles simultaneously; among the respondents, some played both roles at varying degrees and levels at different periods of their lives. The selection of the research sample was justified by the availability of people with possibly diverse artistic and managerial experience from different countries and cultures and their openness to participate in such research. About 33 artists-managers were asked to participate in the study; eventually, 22 agreed to participate in the project. Those who ultimately did not participate in the research stated that they did not consider themselves artists or managers, although – according to the research assumptions – they fully met the criteria. The reason for such behaviour may be the tension between these people's real selves and their imagined false selves, a kind of active denial of one's identity. This issue in itself could be an interesting research problem.

The majority of the sample was from Poland ($n = 12$, 55%), three from the United States (14%), two from the United Kingdom (10%), and one person each from Bulgaria, Nigeria, and Ukraine (4.5% each). In addition, the majority of respondents were men ($n = 16$, 73%), most had artistic experience in the field of classical music ($n = 18$, 82%), and most of the sample did not have formal managerial education ($n = 15$, 68%). No effort was made to balance the gender or age of the participants, according to either the length of their professional experience or the chosen art form. The impact of these elements on the study's results was fully understood, but analyses and conclusions were continued due to the pilot nature of this study. The detailed consequences of the sample characteristics are listed in the Conclusion.

Most of the interviews were conducted as individual conversations, and – due to the COVID-19 pandemic and restrictions on face-to-face meetings – some took the form of an online conversation; several respondents completed a questionnaire with 36 written questions. Interviews with Polish respondents were conducted in Polish, and interviews with other respondents were conducted in English. Non-English interviews were translated into English. The answers are listed in a table along with categories specifying nationality, age, gender, formal education in the arts, management and other fields, and description of activities in the arts and management. The description of the research sample is presented in Table 0.3. Data analysis was performed using NVivo software.

The subchapter "4.2.1. Identity of simple creative personalities" describes the study's conclusions.

Research methodology 4: perception of simple creative personalities

Another undertaken empirical study was an attempt to understand the perception of simple creative personalities (i.e., artist, creator, manager, leader, and entrepreneur) by the environment of these individuals. Based on the literature analysis, the following research hypotheses were established:

H1. the majority of society does not see the difference between creativity and artistry;
H2. creativity and entrepreneurship have a similar perception among society;
H3. Leadership and management have similar perceptions in society.

The tool for quantitative research in the form of a questionnaire was developed based on Stefan Nowak's methodology (Nowak, 2007), consisting in determining the dimensions of the studied phenomenon and then selecting indicators that allow it to describe the studied phenomenon. The initial methodological assumption was to build separate sets of indicators for each dimension. Sets of indicators for individual dimensions began to be built based on the literature in the field of:

1. artistry (Bayrakci et al., 2009; McHugh, 2015; Szostak, 2020; Walter, 2015; Wilson & Brown, 2012; Woodward & Funk, 2010),
2. creativity (Dufour et al., 2020; Lehmann & Gaskins, 2019; Leso et al., 2017; Szostak & Sułkowski, 2020; Taleghani, 2012; Zhou et al., 2008),
3. managerial issues (Baker et al., 2012; Bulei et al., 2014; Elstad & Jansson, 2020; Hallier, 2004; Hatch et al., 2006; Hracs, 2015; Lähdesmäki, 2012; López-Fernández et al., 2018; Lutas et al., 2020),
4. leadership (Adler, 2006; Alvesson & Blom, 2015; Carroll & Levy, 2008; Jankurová et al., 2017; Lord & Brown, 2001; Nikolski, 2015; Postuła & Majczyk, 2018; Raso et al., 2020; Stuke, 2013; Woodward & Funk, 2010),
5. entrepreneurship (Bureau & Zander, 2014; Cardon et al., 2009; Clarke & Holt, 2019; Damásio & Bicacro, 2017; Davidsson, 2006; Enhuber, 2014; Lewis et al., 2016; Postuła & Majczyk, 2018; Toscher, 2019, 2020).

Table 0.3 Identity of creative personalities: description of the research sample

Code	*Nationality*	*Year of birth*	*Sex*[6]	*Formal education in the arts*	*Formal education in management*	*Artistic activity*	*Activity as a manager*
BUL	Bulgaria	1978	M	Master of Musical Arts, instrumentalist	lack	performing chamber, symphonic, and solo recitals with orchestras and various ensembles; conducting master classes, lectures	art manager for two years, managing about 14 artists: impresario activities
NIG	Nigeria	1995	M	musician instrumentalist	Master of Business Management	composer and music director, classical musician, choirmaster	music director of a cultural institution: 60–100 people; choirmaster: 14 people
PL01	Poland	1989	M	Master of Musical Arts, instrumentalist	postgraduate studies	internship: about 15 years of solo and ensemble activity in the philharmonic (on commission) and on his own	manager in a cultural institution: 50 employees
PL02	Poland	1981	M	lack	MBA	creator of origami lamps and graphics; own studio, individual activity	managing own business, related projects, and people (17 years old)
PL03	Poland	1974	M	Master of Musical Arts, vocalist – two diplomas: Polish and German	MBA	singer-soloist of operas, philharmonics, festivals, early music ensembles, CD, radio and television recordings (in Poland and abroad); full-time soloist in opera houses	impresario of the city opera (of international renown), organisation and leading bands of 100–150 people; head of the artistic work organisation department at the National Opera

(*Continued*)

Table 0.3 (Continued)

Code	*Nationality*	*Year of birth*	*Sex*[6]	*Formal education in the arts*	*Formal education in management*	*Artistic activity*	*Activity as a manager*
PL04	Poland	1999	M	music high school, numerous master classes in the field of musical arts	lack	concert musician for 12 years; owner of a private music school; teacher in private music schools. musician of the entertainment band, founder of the orchestra	artists promotion agency; management of four people
PL05	Poland	1980	M	lack	lack	lack	founder and owner of a 15-year-old company, about 50 subordinates
PL06	Poland	1992	M	two master's degrees in musical arts	lack	assistant conductor of the Warsaw Philharmonic, guest conductor at various international institutions	lack
PL07	Poland	1980	M	Doctor of Musical Arts, instrumentalist, studies in Warsaw, Milan, London, and international master classes	Master of Management; completed doctoral studies in management	since 2002, a professional musician (aged 18) at institutions (employment contracts); regular international solo concert activity since 2010 (10 years) on own account (Europe, Asia, North America, South America, Africa), recorded albums	professional manager (higher level of management) since 2004 (16 years old) in companies (employment contracts, functional contracts); responsibility for various areas of the organisation and human teams (10–20 people) in small and medium-sized companies in an international environment

PL08	Poland	1964	F	Doctor of Arts, painter	lack	painter and visual artist since 1997; self-employment and at institutions (artistic associations, universities); individual artistic work	vice president of the artistic association: responsible for the implementation of grant projects, coordination and curation of exhibitions, organisation: 20–25 people; dean of the university faculty: managing a team of field managers (about 30 lecturers) and over 2,000 students
PL09	Poland	1999	F	primary and secondary music schools	lack	publishing a book, publishing music on Internet platforms, playing in a symphony orchestra	art agency: development and promotion manager: small organisation, no subordinates, project management
PL10	Poland	1991	M	Master of Musical Arts, instrumentalist	postgraduate studies: management	for 3 years, a research and didactic employee of an art school, apart from solo concert activity, in chamber ensembles or as a member of an orchestra	promotion and program departments in public cultural institutions of national importance, implementation of original music projects and concerts as part of own non-governmental organisation
PL11	Poland	1952	F	3-year music centre and private lessons, vocalist	Master of Management and Marketing; postgraduate studies of culture managers	choir singer; vocalist of a vocal group; 25 years of cooperation with many entertainment bands as a vocalist	vice president of the national association of popular musicians; president of the performers' association; manager and co-founder of an 80-member song and dance ensemble at the university; impresario of regular jazz concerts

(*Continued*)

Table 0.3 (Continued)

Code	*Nationality*	*Year of birth*	*Sex*[6]	*Formal education in the arts*	*Formal education in management*	*Artistic activity*	*Activity as a manager*
PL12	Poland	1978	F	Master of Musical Arts in Poland and Italy, vocalist	lack	concerts organised as part of own activity and based on contracts for specific work; books published at own expense and journalistic cooperation under employment contracts and orders	concerts in cooperation with the local government and as part of its own business, employing up to a dozen people a year
PL13	Poland	1970	M	Doctor of Musical Arts, singer	lack	30 years on stage, actor, opera singer, public and private institutions, solo work	self-employed, creator of the scene of young musicians; organisation of concerts and own artistic work
PL14	Poland	1982	F	Master of Musical Arts, instrumentalist	lack	violin teacher, a violinist in a piano duo	piano duo manager
UK1	United Kingdom	1948	M	secondary music school in theory and instrument; international master classes	lack	part-time instrumentalist; president of the local musicians' association	27 years of work at British Energy to the degree of Chief Engineer in real-time national electrical load management, work organisation of approximately 4,000 employees

UK2	United Kingdom	1981	M	Master of Musical Arts: performance and choral direction, instrumentalist	lack	solo instrumental concert activity (organ) and choir coach/conductor	head of the music department: director of music, performances, and training, about 50 subordinates; artistic and administrative manager of the concert hall: 5 employees
UKR	Ukraine	1990	M	Master of Literature	postgraduate studies in music management	poet, poetic translator	concert hall director, orchestra director; management of 30–50 people
US1	United States	1965	M	Master of Musical Arts, instrumentalist	lack	music director: organist and choir director, performer of local concerts; lecturer of the instrument (organ) at the university	editorial director and publisher for an international publishing house
US2	United States	1947	M	Master of Musical Arts, instrumentalist	lack	international solo concert activity	manager of his own artistic career
US3	Russia–United States	1977	F	music high school, private organ lessons for over 20 years	lack	independent instrumentalist performing several times a year locally	a senior manager in the technical advertising team at a major publishing company in New York

Source: Author's own elaboration

The analysis of individual groups of indicators showed, however, that, in principle, each indicator selected for individual dimensions can be used to describe all the examined dimensions. Following this conclusion, a single set of 50 indicators was developed and applied unchanged to all five dimensions examined. Thanks to this, it was possible to compare the results of the same indicators for different dimensions after obtaining the answer.

The survey was divided into four parts. The first part included questions (each question concerned one indicator) divided into thematic sections on each of the analysed dimensions: artistry, creativity, managerial issues, leadership, and entrepreneurship. All questions were closed-ended, and answers could be given based on a 5-point Likert scale: definitely not, rather not, hard to say, rather yes, or definitely yes. The second part of the survey asked questions about the relationship of each dimension to each of the other dimensions. In the third part of the survey, the respondents defined their identity regarding each of the analysed dimensions. The fourth part contained questions identifying the respondents in terms of age, education, and nationality.

A non-parametric chi-square test of independence dedicated to small samples that do not have a normal distribution was used to verify the research hypotheses. Pairs of observed values were compared with pairs of expected values for each hypothesis. The p-value of the tests was < 0.001. Data analysis was carried out using IBM SPSS and MS Excel programs. Due to the small sample size, no complex statistics were performed.

The survey was available to survey participants virtually in the form of the professional SURVIO tool for 34 days, i.e., from 20 December 2020 to 23 January 2021. Two identical questionnaires, one in English and the other in Polish, were sent via direct contact and indirect public tools (social networks and collective messages to various communities). Around 2,000 to 3,000 people were asked to participate in the study. Of these, 879 people expressed interest in participating in the survey, which was assessed by clicking on the link leading to the survey, which was recorded by the research tool. Actual participation in the study, consisting of completing the questionnaire, was completed by 160 people, i.e., 18.2% of the number interested in participating. The average time spent completing the survey was 32 minutes and 23 seconds, and the average age of the respondent was 38 years. Among the respondents, women accounted for 42.5% and men for 57.5%; people with higher education (bachelor's, master's, engineering degrees) accounted for 64.57%, people with the titles of doctor, habilitated doctor, or professor made up 18.90%; and people with secondary education accounted for 15.75%. Respondents came from 28 countries, but since the distribution of this characteristic was very diverse, the sample was divided into potentially comparable groups: 74% of developed countries and 26% of developing countries.[7] Also, 71.7% came from European countries, and 28.3% from non-European countries; 49.6% came from Poland, and 50.4% from other countries; 63.8% came from post-communist countries and 36.2% from countries with no experience of communism.

Subsection 4.2.2 in Chapter 4 describes the study's conclusions.

Research methodology 5: complex creative personalities: artist-manager and artist-entrepreneur

This study aims to describe the challenges related to identifying artists-managers and artists-entrepreneurs, as well as the characteristics of these complex creative identities. After analysing the literature in the field of simple creative identities, the following goals needed to be achieved: (1) answering the questions "Who is an artist-manager?" and "Who is an artist-entrepreneur?"; (2) presentation of a proprietary model of creativity development built based on the process of identifying complex creative identities by illustrating the main issues of creativity relating to the identity features of artists-managers and artists-entrepreneurs; and (3) description of the challenges facing empirical research in the field of complex creative identities on the example of artists-managers and artists-entrepreneurs.

Based on these considerations, the following research questions were defined:

1. What are the differences and common features between the identity of an artist and manager and the identity of an artist and entrepreneur?
2. Do artists-managers and artists-entrepreneurs have their own identities?
3. Do artists-managers and artists-entrepreneurs experience identity tensions and paradoxical thinking?
4. Is being an artist an added value to the role of a manager and the role of an entrepreneur?
5. How has the COVID-19 pandemic caused an identity crisis for artists?
6. Do artists-entrepreneurs cope with the identity crisis better than artists without an entrepreneurial identity?
7. Do artists-entrepreneurs look for new forms of activity in times of crisis more often than artists without an entrepreneurial identity?

The practical aim was to verify the aforementioned problems to reduce inner-psychic tensions and the negative consequences of paradoxical thinking among personalities in organisations.

The qualitative study was conducted through in-depth interviews with key informants and autoethnography. The key informants were artists in their professional life, with various experiences in the field of management and entrepreneurship. The research sample was not limited to people who currently hold both roles simultaneously. Among the respondents, some performed both roles in different periods of their lives, to a different extent and at different levels. The choice of the research sample was justified by the availability of people with possibly diverse artistic, managerial, and entrepreneurial experiences from different countries and cultures.

The basis for this study was research methodology 3, "identity and self-perception of simple creative personalities", which was about artists-managers; it was then expanded to include aspects of entrepreneurship. For this study, the cases of 21 artists were analysed. Most of the face-to-face or online interviews were conducted in February and March 2020. Interviews with Polish respondents were conducted in Polish, while interviews with other respondents were conducted in English. Subsequently, all non-English interviews were translated into English. Each respondent's answers were placed in a table along with the basic categories that define them, and the analysis was started using the NVivo software. The description of the research sample is presented in Table 0.4.

Table 0.4 The identity and self-perception of the artist-entrepreneur: a description of the research sample

Nationality	*Year of birth*	*Sex*[8]	*Artistic activity*	*Entrepreneurial activity*
United States	1947	M	international musician-instrumentalist	self-employed entrepreneur in the field of art
United Kingdom	1948	M	musician-instrumentalist	lack
Poland	1952	F	musician-singer (25 years old)	president of music associations; manager and co-founder of a dance group; impresario
Poland	1964	F	painter and visual artist (23 years old)	self-employed artistic entrepreneur; member of artistic associations
United States	1965	M	musician-instrumentalist; choir conductor, lecturer	lack
Poland	1970	M	actor, opera singer (30 years old)	self-employed artistic entrepreneur; creator of the scene of young musicians; organiser of concerts and his artistic career
Poland	1974	M	musician-vocalist (operas, philharmonics, bands)	opera impresario; head of the opera's artistic department
Russia –3 United States	1977	F	musician-instrumentalist	coordinator and designer of artistic projects

Nationality	*Year of birth*	*Sex*[8]	*Artistic activity*	*Entrepreneurial activity*
Bulgaria	1978	M	international musician-vocalist; lecturer	creator, owner, and manager of an international art agency
Poland	1978	F	musician-singer; author of books	self-employed artistic entrepreneur, employing a dozen or so people
Poland	1980	M	international musician-instrumentalist; music lecturer (18 years old)	entrepreneur (own business activity); manager in international companies (16 years old); founder and CEO of an NGO
United Kingdom	1981	M	musician-instrumentalist, choir tutor, choir conductor	head of the music department; concert hall manager
Poland	1981	M	independent creator of origami lamps and graphics	entrepreneur, business owner, and manager (17 years old)
Poland	1982	F	musician-instrumentalist	lack
Poland	1989	M	musician-instrumentalist	creative manager in a cultural institution
Ukraine	1990	M	poet, translator	entrepreneur; concert house director; orchestra manager
Poland	1991	M	musician-instrumentalist	manager of promotion and program departments in cultural institutions, founder of NGOs
Poland	1992	M	international conductor	lack
Nigeria	1995	M	composer, musician-instrumentalist, choir conductor	lack
Poland	1999	M	musician-instrumentalist (12 years old)	creator, owner, and teacher at a music school; founder and director of the orchestra; founder and manager of a promotional agency
Poland	1999	F	musician-instrumentalist	creative manager in an art agency

Source: Author's own elaboration

The majority of the sample came from Poland (n = 11, 52%), three participants from the United States (14%), two from the United Kingdom (10%), and one participant each from Bulgaria, Nigeria, and Ukraine (4.5% each). In addition, most respondents were men (n = 15, 71%) with experience in the music industry (n = 18, 86%). No effort was made to balance participants' gender or age, nor was the sample balanced according to the length of work experience or art form pursued. Due to the qualitative nature of this study, respondents were not differentiated in terms of personal characteristics (e.g., optimist-pessimist, proactive-passive). With full awareness of the impact of these elements on the study results, due to the nature of this study and the rapidly changing pandemic situation, the analysis of results and conclusions was continued.

The study's conclusions are described in subsections 4.3.1 and 4.3.2 in Chapter 4.

Structure

This monograph consists of this Introduction (including a description of the methodology of the entire work), six chapters, a conclusion, a bibliography, a list of figures and tables, and appendices.

Chapter 1, "Management as an Art", focuses on analysing the essence of management and the essence of art in search of common areas between these fields and finally determines the interpenetration of these fields at the colloquial and scientific levels.

Chapter 2, "Art as an Organisational Activity", describes the duality of understanding art management and introduces and presents M. Gołaszewska's theory of the aesthetic situation in detail, showing its components and relations between them in order to draw attention to the complexity of the management process from the point of view of the artist as a manager. The managerial activity of an art creator was described on three levels: self-management, management of the aesthetic situation, and management of cultural institutions and artistic projects. Finally, as an empirical verification of the practical application of the developed theoretical concepts, the results of my qualitative study on the specificity of managing the aesthetic situation by artists within individual art disciplines in the context of virtualisation forced by the COVID-19 pandemic were presented.

Chapter 3, "Application of Aesthetic Theory in Management", describes the phenomenon of the aestheticisation of management, which is a derivative of the phenomenon of the aestheticisation of reality, and then introduces the metaphor of the organisation as a work of art and, in this spirit, analyses the relationship between the manager, the organisation, and its stakeholders, based on the achievements of the aesthetic situation described in Chapter 2; it also analyses the concepts of virtuosity, artistry, and creativity as crucial competencies of a manager.

Chapter 4, "Creative Personality: Identity and Perception", presents the issue of simple and complex creative identities and their perception, as well as problems related to the multiplicity of identities functioning within an individual – especially creative individuals (artists, creators, managers, leaders, and entrepreneurs), i.e., identity tensions, paradoxical thinking, identity crises. It also presents the results and conclusions of the author's quantitative and qualitative research on the identity and perception of simple and complex creative identities and the challenges in identifying these identities.

Chapter 5, "Creativity in Artistic and Managerial Activities – Source, Motive, Inspiration, Improvisation", is devoted to creativity as a desired competence of both managers and artists. Psychological and aesthetic concepts of creativity, sources of artistic creativity, motives and inspirations, and problems faced by a manager who wants to manage himself and his team's creativity are presented. Focus is also placed on the phenomenon of artistic improvisation in order to conclude management from this unusual and demanding form of creativity. The results and conclusions from original empirical research in the field of participation in an aesthetic situation, traditionally and virtually, both from the perspective of the creators of individual fields of art and recipients of particular fields of art, are also presented.

Chapter 6, "Kitsch and Ignorance in Management", presents two attitudes opposite to the aestheticisation of management, i.e., a tendency towards kitsch and ignorance. First, the issue of kitsch is discussed through the analysis of aesthetic and non-aesthetic kitsch, i.e., occurring on the grounds of intellect, education, politics, social processes, and religion, and then leading to the analysis of the phenomenon of organisational kitsch, showing its forms, carriers, and propagators. The problem of ignorance is discussed by showing the diversity of scientific approaches to ignorance, defining the function of ignorance, and showing the potential of ignorance management to develop ways to counteract this phenomenon in the face of the aestheticisation of management.

The substantive chapters are followed by the Conclusion (presenting the conclusions from the entire work, implications for the theory and practice of management, limitations of the undertaken considerations and empirical research, and recommendations for further research).

Notes

1 Not only the problems of the real world, but all elements of the aesthetic situation.
2 A detailed analysis of the aesthetic situation theory is presented in Section 2.2, "Aesthetic Situation".
3 The concepts of efficiency and effectiveness used in the work are not identical and are not used interchangeably. Whenever efficiency is mentioned, both the pursued goal and the costs of its implementation, i.e., the ratio of inputs to the effect obtained, should be taken into account; while when it comes to effectiveness, only the achievement of the chosen goal should be taken into account.

4 RQ – research question. ER – empirical study.
5 The interview questionnaire was placed as an attachment at the end of the monograph.
6 Although varied options in this area could be chosen, all respondents used Male or Female descriptions.
7 Based on Human Development Index: developing countries < 0.71 HDI, developed countries > 0.71 HDI. Source: https://worldpopulationreview.com/country-rankings/developing-countries (accessed: 29 July 2022).
8 Although varied options in this area could be chosen, all respondents used Male or Female descriptions.

References

Adler, N. J. (2006). The arts & leadership: Now that we can do anything, what will we do? *Academy of Management Learning and Education*, *5*(4), 486–499. https://doi.org/10.5465/AMLE.2006.23473209

Ainsworth, G. B., Redpath, S. M., Wilson, M., Wernham, C., & Young, J. C. (2020). Integrating scientific and local knowledge to address conservation conflicts: Towards a practical framework based on lessons learned from a Scottish case study. *Environmental Science and Policy*, *107*, 46–55. https://doi.org/10.1016/j.envsci.2020.02.017

Alvesson, M., & Blom, M. (2015). Less followership, less leadership? An inquiry into the basic but seemingly forgotten downsides of leadership. *M@n@gement*, *18*(3), 266–282.

Baker, S., Marshburn, D. M., Crickmore, K. D., Rose, S. B., Dutton, K., & Hudson, P. C. (2012). What do you do? Perception of nurse manager responsibilities. *Nursing Management*, *43*(12), 24–29. https://doi.org/10.1097/01.NUMA.0000422890.99334.21

Bayrakci, B., Forouz, A., Şahin, A. B., Abali, M., & Aliyeva, G. Z. (2009). Disease painting or painting disease: How does illness and hospitalisation affect children's artistry? *Perception*, *38*(11), 1721–1727. https://doi.org/10.1068/p6138

Biehl-Missal, B. (2011). *Wirtschaftsästhetik: Wie Unternehmen die Kunst als Inspiration und Werkzeug nutzen*. Gabler Verlag.

Bulei, I., Mihalcioiu, V., & Tucmeanu, A. (2014). The professional vs. the manager – identity issues and key features. *Valahian Journal of Economic Studies*, *5*(3), 31–36.

Bureau, S., & Zander, I. (2014). Entrepreneurship as an art of subversion. *Scandinavian Journal of Management*, *30*(1), 124–133. https://doi.org/10.1016/j.scaman.2013.12.002

Cardon, M. S., Wincent, J., Singh, J., & Drnovsek, M. (2009). The nature and experience of entrepreneurial passion. *Academy of Management Review*, *34*(3), 511–532. https://doi.org/10.5465/AMR.2009.40633190

Carroll, B., & Levy, L. (2008). Defaulting to management: Leadership defined by what it is not. *Organization*, *15*(1), 75–96. https://doi.org/10.1177/1350508407084486

Chen, V. Z., & Hitt, M. A. (2021). Knowledge synthesis for scientific management: Practical integration for complexity versus scientific fragmentation for simplicity. *Journal of Management Inquiry*, *30*(2), 177–192. https://doi.org/10.1177/1056492619862051

Clarke, J. S., & Holt, R. (2019, June). Images of entrepreneurship: Using drawing to explore entrepreneurial experience. *Journal of Business Venturing Insights*, *11*, 2019–2021. https://doi.org/10.1016/j.jbvi.2019.e00129

Craig, S. L., Eaton, A. D., Pascoe, R., Egag, E., McInroy, L. B., Fang, L., Austin, A., & Dentato, M. P. (2020). QueerVIEW: Protocol for a technology-mediated qualitative

photo elicitation study with sexual and gender minority youth in Ontario, Canada. *JMIR Research Protocols*, *9*(11). https://doi.org/10.2196/20547
Dahlhaus, C. (2007). *Estetyka muzyki*. Wydawnictwa Uniwersytetu Warszawskiego.
Damásio, M. J., & Bicacro, J. (2017). Entrepreneurship education for film and media arts: How can we teach entrepreneurship to students in the creative disciplines? *Industry and Higher Education*, *31*(4), 253–266. https://doi.org/10.1177/0950422217713110
Davidsson, P. (2006). Nascent entrepreneurship: Empirical studies and developments. *Foundations and Trends® in Entrepreneurship*, *2*(1), 1–76.
DeFillippi, R., Grabher, G., & Jones, C. (2007). Introduction to paradoxes of creativity: Managerial and organizational challenges in the cultural economy. *Journal of Organizational Behavior*, *28*, 511–521. https://doi.org/10.1002/job
Drucker, P. F. (2006a). *The effective executive*. HarperCollins.
Drucker, P. F. (2006b). *The practice of management*. HarperCollins.
Drucker, P. F. (2009). *Sztuka zarządzania według Petera Druckera*. Harvard Business Review Polska.
Dube, T. J., & İnce, G. (2019). A novel interface for generating choreography based on augmented reality. *International Journal of Human Computer Studies*, *132*, 12–24. https://doi.org/10.1016/j.ijhcs.2019.07.005
Dufour, L., Maoret, M., & Montani, F. (2020). Coupling high self-perceived creativity and successful newcomer adjustment in organizations: The role of supervisor trust and support for authentic self-expression. *Journal of Management Studies*, *57*(8), 1531–1555. https://doi.org/10.1111/joms.12547
Dunne-Howrie, J. (2020). Documenting performance: The contexts & processes of digital curation and archiving. *International Journal of Performance Arts and Digital Media*, *16*(2), 217–218. https://doi.org/10.1080/14794713.2020.1778840
Elstad, B., & Jansson, D. (2020). From artist to manager – working conditions, career satisfaction, and professional identity among graduated arts management students. *Journal of Arts Management Law and Society*, *50*(3), 184–198. https://doi.org/10.1080/10632921.2020.1746717
Enhuber, M. (2014). How is Damien Hirst a cultural entrepreneur? *Artivate: A Journal of Entrepreneurship in the Arts*, *3*(2), 3–20. https://repository.asu.edu/attachments/146224/content/ArtivateVol3No2pages3–20Enhuber.pdf
Fancourt, D., Baxter, L., & Lorencatto, F. (2020). Barriers and enablers to engagement in participatory arts activities amongst individuals with depression and anxiety: Quantitative analyses using a behaviour change framework. *BMC Public Health*, *20*(1). https://doi.org/10.1186/s12889-020-8337-1
Gołaszewska, M. (1967). *Odbiorca sztuki jako krytyk*. Wydawnictwo Literackie.
Gołaszewska, M. (1984a). *Estetyka rzeczywistości*. Instytut Wydawniczy PAX.
Gołaszewska, M. (1984b). *Zarys estetyki*. PWN.
Gołaszewska, M. (1986a). *Kim jest artysta?* Wydawnictwa Szkolne i Pedagogiczne.
Gołaszewska, M. (1986b). *O naturze wartości estetycznych*. Uniwersytet Jagielloński.
Gołaszewska, M. (2001). *Estetyka współczesności*. Wydawnictwo Uniwersytetu Jagiellońskiego.
Gołaszewska, M. (2005). *Estetyka możliwości*. Wydawnictwo Uniwersytetu Jagiellońskiego.
Griffin, R. W. (2005). *Podstawy zarządzania organizacjami*. Wydawnictwo Naukowe PWN.
Guidry, K. R. (2014). *Non-response bias on web-based surveys as influenced by the digital divide and participation gap. Submitted to the faculty of the University Graduate*

School in partial fulfillment of the requirements for the degree Doctor of Philosophy [Indiana University]. ProQuest Dissertations and Theses. www.proquest.com/openview/903c5e492b5d82315a69054cb56e8b63/1?pq-origsite=gscholar&cbl=18750

Guillet de Monthoux, P. (2004). *The art firm: Aesthetic management and metaphysical marketing*. Stanford University Press.

Guo, L., Lu, R., Zhang, H., Jin, J., Zheng, Z., Wu, F., Li, J., Xu, H., Li, H., Lu, W., Xu, J., & Gai, K. (2020). A deep prediction network for understanding advertiser intent and satisfaction. *International Conference on Information and Knowledge Management, Proceedings*, 2501–2508. https://doi.org/10.1145/3340531.3412681

Habelsberger, B. E. M., & Bhansing, P. V. (2021). Art galleries in transformation: Is COVID-19 driving digitisation? *Arts*, *10*(48), 1–23. https://doi.org/10.3390/arts10030048

Hallier, J. (2004). Embellishing the past: Middle manager identity and informality in the implementaion of new technology. *New Technology, Work and Employment*, *19*(1), 43–62. https://doi.org/10.1111/j.1468-005X.2004.00127.x

Hatch, M. J., Kostera, M., & Koźmiński, A. K. (2006). The three faces of leadership: Manager, artist, priest. *Organizational Dynamics*, *35*(1), 49–68. https://doi.org/10.1016/j.orgdyn.2005.12.003

Hobbs, R., & Tuzel, S. (2017). Teacher motivations for digital and media literacy: An examination of Turkish educators. *British Journal of Educational Technology*, *48*(1), 7–22. https://doi.org/10.1111/bjet.12326

Hracs, B. J. (2015). Cultural intermediaries in the digital age: The case of independent musicians and managers in Toronto. *Regional Studies*, *49*(3), 461–475. https://doi.org/10.1080/00343404.2012.750425

Ingarden, R. (1970). *Studia z estetyki. Tom III*. Wydawnictwo Naukowe PWN.

Ingarden, R. (1981). *Wykłady i dyskusje z estetyki*. Państwowe Wydawnictwo Naukowe.

Isaksen, A., & Nilsson, M. (2013). Combined innovation policy: Linking scientific and practical knowledge in innovation systems. *European Planning Studies*, *21*(12), 1919–1936. https://doi.org/10.1080/09654313.2012.722966

Jackson, K. (2017). Music and virtuosity: A higher vision for business. *Humanistic Management Journal*, *2*(1), 15–36. https://doi.org/10.1007/s41463-017-0020-z

Jankurová, A., Ljudvigová, I., & Gubová, K. (2017). Research of the nature of leadership activities. *Economics and Sociology*, *10*(1), 135–151. https://doi.org/10.14254/2071-789X.2017/10-1/10

Jarrier, E., & Bourgeon-Renault, D. (2019). The role of digital mediation devices in the satisfaction of art museum audiences. *Le Rôle Des Dispositifs Numériques de Médiation Dans La Satisfaction Des Publics de Musée d'art*, *5*(3), 67–84. https://search.ebscohost.com/login.aspx?direct=true&db=bth&AN=146420604&lang=es&site=ehost-live

Kociatkiewicz, J., & Kostera, M. (2013). Humanistic management: Agenda outline. *Problemy Zarzadzania*, *11*(44), 9–19. https://doi.org/10.7172/1644-9584.44.1

Kostera, M. (2014). *Occupy management! Inspirations and ideas for self-organization and self-management*. Routledge. https://doi.org/10.4324/9780203795033

Kostera, M. (2019). *Organize ourselves! Inspirations and ideas for self-organization and self-management*. Mayfly Books. https://ruj.uj.edu.pl/xmlui/bitstream/handle/item/72058/kostera_organize_ourselves_2019.pdf?sequence=1&isAllowed=y

Kostera, M., & Woźniak, C. (2022). *Aesthetics, organization, and humanistic management*. Routledge.

Kotler, P., & Keller, K. L. (2016). *Marketing mangement*. Pearson Edition Limited.

Koźmiński, A. K. (2005). *Zarządzanie w warunkach niepewności: Podręcznik dla zaawansowanych*. PWN.

Koźmiński, A. K., & Piotrowski, W. (1999). *Zarządzanie: Teoria i praktyka*. Wydawnictwo Naukowe PWN.

Lähdesmäki, M. (2012). Construction of owner-manager identity in corporate social responsibility discourse. *Business Ethics*, *21*(2), 168–182. https://doi.org/10.1111/j.1467-8608.2011.01644.x

Lee, H. J. (2011). Book reviews: Joystick soldiers: The politics of play in military video games. *Journal of Communication Inquiry*, *35*(3), 295–299. https://doi.org/10.1177/0196859911415408

Lehmann, J., & Gaskins, B. (2019). Learning scientific creativity from the arts. *Palgrave Communications*, *5*(95), 1–5. https://doi.org/10.1057/s41599-019-0308-8

Leso, G., Dias, G., Ferreira, J. P., Gama, J., & Couceiro, M. S. (2017). Perception of creativity and game intelligence in soccer. *Creativity Research Journal*, *29*(2), 182–187. https://doi.org/10.1080/10400419.2017.1302779

Levinson, J. (2003). *The Oxford hanbook of aesthetics*. Oxford University Press.

Lewis, K. V., Ho, M., Harris, C., & Morrison, R. (2016). Becoming an entrepreneur: Opportunities and identity transitions. *International Journal of Gender and Entrepreneurship*, *8*(2), 1–6. https://doi.org/10.1108/IJGE-02-2015-0006

Linstead, S., & Höpfl, H. J. (2000). *The aesthetics of organization*. SAGE Publications Ltd. https://uk.sagepub.com/en-gb/eur/the-aesthetics-of-organization/book205791#preview

Liu, Y. N., Li, K., & McLean, A. (2017). Practical scientific knowledge education based on Herbert Spencer's "what knowledge is of most worth?" *Eurasia Journal of Mathematics, Science and Technology Education*, *13*(7), 4291–4299. https://doi.org/10.12973/eurasia.2017.00836a

López-Fernández, M., Romero-Fernández, P. M., & Aust, I. (2018). Socially responsible human resource management and employee perception: The influence of manager and line managers. *Sustainability (Switzerland)*, *10*(12), 1–19. https://doi.org/10.3390/su10124614

Lord, R. G., & Brown, D. J. (2001). Leadership, values, and subordinate self concepts *The Leadership Quarterly*, *12*, 133–152.

Lutas, M., Nistor, R., Radu, M., & Beleiu, I. (2020). Perceptions regarding the profile of an ideal project manager. *Amfiteatru Economic*, *22*(54), 608–622. https://doi.org/10.24818/EA/2020/54/608

McHugh, K. E. (2015). Touch at a distance: Toward a phenomenology of film. *GeoJournal*, *80*(6), 839–851. https://doi.org/10.1007/s10708-015-9650-6

Melé, D. (2016). Understanding humanistic management. *Humanistic Management Journal*, *1*(1), 33–55. https://doi.org/10.1007/s41463-016-0011-5

Minahan, S. (2020). *Aesthetic turn in management*. Routledge. https://doi.org/10.4324/9781351147965

Mintzberg, H. (2012). *Zarządzanie*. Wolters Kluwer Polska.

Nikolski, K. (2015). Leadership and management: Practice of the art of influence. *Annals of the "Constantin Brâncuşi" University of Târgu Jiu, Economy Series*, *2*(1), 31–39.

Nowak, S. (2007). Metodologia Badań Społecznych. In *Metodologia Badań Społecznych*. Wydawnictwo Naukowe PWN.

Ossowski, S. (1949). *U podstaw estetyki*. Spółdzielnia Wydawniczo-Oświatowa Czytelnik.

Ostrowicki, M. (1997). Teoria sytuacji estetycznej M. Gołaszewskiej jako fundament estetyki. http://www.sideymyoo.art.pl/old/Teoria_sytuacji_estetycznej.pdf

Park, H. J., & Lim, K. H. (2015). A study on experiential digital art user experience. *International Journal of Multimedia and Ubiquitous Engineering*, *10*(4), 379–386. https://doi.org/10.14257/ijmue.2015.10.4.36

Phillips, M. (2000). The Sadeian interface: Computers and catharsis. *Digital Creativity*, *11*(2), 75–87. https://doi.org/10.1076/1462-6268(200005)11:2;1-r;ft075

Pianzola, F., Toccu, M., & Viviani, M. (2021). Readers' engagement through digital social reading on Twitter: The TwLetteratura case study. *Library Hi Tech*, 1–17. https://doi.org/10.1108/LHT-12-2020-0317

Porter, M. E. (1980). *Competitive strategy: Techniques for analyzing industries and companies*. Free Press.

Postuła, A., & Majczyk, J. (2018). Managers and leaders in need of entrepreneurial competences. *Entrepreneurial Business and Economics Review*, *6*(1), 91–103. https://doi.org/10.15678/EBER.2018.060105

Quattrini, R., Pierdicca, R., Paolanti, M., Clini, P., Nespeca, R., & Frontoni, E. (2020). Digital interaction with 3D archaeological artefacts: Evaluating user's behaviours at different representation scales. *Digital Applications in Archaeology and Cultural Heritage*, *18*. https://doi.org/10.1016/j.daach.2020.e00148

Raso, R., Fitzpatrick, J. J., & Masick, K. (2020). Clinical nurses' perceptions of authentic nurse leadership and healthy work environment. *Journal of Nursing Administration*, *50*(9), 489–494. https://doi.org/10.1097/NNA.0000000000000921

Sereenonchai, S., & Arunrat, N. (2020). Practical agricultural communication: Incorporating scientific and indigenous knowledge for climate mitigation. *Kasetsart Journal of Social Sciences*, *41*(1), 60–67. https://doi.org/10.1016/j.kjss.2018.05.014

Sosnowska, E. (2015). Touch, look and listen: The multisensory experience in digital art of Japan. *Journal of Science and Technology of the Arts*, *7*(1), 63. https://doi.org/10.7559/citarj.v7i1.147

Strati, A. (1999). *Organization and aesthetics*. SAGE Publications Ltd. https://sk.sagepub.com/books/organization-and-aesthetics

Stuke, K. B. (2013). Understanding leadership through leadership understandings. *Journal of Leadership Studies*, *7*(2), 55–61. https://doi.org/10.1002/jls.21291

Sułkowski, Ł. (2007). Problem demarkacji nauk o zarządzaniu. *Przegląd Organizacji*, *1*, 12–14. https://doi.org/10.33141/po.2007.01.02

Sułkowski, Ł., & Lenart-Gansiniec, R. (2021). *Epistemologia, metodologia i metody badań w naukach o zarządzaniu i jakości*. Wydawnictwo Społecznej Akademii Nauk.

Szostak, M. (2020). Creativity and artistry in organ music. *The Organ*, *391*, 24–31. https://depot.ceon.pl/handle/123456789/19170

Szostak, M. (2021a). Artistry, management, and creativity: Links and common denominators. *Discourses on Culture*, *16*(1), 23–54. https://doi.org/10.36145/DoC2021.08

Szostak, M. (2021b). *The organ as a source of inspiration: The rebirth of a giant (Paris – Vatican – Licheń)*. SINDRUK-DIMK.

Szostak, M., & Sułkowski, Ł. (2020). Manager as an artist: Creative endeavour in crossing the borders of art and organizational discourse. *Creativity Studies*, *13*(2), 351–368. https://doi.org/10.3846/cs.2020.11373

Szostak, M., & Sułkowski, Ł. (2021a). Identity crisis of artists during the COVID-19 pandemic and shift towards entrepreneurship. *Entrepreneurial Business and Economics Review*, *9*(3), 87–102. https://doi.org/doi.org/10.15678/EBER.2021.090306

Szostak, M., & Sułkowski, Ł. (2021b). The challenges in identification of artists-managers: Consequences for creativity. *Creativity Studies*, *14*(1), 112–124. https://doi.org/10.3846/cs.2021.13822

Szostak, M., & Sułkowski, Ł. (2021c). The identity and self-perception of artists-managers. *Problems and Perspectives in Management*, *19*(1), 372–386. https://doi.org/10.21511/ppm.19(1).2021.32

Taleghani, M. (2012). Impact of attitudes on managers creativity. *Procedia – Social and Behavioral Sciences*, *40*, 65–70. https://doi.org/10.1016/j.sbspro.2012.03.162

Tatarkiewicz, W. (2015). *Historia estetyki: Tom I*. PWN.

Toscher, B. (2019). Entrepreneurial learning in arts entrepreneurship education: A conceptual framework. *Arti*, *8*(1), 3–22.

Toscher, B. (2020). Blank canvas: Explorative behavior and personal agency in arts entrepreneurship education. *Artivate: A Journal of Entrepreneurship in the Arts*, *9*(2), 19–44. https://doi.org/10.34053/artivate.9.2.115

Walter, H. M. (2015). *Artist, professional, gentleman: Designing the body of the actor-manager, 1870–1900*. Royal College of Art.

Welsch, W. (2005). Procesy estetyzacji. Zjawiska, rozróżnienia, perspektywy. In *Estetyka poza estetyką: o nową postać estetyki* (pp. 31–73). Universitas.

Wilkoszewska, K. (2007). *Wizje i re-wizje: Wielka księga estetyki w Polsce*. Towarzystwo Autorów i Wydawców Prac Naukowych Universitas.

Wilson, C., & Brown, M. (2012). Sound, space, image and music: Hybridity in creative process through technology, interactivity and collaboration. *Journal of Music, Technology and Education*, *5*(1), 89–107. https://doi.org/10.1386/jmte.5.1.89_1

Woodward, J. B., & Funk, C. (2010). Developing the artist-leader. *Leadership*, *6*(3), 295–309. https://doi.org/10.1177/1742715010368768

Wu, Y., Zhang, L., Bryan-Kinns, N., & Barthet, M. (2017). Open symphony: Creative participation for audiences of live music performances. *IEEE Multimedia*, *24*(1), 48–62. https://doi.org/10.1109/MMUL.2017.19

Zhou, J., Shin, S. J., & Cannella, A. A. (2008). Employee self-perceived creativity after mergers and acquisitions: Interactive effects of threat-opportunity perception, access to resources, and support for creativity. *Journal of Applied Behavioral Science*, *44*(4), 397–421. https://doi.org/10.1177/0021886308328010

Zollo, L., Rialti, R., Marrucci, A., & Ciappei, C. (2021). How do museums foster loyalty in tech-savvy visitors? The role of social media and digital experience. *Current Issues in Tourism*. https://doi.org/10.1080/13683500.2021.1896487

1 Management as an art

The turn of the 21st century is a time when management practitioners and theoreticians opened up to the world of art, looking for answers to their doubts, the crisis of values, and the need for a creative approach to the changing reality (Morozova et al., 2016; Woodward & Funk, 2010). There is a diametrical difference in the way people from the world of technical sciences think compared to people from the humanities; a more significant the difference can be found in the way of thinking of people from the world of science and the world of art. Modern organisations – full of analysts and technocrats – need creativity in using so-called "hard" resources to build, develop, and maintain their competitive advantages effectively (Watkins & King, 2002), especially since the dynamics of change are becoming faster and more profound. Building strategies that will be sensible and worth implementing in these conditions requires an unconventional approach instead of a logical choice from solutions that have worked well in the past (Adler, 2006).

It is common to encounter a statement that opposes science and art, and the axis of the apparent division is considered to be the issues of objectivism (allegedly belonging only to science) and subjectivism (allegedly belonging only to art). Just as science can be subjective – e.g., due to the researcher's interests or personal choice and combination of concepts, or the current (incomplete) state of knowledge – art can be objective, if only because of the values it refers to (Mercier, 1985). The optimal solution here will be a synthetic approach recognising the mutual complementarity of science and art: art has much to offer science, and the scientific approach to art is beyond doubt. Even such an abstract concept as beauty can be the subject of scientific analysis in art (Barbone, 1997).

Beauty, the primary research problem of aesthetics, answers many questions about contemporary managers. In its search for creativity, the world demands a permanent redefinition of who we are as human beings. Today's society longs for leadership of opportunity based more on hope, aspirations, wisdom, meaning, and innovation than on replicating historic pragmatic solutions (Adler, 2015). For this reason, attention was drawn to the fact that the

DOI: 10.4324/9781003458029-2

existing, strictly scientific academic programs in developing managers' creativity ceased to meet the expectations of modern organisations (Gosling & Mintzberg, 2004; Mangham, 1990). Art has become a remedy for these problems, all the more so as it has become the foundation of the new spirit of global capitalism (Watson, 2001), and reflections on creative management are developed through a critical approach to classical management theories (Beirne & Knight, 2007).

This chapter focuses on analysing the essence of art and management in search of common areas between these fields to formulate a research gap that is the subject of interest in subsequent chapters.

1.1 Essence of art

Defining the essence of art has been divided into three considerations: (1) art and creativity, (2) beauty and reality, and (3) aesthetics and ethics, emphasising the role of values and evaluation criteria.

1.1.1 Art and creativity

Art has existed in human life since the earliest ages; it allows you to see, hear, and feel more. And although aesthetics (Greek: to perceive, perception) as an autonomous science was separated from philosophy relatively late – in the 18th century, thanks to Alexander Gottlieb Baumgarten (1714–1762) – it was present in philosophical discourses from the beginning of abstract thought (Ingarden, 1981, p. 19). Because art is an ephemeral phenomenon that can be noticed empirically only in the form of a more or less tangible work of art (e.g., a sculpture) or during the creative process (e.g., a ballet performance), attempts to define this phenomenon have also been numerous and resulted in different perspectives. No matter how one tries to define art, its essence can be contained in three perception models (Gołaszewska, 1967, p. 17):

1. art as a complement to life – by creating or drawing attention to additional dimensions of reality, everyday life does not have to consist only in carrying out mundane activities related to physical survival; art can be an extension of reality (aestheticisation) or even additional independent dimensions in which functioning, apart from physicality, takes place in the world of universal values; this model draws attention to the fact that life would be poorer without art;
2. art as an artist's expression – being a field of creative expression of individuals with a developed creative personality, it allows in an almost unlimited way to formulate artistic messages that are often a more eloquent form of communication than scientific argumentation;

3. art as an independent reality – the richness of artistic reality, taking place at the junction of the real world and the world of values, unlike physical reality, is immeasurable and unlimited; it is governed by other laws and rules, which makes it justified to consider it as an independent reality on an equal footing with physical reality.

It is a kind of paradox that a modern individual, having access to all works of art (physically and in reality, in a digitised form or employing remote communication), falls into considering the meanders of very narrow classes of cases, which makes understanding the essence of art even more complicated (Dutton, 2019, p. 97). However, to understand the area of interest to us, we must not forget about the differences between art and creativity and the key value of art, which is beauty. Moreover, although the concept of beauty evolves with the human, every recipient dealing with a real work of art will still feel that he is dealing with a real universal value in its more or less perfect edition (Eco, 2004).

Although some researchers claim that the essence of art cannot be encapsulated in terms at all due to the constant redefinition of its borders (Gombrich, 1966), it is worth looking at the attempts made in this regard over the centuries.

Initially, the concept of individual creativity was not distinguished, and art was understood as the ability to combine three factors: the material factor (given by nature), the knowledge factor (derived from tradition), and the work factor (derived from people). It can be said that the initial meaning of art was close to the modern definition of craft. Creativity was initially perceived passively as imitation (mimesis). Defining and analysing the phenomenon of individual creativity, which is essential in our considerations, began much later (Tatarkiewicz, 2015). The Middle Ages developed a division of the arts because they involved only the mind (called the liberal arts, *Artes Liberales*: arithmetic, astronomy, geometry, grammar, logic, music, and rhetoric) or also requiring physical effort (common/utilitarian/mechanical arts, *Artes Vulgares*: sculpture, painting, architecture, and others). The Renaissance was a period of attempts to make art independent of craft and science. In the 18th century, the term "fine arts" (French: beaux-arts) was introduced, including architecture, painting, music, poetry, sculpture, dance, theatre, and speech. The contemporary view of art is radically different from the indicated historical views. It is said that beauty has gone beyond art, no longer being a distinctive value for art. Analysing the vast majority of contemporary works, it is no exaggeration to say that beauty is no longer essential to art. We must not forget about the phenomenon of commercialisation, which has always been present, but nowadays, it has become a value in itself and a kind of test of art, and by creating an entertainment industry, art – usually low-flying – has become an independent branch of industry.

The Austrian poet Rainer Maria Rilke (1875–1926), emphasising the universalist aspirations of art and its translation of reality, considered art to be a view of life (worldview) or a way of being in which imagination plays a key role (Rilke, 2010). Going further, a look at reality transferred from the aesthetic situation (Gołaszewska, 1984) on the ground of everyday life enables its creative view, constructing meaning and reaching the circles of universals and beauty (Żak, 2015).

The German philosopher Hans Georg Gadamer (1900–2002) proposed the concept of "art as a game", where the key attributes become (Gadamer, 1994):

1. variability of movement – requiring space and life;
2. reason – with its discipline and order;
3. interplay – requiring communicativeness;
4. identity – with the awareness of rules;
5. reflection – as an action and as a result.

In turn, the British art critic Clive Bell (1881–1964) defined art as having a significant form. Having this significant form meant evoking an aesthetic emotion in the recipient (Levinson, 2003, p. 140).

The definitions of art use specific repetitive components that are combined in various configurations and proportions by those who try to operationalise the concept of art. These are: (1) theoretical knowledge, (2) practical skills, (3) creativity, (4) improvement, and (5) direction of activities. Each discipline of art requires theoretical knowledge (general and related to a given discipline), which allows you to embed practical activities in specific contexts and consciously navigate through the achievements of a given field so far (da Vinci, 1930, p. 194). However, knowledge of the theory is insufficient because the essence of creativity is practice. Moreover, the same theoretical knowledge provided to a group of adepts of a given discipline does not guarantee an equal probability of each appearing on the art market. It is in the area of practice that artists develop their style, preferred techniques, or the way of creative work. In addition to theoretical preparation and creative techniques developed through their practice, creativity is another component that constitutes the creator of art. Without this resource, artistic activities will only copy or imitate the activities of other creators. The presence of the creative element, creating something new or in a new way, makes both theory and practice come to life, becoming a means and not an end. Perfection is an inherent quality of the creator; it concerns all aspects of activity: from theoretical knowledge, through practical skills, to the ability to stimulate and use the resources of one's creativity. Although artists are often perceived as chaotic individuals, functioning in so-called creative disarray, the components discussed are not combined by chance; the creator is goal-oriented and subordinates all his actions to this goal.

In addition to attempts to describe the essence of art in the form of a definition, some art theoreticians went in the direction of creating various types of classifications of art's features (being aware of the different saturation of individual features depending on cultural differences). Thus, according to the philosophy of art, these features should be included (Dutton, 2019, pp. 100–112):

1. the direct pleasure of communing with beauty or from the aesthetic activity itself;
2. the proficiency and virtuosity necessary in creators and performers for a work of art to fully exist;
3. the style (or lack thereof) in which a particular artist creates and in which the work has been maintained;
4. innovation and creativity manifested in both originality and the ability to surprise the recipient;
5. openness to criticism and the fact that criticism takes nothing away from a true work of art;
6. imitation (representation) of physical or metaphysical reality in a work that gives the viewer the pleasure of recognising the content of the work;
7. a special place (uniqueness) of a work of art, which manifests itself in its physical presentation (lighting, distinction, rituals) and adds unusualness to the work;
8. expressing individuality, e.g., personality, phenomenon, situation;
9. emotional saturation imparting to the recipient of the work (according to the basic types of emotions according to empirical psychology: disgust, contempt, joy, sadness, fear, surprise, anger);
10. an intellectual challenge that stimulates the ability to interpret sensory impressions;
11. traditions and art institutions that give the work of art additional senses and meanings;
12. imagination (imaginative experience), which is required from both the creator and the recipient.

Art fulfils various functions, which are not its essence (Gołaszewska, 1984, pp. 143–147). The following functions of art are distinguished (listed alphabetically):

1. adaptive – extends human experience, facilitating understanding of the environment and living in communities;
2. didactic (cognitive) – allows you to learn about historical figures, events, and phenomena;
3. expressive – allows individuals to express themselves and fulfil themselves creatively;
4. aesthetic – evokes aesthetic experiences in the recipient;
5. humanising – adding additional (aesthetic) dimensions to the world of nature and culture;
6. ideological – conveys (not always) specific political, social, and ideological attitudes; integrates individuals around ideas;

7. integrative – mitigates national and social divisions, integrates communities at all levels – from global to small local groups;
8. cathartic – allows experiencing of catharsis, release from intrusive thoughts, or negative emotional states;
9. communicative – the creator communicates with the recipient through his work;
10. breaking stereotypes – shows the natural otherness of the world and allows one to look at the world and himself from a different perspective;
11. therapeutic – it can be an element of art treatment (music therapy) or allow for escapism in medically hopeless situations;
12. educational – shaping attitudes, it stimulates the imagination, engaging feelings.

It is worth considering the question of why art is essential to humans. The answers to this question can be grouped into three categories (Figure 1.1):

1. related to the creation of space understood as an additional dimension of reality,
2. related to generating economic value,
3. related to the creation of communities and the involvement of their members.

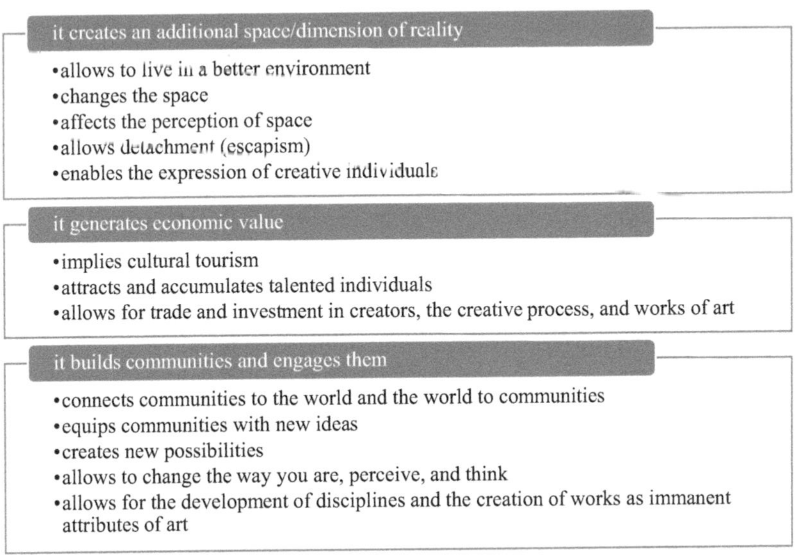

Figure 1.1 The role of art in human life

Source: Author's own elaboration

In terms of creating an additional dimension or space of reality, art allows one to live in a better, multidimensional environment and also changes the space, at the same time influencing the perception of this space. This multidimensionality also allows for escapism, i.e., detachment from everyday life focused on a specific dimension of reality, in order to move to another dimension through art; art is also a form of expression of creative individuals, allowing them to express themselves on specific topics using the language of art referring to metaphysical reality. Regarding generating economic value, art attracts and accumulates talented individuals and allows for trade and investment in creators, the creative process, and the works of art themselves, whose turnover is primarily implied by the capital investment function. In addition, it attracts tourists and implies the mobility of art creators and recipients, stimulating the creative economy, which is about 10% of the global GDP (UNESCO, 2017). When it comes to creating communities and engaging their members, art connects communities with the world and the world with communities, endowing these communities with new ideas and possibilities, allowing them to change the way they are, perceive, and think, and – what from the point of view of aesthetics is most important – it allows the development of disciplines and the creation of works as immanent attributes of art.

1.1.2 Beauty and reality

At this point, we should focus on the concept of beauty, which is the main subject of interest in aesthetics, and – which will be discussed in greater detail in later chapters – is the fundamental and superior aesthetic value in the theory of the aesthetic situation (Gołaszewska, 1984, p. 76).

Tatarkiewicz proposed a duality of the notion of beauty (Tatarkiewicz, 2004, p. 123):

1. beauty *sensu largo* (broader scope) – encompassing everything that we perceive and imagine with pleasure and appreciation; it contains grace, subtlety, sublimity, and appropriateness;
2. beauty in the strict sense (narrower scope) – covering everything that we perceive and imagine with pleasure and appreciation due to the arrangement; it contains proportion, order, and form; it can therefore be said that beauty *sensu stricto* (the beauty of form) is a variety (category) of beauty *sensu largo*.

Just as the concept of art can be considered through various methodologies, the concept of beauty is a complex matter. Beauty can be the subject of a dialectical dispute regarding its opposite, ugliness, but it can be considered objectively and subjectively (Tatarkiewicz, 2004, p. 129).

The first ancient canons of beauty concerned the Stoic objectivity of phenomena such as harmony, order, proportion, and measure based on numbers, which resulted in the concept of symmetry (Greek: commensurability), and the subjective approach of the sophists that "man is the measure of all things", and therefore also beauty. The Middle Ages absorbed the objectivism of beauty, although a distinction was made between "beauty in itself" and "beauty concerning something or for someone". The objectivism of beauty was also dominant in the Renaissance, where harmony, conformity, and arrangement of parts were emphasised as the absolute and highest law of nature, something innate (*innatum*); and the artist was allowed to add decorations (*ornamentum*), which anyway results from necessity and not creative freedom. Baroque was based on the Renaissance concept of beauty, although the latter developed the former extremely; beauty was seen in the rules, and artistry manifested itself precisely in these rules of observance. In the eighteenth century, the subjectivism of beauty dominated its objective optics, as evidenced by the lack of universality in judgements about beauty; the search for universal principles and rules of beauty was abandoned in favour of its psychological determinants: imagination, taste, the process of associating. There was also an independent sense – the "sense of beauty". Published only in 1790 by Immanuel Kant, "Kritik der Urteilskraft" (German: "Critique of Judgment") reconciled objectivism and subjectivism in the perception of beauty, emphasising the values of both optics (Kant, 2015). At the turn of the 19th and 20th centuries, beauty began to be treated as an exclusively psychological phenomenon, which was supported by the following arguments:

1. there is not a single feature common to all beautiful objects, but there are common features of an aesthetic attitude towards objects;
2. aesthetic experience depends on taking an aesthetic attitude, which can apply to virtually any object;
3. the concept of an aesthetic object is of a psychological nature.

The 20th century is a conglomerate of many approaches to beauty; it is worth paying attention to the following:

1. sociology – beauty depends on the social order (each system has its own beauty);
2. historicism – beauty depends on the historical situation (each epoch has its own beauty);
3. conventionalism – beauty depends on the adopted convention (each convention has its own beauty).

The concept of beauty has evolved along with the development of humanity, and it has recently faded into the shadows compared to other values in art, such as form or deformation, construction or deconstruction, and logic (Tatarkiewicz, 2004, pp. 129–150). An example of this evolution may be musical works from the trend of dodecaphony or serialism, which can be explained logically and coherently in a scientific way; but when perceived by the sense of hearing, the vast majority of recipients give the impression of chaos and randomness without any classic signs of beauty.

Aesthetics has developed a division of beauty into four areas (Gołaszewska, 1984, p. 84):

1. the existing beauty – which is independent of humans and different from everything that humans are able to produce; this area includes the beauty of nature;
2. the beauty of art – concerning specialised beauty, appearing in connection with the products of humans and their deliberate action; it is a kind of opposite of the existing beauty;
3. beauty as a by-product of human activities – manifested in products whose basic functions are other than aesthetic (e.g., utilitarian functions such as technical devices, machines, and infrastructure); these products are beautiful "by the way" of being useful;
4. the beauty of events – manifested in the arrangement of processes taking place in reality, which can be attributed to aesthetic qualifications.

1.1.3 Aesthetics and ethics: values and criteria

Aesthetics, whose roots come from philosophy, is a theoretical discipline. Nevertheless, it is hard to deny the role it brings to creative artistic practice. The artist, equipped with the theoretical tools of aesthetics, will be more aware of the various aspects that his work can bring to the life of the recipient. Within the framework of theoretical aesthetics, three attitudes or optics towards the subject of study are distinguished – it should be remembered that these attitudes are interdependent and should not be treated as separate categories (Ingarden, 1981, pp. 19–20):

1. subjectivist (called aesthetics), which, dealing with the human attitude towards beauty, leads to the creation of a theory of aesthetic experience (knowledge); deals with the analysis of a work of art, regardless of its value (there arises a doubt whether the subject of research should belong to the scope of interest of psychologists, or whether an autonomous discipline should be separated, which could be phenomenology, dealing with human behaviour towards the work);
2. objectivist, which deals with beauty and its components (called the general theory of art); focuses on the value of the work;
3. subjectivist-objectivist, emphasising the inseparable relationship between the two previous views, characterised by the meeting and interaction of the subjective element (man and his experience) with the objective element (existing

work with its features); the essence of the subjectivist-objectivist attitude is the transformation of what a person experiences and the transformation of the existing work that this experience has caused.

The analysis of the aesthetic experience or the work itself leads directly to the question of their evaluation, and thus – of valuation; the approach to evaluation and evaluation is closely related to the optics mentioned earlier. Aesthetic values are not an unambiguous concept, and researchers indicate different approaches: from the attitude that (1) there is only one aesthetic value and that is beauty (which should not be confused with prettiness), so only outstanding works should be analysed (there remains the question of which works and on what basis to be considered outstanding) to the perspective that (2) aesthetic values extend on the scale between beauty and ugliness, therefore they analyse works of different qualitative scale. In addition to beauty, there is often another aesthetic value – sublimity, which, in addition to aesthetic criteria, also adds ethical criteria. Other researchers claim that there are no values at all, only specific judgments or behaviours; Therefore, there is no such thing as objective beauty (Ingarden, 1981, pp. 20–21).

It seems impossible to create aesthetic criteria that could be applied universally to all works and all experiences. It is true that within individual stylistic epochs, certain canons of beauty were created (and still are being created); however, an attempt to evaluate and gradate them is basically impossible to achieve (Ingarden, 1981, p. 22).

For the clarity of further considerations, it should be mentioned that aesthetic issues can be divided into three levels, which in fact are interrelated and mutually

Figure 1.2 The Platonic triad as the completion of ethics and aesthetics

Source: Author's own elaboration

condition each other (Gołaszewska, 1984, p. 78): (1) pro-aesthetic – when individual cases are considered; (2) aesthetic – when scientific facts are considered; and (3) meta-aesthetic – when theories are considered. In this book, the level of meta-aesthetics is analysed with the support from the level of aesthetics.

Reaching the Platonic triad, which includes the ideal, eternal, and unchanging universal values of truth, goodness, and beauty, we will also notice the mutual *complementation of aesthetics and ethics*[1] (Figure 1.2). While ethics, based on the value of good, refers to what is good and how to act, aesthetics, referring to the value of truth (as opposed to kitsch based on pretence) and the value of beauty (much more complex than superficial beauty) expands reality with further transcendental dimensions. None of these three values is more important than the others, and the elimination of any of them impoverishes the perception of the others. Thanks to these ethical and aesthetic standards, human activity gains depth, meaning, and motivation. These human aspirations and searches for truth, good, and beauty are realised through the choices made in actions and, consequently, build the culture (Klamer, 2017, pp. 11–19; Tatarkiewicz, 2015, pp. 131–161).

1.2 Essence of management

The issue of the essence of management will be discussed based on: (1) definitions and features of management, (2) levels and functions of management, and (3) the issue of self-management as a particular type of management in the context of the problems considered in this monograph.

1.2.1 Definitions and features of management

Management – in a more or less conscious way – has accompanied humanity since primitive times; organisation, division of tasks, and specialisation to achieve goals were later reflected in the theory of organisation and management. From the beginning of the 20th century, when attempts were made to base management on scientific grounds, until around the 1960s, management was understood as a managerial activity involving the so-called classic management functions defined by Henri Fayol (1841–1925) as planning, organising, deciding, motivating, and controlling (Listwan & Witkowski, 2001). The evolution of considerations in this area has left the following *definitions of management*:

1. the art[2] of combining the means at the disposal of the company so that it achieves its goals with maximum efficiency; this definition of management should not be confused with management that is the essence of decision-making and is a set of activities aimed at achieving positive financial results at the end of specific periods; the selection, distribution, and application of the enterprise's resources, as well as the relations of any kind it may have with other legal persons (Caude & Moles, 1964, p. 450);

2. managerial activity consisting in setting goals and causing their implementation in organisations subordinate to the manager, based on the ownership of means of production or at their disposal (Gliński, 1974, p. 929);
3. the act of disposing of resources; the most important resources are people and money; people are influenced by money; management is related to management, and very often, the terms "organisation and management" and "direction and management" are used together (Pszczołowski, 1978, p. 288);
4. exercising power over people, resulting from the ownership of things that are necessary objects or work tools for people (necessary to obtain means of subsistence) or from the authorisation received from the owner of these things (Zieleniewski, 1982);
5. wandering through chaos understood as constructing reality from available elements: ideas, people, formal and legal institutions, material and financial resources, as well as the right to dispose of them (Koźmiński & Piotrowski, 1999, p. 130);
6. mastering diversity and transforming potential conflict into cooperation (Koźmiński & Piotrowski, 1999, p. 130);
7. action set (planning, organisation, motivating, control) aimed at the organisation's resources (human, financial, material, informative) used with the intention of achieving the objectives of the organisation (Griffin, 2005, p. 6);
8. a conscious, well-thought-out, and systematised process conducted in accordance with applicable law by persons who have been granted appropriate decision-making powers and scope of responsibility, extending to a number of complex, formal activities aimed at ensuring the current functioning of the organisation and stable development in the future, under the set goals and adopted strategy (Walczak, 2014).

Repetitive elements in the quoted definitions include goal achievement, efficiency, decisions, actions, processes, and resources. It can be summarised that management is a broadly understood range of activities undertaken as a result of well-thought-out decisions regarding the efficient use of resources to achieve specific goals. For this work, management will be understood as *achieving goals in an efficient manner*.

Peter Drucker (1909–2005) points to the following characteristics of management: (1) it concerns mainly people; (2) it is embedded in the culture; (3) it requires simple and understandable values, goals, and tasks for the organisation's participants; (4) it should lead to learning by the organisation; (5) it requires communication; (6) it requires indicators; and (7) it should be oriented towards the organisation's customer satisfaction (Drucker, 2006a, 2006b).

Looking at changes in the goals of managing a business organisation over the decades, the following general evolution can be observed:

1. in the 19th century, management aimed to organise the production process as efficiently as possible to produce the largest amount of goods in the shortest

time and at the lowest cost; in principle, any quantity of goods was saleable, as the limited possibilities of producing goods so far were not sufficient to meet the growing needs of societies;
2. in the 20th century, the goal of management was to increase the value of the company from the point of view of the owners (shareholders); therefore, not only organisational efficiency in the field of production processes but also managerial skills in the field of selling these products; the market began to fill up with goods produced more and more efficiently and faster, and selling them became an art;
3. in the 21st century, the goal of management – apart from the ability to organise production processes and sales efficiency with good effect for the increase in the value of the company and thus the property of the owners – has become caring for people; people are no longer just a mode of organisation and a means to achieve an economic goal (as a stakeholder of the organisation), but are perceived primarily as a sentient being whose well-being is no less important than the well-being of the company's owners.

Interesting conclusions on the evolution of crucial management problems at the turn of the 20th and 21st centuries are provided by the analysis of one of the essential Polish academic textbooks in management: *Zarządzanie. Teoria i praktyka* (English: *Management: Theory and Practice*) edited by A. Koźmiński and W. Piotrowski. In the 1999 edition, the emphasis is on the world of organisation, management process, strategic management, planning, control and controlling, production management, organisational structures, organisational behaviour, management of the social potential of the organisation, international management, intercultural management, and management concepts (Koźmiński & Piotrowski, 1999). In 2013, the same manual underwent the following changes: production management was removed, and organisational decision-making, project management, and change management were added. Judging from these modifications, the entire management world changed profoundly in only 14 years. Secrets of production management in the field of technology, methods of production regulation and production systems lost their original (so to speak, 19th-century) keyness in favour of the ability to reason in order to make organisationally appropriate decisions, the ability to manage periodic projects, and the ability to cope with organisational changes. The world has accelerated, and changes have become an immanent component of organisational life; no longer the ability to calibrate the organisation once and for all, but the ability to cope with turbulence in the environment and the need to adapt the organisation to the consequences of these changes quickly have become the key to survival and success. Long-term stability has given way to periodic projects that are created as a reaction to the current situation; after the end of the project (and often even before its completion,

According to Henry Mintzberg (born 1939), the key management issues are dynamics, models, dilemmas, and effectiveness (Mintzberg, 2012). M. Kostera and M. Śliwa, writing about management in the 21st century, consider it crucial (Kostera & Śliwa, 2012):

1. contexts: globalisation, corporate social responsibility, also known as corporate social responsibility, post-colonialism;
2. interculturality: cultural differences, cultural conditions, cultural assumptions, dimensions and levels of culture analysis;
3. quality: quality in management, quality in services, quality definition, ethics and policy in quality management;
4. creativity: the state of flow, the story of the organisation, myths and archetypes, art management and the art of management, sensations, irony and humour, entrepreneurship and innovation;
5. culture: organisational culture, identity, organisational space, spirituality, management culture, diversity management.

The juxtaposition of possible forms of action is of crucial pragmatic importance because, thanks to theoretical analysis, these solutions are automatically implemented in organisational activities, and the decision taken becomes a regulator of variants covering the scale of available possibilities. Based on dialectics, general guidelines are distinguished that constitute the *antinomies of efficient action*, which can be grouped into opposing pairs (Kieżun, 1997, pp. 23–24):

- specialisation and universalisation,
- the anticipation of the right moment and anticipation,
- activation and limitation,
- concentration and distraction,
- maintenance of a specific type of resources versus full use of resources.

Like any living discipline of knowledge, management sciences are also subject to evolution. The growing separation from other knowledge disciplines manifests the management sciences development. In the 1980s, dependence on psychology, economics, and sociology began to be broken and was expressed in "borrowing" concepts and explanations in favour of clearly observable own terminology, questions, and research methods. This situation results from the need to keep up with practice and shape managerial practice (Czakon, 2019). Looking from the point of view of scientific disciplines, the discipline of management sciences – by the Resolution of the Central Commission for Degrees and Titles in Poland of 23 June 2003, on defining the fields of science and the fields of art as well as scientific and artistic disciplines – was divided into two equal scientific fields: management within the framework of economic sciences, and management within the framework of humanities.[3] Undoubtedly, this is additional proof that the 21st century is widely open to the humanistic trend in management. Nevertheless, on the other hand, the 19th-century technological and engineering precision and the 20th-century economic efficiency in the context of market requirements gained the third force in the form of the 21st-century view of the person as a being living in a much larger number of dimensions of reality, e.g., psychological, sociological, ethical, and aesthetic.

1.2.2 Management levels and functions

Management is a ubiquitous phenomenon, and practically everything can be managed. The main subjects of management include management of, among others: time, documentation, finance, quality, intangible capital, culture, real estate, organisation, processes, projects, enterprise, relationships, risk, stress, environment, rights, value, knowledge, and human resources.

Management can be carried out at different *levels of generality* (strategic, tactical, operational) or in different *time perspectives* (long term, medium term, short term).

The *classic management functions* defined by H. Fayol in the form of a sequence of actions (i.e., planning, organising, deciding, motivating, and controlling) seem to be the backbone of all theories defining the critical result of the management process. Researchers extend this classic set of management functions with new components – e.g., planning, organising, information and knowledge managing, organisation's financial managing, operations managing, personnel policy managing, marketing and public relations, negotiating, and controlling (Koźmiński & Jemielniak, 2008, pp. 19–21) – however, all evolutions in this area can usually be reduced to the classic prototype.

1.2.3 Self-management

Considerations regarding managerial issues in the artist's activity can be placed in the subject of interest in self-organisation and self-management, where self-awareness and the ability to reflect play a key role. This self-management, which can be described as "occupy management" from the title of M. Kostera's monograph, is a response, on the one hand, to the erosion of the role of the nation-state and, on the other hand, to the growing power of corporations, which take over an increasing range of everyday spheres. In between all this, there is a modern person who is increasingly better equipped with the knowledge and skills to organise his own life without the participation of institutional support (Kostera, 2014). However, we also see that the hitherto guarantors of the good of humanity – in the form of technological progress, democracy, and science – are no longer valid, and in each of these areas, we notice negative sides in the form of callousness, populism, or the use of the results of progress for selfish purposes.

Referring to selected classic management functions, Kostera (2019) considers the principal axes of self-management to be:

1. as keys to planning – 3I: imagination, inspiration, intuition;
2. as keys to organising – 3S: structure, space, synchronicity;

3. as keys to motivation – 3L: leadership, learning, love;
4. as keys to control – 3E: ethos, ethics, ecology.

The indicated areas are nothing more than the aestheticisation of reality through the aestheticisation of management (more on this subject in Section 3.1, "Aestheticisation of management"). Classic management functions are shown from a new perspective – although we are talking about self-management, the keys to these functions are at the macro level. It is the opposite of what the classics of organisational management had in mind – they wanted to manage organisations (mezzo level) but focused on organising resources (including people treated as resources; their keys were at the micro level). To put this matter metaphorically: if a musician, during the performance of a piece, focuses on individual notes, being careful not to make a mistake in organising them, sooner or later he will stumble; while the same musician, when he focuses on interpreting the work, and presenting the emotions and values that the work carries, will be able to reach heights unattainable in the first situation.

1.3 Art and management boundaries interpenetration

The issues raised in Sections 1.1 and 1.2 indicate that art and management have some common components and issues that make the scopes of both areas interpenetrate. Therefore, the analysis of this problem will be carried out on two levels: (1) on the colloquial level, i.e., a review of literature in the field of management, which somehow refers to the art or its components; and (2) on the level of management aesthetics, i.e., a relatively new area dealing with the issue of art in management professionally and substantively.

1.3.1 Colloquial understanding of art in management

In the management literature, which does not refer directly to aesthetics, the term "art" is used sporadically but always as a spell-key, which the authors, translators or publishers intend to distinguish these specific items from other "ordinary" publications. Here is an analysis of the content of sample monographs:

1. *The Art of Management According to Peter Drucker* (Drucker, 2009) touches on the subject of the manager's tasks and missions, challenges facing the manager, his effectiveness, "human" treatment of employees, or self-management, but it does not refer to the title "art" in its content;
2. *The Art of Managing Finance* (Davies, 1997), apart from describing the technical issues related to financial statements, ratio analysis, costs, and ways of financing the business, does not mention anything about the art components;
3. *The Art of Project Management* (Berkun, 2006) contains a technical analysis of classic project management problems; however, we will not find any reference to any aesthetic issues in it;

4. *Berufstress ade!* (Knoblauch, 2004), translated into Polish and given a slightly exaggerated title, *Sztuka zarządzania sobą* (English: *The Art of Managing Yourself*) contains advice on physical, intellectual, and spiritual development (by the way, forgetting about emotions), but it also does not refer to the title aspect of art;
5. *Sztuka skutecznego zarządzania: kierowanie firmą z myślą o jutrze i procesach integracji z Unią Europejską* (English: *The Art of Effective Management: Managing the Company with a View to Tomorrow and the Processes of Integration with the European Union*) (Penc, 2006) touches on selected issues in the field of management without referring to the components of art;
6. *Sztuka zarządzania organizacjami. Zasoby, sposoby, perspektywy* (English: *The Art of Managing Organisations. Resources, Ways, Perspectives*) (Galata, 2006) addresses the topics of general characteristics of organisational activities, organisational resources (only human resources, knowledge and energy resources), management of modern organisations (evolution of management theory and practice, decision-making process, dilemmas and errors in managerial activity, strategic management), the role of economic information in management, and the moral and ethical context of management; we will not find any references to aesthetics or the title art;
7. Only *Miteinander Reden. Kommunikationspsychologie für Führungskräfte* (German: *Talking to Each Other: Psychology of Communication for Executives*), ennobled in Polish translation as *Sztuka zarządzania: psychologia komunikacji dla szefów i liderów* (Polish: *The Art of Management: The Psychology of Communication for Bosses and Leaders*) (Schulz von Thun et al., 2004), goes a step further, because, in the titles of several chapters and subchapters, it contains loose references to the language of art (e.g., "consonant management", "creative mess"), while in the substantive layer, it remains a scientific analysis of the psychology of communication.

Analysing these examples, one can draw a particular analogy to the participation of society in art: basically, everyone knows the word "art" and has own idea of it, but the vast majority of society, not being interested in this area of reality, limits itself to defining as art vague and closer undefined mysterious areas that others occupy. Similarly, in the aforementioned publications, without more profound reflection, they were defined as "art", probably wanting to add an element of mystery and secret recipes for the so-called "success" – which can be considered a manifestation of kitsch (see Section 6.2.2, "Educational kitsch"). Referring to the theory of value (see Section 2.2.7, "A world of values"), it can be said that this "art" is, for authors, translators, or publishers, a superior value in itself, which they want to strive for.

Going further, it can be concluded that the term "art of management" used in the colloquial sense includes unspecified phenomena/areas related to management, which cannot be easily described with complex or quantifiable tools and theories that dominate in the literature on the subject.

Among these measurable, deeply researched, and widely described disciplines within the management area, we have structured knowledge in the field of goals and strategies, structures, processes, projects, and quality or management of various types of resources requiring specialist proficiency in finance, economics, sociology, and psychology. We can call these elements measurable components of management. Apart from them, immeasurable components (although they should rather be called "less measurable") commonly refer to the art of management; the creativity of individuals and groups, innovation, entrepreneurship, and leadership can be mentioned here (Figure 1.3).

As shown in Section 1.1, "Essence of art", art and the aesthetics that describe it are equipped with an extensive conceptual apparatus and can describe abstract, intangible phenomena in a possible objective and legible way. This achievement is significant and desirable when dealing with management aesthetics. Therefore, one of the goals of this work is to use the achievements of aesthetics to describe the "art of management" as precisely as possible, so that it is not a catchphrase but is deep and full of specific meanings, and that the component of "art" in management is easier to understand, and thus more "teachable", to the benefit of not only theory but also management practice.

Management is both an art and a science because it combines components of both approaches. Thanks to the optics of science, having an organised body of knowledge, it presents certain universal truths. Thanks to the optics of art, it

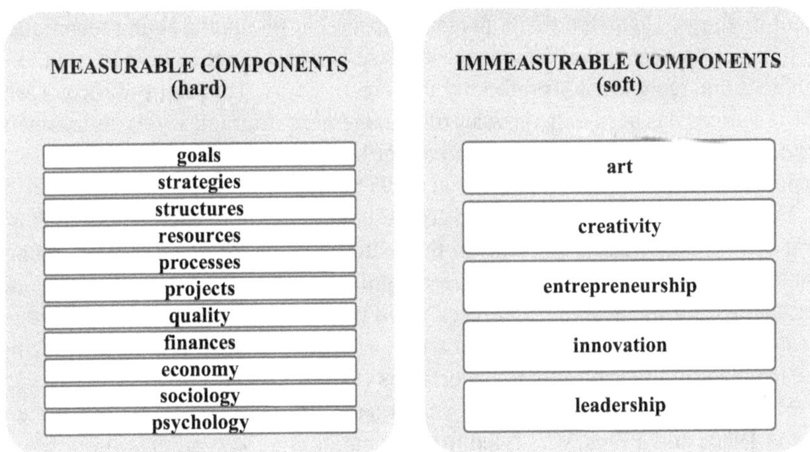

Figure 1.3 Measurable and immeasurable components of management

Source: Author's own elaboration

requires specific skills that are personal properties of managers. These skills cannot be easily taught; they need to be worked out and refined within one's practice (Mangham, 1990). Today's effective manager should be proficient in scientific knowledge and the art of applying this knowledge. In this context, science and the art of management are not mutually exclusive but complementary.

This analysis of the definition of the essence of management and art leads to the formulation of a research gap, which can be defined as the *lack of a holistic aesthetic approach to management theory*. Instead, there are many fragmentary approaches, selecting a specific phenomenon from the areas of art and aesthetics and their application in the management field. It seems, however, that both these areas (management and art) have much more in common than just occasional attempts to use each other's concepts.

1.3.2 Management aesthetics and humanistic management

Professional consideration of the issue of art in management is dealt with by the field called management aesthetics or organisational aesthetics (if we are talking about managing an organisation). Publications from this trend show that management and art cross their borders for mutual benefits, and many organisational problems can be understood or even solved through creative practices or approaches based on theories derived from the art world.

The development of managerial literature relating to art began after World War II, and the first attempts to find similarities between management and art date back to the 1960s. William Ingram was one of the first to draw attention to the importance of creativity in using organisational resources and learned management methods. He stated that a person educated in the methods and techniques of management is not yet a manager because he must practice how to use these methods and techniques – preferably in a creative way. This ability to creatively use resources has been called the art of management (Ingram, 1965). Subsequent researchers searched for common areas for both fields, initially including craft, vision, and communication (Boettinger, 1975).

Then, attention began to be paid to the intangible dimension of the manager's activity: efficiency, not only in the material or financial dimension. Many analogies (more or less significant) were pointed out between management and art, comparing the analysis and research in the field of management with areas related to the theory of art – e.g. aesthetics, art history, and art criticism – placing the manager in the centre of considerations (Degot, 2007).

The aesthetic dimension of work and organisational life occupied researchers in the 1980s and 1990s, which led to the separation of four *main approaches in research on organisational aesthetics*:

1. an archaeological approach that privileges the symbolic dimension of aesthetic understanding;

2. an empathic-logical approach that tries to capture the pathos of the organisation's life;
3. an aesthetic approach that emphasises negotiating organisational aesthetics;
4. an artistic approach that explores flow, creativity, and play, e.g., through analysing inspiring and imaginative organisational archetypes (Kostera, 2012).

However, most researchers dealt with the intellectual approach to studying organisations, emphasising mental, cognitive, and rational dimensions of social activities while neglecting the material, sensual, and emotional dimensions of labour relations in organisations (Strati, 2010).

Antonio Strati, whose articles from the 1990s are considered the father of organisation's aesthetics (Strati, 1992, 1996), and the monograph *Organisation and Aesthetics* from 1999 (Strati, 1999) paved the way for the aesthetic dimension of organisation and management as a legitimate trend in management science (Taylor, 2019). Theories and models in the field of aesthetics began to be considered crucial in formulating thoughts, with particular emphasis on the trend in management discourse treated as a creative endeavour similar to art (Sułkowski & Patora-Wysocka, 2018). Aesthetics in organisational theory is called a way of understanding through the senses, thoughts, and feelings (Minahan, 2020).

After defining and initially solidifying a new direction of research, at the turn of the third millennium, there was a flourishing of publications showing the benefits of combining the broadly understood world of art with management and the world of organisations (business, state and local government administration): from group artistic activities for communities in different cultures to business patronage over artists and artistic activities for organisations (Adler & Ippolito, 2018). The benefits of cooperation between the two areas show added value for both sides, although they spread with different intensities depending on the scope of cooperation. Business, thereby patronising artists, tries to build a specific marketing narrative or corporate social responsibility; artists, in turn, become subjects who share values, skills, and techniques of their choice to obtain funds for proper creative activity.

New horizons resulting from this marriage began to appear: the effective development of leadership skills in management (Purg & Walravens, 2015), self-analysis processes, or self-development activities (Guranda & Nagy, 2011). The effectiveness of artistic methods in improving managerial practices was emphasised, for example: directing attention – drawing contours; seeing contexts – drawing space as a negative; change of perspective – turning "upside down" and looking at the canvas from a distance; studying art – improving the skills of observation and diagnosis. Attention was also paid to art criticism as a method of solving organisational problems when business optics based solely on profitability and efficiency could not help. Scientists began to emphasise phenomena in the field of art: values, artistry, aesthetics, and culture (Chiapello, 2004).

The reasons for the increased interest in the potential of artistry in improving management skills at the individual and group levels (including organisational) include the following phenomena (Adler, 2006, 2011; Sutherland, 2013):

1. globalisation of trends and opinions;
2. the growing dominance of market forces compared to the world of universal values and ideas;
3. the increasing complexity and chaotic nature of the broadly understood business environment;
4. a decrease in the cost of experimenting with organising relative to the potential benefits of innovation;
5. attempts to search for a deeper meaning in one's actions.

Literature in the area of management that touches on or draws from the area of art can be divided into the following thematic groups:

1. management in artistic activity, i.e., attempts to demonstrate the specificity of art management, and even individual art disciplines, as a separate management discipline (Elstad & Jansson, 2020; Kleppe, 2018; Morozova et al., 2016);
2. the use of art (or its selected issues) in the management of specific types of organisations or specific social processes, e.g., in health care (Dewey Lambert & Sonke, 2019), education (Cuyler, 2013; Guranda & Nagy, 2011; Komandyshko & Semenova, 2017; Purg & Sutherland, 2017; Purg & Walravens, 2015), tourism and the hotel industry (Cheng et al., 2018; Hager & Sung, 2012; Nugraheni et al., 2019; Zhai, 2021), and the creative sectors (Latilla et al., 2018; Major et al., 1998);
3. artistic interventions consisting in introducing an artist (usually a painter, visual artist, actor, or dancer) to the organisation, whose creative potential would stimulate specific behaviours of members or the entire organisation (Antal, 2011; Antal et al., 2016, 2018, 2019; Cheng et al., 2018; Johansson-Sköldberg & Woodilla, 2014; Millward et al., 2019; Schnuugg, 2019; Skoldberg Johansson et al., 2015; Zambrell, 2016);
4. searching for the characteristics of an artistic personality in order to transfer them to the field of management (Bass, 2017; Borowiecki & Dahl, 2021; Elstad & Jansson, 2020; Emrali, 2017; Kosmala, 2007; Randrianasolo & Sala, 2016; Schediwy et al., 2018; Szostak, 2020, 2021a, 2021b, 2022, 2023; Szostak & Sulkowski 2021a, 2021c; Travis, 2020);
5. transfer of creativity competences from the area of art to management (Ancelin-Bourguignon et al., 2020; Gahan et al., 2007; Hirschmann et al., 2020; Larso & Saphiranti, 2016; Ridwan et al., 2020; Schiuma & Lerro, 2017);
6. art as an inspiration for managerial activity (Beirne & Knight, 2005; Mangham, 1990);

7. art as inspiration for leadership (Adler, 2015; Adler & Ippolito, 2018; Ibbotson & Darsø, 2008; Kerr & Lloyd, 2008; Minocha & Reynolds, 2013; Nikolski, 2015; Purg & Walravens, 2015; Szczepaniak, 2018);
8. art as an inspiration for entrepreneurship (Bureau & Zander, 2014; Enhuber, 2014; Ferriani et al., 2009; Fillis & Rentschler, 2005; Larso & Saphiranti, 2016; Penaluna & Penaluna, 2020; Schiuma & Lerro, 2017; Szostak & Sułkowski, 2021b).

Attempts to justify the similarities between management and art can be grouped as follows:

1. combining and looking for analogies between the areas of management and art – e.g., organising + innovation + mimesis (Atkinson, 2007, pp. 202–208) – or looking for analogies between the narrow concepts of one field and attempts to find their meaning for the other field (Chountasi et al., 2021; Madeira et al., 2018; Parush & Koivunen, 2014; Reinhold et al., 2018);
2. transfer of artistic skills by involving members of the organisation in the creative process (e.g., creating masks, collages) in order to find layers of creativity (Latilla et al., 2018, 2019; Skoldberg Johansson et al., 2015);
3. techniques of projecting ideas into reality (Aurangzeb et al., 2021; Avram, 2013);
4. techniques of finding the "quintessence" of a problem before it becomes real in the matter (Taylor & Ladkin, 2009).

Researchers trying to answer whether management can be considered an art form have extensively used philosophical and aesthetic theories for this purpose. Some concluded that management is neither a science nor an art nor a craft (Atkinson, 2007). Some postulated to maintain clear boundaries between these areas, recognising that the concept of "art of management" has an internal contradiction because the implementation of this concept causes far-reaching deviations for both art and management, and all attempts to find similarities are based on the naivety of researchers (Pelzer, 2006). Such formalised criticism, however, is relatively rare.

The problems of management aesthetics are usually addressed in publications belonging to the humanistic management trend, which, in response to efficiency reductionism and economic exploitation present in mainstream management theory and practice, try to broaden the horizons of perception with the human condition, concern for dignity, emancipation, and the common good, as well as for reflection on reality, openness, and appreciation for the irreducible complexity of existence. Therefore, the following items (in chronological order) should be considered essential monographs that aestheticise management:

1. *Organisation and Aesthetics* (Strati, 1999) – considered to be the first extensive publication in this field, discussing:

    a. the role of emotions in organisations,
    b. the meaning of the symbol,

c. empathy as a way of understanding the organisation,
d. the beauty of organisation,
e. the symbolism of representativeness of organisational beauty,
f. the subjective impact of culture,
g. the aesthetics of the non-human and the artistry of the human,
h. learning and cognition processes,
i. awareness of aesthetics and aesthetics of consciousness.

2. *The Aesthetics of Organisation* (Linstead & Höpfl, 2000), consisting of a dozen or so loosely related chapters, touches on the following issues:

   a. the essence of the aesthetics of organising,
   b. organisation poetics,
   c. aesthetics of restraint,
   d. the aesthetics of mundane and routine pleasures,
   e. the relationship between the observer and the audience,
   f. restoring the aesthetics of existence as an alternative to business ethics,
   g. relationship between jazz improvisation and self-organisation.

3. *The Art Firm: Aesthetic Management and Metaphysical Marketing* (Guillet de Monthoux, 2004), dealing with problems such as:

   a. key figures in philosophy who laid the foundations for the aesthetics of creativity and artistry,
   b. relationship between the critic and the recipient of the work,
   c. the double dilemma of the totality and banality of a work of art,
   d. metaphysics as the marketing of artistic companies,
   e. aesthetic philosophy of added value,
   f. management practices in artistic companies.

4. *Economic Aesthetics: How Companies Use Art as Inspiration and Tool* (German: *Wirtschaftsästhetik. Wie Unternehmen die Kunst als Inspiration und Werkzeug nutzen*) (Biehl-Missal, 2011) discusses the following issues:

   a. the theory of enterprise aesthetics,
   b. aesthetic research methods,
   c. aesthetic and artistic forms of representation,
   d. aesthetic phenomena in the context of particular fields of art,
   e. metaphors from the world of the art regarding the organisation, management, and actors of the enterprise,
   f. artistic interventions,
   g. improvised activities,
   h. the application of art criticism on the ground of the organisation.

5. *Zarządzanie w XXI wieku. Jakość, twórczość, kultura* (English: *Management in the 21st century: Quality, Creativity, Culture*) (Kostera & Śliwa, 2012) is a Polish-language monograph that was the first to start describing management

problems more extensively, partly through the optics of aesthetics; the authors consider creativity, which they analyse through:

a. focus on the state of flow (flow),
b. organisational stories,
c. organisation myths and archetypes,
d. management of individual art disciplines and the art of management,
e. sensations,
f. irony and humour,
g. entrepreneurship and innovation.

6. *Occupy Management! Inspirations and Ideas for Self-Organisation and Self-Management* (Kostera, 2014) was further developed in *Organize Ourselves! Inspirations and Ideas for Self-Organisation and Self-Management* (Kostera, 2019); both publications address the following issues of management aesthetics:

a. in the context of the planning function (3I): imagination, inspiration, intuition,
b. in the context of the organising function (3S): structure, space, synchronicity,
c. in the context of the motivating function (3L): leadership, learning, love,
d. in the context of the control function (3E): ethos, ethics, ecology.

7. *Aesthetic Turn in Management* (Minahan, 2020) discusses:

a. aesthetic understanding of organisational life,
b. searching for form,
c. narrative views on strategic discourse,
d. organisational kitsch,
e. rhetoric and myth in fashion for management,
f. analysis of the fantasy topic in the context of a learning organisation,
g. dissemination of management practices by the popular press,
h. fashion for management seen as an image spectacle in the context of best-selling management books,
i. combining narrative and scientific knowledge in organisational research,
j. theatre and management performance – management as a performing art,
k. cultural representation of control,
l. spectacular metaphors: from theatre to cinema,
m. improvisation in management – improvisation as a way of thinking in organisational analysis.

8. *Aesthetics, Organisation, and Humanistic Management* (Kostera & Woźniak, 2022) deals with the following issues:

a. an attempt to understand the role of management in the surrounding reality,
b. personal reflections on the relationship between art and management,

c. the importance of reinterpretation in management sciences,
d. transposition of issues in the field of audiovisual art into organisational control,
e. the role of dreams and imagination,
f. recalling and analysing the activities of figures from the history of art that can be an inspiration for theoreticians and practitioners of management,
g. artistic interventions in organisations,
h. accepting feelings,
i. organisational creativity,
j. creating organisational identity through art.

However, in the quantitatively limited Polish-language literature in the field of humanistic management, we will not find much on issues related to the aesthetics of management:

1. *Humanistyczne aspekty w zarządzaniu i biznesie* (English: *Humanistic Aspects in Management and Business*) (Gierasimczuk & Daszkiewicz, 2001) touches on:

    a. the problem of managing society in ancient philosophy,
    b. management problems in medieval and renaissance philosophy,
    c. issues of management in philosophers of the 17th, 18th, and 19th centuries,
    d. the problem of management in German philosophy of the 18th and 19th centuries,
    e. the problem of freedom in a market economy,
    f. rationalism and institutionalism in contemporary management,
    g. philosophy of success in management and business,
    h. an anthropological and ethical theme in the contemporary philosophy of management.

As can be seen, none of these works issues references to aesthetics.

2. *Zarządzanie humanistyczne* (English: *Humanistic Management*) (Sułkowski & Woźniak, 2014), in the form of loosely related chapters, discusses the following topics:

    a. referring to humanistic and ethical issues:

        i. humanistic aspects of the economy focused on seniors,
        ii. communicating in the context of humanistic aspects of the professional role of a manager,
        iii. the organisational perspective of public trust,
        iv. characteristics of humanistic and public management in Poland,
        v. the possibility of influencing the functioning of domestic enterprises by international corporations,

vi. knowledge workers as suppliers of a strategic resource in the organisation,
vii. definitional differences in the meaning of categories of knowledge,
viii. manager's authority,
ix. reflections on freedom in Lew Trotsky's thought;

b. referring to aesthetics issues:

i. analysis of the marketing potential of the universe of two volumes of A. Sapkowski's stories in terms of identifying the objects described therein.

3. *Zarządzanie humanistyczne* (English: *Humanistic Management*) (Nierenberg et al., 2015), in the form of loosely connected chapters, deals with:

a. humanistic and ethical issues:

i. the essence of humanistic management and the essence of human management,
ii. humanistic freedom and humanitarian solidarity in the context of post-socialist societies,
iii. the nature of social reality and the history of Polish social sciences,
iv. scientific approaches to humanistic management: functionalist, systemic, and positive,
v. the needs of humanistic management and attempts to define the principles of humanistic management in the media and universities,
vi. humanistic management paradigms,
vii. humanistic entrepreneurship,
viii. making decisions in the field of education,

b. aesthetic issues:

i. values in the world of management,
ii. the benefits of reading literature on management science,
iii. art and reason,
iv. understanding and using order in the context of using the Internet,
v. projection techniques in the context of university management.

Humanistic management can be viewed from three following perspectives (Sułkowski & Woźniak, 2014, pp. 91–105):

1. the perspective of humanistic functionalism – assuming that social reality is order rather than chaos and that societies cooperate internally rather than fall apart; hence, human-made social structures are characterised by functional purposefulness;
2. the humanistic-systems perspective – assuming the understanding of organisations within the framework of broad, transdisciplinary theories and

understanding organisations as a particular type of social structure in which dynamics occurring in complex systems can be recognised;

3. the positivist perspective – based on the unity of the scientific method, searching for cause-and-effect relationships, faith in empirical data, excluding value judgements from the scientific process, and basing reasoning on the principles of logic and mathematics.

Analysing the growing interest in humanistic management among researchers worldwide (Koon, 2021), one can presume that the aestheticisation of management will also be more and more frequent in the literature on the subject and, most importantly, in the practice of management.

1.4. Summary

A kind of duality in the definitions of the management process related to the artistic and scientific components is natural and results from the essence of the management process. The art component is no less important in effective management than the science component – they should be treated as mutually complementary. It has been proven that – apart from the science component – the art component is a capacious concept under which phenomena that do not fit into the empirical scientific framework should be placed. The factor of art in management, thanks to the achievements of aesthetics, has been shown as no less structured and with a rich conceptual, semantic, and practical achievement.

Undoubtedly, aestheticisation can bring added value to management in the theoretical dimension in terms of paying attention to universal values and to a person as a living and feeling being, who should be reflected in the practical dimension of management in the form of broadening the approach to the organisation as a set of individuals, and not only as a machine aiming to pursue economic goals ruthlessly. It is not without reason that management, in the spirit of efficiency and marketing, is commonly associated with exploiting employees and the environment. The change of optics of managers, employees, and owners should positively impact the change in the perception of management. The aestheticisation of management flows directly from the widely described trend of the aestheticisation of reality,

In addition to ethics and corporate social responsibility, aestheticisation can be an additional qualitative dimension drawing attention to the issues of universal values in management. This is due to two reasons. First, ethics (based on the universal value of good) refers to morality, while aesthetics (based on the universal values of truth and beauty) broadens the qualitative perspective. It is not enough for managers and organisations to focus on morality, that is, to act ethically. Only ethical action, simultaneously extended to the issues of truth and beauty, becomes fuller and refers to a much more comprehensive range of arguments. Secondly, one can get the impression of a kind of hypocrisy among many organisations implementing specific policies in the field of business ethics or conducting widely advertised activities related to their social responsibility. This is because, most often, these ethical-responsibility programs only play the role of a fig leaf or a bandage for a bleeding wound. To help a patient with a bleeding wound, first, we need to stop the bleeding, clean the wound, and then dress it. On the one hand, carrying out activities that destroy the environment and, on the other hand, helping the environment mean transferring resources from one pocket to another instead of improving the net situation. From these actions, the number of resources will not change.

Notes

1 It should be kept in mind that today's understanding of Plato's triad is somewhat different from the understanding of the author himself. Plato did not consider these three values to be a closed whole, but added to them the specification "and everything like" while listing these virtues (Tatarkiewicz, 2015, p. 133).
2 The word "art" is used here rather to add some mystery than as a reference to the artistry.
3 In the consequence of the next circumstances, this division was withdrawn a few years later.

References

Adler, N. J. (2006). The arts & leadership: Now that we can do anything, what will we do? *Academy of Management Learning and Education*, *5*(4), 486–499. https://doi.org/10.5465/AMLE.2006.23473209

Adler, N. J. (2011). Leading beautifully: The creative economy and beyond. *Journal of Management Inquiry*, *20*(3), 208–221. https://doi.org/10.1177/1056492602111007

Adler, N. J. (2015). Finding beauty in a fractured world: Art inspires leaders-leaders change the world. *Academy of Management Review*, *40*(3), 480–494. https://doi.org/10.5465/amr.2015.0044

Adler, N. J., & Ippolito, L. M. (2018). Musical leadership and societal transformation: Inspiration and courage in action. *Kwartalnik Ekonomistów i Menedżerów*, *50*(4), 41–65. https://doi.org/10.5604/01.3001.0013.0629

Ancelin-Bourguignon, A., Dorsett, C., & Azambuja, R. (2020). Lost in translation? Transferring creativity insights from arts into management. *Organization*, *27*(5), 717–741. https://doi.org/10.1177/1350508419855716

Antal, A. B. (2011). *Managing artistic interventions in organisations : A comparative study of programmes in Europe*. TILLT Europe.

Antal, A. B., Debucquet, G., & Fremeaux, S. (2016). Addressing identity tensions through paradoxical thinking: Lessons from artistic interventions in organizations. *Management International*, *21*(1), 25–40. https://doi.org/10.7202/1052495ar

Antal, A. B., Debucquet, G., & Frémeaux, S. (2018). Meaningful work and artistic interventions in organizations: Conceptual development and empirical exploration. *Journal of Business Research*, *85*, 375–385. https://doi.org/10.1016/j.jbusres.2017.10.015

Antal, A. B., Debucquet, G., & Frémeaux, S. (2019). When top management leadership matters: Insights from artistic interventions. *Journal of Management Inquiry*, *28*(4), 441–457. https://doi.org/10.1177/1056492617726393

Atkinson, D. M. (2007). *Thinking the art of management*. Palgrave Macmillan. https://doi.org/10.1057/9780230589988

Aurangzeb, W., Mehmood, A., & Khan, S. (2021). Gendered perceptions' regarding career guidance needs at higher education level. *International Journal of Innovation in Teaching and Learning (IJITL)*, *6*(2), 48–62. https://doi.org/10.35993/ijitl.v6i2.810

Avram, H. (2013). The convergence effect: Real and virtual encounters in augmented reality art. *M/C Journal*, *16*(6). https://doi.org/10.5204/mcj.735

Barbone, S. (1997). Analityczna postawa wobec piękna sztuki. In M. Gołaszewska (Ed.), *Estetyka w świecie: wybór tekstów: Tom V* (pp. 71–80). Uniwersytet Jagielloński.

Bass, A. E. (2017). Identity discovery and verification in artist-entrepreneurs: An active learning exercise. *Organization Management Journal*, *14*(2), 90–103. https://doi.org/10.1080/15416518.2017.1322485

Beirne, M., & Knight, S. (2005). The performing art of management: Theatre, drama and active management learning. https://www.academia.edu/907823/The_performing_art_of_management_theatre_drama_and_active_management_learning

Beirne, M., & Knight, S. (2007). From community theatre to critical management studies: A dramatic contribution to reflective learning? *Management Learning*, *38*(5), 591–611. https://doi.org/10.1177/1350507607083209

Berkun, S. (2006). *Sztuka zarządzania projektami*. Helion S. A.

Biehl-Missal, B. (2011). *Wirtschaftsästhetik: Wie Unternehmen die Kunst als Inspiration und Werkzeug nutzen*. Gabler Verlag.

Boettinger, H. M. (1975). Is management really an art? *Harvard Business Review*, *53*(1), 54–64. https://hbr.org/1975/01/is-management-really-an-art

Borowiecki, K. J., & Dahl, C. M. (2021). What makes an artist? The evolution and clustering of creative activity in the US since 1850. *Regional Science and Urban Economics*, *86*, 1–23. https://doi.org/10.1016/j.regsciurbeco.2020.103614

Bureau, S., & Zander, I. (2014). Entrepreneurship as an art of subversion. *Scandinavian Journal of Management*, *30*(1), 124–133. https://doi.org/10.1016/j.scaman.2013.12.002

Caude, R., & Moles, A. (1964). *Methodologie vers une science de l'action*. Gauthier-Villars.

Cheng, J. S., Xiang, Y., Sher, P. J., & Liu, C. W. (2018). Artistic intervention, intellectual capital, and service innovation: A case study of a Taiwan's hotel. *Service Business*, *12*(1), 169–201. https://doi.org/10.1007/s11628-017-0342-9

Chiapello, E. (2004). Evolution and co-optation. *Third Text*, *18*(6), 585–594. https://doi.org/10.1080/0952882042000284998

Chountasi, M., Dafiotis, P., & Sylaiou, S. (2021). Newness and openness in new media arts and digital performances: Contextualizing Greece in the Balkan scene. *International Journal of Performance Arts and Digital Media*, *17*(3), 316–335. https://doi.org/10.1080/14794713.2020.1856552

Cuyler, A. C. (2013). Affirmative action and diversity: Implications for arts management. *Journal of Arts Management Law and Society*, *43*(2), 98–105. https://doi.org/10.1080/10632921.2013.786009

Czakon, W. (2019). Tożsamość nauk o zarządzaniu: rozwój, legitymizacja, wyróżniki. In *Ewolucja nauk ekonomicznych: Jedność a różnorodność, relacje do innych nauk, problemy klasyfikacyjne*. Polska Akademia Nauk.

da Vinci, L. (1930). *Pisma wybrane: Tom II*. Wydawnictwo J. Mortkowicza.
Davies, D. (1997). *Sztuka zarządzania finansami*. Wydawnictwo Naukowe PWN.
Degot, V. (2007). Portrait of the manager as an artist. *Aesthesis: International Journal of Art and Aesthetics in Management and Organizational Life*, *1*(3), 6–42.
Dewey Lambert, P., & Sonke, J. (2019). Professionalizing arts management in healthcare facilities. *Journal of Arts Management Law and Society*, *49*(3), 155–170. https://doi.org/10.1080/10632921.2018.1559264
Drucker, P. F. (2006a). *The effective executive*. HarperCollins.
Drucker, P. F. (2006b). *The practice of management*. HarperCollins.
Drucker, P. F. (2009). *Sztuka zarządzania według Petera Druckera*. Harvard Business Review Polska.
Dutton, D. (2019). *Instynkt sztuki*. Copernicus Cener Press.
Eco, U. (2004). *On beauty*. Secker & Warburg.
Elstad, B., & Jansson, D. (2020). From artist to manager – working conditions, career satisfaction, and professional identity among graduated arts management students. *Journal of Arts Management Law and Society*, *50*(3), 184–198. https://doi.org/10.1080/10632921.2020.1746717
Emrali, R. (2017). Today's artist identity as multicultural and hybrid identity. *Global Journal of Arts Education*, *6*(4), 115–119. https://doi.org/10.18844/gjae.v6i4.1826
Enhuber, M. (2014). How is Damien Hirst a cultural entrepreneur? *Artivate: A Journal of Entrepreneurship in the Arts*, *3*(2), 3–20. https://repository.asu.edu/attachments/146224/content/ArtivateVol3No2pages3–20Enhuber.pdf
Ferriani, S., Cattani, G., & Baden-Fuller, C. (2009). The relational antecedents of project-entrepreneurship: Network centrality, team composition and project performance. *Research Policy*, *38*(10), 1545–1558. https://doi.org/10.1016/j.respol.2009.09.001
Fillis, I., & Rentschler, R. (2005). Using creativity to achieve an entrepreneurial future for arts marketing. *International Journal of Nonprofit and Voluntary Sector Marketing*, *10*(4), 275–287. https://doi.org/10.1002/nvsm.26
Gadamer, H. G. (1994). Sztuka jako gra. In M. Gołaszewska (Ed.), *Estetyka w świecie: wybór tekstów: Tom IV* (pp. 49–58). Uniwersytet Jagielloński.
Gahan, P., Minahan, S., & Glow, H. (2007). A creative twist: Management theory, creativity and the arts. *Journal of Management & Organization*, *13*(1), 41–50. https://doi.org/10.1017/s1833367200003898
Galata, S. (2006). *Sztuka zarządzania organizacjami: Zasoby, sposoby, perspektywy*. Difin.
Gierasimczuk, A., & Daszkiewicz, J. (2001). *Humanistyczne aspekty w zarządzaniu i biznesie*. Poligrafia Wyższego Seminarium Duchownego.
Gliński, B. (1974). *Mała encyklopedia ekonomiczna*. Państwowe Wydawnictwo Ekonomiczne.
Gołaszewska, M. (1967). *Odbiorca sztuki jako krytyk*. Wydawnictwo Literackie.
Gołaszewska, M. (1984). *Zarys estetyki*. PWN.
Gombrich, E. H. (1966). *Reflections on teaching art history in art schools*. https://gombricharchive.files.wordpress.com/2011/04/showdoc34.pdf
Gosling, J., & Mintzberg, H. (2004). The education of practicing managers. *MIT Sloan Management Review*, *45*(2), 26–32. http://dialnet.unirioja.es/servlet/articulo?codigo=2316408
Griffin, R. W. (2005). *Podstawy zarządzania organizacjami*. Wydawnictwo Naukowe PWN.

Guillet de Monthoux, P. (2004). *The art firm: Aesthetic management and metaphysical marketing*. Stanford University Press.
Guranda, M., & Nagy, D. (2011, May 26–28). Educational management – art or science? *International Conference Of Scientific Paper Afases 2011, Brasov*, 427–433.
Hager, M. A., & Sung, H. K. (2012). Local arts agency participation in cultural tourism management. *Journal of Heritage Tourism*, *7*(3), 205–217. https://doi.org/10.1080/1743873X.2012.677140
Hirschmann, T., Hartley, N., & Roth, S. (2020). Can we build resilience by way of creativity? Artistic ventures in a London hospice. *International Journal of Entrepreneurship and Innovation Management*, *24*(2–3), 116–131. https://doi.org/10.1504/IJEIM.2020.105779
Ibbotson, P., & Darsø, L. (2008). Directing creativity: The art and craft of creative leadership. *Journal of Management and Organization*, *14*(5), 548–559. https://doi.org/10.5172/jmo.837.14.5.548
Ingarden, R. (1981). *Wykłady i dyskusje z estetyki*. Państwowe Wydawnictwo Naukowe.
Ingram, W. T. (1965, August). Management art or science. *Industrial Management*, 2–4.
Johansson-Sköldberg, U., & Woodilla, J. (2014, September). Mind the gap! Strategies for artistic interventions in organizations. *19th DMI: Academic Design Management Conference Design Management in an Era of Disruption London*, 538–561. www.dmi.org/?page=ADMC2014
Kant, E. (2015). *Kritik der Urteilskraft*. Anaconda Verlag.
Kerr, C., & Lloyd, C. (2008). Pedagogical learnings for management education: Developing creativity and innovation. *Journal of Management and Organization*, *14*(5), 486–503. https://doi.org/10.5172/jmo.837.14.5.486
Kieżun, W. (1997). *Sprawne zarządzanie organizacją*. Szkoła Główna Handlowa w Warszawie.
Klamer, A. (2017). *Doing the right thing: A value based economy*. Ubiquity Press. https://doi.org/10.5334/bbb
Kleppe, B. (2018). Managing autonomy: Analyzing arts management and artistic autonomy through the theory of justification. *Journal of Arts Management Law and Society*, *48*(3), 191–205. https://doi.org/10.1080/10632921.2017.1377661
Knoblauch, J. (2004). *Sztuka zarządzania samym sobą*. Oficyna Wydawnicza Vocatio.
Komandyshko, E. F., & Semenova, E. A. (2017). Educational tourism: Adoption of art management technologies in the activity of universities. *Journal of Environmental Management and Tourism*, *8*(6), 1183–1188. https://doi.org/10.14505/jemt.v8.6(22).04
Koon, V. Y. (2021). Bibliometric analyses on the emergence and present growth of humanistic management. *International Journal of Ethics and Systems*, *37*(4), 581–598. https://doi.org/10.1108/IJOES-03-2021-0062
Kosmala, K. (2007). The identity paradox? Reflections on fluid identity of female artist. *Culture and Organization*, *13*(1), 37–53. https://doi.org/10.1080/14759550601167271
Kostera, M. (2012). *Organizations and archetypes*. Edward Elgar Publishing.
Kostera, M. (2014). *Occupy management! Inspirations and ideas for self-organization and self-management*. Routledge. https://doi.org/10.4324/9780203795033
Kostera, M. (2019). *Organize ourselves! Inspirations and ideas for self-organization and self-management*. Mayfly Books. https://ruj.uj.edu.pl/xmlui/bitstream/handle/item/72058/kostera_organize_ourselves_2019.pdf?sequence=1&isAllowed=y

Kostera, M., & Śliwa, M. (2012). *Zarządzanie w XXI wieku: Jakość, twórczość, kultura*. Wolters Kluwer Polska.
Kostera, M., & Woźniak, C. (2022). *Aesthetics, organization, and humanistic management*. Routledge.
Koźmiński, A. K., & Jemielniak, D. (2008). *Zarządzanie od podstaw*. WAiP.
Koźmiński, A. K., & Piotrowski, W. (1999). *Zarządzanie: Teoria i praktyka*. Wydawnictwo Naukowe PWN.
Larso, D., & Saphiranti, D. (2016). The role of creative courses in entrepreneurship education: A case study in Indonesia. *International Journal of Business*, *21*(3), 216–225.
Latilla, V. M., Frattini, F., Messeni Petruzzelli, A., & Berner, M. (2018). Knowledge management, knowledge transfer and organizational performance in the arts and crafts industry: A literature review. *Journal of Knowledge Management*, *22*(6), 1310–1331. https://doi.org/10.1108/JKM-08-2017-0367
Latilla, V. M., Frattini, F., Messeni Petruzzelli, A., & Berner, M. (2019). Knowledge management and knowledge transfer in arts and crafts organizations: Evidence from an exploratory multiple case-study analysis. *Journal of Knowledge Management*, *23*(7), 1335–1354. https://doi.org/10.1108/JKM-11-2018-0699
Levinson, J. (2003). *The Oxford hanbook of aesthetics*. Oxford University Press.
Linstead, S., & Höpfl, H. J. (2000). *The aesthetics of organization*. SAGE Publications Ltd. https://uk.sagepub.com/en-gb/eur/the-aesthetics-of-organization/book205791#preview
Listwan, T., & Witkowski, S. (2001). *Sukces w zarządzaniu: Problemy organizacyjno-zarządcze i psychospołeczne*. Wydawnictwo Akademii Ekonomicznej.
Madeira, C., Salazar, D., & Marçal, H. (2018). Performance art temporalities: Relationships between museum, university, and theatre. *Museum Management and Curatorship*, *33*(1), 79–95. https://doi.org/10.1080/09647775.2017.1419828
Major, S., Zealand, N., & Connell, A. (1998). From arts management to creative industries. *Media*, 1–6.
Mangham, I. L. (1990). Managing as a performing art. *British Journal of Management*, *1*(2), 105–115. https://doi.org/10.1111/j.1467-8551.1990.tb00166.x
Mercier, A. (1985). Nauka a sztuka. In M. Gołaszewska (Ed.), *Estetyka w świecie: wybór tekstów: Tom I* (pp. 163–182). Uniwersytet Jagielloński.
Millward, H. A., Kelemen, M. L., Mangan, A. M. L., Millward, H. A., & Kelemen, M. L. (2019). Co-producing community and individual change through theatrical interventions. *Organizational Aesthetics*, *8*(1), 34–50.
Minahan, S. (2020). *Aesthetic turn in management*. Routledge. https://doi.org/10.4324/9781351147965
Minocha, S., & Reynolds, M. (2013). The artistry of practice or the practice of artistry: Embodying art and practice in a business school context. *Journal of Management Inquiry*, *22*(2), 173–192. https://doi.org/10.1177/1056492612451652
Mintzberg, H. (2012). *Zarządzanie*. Wolters Kluwer Polska.
Morozova, O., Nozdrenko, E., Zhukovskaya, L., & Kostylev, S. (2016). Management and art-management: Dimensions of conceptual interaction. *Economic Annals-XXI*, *158*(3–4), 61–65. https://doi.org/10.21003/ea.V158-14
Nierenberg, B., Batko, R., & Sułkowski, Ł. (2015). *Zarządzanie humanistyczne*. Wydawnictwo Uniwersytetu Jagiellońskiego.

Nikolski, K. (2015). Leadership and management: Practice of the art of influence. *Annals of the "Constantin Brâncuşi" University of Târgu Jiu, Economy Series*, *2*(1), 31–39.

Nugraheni, T., Budiman, A., & Sukmayadi, Y. (2019). Entrepreneurship and art education tourism: A study on results of management skills training program for students. *Harmonia: Journal of Arts Research and Education*, *19*(2), 193–203. https://doi.org/10.15294/harmonia.v19i2.22674

Parush, T., & Koivunen, N. (2014). Paradoxes, double binds, and the construction of "creative" managerial selves in art-based leadership development. *Scandinavian Journal of Management*, *30*(1), 104–113. https://doi.org/10.1016/j.scaman.2013.12.001

Pelzer, P. (2006). Art for management's sake? A doubt. *Culture and Organization*, *12*(1), 65–77. https://doi.org/10.1080/14759550500490592

Penaluna, A., & Penaluna, K. (2020). In search of entrepreneurial competencies: Peripheral vision and multidisciplinary inspiration. *Industry and Higher Education*, *20*(10), 1–14. https://doi.org/10.1177/0950422220963796

Penc, J. (2006). *Sztuka skutecznego zarządzania: kierowanie firmą z myślą o jutrze i procesach integracji z Unią Europejską*. Oficyna Ekonomiczna.

Pszczołowski, T. (1978). *Mała encyklopedia prakseologii i teorii organizacji*. Ossolineum.

Purg, D., & Sutherland, I. (2017). Why art in management education? Questioning meaning. *Academy of Management Review*, *42*(2), 382–396. https://doi.org/10.5465/amr.2016.0047

Purg, D., & Walravens, A. (2015). Arts and leadership: Vision and practice at the IEDC-Bled School of Management. *Journal of Leadership Studies*, *9*(1), 42–47. https://doi.org/10.1002/jls

Randrianasolo, A., & Sala, J. (2016). Artist brand personality, cognitive identification, and music consumption. *AMA SummerEducators' Conference Proceedings*, *27*, B-7–B-8. http://web.a.ebscohost.com/ehost/detail/detail?vid=0&sid=1877bd63-4462-4134-8703-d823806c34c4%40sessionmgr4008&bdata=Jmxhbmc9ZnImc2l0ZT1laG9zdC1saXZl#AN=119995552&db=bth

Reinhold, E., Schnugg, C., & Barthold, C. (2018). Dancing in the office: A study of gestures as resistance. *Scandinavian Journal of Management*, *34*(2), 162–169. https://doi.org/10.1016/j.scaman.2018.05.001

Ridwan, R., Narawati, T., Karwati, U., & Sukmayadi, Y. (2020). Creativity and innovation of artist in maintaining and developing the Songah tradition art. *Harmonia: Journal of Arts Research and Education*, *20*(2), 213–222. https://doi.org/10.15294/harmonia.v20i2.25169

Rilke, R. M. (2010). *Druga strona natury: Eseje, listy i pisma o sztuce*. Wydawnictwo Sic!

Schediwy, L., Bhansing, P. V., & Loots, E. (2018). Young musicians' career identities: Do bohemian and entrepreneurial career identities compete or cohere? *Creative Industries Journal*, *11*(2), 174–196. https://doi.org/10.1080/17510694.2018.1489197

Schiuma, G., & Lerro, A. (2017). *Integrating art and creativity into business practice*. IGI Global. https://doi.org/10.4018/978-1-5225-2050-4

Schnuugg, C. (2019). *Creating artscience collaboration: Bringing value to organizations*. Palgrave Macmillan.

Schulz von Thun, F., Ruppel, J., & Stratmann, R. (2004). *Sztuka zarządzania: psychologia komunikacji dla szefów i liderów*. Wydawnictwo WAM.

Skoldberg Johansson, U., Woodilla, J., & Antal Berthoin, A. (2015). *Artistic interventions in organizations research, theory and practice*. Routledge. www.routledge.com/

Artistic-Interventions-in-Organizations-Research-Theory-and-Practice/Skoldberg-Woodilla-Antal/p/book/9781138497436%0A

Strati, A. (1992). Aesthetic understanding of organizational life. *The Academy of Management Review*, *17*(3), 568–581. Taylor and Francis. https://doi.org/10.4324/9781351147965-1

Strati, A. (1996). Organizations viewed through the lens of aesthetics. *Organization*, *3*(2), 209–218. https://doi.org/10.1177/135050849632004

Strati, A. (1999). *Organization and aesthetics*. SAGE Publications Ltd. https://sk.sagepub.com/books/organization-and-aesthetics

Strati, A. (2010). Aesthetic understanding of work and organizational life: Approaches and research developments. *Sociology Compass*, *4*(10), 880–893. https://doi.org/10.1111/j.1751-9020.2010.00323.x

Sułkowski, Ł., & Patora-Wysocka, Z. (2018). *HEI quality culture in Poland – multi-paradigm view* (pp. 423–434). Springer. https://doi.org/10.1007/978-3-319-60018-5_42

Sułkowski, Ł., & Woźniak, A. (2014). *Zarządzanie humanistyczne*. Wydawnictwo Społecznej Akademii Nauk.

Sutherland, I. (2013). Arts-based methods in leadership development: Affording aesthetic workspaces, reflexivity and memories with momentum. *Management Learning*, *44*(1), 25–43. https://doi.org/10.1177/1350507612465063

Szczepaniak, K. (2018). Arts for business: Creative co-operation for innovation and sustainable development of the company as a brand and community. *Kwartalnik Ekonomistów i Menedżerów*, *50*(4), 127–141. https://doi.org/10.5604/01.3001.0013.0639

Szostak, M. (2020). Does creativity influence the perception of creative identities? *European Research Studies Journal*, *23*(4), 312–333. https://doi.org/10.35808/ersj/2444

Szostak, M. (2021a). Does Polish post-communist cultural Burden influence the perception of creative identities? *Journal of Intercultural Management*, *13*(2), 29–58. https://doi.org/10.2478/joim-2021-0060

Szostak, M. (2021b). Perception of creative identities by leaders and non-leaders: Consequences for theory and practice of management. *European Research Studies Journal*, *XXIV*(4), 211–232.

Szostak, M. (2022). Perception of creative identities by managers and non-managers: Does a manager see more? *Entrepreneurship and Sustainability Issues*, *9*(3), 24–49. https://doi.org/10.9770/jesi.2022.9.3(2)

Szostak, M. (2023). Perception of creative identities by artistic and non-artistic individuals: Consequences for management. *Creativity Studies*, *16*(1), 1–25. https://doi.org/10.3846/cs.2023.15081

Szostak, M., & Sułkowski, Ł. (2021a). Artist, creator, manager, entrepreneur, leader: How society perceive these identities? *Economics and Sociology*, *14*(2), 209–221. https://doi.org/10.14254/2071-789X.2021/14-2/11

Szostak, M., & Sułkowski, Ł. (2021b). The challenges in identification of artists-managers: Consequences for creativity. *Creativity Studies*, *14*(1), 112–124. https://doi.org/10.3846/cs.2021.13822

Szostak, M., & Sułkowski, Ł. (2021c). The identity and self-perception of artists-managers. *Problems and Perspectives in Management*, *19*(1), 372–386. https://doi.org/10.21511/ppm.19(1).2021.32

Tatarkiewicz, W. (2004). *Wybór pism estetycznych*. Towarzystwo Autorów i Wydawców Prac Naukowych Universitas.

Tatarkiewicz, W. (2015). *Historia estetyki: Tom I.* PWN.

Taylor, S. S. (2019). Our father, twenty years on. *Organizational Aesthetics*, *8*(1), 8–10.

Taylor, S. S., & Ladkin, D. (2009). Understanding arts-based methods in managerial development. *Academy of Management Learning and Education*, *8*(1), 55–69. https://doi.org/10.5465/AMLE.2009.37012179

Travis, S. (2020). Flashpoints of artist identity formation. *Art Education*, *73*(5), 16–25. https://doi.org/10.1080/00043125.2020.1781438

UNESCO. (2017). Reshaping cultural policies advancing creativity for development. *2018 Global Report*, 7. https://en.unesco.org/creativity/sites/creativity/files/global_report_fact_sheet_en.pdf

Walczak, W. (2014). *Cele i funkcje zarządzania w teoriach naukowych a praktyka – próba diagnozy źródeł występujących rozbieżności*. E-Mentor. www.e-mentor.edu.pl/artykul/index/numer/44/id/917

Watkins, C., & King, I. W. (2002). Organizational performance: A view from the arts. *TAMARA: Journal of Critical Postmodern Organization Science*, *2*(1), 31–46.

Watson, T. J. (2001). *In search of management: Culture, chaos and control in managerial work* (1st ed.). Cengage Learning EMEA.

Woodward, J. B., & Funk, C. (2010). Developing the artist-leader. *Leadership*, *6*(3), 295–309. https://doi.org/10.1177/1742715010368768

Żak, J. (2015). Postrzeganie dzieł sztuki jako proces tworzenia. In K. Pankowska (Ed.), *Sztuka i Twórczość*. Wydawnictwo Akademickie Żak.

Zambrell, K. (2016). Managers' identity construction at work: Artistic interventions as triggers for identity work. *Organizational Aesthetics*, *5*(2), 34–67.

Zhai, L. (2021). Research on tourism management education under the background of new liberal arts construction. *International Journal of Electrical Engineering and Education*. https://doi.org/10.1177/00207209211005259

Zieleniewski, J. (1982). *Organizacja zespołów ludzkich: Wstęp do teorii organizacji i kierowania*. PWN.

2 Art as an organisational activity

Art can be understood by analysing certain practices in specific configurations and regimes of identification (Dronsfield et al., 2008), or by analysing the results (works) that practising art generates. In order to present the full range of managerial problems the artist faces, it is best to use the theory of the aesthetic situation for this purpose. After one analyses the components of the aesthetic situation and the relationships between these components, a structured space will appear that allows for the analysis of the multitude of decision-making problems faced by the creator of a given field of art who wants to achieve a specific artistic goal.

This chapter looks at artistic activity as an organisational activity in art. Although artistic creation appears to be a chaotic activity, it is a deeply structured process – what is more, it can be said that the structure of artistic activities is much more complex than the structure of non-artistic activities. The apparent chaos of artistic activity results from the observers' misunderstanding of its essence and the assessment based on inadequate criteria. This chapter answers the following questions: (1) At what levels can artistic activity be considered an organisational activity? (2) To what extent can Gołaszewska's theory be used to illustrate organisational activity in the field of artistic activity? (3) In what dimensions do art creators manage the creative process, and how do changes in this process affect the quality of a work of art? The results of these considerations will then be implemented in subsequent chapters to the entire management process and its components.

2.1 Art management

Literature in the field of management under the term "art management" (management of arts) understands managerial activity in the organisational and financial scope of individual artistic disciplines: management of an artistic ensemble (orchestra, chamber ensemble, choir, theatre group, or ballet group), managing a cultural institution (philharmonic, theatre, gallery, museum), organising exhibitions, and managing film and television (Kostera, 2013; Kostera & Śliwa, 2012, pp. 203–205; Røyseng, 2008).

DOI: 10.4324/9781003458029-3

Without belittling the importance of scientific, practical, and instrumental knowledge characteristic of organisational activity within individual artistic disciplines, one should emphasise the aspect of self-awareness, barely outlined in the discourse, called self-organisation or self-management (Kostera, 2014; Linstead & Höpfl, 2000, pp. 228–243). The essence of self-management in the field of art is crucial and lies in the complex characteristics of the creative process, the multidimensionality of the work of art, and the non-standard nature of the process of perception of the work by art recipients. It should be emphasised that these issues apply equally to all art disciplines and are well-defined, established, and analysed in the aesthetic literature.

Management representatives should be aware that art (and aesthetics) is an internally very ordered field with a much longer tradition than management. Hence: (1) the management of visible aspects within individual art disciplines cannot ignore the dimension of artistic self-awareness and artistic self-management; and (2) the application of issues in the field of art and aesthetics in management cannot be selective, fragmentary, or devoid of context. In order to embrace the issue of art management holistically, it is necessary to internalise both the adequate achievements of aesthetics and the adequate achievements of management. This chapter fills that gap.

Many aesthetic theories may refer to considerations in the field of art management in particular scopes. However, the most adequate, coherent, and simultaneously capacious and flexible is the theory of the "aesthetic situation" by Maria Gołaszewska (1926–2015), a philosopher and ethicist associated with the Jagiellonian University. Surprisingly, this exceptional achievement is entirely unnoticed in the world, despite many publications in English.

2.2 Aesthetic situation

Maria Gołaszewska, based on the achievements of Ingarden's phenomenology (Ingarden, 1970, 1981), translated her own theory of the "axiological situation" (Gołaszewska, 1986b, pp. 23–38) into the area of aesthetics, calling it the "aesthetic situation" (Gołaszewska, 1984, pp. 27–30). The main components of the aesthetic situation are: the creator, the work of art, the recipient, the natural world, and the world of values. The fundamental relationships between the listed components are as follows: the creator in the creative process creates a work of art; the recipient receives the work of art in the reception process; all these elements have connections and interactions with the world of values, but they happen in the real world (Figure 2.1).

The model proposed by Gołaszewska is fundamental, universal, and systemic. The fundamentality of the model manifests itself in considering all the problems and phenomena belonging to the consideration of aesthetics. Literature in the field of aesthetics abounds in theories addressing the essence of individual

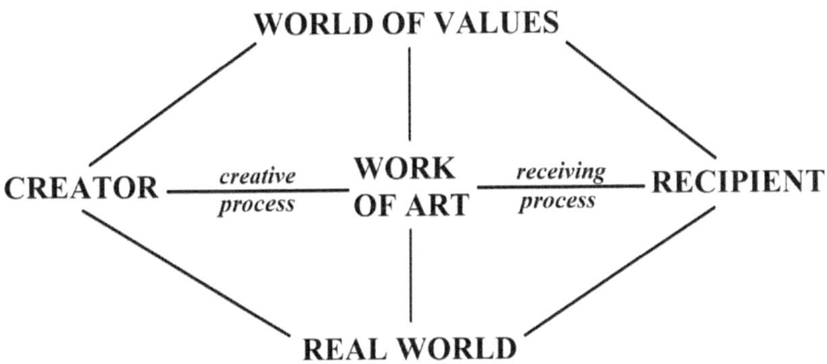

Figure 2.1 Scheme of the aesthetic situation according to M. Gołaszewska

Source: Author's own elaboration based on Gołaszewska (1984)

aesthetic problems, but there is a lack of metatheories that would be able to cover all these problems and carry their multitude and diversity. The universality of the model consists in its adequacy both for consideration of problems concerning aesthetics as a whole, as well as for detailed problems, the placement of which in the diagram shows their importance in the entire aesthetic situation. The systemic nature of the model draws attention to the fact of interconnections between elements and the consequences of modifying one element affecting the remaining elements (Ostrowicki, 1997).

Probably the closest metamodel to M. Gołaszewska's theory was proposed by Linstead and Höpfl, who described the theory of "disorganized aesthetics" (Linstead & Höpfl, 2000, p. 58). According to the authors, this disorganisation of aesthetics should occur through a totalitarian implosion or a trivialised explosion of components in the form of authors, technicians, audiences, and critics. In the centre of the model is a work of art, which is the result (implosion) or effect (explosion) of the creative process that takes place between the authors of the work (e.g., composer) and the technicians performing the author's records (e.g., musicians-performers), and the process of interpretation that takes place between the audience that receives the performances of the technicians and the critics, who are a specialised audience able to explain a less understandable work in a more accessible way (Figure 2.2).

The theory of the aesthetic situation by M. Gołaszewska is the central axis of consideration in this work. Due to these connections and interactions, it is not an easy task to analyse the individual components of the aesthetic situation in isolation from each other. Despite these difficulties, for the success of further considerations, it is necessary to know the main problems of this area, i.e., the creator, the creative process, the work, the reception process, the recipient, the world of values, and the real world.

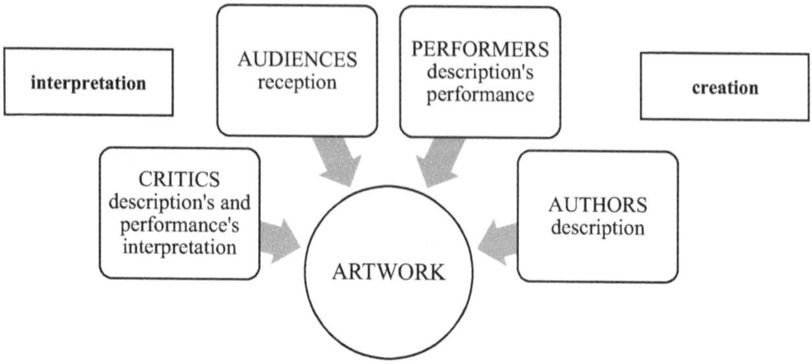

Figure 2.2 Aesthetics disorganised by totalitarian implosion or trivialised explosion

Source: Author's own elaboration based on Linstead and Höpfl (2000, p. 58)

2.2.1 Creator

Virtuosity, *creativity*, and *artistry* sare independent properties, but their coexistence is desirable and mutually catalyses. The order in which they are listed is also significant: first virtuosity, then (in parallel) creativity and artistry – although one can argue about the equality of creativity and artistry. To explain this reasoning, it is worth using the concepts characteristic of identity management, i.e., "becoming" as opposed to "being". Building the identity of an artist (a creator in the field of art) begins with learning the theory, then developing technical skills and mastering the technique, which together we refer to as virtuosity (or becoming a virtuoso, although not every adept of art will become a virtuoso in his field, and, moreover, the virtuoso has its weaknesses); see Figure 2.3.

Another argument confirming the reasoning described earlier is the didactic process in the field of art: it begins with an individual's development of technical skills (virtuosity), and only after mastering a certain range of skills (not everyone reaches the heights in this area) does that individual work on the development of creativity and artistry (or of artistry and creativity). Looking at the nomenclature of diplomas in artistic education on the example of musical arts, it can be seen that: at the level of primary education, the diploma speaks of "playing a specific instrument"; at the level of secondary education, the title of "instrumentalist musician" can be seen on the diploma (which should be related to the concept of a craftsman in a given field); while at the higher education level, the title "artist musician" appears on the diploma. The next stages of development will be associated with further development of virtuosity as well as creativity and artistry. Depending on which element (virtuosity, creativity, or artistry) will dominate in the activity of an individual, that individual is defined as a virtuoso of a given field (when technical skills and mastery emanate from the works), a creative creator (when the works are innovative), or an artist

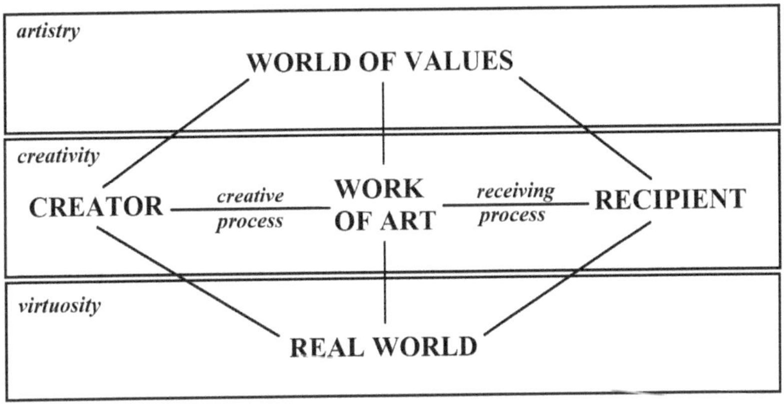

Figure 2.3 Virtuosity, creativity, and artistry in an aesthetic situation

Source: Author's own elaboration

(when creativity reaches the recipients, giving them a sense of communing with metaphysics, with the world of values).

As you can see, the concept of artistry is ennobling, being a kind of crowning achievement (or reaching a certain level) of development in the field of art (though not only art). These three key concepts (virtuosity, creativity, artistry) should be disenchanted, because they do not have to refer only to activities in the field of art and cleansed of their common – usually interchangeable – understanding and use. For this purpose, they will be discussed in detail next.

Virtuosity

Virtuosity is a complex phenomenon, and its essence has changed along with the epochs of cultural evolution. The contemporary, dictionary definition of virtuosity – as outstanding (above average) technical perfection in performing specific activities (usually artistic) and presenting high craftsmanship in a specific scope (Virtuosity, 2022) – this is due to the development of musical instruments in the 19th century and the glorification of the artist as a divine entity endowed with extraordinary qualities.

Romantic musicians outdid each other in technical prowess, which became an end in itself. Artistic values were put aside, focusing on technical prowess to amaze listeners. How much people worshiped and believed in the power of virtuosity can be seen in the example of the pianist and composer Robert Schumann (1810–1856), who, apart from backbreaking exercises at the piano keyboard, used an apparatus he had designed to mechanically stretch and improve his fingers, which resulted in permanently damaged hands (Jensen, 2012). It was not uncommon to find supernatural (then described as devilish) sources of this technical proficiency in 19th-century virtuosos, such as the violinist Niccolo Paganini or the pianist Ferenc Liszt (Ginsborg, 2018).

The second key factor in such an understanding of virtuosity is the desire to imitate the intention of the creator of the work (composer) in an ideal way by the performer (instrumentalist musician). With this approach, the individuality of the performer, his contribution to the work, or the circumstances of the specific performance did not matter; the performer – following the example of the printing press – was always everywhere and in an ideal situation to reflect the composer's intention (Kaiser, 2018). Hence, the easy way is to compare a virtuoso to a "trained monkey with an empty head" (Ginsborg, 2018).

The twentieth century, and especially its last decades, began to break with the romantic vision of mechanical virtuosity (virtuoso-machine). Yes, the ability to efficiently use the technical workshop is still crucial, but the individual factor, personality, or context becomes no less important when defining contemporary virtuosity (Leech-Wilkinson, 2018). In these circumstances, the concept of virtuosity has now become a rather theoretical rhetorical figure, and from the practical side, it began to evolve towards artistry (more on this subject in the subsection "Artistry"). This technical proficiency has been subordinated to the overarching goal, i.e., the communication of specific universal values contained in a work of art to the recipient (Leech-Wilkinson, 2020). The argument that virtuosity itself is not the essence of art states that although we currently have the possibility of obtaining a perfectly perfect performance in terms of precision using artificial intelligence (computers controlling the instruments), we are still looking for human performers who are not as technically perfect as machines, but who are able to infuse the work with an invigorating spirit of artistry.

Analysing historical definitions of virtuosity, we find the following characteristics (Ginsborg, 2018):

1. originally the term was applied to theoreticians and composers, whereas nowadays it applies to performers;
2. it may be a gift and/or it may result from the educational process;
3. it concerns eminence and uniqueness;
4. it applies to both technology and art.

Contemporary research in the field of art shows that the concept of virtuosity is still not an unambiguous phenomenon – even for professionals and students of the same field, e.g., musical arts. Professional musicians consider the ease of meeting the requirements of the work and the level of technical skills to be the most important features of virtuosity; self-identification as a virtuoso, mastery in one's field, personal qualities, self-confidence, and uniqueness were ranked further down with much less importance. On the other hand, students of musical arts define virtuosity mainly through the level of technical skills, mastery in their field, and personal characteristics (Ginsborg, 2018). There is also a researched relationship between the creator's intelligence and his virtuosity, which requires imagination, awareness, mental navigation, anticipation, adaptation, and speed (Stachó, 2018).

Research conducted on musicians shows how many factors constitute the phenomenon of virtuosity in the consciousness of the creator of art. There are five main problems and several possibilities within each of them (Ginsborg, 2018):

1. aspirations:
   a. considered as a prerequisite – without aspirations, it is difficult to talk about the success of achieving high technical skills due to the fact that they require a lot of effort;
   b. personal perfection – a kind of deeply internalised goal of self-improvement and development, more as a permanent action than a target state;
   c. something that should be achieved but at a later stage;
   d. the utter needlessness of aspiration; ambition is not essential in achieving virtuosity;
2. the relationship between virtuosity and "magical" artistry:
   a. artistry considered superior to virtuosity;
   b. the crucial relationship between virtuosity and artistry;
   c. virtuosity as a tool of artistry;
   d. a complete lack of relationship between virtuosity and artistry;
3. characteristics of virtuosity:
   a. technical skills;
   b. component of mastery in its field;
   c. constitutive of self-confidence;
   d. ease of movement in the matter of the art discipline;
   e. virtuosity as an expression of the artist's personality;
   f. virtuosity that gives the artist uniqueness;
   g. relativity of virtuosity as a function of definition;
4. ways to achieve virtuosity:
   a. hard and systematic work;
   b. as a natural gift, or talent;
   c. as a result of experience in a given field – greater experience, greater virtuosity; this element indicates that ambition is not important in achieving virtuosity;
   d. as a combination of the first three elements;
5. communication:
   a. artist with co-performers;
   b. the artist with the audience (as a set of individual recipients);

c. spectacularity – giving the work the character of an unusual event; this element is related to the lack of relationship between virtuosity and artistry and means virtuosity for the sake of virtuosity;
d. the important role of the recipient's activity in the reception process;
e. as carrying a message from the creator to the recipient.

Having a choice of factors constituting virtuosity, most musicians indicate that it results from hard work, and experience and talent are only secondary factors (Ginsborg, 2018). The entire phenomenon is depicted in Figure 2.4. Despite the continuous evolution of the concept of virtuosity, it is still an important factor, and even a kind of synthetic indicator, of the quality of a performer of art (Heredia-Carroza, 2019).

Creativity

The term "artist" has a narrower meaning than the term "creator" (in the sense of a creative individual). An artist produces works of art, while a creator produces results of various kinds: scientific, cultural, and also artistic (Gołaszewska, 1986a, p. 7).

In order to answer the question of what makes a person undertake creative activity in the field of art, and thus become an artist, we must refer to the achievements of aesthetics, which distinguished two types of personality by developing the concepts of "basic personality" and "creative personality" (Gołaszewska,

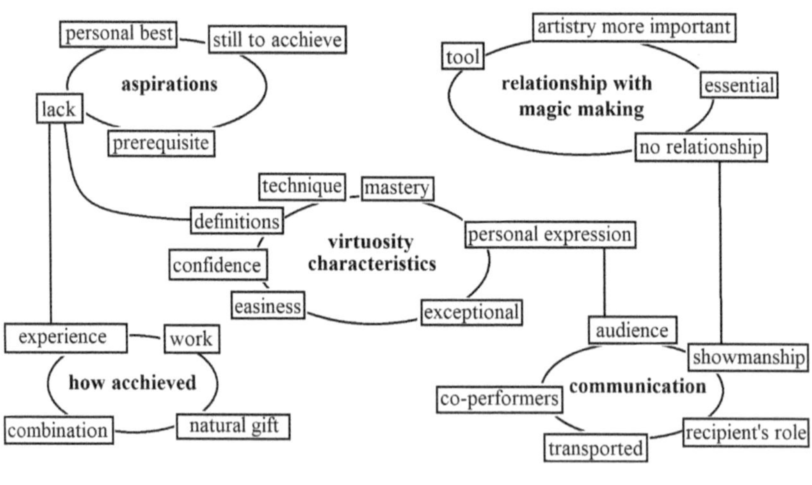

Figure 2.4 What does virtuosity mean for art creators?

Source: Author's own elaboration based on Ginsborg (2018, p. 470)

1984, pp. 167–175). Basic personality is nothing more than all the features that make up the characteristics of an individual: introversion-extroversion, slowness-agility, high-low cognitive abilities. Creative personality, on the other hand, is the choice of basic personality traits that determine the beginning of creative activity and its continuation, and that give shape to work. Some features manifest themselves at work, while others are a prerequisite for undertaking creative work. The creative personality develops against the background of the basic personality. We will never find a complete reflection of any personality in a work, although we can deduce traces of a creative personality from the work. To notice the characteristic features of the artist's imagination, you need to familiarise yourself with all the artist's work. The issue of creative personality is connected with artistic style, while the overall output of the artist allows us to reconstruct the artist's creative personality.

Researchers analysing artists' creative process divided it into its conceptual, experimental, implementation and post-implementation phases. As a result, it became possible to create a typology of creative personalities (Gołaszewska, 1984, pp. 176–189):

1. creative personality of the intuitive type – characterised by a close entanglement of the phases of experience and realisation, and the participation of pre-reflective awareness; the work process is quick and with a sense of well-made decisions; the most important creative moments are realised based on acts of intuition without discursive motivation, without the participation of full consciousness (musical improvisers);
2. creative personality of the reflective type – characterised by a clear separation of phases, where the experience phase precedes the implementation phase; full awareness is involved here; has a complicated structure, with hesitation in choosing the concept and means of expression; the creative process is long; the artist controls his intentions, creates a concept, and then implements it more or less consistently; the reflexivity of the creative process is special – it is not only an intellectual reflection but also emotional, concerning personal matters and revolving around experience;
3. creative personality of the behavioural type – characterised by the separation of the phases of the creative process, with the exception that the phase of implementation to some extent precedes the phase of experience; includes both types of consciousness (pre-reflective and reflective); it is a kind of trial-and-error method: the artist does not know what the final work should look like and does not feel the need to take this or that step; it is about incorporating an artistic vision that is not entirely clear into further real shapes.

It should be noted that the distinguished types of creative personality do not actually appear in pure forms, but as a mixture of individual types in various proportions (Gołaszewska, 1984).

People working on the development of their own creativity often ask the question, where should the creator look for his creativity? Based on the theory of personality (Gołaszewska, 1984, pp. 176–189), the answer points to the search for one's own creativity within oneself, within one's own personality. Looking for your own creativity in the works of other artists leads to copying or imitation. The natural source of one's own creativity is found in the creative personality. This personality, which can be compared to a "creative child", should be brought up and constantly developed; the growth and flowering of one's own creativity should be the natural goal of every conscious individual.

These facts also imply the conclusion that a look at the aesthetic theory of creativity may be of primary importance here, as opposed to looking for correlations with dimensions of secondary importance. The sources of artistic creativity may result from the following (Arbuz-Spatari, 2019; Gołaszewska, 1984, pp. 189–198; Jung, 2014):

1. inspiration;
2. the act of creating in the image of nature;
3. discovering timeless ideas and incorporating them into your work;
4. imitation of divine creativity;
5. meeting the needs of a social group (sociological theory of creativity);
6. excess energy that remains after satisfying basic needs (physiology of human life);
7. the state of culture and the approach to artistic ideals at a given level of human development (cultural approach);
8. the sum of the socio-economic (ideological) conditions in which the artist lives (historical approach);
9. expressing the creator's personality (psychological approach).

The psychological theories of artistic creativity, which may be crucial in the analysis of the phenomena of managerial creativity, include (Dai & Cheng, 2017; Ekmekçi et al., 2014; Gołaszewska, 1984, pp. 189–204; Shi et al., 2017; Sternberg, 1985, 2003; Tarnopolski, 2017):

1. creativity as inspiration – in this model, the artist achieves particularly significant artistic effects thanks not to his knowledge or skills, but to inspiration (a set of factors that may not be rationally explained, but which come to the fore in spontaneous moments); the results of inspiration are unpredictable; the uniqueness of the work here results from the uniqueness of the conceptual process that leads to the creation of the work; it is a combination of the theory of inspiration with the theory of genius and individualism;
2. creativity as work – this model indicates the key importance of work, effort, and overcoming obstacles; people have natural abilities, but must work on them to create authentic works of art; the necessary conditions for creativity

in this model are the awareness of the rules of creation and the ability to use them; work becomes an indispensable component of the creative process;
3. creativity as an expression of personality – this model suggests that the creator can express what others feel through his own expression; the creator's consciousness controls the expression that underlies creativity; art is a form of communication, and its function is to communicate internal states; artists externalise their states of mind to enable audiences to achieve similar states;
4. creativity as an essential component of wisdom – this model suggests that an individual who is both intelligent and wise has creative skills; it should be emphasised here that wisdom is also a manageable quality, which Aristotle described as a combination of intellect, scientific knowledge, instrumental knowledge, practical knowledge, and particular auxiliary virtues such as ingenuity, prudence, and cunning.

Dictionaries define creativity as a multifaceted phenomenon resulting in the creation of new and valuable products. As can be seen, the phenomenon of creativity refers to the component of creativity (novelty) and the component of quality (valency of the effect). The concept of creativity applies to both the process of creation and the creative output, i.e., the totality of works created by the creator.

Creativity is usually defined from the perspective of its effects, which can be classified according to the specificity of the creator's domain. Four types of values are proposed, which can be assigned to the corresponding domains of creativity (Nęcka, 2000): (1) cognitive values, (2) aesthetic values, (3) pragmatic values, and (4) ethical values. Art, as a domain of creativity, is in this classification related to aesthetic values connected with the search for and creation of beauty. Unfortunately, the perception of these aesthetic values is ephemeral, changeable, and individualised, so their blurred boundaries are not clearly defined (Mendecka, 2010, p. 15).

Artistry

Before analysing the meanders of the meaning of the concepts of artistry and artist, one should break away from their common understanding: a person painting pictures is not an artist, but a painter; the person playing on the stage is not an artist, but an actor; a person playing an instrument is not an artist, but a musician. All these people, despite dealing with the spheres commonly associated with artistry, are simply doing their jobs. To be an artist in a given area, one needs more than just physical activities, even those commonly referred to as artistic. In order to obtain the right to use the name of an artist, apart from practising a given profession, one should also refer to universal values in a given activity; without universal values, the performed activities remain only in the real world, at the most deserving a name of craft if they are done finely from the technical side (virtuosity).

The Latin *artist* means a fine arts student (Gołaszewska, 1986a, p. 6). According to the dictionary definition, an artist is "someone who creates things with great skill and imagination" (Artist, 2023a). Medieval practical perception of art, said an artist, is "someone who, according to art, works with tools in a specific matter". The synonyms of the artist are master, expert, geek, guru, virtuoso, and wizard, while the antonyms are amateur, inexperienced person, and non-expert (Artist, 2023b). The concept of the artist has changed over time and with the evolution of art so much that nowadays, there is even talk of its redefinition, i.e., the loss of its homogeneous meaning and even the loss of constant features that allow capturing the essence of the concept of an artist in the form of a permanent definition (Sztabiński, 2002).

Ancient aesthetics distinguished several key issues that defined the artist (Tatarkiewicz, 2015): (1) imagination, (2) thought, (3) knowledge, (4) wisdom, (5) idea in mind, and (6) ability to use the rules of art; in art, only the artist is the legislator. Expanding this list with the achievements of subsequent eras, one cannot forget about such features as (Gołaszewska, 1984, 1986a): (1) creativity, (2) sensitivity, (3) intuition, (4) "getting lost" in the creative process (from conceptualisation to implementation), (5) devoting everything to the creative process, (6) self-analysis, and (7) self-correction.

Also, the artist's goals have changed over time, although the most unchanging are: (1) materialisation, (2) giving form to universal ideas, (3) conveying values, (4) giving satisfaction and pleasure to the recipient, (5) enabling the recipient of the experience to a state of catharsis, and (6) transforming ugliness into beauty.

Going further, we can distinguish the features of an artist necessary for the effective implementation of artistic goals: perseverance/consistency, hard work from an early age and throughout life, self-discipline, mental toughness, responsibility, the ability to set goals, the ability to achieve goals, the ability to observe the world, perceptiveness, openness.

An attempt to understand the artist's meaning based on the concept's evolution will not be complete. A contextual approach should be used here: to see the artist in the system of all the phenomena that influenced him and those he somehow shaped. After all, an artist is an individual from a given community, subject to the same laws, and at the same time grows into someone separate and unique due to an individual creative personality. An artist can be seen as a model example of a creator (Gołaszewska, 1986a, pp. 5–6).

Based on the theory of the psychiatrist Ernst Kretschmer (1888–1964), who claimed that the artist has a personality of the marginal (extreme) type, i.e., oscillating between health and mental illness, it can be concluded that the artist has a personality exceeding the norms; hence, including it in the definitions is certainly a difficult task, and possibly even an impossible one. An artist works in the same world as non-artists, but he sees and feels more and adopts a radicalised, even extreme, attitude. Despite the above difficulties, the manifestations of the artist's uniqueness can be characterised by the following issues (Gołaszewska, 1986a, pp. 51–56):

1. making the improbable a reality – defining the concept of artist borders on impossible; analysing the most significant creators of art, we often come to the conclusion that this person lacks some essential feature resulting from the definition of an artist; a work of art deprived of its proper cultural context becomes an ordinary artefact; creates something out of nothing, and very often puts together existing elements; despite these issues, the artist creates closed works, capable of lasting;
2. knowledge without arguments – which can be described as intuition or scientificity; the artist finds the answer to the question without analysing the arguments, often the answer precedes the appearance of the question; many artists are considered precursors of theory (Fyodor Dostoyevsky, Jules Verne, Leonardo da Vinci); the artist has trouble analytically explaining his creative process;
3. generalised sensitivity – both to internal and external stimuli, to biological and mental states; sensitivity generates a state of solid tension in the layer of creative personality and basic personality; this causes a strong complication of personality, which makes it difficult to understand or systematise it according to generally applicable standards;
4. absolutised freedom – above all, "freedom from", which, as a consequence, often appears to the artist as "freedom to"; apparently, it is a liberating state, but ultimately the artist must create his own rules and limitations, which – being visible only to him – often drive him into deep dilemmas, even ending in suicide;
5. objectivised subjectivism – the artist's individualism and uniqueness become objectively significant and valued; the artist should be himself, not imitate anyone or anything, not look for patterns anywhere; he becomes a reference point for himself; he often defends himself against being included in a particular current, because any assignment appears as an objective loss of subjective individuality;
6. self-destructive awareness – because art is a protest and an act of disagreement with the world, the artist sees gaps and contradictions in the world and rebels against repetition and mediocrity; it can be assumed that these rebellions also serve to improve oneself and enhance the artist's uniqueness;
7. functional autotelism – the artist strives for the artistic perfection of his work, while the functionality of the work (large, gloomy, terrifying) is secondary (just opposite to the world of technology, where a machine can be defective as long as it produces valuable products);
8. rationalisation of the non-rational – although humanity's ability to understand reality rationally is limited at every stage of development, the artist is able,

even in the absence of knowledge in a given field, to rationalise what is not rational at the moment; science rationalises by repressing the irrational, while the artist reaches the essence of the irrational, he puts the irrational into his artistic categories, finding aesthetic values there and bringing them closer to people in the form of a work of art (e.g., irrational love can be perfectly conveyed by art when its analytical understanding by science is imperfect); Here the question arises whether at some stage of the technical development of humanity, science, which will be able to answer all questions and doubts, will supplant art in general.

The 20th-century postmodern meanings of the artist concept have been discarded to simplify further considerations.

It is much more challenging to answer what characterises a good artist. First, it should be understandable; however, we find many examples of artists incomprehensible to their contemporaries, and after years/centuries, they were pillars in their fields (e.g., J. S. Bach). It should be popular, which would mean that it reaches the audience's awareness; however, popularity is also not a good indicator, as it does not reflect the quality of the artwork. The only answer that resists criticism is that a good artist should be true by referring to universal values and ideas that are understandable and relevant to humanity in the long term, regardless of the era.

Summarising these considerations, for the purposes of this book, the artistry will be considered as taking into account universal values in one's activity (not only in the field of art) in order to influence recipients through one's products.

2.2.2 Creative process

Although the most important values from the point of view of aesthetics are universal values, and the most visible symptom of creativity is the work of art itself, it is in the person (mind, consciousness, subconsciousness) of the creator that the most important processes that make up the phenomenon of creativity take place. The theory of creativity in empirically oriented aesthetics will be used to thoroughly trace the creative process in the field of art (Gołaszewska, 1984). Figure 2.5 shows the diagram of the creative process.

Taking up artistic creativity is influenced by several conditions, which are collectively called a creative disposition or attitude:

1. personality determinants (abilities and interests leading to an attitude of interest in creating and appreciating art);
2. social conditions (influence of the environment and education, and public opinion regarding the position of art and the evaluation of the works of other artists);
3. richness of experience (the sum of the artist's individual experiences).

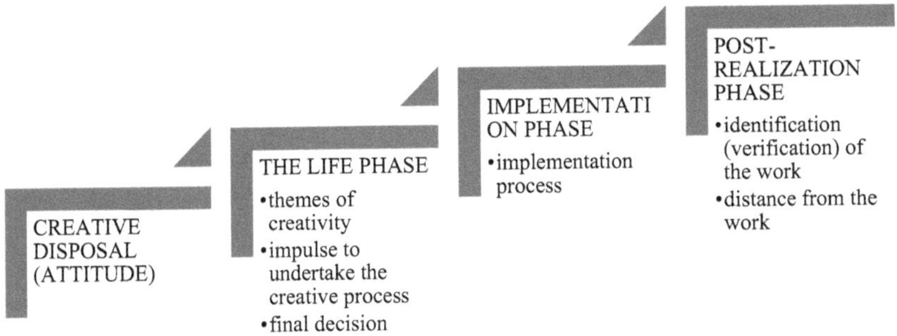

Figure 2.5 Diagram of the creative process in the context of the aesthetic situation

Source: Author's own elaboration based on Gołaszewska (1984, p. 199)

In order to start the creative process, a creative attitude alone is not enough – one also needs motives for undertaking a creative activity, and these are of two types:

1. assigned – directly affecting the shaping of the work, can be implemented with the participation of creative work:
   a. taking into account oneself, i.e., the desire to create a work that meets and expresses the creator's expectations;
   b. consideration of the work, i.e., attention focused on the perfection of the work, realising high aesthetic value;
   c. consideration of the recipient, i.e., the desire to provide others with the experience that a work of art can bring;
2. unassigned – marked indirectly in the work and possibly also implemented through other activities; additionally activating creative forces (economic reasons, social coercion, compliance with stereotypes).

In order for a work to be created, there must be a direct impulse to undertake the creative process, i.e., mental stimulation through an external or internal stimulus in the form of:

1. lack of perception in a world that allows or requires fulfilment (seeing imperfection, the artist decides to enrich reality with a new value);
2. fascination with the world and reality (the artist wants to show his admiration for the world and things in the world and save this state from oblivion);
3. the excess of his own experiences from which the artist wants to free himself (wanting to present them to others, looking for a way to express them in an artistic form).

The sum of the previous elements in the form of internal coercion leads to the final decision to start the creative process; then, there is real preparation for creative work and the first efforts. Sometimes the artist begins work immediately, but more often, the creation of the work is preceded by three stages: conceptualisation of the work, its artistic vision, and crystallisation of the artistic intention.

The physical process of realisation begins when the artist begins to actually objectify his intention by shaping the material to realise a certain aesthetic value; the critical phases at this stage aim to shape the material so that the work is equivalent to the artistic vision. It is worth paying attention to situations unforeseen in the concept of the work (the so-called accidents at work) and resulting from chance, coincidence, or even a mistake at the stage of implementation (e.g., unnecessary but irreversible movement of the sculptor's chisel); injecting the unintended result of action as a valuable and immanent part of the work of art requires the artist's reflexes, observational skills, and creativity (more on this subject in Section 5.3, "Artistic improvisation").

After the physical creative process is completed, there is a post-implementation phase consisting in verifying the work in terms of materialising the intended artistic concept. With time from the end of the creative process, there is a process of gaining the artist's distance to the work, the purpose of which is for the artist to break the creative bond with the work to become the recipient of his work.

This distance of the artist from his work has a twofold character:

1. short-term – a musician hears a piece performed by him/her differently during the creative process, and differently when listening to a recording of the same performance;
2. long-term – it usually takes much time for the creator of the work to "forget" all the analytical activities that he carried out during the creative process (usually it is a catalogue of mistakes, searches, problems, and adversities) so that he can give himself over to his work as a creatively unbound recipient.

2.2.3 Work of art

A work of art is an object made by an artist with outstanding skills, a product of one of the fine arts or something that gives the recipient high aesthetic satisfaction (Work of Art, 2023). From this dictionary definition, it is clear that the work is an element between the artist and the recipient – evident in the illustration of the aesthetic situation (see Figure 2.1). A work of art is a closed whole, separated from the environment (e.g., through a picture frame); it is an object deliberately created by the artist, but it persists among other objects of the real world, although endowed with a special meaning due to its aesthetic value. Resulting from the essence of the creative process, a work of art concentrates the artist's effort, which aims to give the work the perfect form so that it speaks for itself, creating its world through the implemented artistic structures (Gołaszewska, 1967, p. 19). The work is independent of the creative process, and the creative process is independent of the creator's core personality (Gołaszewska, 1984).

It is worth looking at the following definitions of a work of art: any creative composition of one or more media (means of expression) whose primary function is to communicate an aesthetically valuable purpose (Lind, 1992); something created with the intention of conveying the possibility of satisfying aesthetic interest (Beardsley, 1983); an artefact that, under standard conditions, provides the recipient with an aesthetic experience (Schlesinger, 1979); physically embodied and culturally embodied being (Margolis, 1986); the object was created only as one of the critical forms of its time to fulfil the function of art at a given time (Gaut & McIver Lopes, 2001, p. 176).

The work is a unique phenomenon, containing a message (materialised by the creator) which could not be formulated in any other way. In order to read and understand this message, a specific attitude of the recipient is needed, which is a function of many factors: knowledge, experience, sensitivity, and openness. A work of art, constituting a closed space filled with specific meanings, is perceived by the viewer who – saturated with his everyday problems – must show an activity that often requires much effort (Gołaszewska, 1967, p. 271).

Looking at a work of art only from the perspective of the real world, without embedding the entire process of cognition in contexts, the recipient may have a real problem distinguishing a work of art from ordinary objects – especially when we consider avant-garde art (Danto, 1991).

2.2.4 Recipient

The recipient of art is the one who is not indifferent to art, who – due to the values of art – feels the need to commune with art and strives to realise his aesthetic interests (Gołaszewska, 1967, p. 29). The main interest of aesthetics is in the current recipients of art. However, one should not forget about the potential recipients, who – after appropriate preparation and the maturation process – can dominate the population of current recipients and be radically different from the previous ones.

From the recipient's point of view, the reception process focuses on the work, which contains the artist's intentions regarding the message of the work (taking into account certain values) materialised in elements of the real world – depending on the art discipline: stone, sounds, words, colours, movement.

Although the creator stands outside the work of art (except, of course, the performative work), because the work is independent and it is in the work that the creator has included everything he wanted to – or managed to – convey, often the recipient does not stop at contemplating the work itself but tries to get to know the interesting person that is the creator. The creator may also be of interest to the recipient when the work itself does not have sufficient artistic potential to convey a message or when the recipient cannot understand this message. For example, a work that is full and absorbs the viewer is perfect. On the other hand, a work that confuses the recipient is incomprehensible, fails the recipient's expectations, and implies the process of searching for reasons for this state by the recipient; here, the list of potential reasons is short: (1) an artist who did not realise his intention, (2) defective work, or (3) unskilful perception of the recipient. In such a situation, the recipient has the following options: (1) condemn the artist, (2) reject the work, and (3) undertake the process of understanding the work (Gołaszewska, 1967, pp. 19–20).

Since the recipients of art constitute a large community, it is natural to try to divide the recipients into smaller groups, which facilitates the possibility of reaching the individual with the artistic message. However, sociological attempts to divide, such as based on age, gender, and education, do not work because the individuality of the art reception process (as opposed to the reception of a kitsch artefact) is based on more qualitative factors that determine the recipient's attitude towards art. Among these factors are (Gołaszewska, 1967, pp. 68–69):

1. frequency of the recipient's contact with works of art – both intentional and unintentional, deep and superficial contacts, because each of the contacts shapes the aesthetic sensitivity of the recipient, while the recipient interested in art will strive for these contacts;
2. theoretical preparation and knowledge of the recipient – especially in the field of knowledge about art; less important (although not without significance) is general education;
3. mental characteristics of the recipient – both innate and acquired: aesthetic sensitivity, interests, tastes, attitudes towards art, emotionality, intellectual ability, ability to think abstractly, ability to generalise;
4. the degree of the recipient's activity in the reception process – expressed in the degree of self-reliance and independence in terms of reaction to the works.

Taking into account the aforementioned factors differentiating the recipients of art, recipients can be divided into four types (Gołaszewska, 1967, pp. 69–72):

1. naive recipient – characterised by rare and accidental contact with works; is unable to select the works with which he would like to commune; has little knowledge of art in general; may have an inborn aesthetic sensitivity or show interest in art; however, they are unaware of the specificity of works, based on their own or observed habits of other recipients; art appears to him as entertainment and the possibility of imitating the real world; he perceives art passively, and formulates apparent judgments focused on his emotional reactions, without delving into the structure of the work;
2. inauthentic (secondary) recipient – usually characterised by frequent contact with works of art; however, contacts are not deep; these contacts result

from an external necessity (fashion, habits) and not from an internal need; knowledge is quite extensive but secondary, and uncritically duplicating the opinions of authorities; sensitivity is low or suppressed by the necessities previously mentioned, fashions, and external opinions; usually has a passive attitude, with inhibition of own spontaneous reactions due to the lack of certainty as to the value of one's assessments;

3. critical recipient – usually frequent contact with works characterised by a critical attitude (not to be confused with criticism); treats art as an opportunity to form judgements and therefore needs frequent contact with it, as thanks to the practice of criticism, he gains skill and experience in it; knowledge is usually extensive, although not always complete; possessing deep systematic knowledge, can act as an art critic; aesthetic sensitivity is proportional to knowledge; independent and independent courts; active attitude towards art;
4. art lover – frequent contact with works of art resulting from the need for artistic experiences, although they usually concern a selected (favourite) type of art; conscious and planned contacts; there is a desire to create one's artistic creation or to collect works; extensive, though unsystematic, knowledge focused on a selected area; high and conscious sensitivity shaped by frequent and deep contact; active attitude and the degree of independence in formulating judgments high.

The psychological distinction assuming the existence of pre-reflective, reflective, and secondarily non-reflective awareness in people has significant consequences for explaining the formation of awareness of aesthetic phenomena – in particular subjective conditions of the aesthetic situation and various forms of beauty. Depending on the level of consciousness on which the aesthetic experiences of the recipient take place, the aesthetic experience and contact with aesthetic values are shaped in different ways (Gołaszewska, 1984, p. 77).

2.2.5 Reception process and role of criticism

The *reception process* of a work of art is complicated, which results from the need to meet many conditions for the recognition of the quality and artistic value of the work to be accurate (Gołaszewska, 1967, p. 271). The recipients of a work of art are specific people (when the work was done according to a specific order), or all potential recipients who come into contact with the work intentionally or accidentally. The recipients can give the artist feedback about the work and the values read from the work. In art, the artist, noticing reactions to his work, can associate his intentions with the actual reception and use this knowledge to create new works or modify the analysed work. The reception process (called the aesthetic process) consists of the sensual reception of the message located in the work. The process of receiving a work of art begins with ignorance (see Section 6.4, "Ignorance in management") and ends with an interpretation (Woodward & Funk, 2010).

It is worth distinguishing a work of art as a product of the intentional actions of the creator from the concretisation of the work by the recipient, which is a reconstruction of the work which takes place in the process of reception. This concretisation of the work concerns the reconstruction of what the author included in the work, but also partial completion and updating of the work with contexts and meanings contemporary to the recipient. It is through concretisation that the work acquires its full or fuller face; it can be said that each work appears to the recipient in some concretisation. A work of art can be perceived on two levels: (1) non-aesthetically – e.g., scientifically or consumptively, in order to get maximum pleasure from communing with the work or to learn something about a topic; and (2) aesthetically – in the development of aesthetic experience (if concretisation occurs in the aesthetic attitude, an aesthetic object). At both levels, the recipient decides whether the reception process will be directed at concretisation as faithful to the author as possible, or at self-concretisation, consistent with one's preferences (Ingarden, 1981, pp. 266–287).

The essence of the process of receiving a work of art is the aesthetic experience, which is the experience of a human interacting with works of art or creations of nature, thanks to which he reaches the aesthetic values inherent in them. Contemplating the quality of sensual things is a necessary condition for an aesthetic experience (Ossowski, 1949, pp. 282–292).

The key in the reception process is interpretation, which is a contextual study (analysis and synthesis) aimed at extracting and explaining the inner meaning of the considered phenomenon (things, events). It juxtaposes the analysed phenomenon with specific traditions and conventions and considers mutual relations (Ossowski, 1949, pp. 17–22). The selection of the contextual background on which the phenomenon is interpreted depends on the adopted research method.

The process of interpretation is related to the deconstruction approach, drawing attention to the multiplicity of possible interpretations of cultural products (Nycz, 2000). Deconstruction can be analytical to understand the meaning of the whole or the nature of the action itself, multiplying the meanings of the interpreted phenomenon, which ultimately does not lead to understanding the whole.

At this point, it is also worth considering the phenomenon of metaphor, which is common and sometimes even crucial in the perception of works of art. A metaphor, considered a particular type of making an analogy, is a stylistic (not only linguistic) device in which means (words) with foreign meanings are juxtaposed, thus creating a (phraseological) relationship with a different meaning from that of the literal meaning of the means (words) used. Although a metaphor is a typical artistic device, it is also used colloquially. Metaphor is considered a kind of higher form of imaging, in opposition to the literal representation of the phenomenon. A metaphor can be understood in one of four ways: (1) as a symbol; (2) as a result of the interaction between the means of expression used; (3) as a result of the interaction between the elements of the structure, in which these elements occur (e.g., the same work of art); or (4) as a form of processing the previously used means of expression. Metaphor is an essential means of interpreting a work of art (Gaut & McIver Lopes, 2001, pp. 285–295).

In the reception process, paying attention to the role of criticism (as opposed to criticism) and to critics is necessary. The role of criticism is to help the recipients perceive the work and show its beauty when it is hidden in meaning from an unprepared recipient. Critics are a special form of recipients of the work, who know or know more and what they use for the recipients. Artists, unlike producers of kitsch, also benefit from criticism, which allows them to assess the accuracy of their artistic ideas and the quality of their materialisation.

2.2.6 The real world

The most researched and described component of the aesthetic situation is the real world, i.e. the material side of the aesthetic situation that can be felt with the senses. It includes all physical matter (including tools and instruments) used by the artist within a given discipline of art (sounds, colours, textures, visual materials, words, gestures, movement), as well as the entirety of material reality providing reference points, contexts, and inspiration necessary for both the creator in the creative process and the recipient in the process of perception.

Before becoming a recipient of a work of art in a specific aesthetic situation, the human being belongs to the natural world and comes into contact with the world that shapes him physically and emotionally, but also intellectually and spiritually. Some experiences resulting from contact with the real world are accumulated in a person, and some fall into a state of unconsciousness, although it manifests itself in the form of intuition or consolidated experience (Gołaszewska, 1984, p. 77).

2.2.7 A world of values

Even though the values are not visible, the effects of believing in or considering them in the activity are quite the opposite. The problem of values in art is not homogeneous and can be considered in various ways. Roman Ingarden distinguished three areas of values (Ingarden, 1970, pp. 220–257):

1. vital values and related utilitarian and pleasure values, e.g., health, age, strength, satiety;
2. cultural values, which include:

    a. cognitive values, e.g., wisdom, colour, size;
    b. aesthetic values, e.g., beauty, ugliness, grace, sublimity, harmony;
    c. social (custom) values, e.g., what is appropriate and what is not appropriate;

3. moral values, e.g., goodness, responsibility, justice, generosity, courage, and nobility.

According to Ingarden, none of the listed categories is superior to the other categories, and attempts to determine what distinguishes some values from others are also unsatisfactory. Moreover, value is not the same as the attitude in which the value is perceived.

Charles Sanders Pierce (1839–1914), the founder of pragmatism, formulated a three-element list of universal categories, also called the categorical scheme of creation (Nowak, 1986):

1. first (monadic) categories – being the mode of being of what is, as it is, positively and without reference to anything else; they concern what is possible (pure qualities, in themselves);
2. second (dyadic) categories – being the mode of being of what is, how it is concerning something else, but without taking into account anything of the third; they concern what is real (the world of things and events);
3. third (triadic) categories – being the mode of being of what is, how it is, constituting a relationship between something else and something third; they concern what is necessary (the world of thoughts, judgements, desires; the domain of representation).

Levinson proposed to distinguish values on three levels (Levinson, 2003, pp. 305–324): (1) meta-aesthetic – analysing the nature of the judgement of aesthetic value; (2) ontological – concerning the nature of the value itself; and (3) normative – focusing on the question of "what" is artistically valuable in art and how to use various valuable features of a work to evaluate it.

The *objectivistic approach to values* says that whatever their categorisation, values are not something in themselves but are the value of something (Ingarden, 1970, p. 228). The primary status of values is their "should-ness" – values are not something that "is", but something that "should be" and at the same time "must not be". People realise values; values exist concretely but differ from ideals and ideas (although Plato recognised values as ideal beings) and intentions. Values and their use distinguish conscious beings from unconscious ones; thus, they are an essential determinant of humanity. Similarly, individuals who reject values (e.g., truth, goodness, beauty) reduce themselves to an animal, extra- or anti-human being. There is also a particular paradox here that a person cannot directly realise values (e.g., being good) because then he focuses on himself (pharisaism) and not on actually doing good; values are realised indirectly, e.g., by recognising the needs of others and helping them (Gołaszewska, 1986b, pp. 23–26; Ingarden, 1970, p. 242).

In addition to the objectivist approach, there is also a *relativistic approach to values*. It is characterised by the statement that value is not a property of things but is a relation between one thing and another, for which the first thing performs some services. If the other thing is a person or a society, one can speak of a social sanction that gives value to a worthless thing. In the extreme case, the relativistic approach to values is a contradiction of the objectivist approach to values and refers to the subjectivity of values (Ingarden, 1970, pp. 229–230).

The values' description, analysis, and interpretation can be made using different methodologies. One of the most popular methodologies in this area is *dialectics*, i.e., opposing thesis and antithesis to emerge the essence of the studied phenomenon based on this discourse (Gołaszewska, 2005, p. 147). It should not be forgotten that eliminating the world of universal values from a work of art leads straight into the embrace of kitsch, which should be avoided or at least consciously controlled (see Section 6.1, "Kitsch in aesthetics").

2.3 Artist's organisational activity

The organisational activity of art creators may concern three dimensions: (1) self-management, (2) management of the aesthetic situation, and (3) management of a cultural institution if an artist with managerial skills is employed for this purpose. This section focuses primarily on the first two dimensions, only mentioning the third dimension, which is widely described in the literature.

2.3.1 Self-management

Considerations regarding managerial issues in the artist's activity can be placed in the subject of interest of the so-called "occupy management" concerning self-organisation and self-management, where self-awareness and the ability to reflect play a key role (Kostera, 2014).

The profile of the manager is described in the other part of this work (see Section 3.2.1, "Manager as creator"); however, in order to fully implement the idea of this chapter, it is necessary to emphasise the key features of this character, which directly result from the definition and function of management, and therefore: the manager should be an effective organiser in achieving specific goals.

The creators' identity does not confirm the common perception of the artist as a disorderly person functioning in a chaotic space. What is more, it concerns only the superficial and easily visible layer of reality, not touching the essence of the organisation of the creative process. The optimal explanation of the organisational component of the artist will be the analysis of the aesthetic situation discussed earlier, together with its elements and the relationships between them. It should be emphasised that the order of the issues discussed in this section is not evaluative.

According to the aesthetic situation theory, the artist's organisational activities take place on three levels:

1. the world of values (artistry),
2. a work of art (creativity),
3. the real world (virtuosity).

Managing an artist at the level of the world of values, i.e., artistry management, can be compared to strategic management. It is responsible for defining the organisation's vision, mission, and strategic goal(s). Decisions at this level determine the further direction of processes. Artists tend to be focused on specific values, exploring them over long periods of creativity, or they change the subject of their creative interests depending on various internal and external factors. The chosen strategies for achieving the goals can be permanent or changeable – adapted to the circumstances.

Management at the level of a work of art, i.e., creativity management, can be compared to tactical management. Specified goals and strategies are translated into directional decisions regarding the creative process, ending with the creation of the work, taking into account the recipient's process of receiving the work. It should be remembered that the artist's intention is not to create the work itself, but to influence the recipient through the created work in a planned way through the values to which the work refers. This fact is not without significance for the process of receiving the work, which depends on many factors discussed earlier.[1]

Management at the level of the real world, i.e., virtuosity management, is an analogy of managing operational activities. This includes decisions regarding the choice of the content and form of the work, the use of specific material (sculpture, colours, structures, musical scales, gestures, language) and its processing techniques. The vast majority of the literature deals with any field of art, and the majority of the didactic process concerns this management level. It is understandable because this level is the most tangible, visible, and modellable, and the effects of this modelling are measurable.

A certain explanation for the apparent chaos surrounding some artists during the creative process is precisely the characteristics of the artist's management of the entire aesthetic situation. Unlike traditional organisation management, where the hierarchy of management levels is preserved (from strategy, to tactics, to operations), managing the creative process is much more dynamic. Despite the analytical separation of these three levels, the artist somehow manages them simultaneously, immediately adapting the actions on the other levels when a change is made in one of them. The whole process, however, is not chaotic in essence; it is highly effective, even though it may look chaotic from the outside. It is because a slight change in the level of the world of values can determine many adjustments at the level of a work of art,

2.3.2 Management of the aesthetic situation

In order to analyse the issue of managing the aesthetic situation from the perspective of the creator, one should be aware of the components of the aesthetic situation and their mutual relationships (a complete discussion of the issue can be found in Section 2.2, "Aesthetic situation"). In short, it can be said that a work of art is a key component of the aesthetic situation, but it needs an artist who will include universal values in the work in the form of elements of the real world, as well as a recipient who will read universal values in the elements of the real world through the process of receiving the work.

In this context, the artist plays the role of manager of the aesthetic situation because the content of the message (the selection of values and their placement in elements of the real world) and its form (applied schemes, styles, or formal solutions) will depend on the artist. For this purpose, the creator has three streams of influence: virtuosity, artistry, and creativity. A conscious creator manages these streams in a controlled manner – both at the stage of building their competencies in this area and, above all, at the stage of using them in the creative process. Not every work requires highly virtuosic solutions: artists often refer to brutalist solutions (e.g., rough sculptural material) to draw the recipient's attention to specific issues. On the other hand, not every work requires many sophisticated references to the world of values – often, the simplicity of the message is more substantial. In the same way, creativity does not have to be characteristic of every work –an innovative form will not always be more understandable than traditional solutions.

The artist, as the manager of the aesthetic situation – by designing the work – also determines the process of its reception. Of course, in each of the disciplines of art, the creator has a different influence on the process of reception: authors of plays or composers of opera performances quite strongly define the requirements for the process of creating a work; however, the directors also have a lot to say in the process of making it. The director of the performance is also a creator, and he also manages his own creative process and reception process; in many cases, the director will have a greater influence on the final shape of the work than the author of the play or the composer of the opera. On the other hand, the creator in the field of visual arts (painter, graphic artist), after making a work, separates himself from it and is unable to influence the reception process: the recipient can shape the circumstances of contemplation (time, exposure length, contexts) at your discretion. As you can see, the creator does not have a total influence on the reception process, because the reception process depends on many factors independent of the creator, including, above all, the recipient's level of activity.

In order to show the complexity of managing the aesthetic situation by the artist, an original qualitative study was conducted in the form of structured face-to-face interviews with the creators of individual art disciplines. The search for a universal context for all art disciplines that could serve as an independent variable was met by life and the global COVID-19 pandemic. The consequences of the pandemic had a powerful impact on the functioning of all art disciplines in the entire aesthetic situation: artists, cultural institutions and recipients, and traditional forms of participation in art began to modulate into digital and virtual forms overnight (Demiańczuk, 2022). What is the essence of art – i.e., the contact of the creator with the work and the work with the recipient – that has been taken by the deadly virus into brackets as a threat to health and life? This ubiquitous and irreversible change served as the primary context for showing the specificity and mechanisms of managing the aesthetic situation from the artist's perspective.

The methodology used in this study is described in the Introduction to this study (see the "Research methodology 1" section). The conclusions from the study regarding the management of the creative process by artists and the artists' perspective on the other components of the aesthetic situation were presented and broken down into three fields of art: musical arts, literary arts, and visual arts.

Musical arts

The analysis of the impact of restrictions resulting from the COVID-19 pandemic on the creative process from the perspective of a music artist is as follows.[2] While the lack of live public performances (question 9) was assessed rather negatively by music artists (rating: −0.79), the very fact of transferring their own artistic activities to virtual reality (10) is a more neutral issue for artists (−0.05); the conclusion may be the thesis that for the creator of musical arts, the possibility of conducting artistic activities is more important than their form (traditional or virtual). The ability of recipients to participate in musical arts in accordance with their personal preferences, i.e., the ability to shape the time and length of participation or adjust the parameters of the work (volume, timbre, etc.), was assessed by the creators at −0.42; that is, between rather negative and neutral (11). Restrictions on real contacts with one's band or members of an artistic group were assessed much more negatively (question 12, rating: −1.05), as were restrictions on real contacts with other artists in the field of musical arts (13, −0.84) and limitations regarding real contacts with creators of other artistic disciplines (14, −0.63). The creators of musical arts considered the limitation of their real contact with people the strongest negative factor (15, −1.26). However, the pandemic restrictions also had positive sides – in the form of more time to relax (question 16, 0.42), to develop one's artistic knowledge by reading and watching content (17, 0.68), and an increase in creativity manifested by the search for new creative abilities (19, 0.37),

To illustrate these analytical results, it is worth following a few selected quotes from the statements of the study participants. For instance, "As an introvert, the reduction of interpersonal contacts was not a problem; however, it clearly limited or even prevented many projects that were previously planned – including international concert tours" [MUS19]. The following three statements confirm the increase in the dynamics of my creativity in the context of the new reality: (1) "I gave more concerts than ever for two reasons: I was able to organise live concerts at times when it was difficult (e.g., as a physicist I calculated the concept of ventilation of our hall so that live events could almost always be organised), and during periods when live concerts were not allowed, I organised recordings and virtual concerts" [MUS03]; (2) "The new normal has opened new perspectives, and for me it is a positive development" [MUS16]; (3) "Even if some aspects may seem negative, by changing areas or rethinking the creative process, we can still make the most of our time and work on other aspects. . . . For some, it is negative, but at the same time, positive for the result itself. Just different methods to achieve the main goal" [MUS18]. When analysing these types of average scores, the complexity of creative individuals must be taken into account: "Personally, I hate interacting with people virtually – whether on a personal, professional, or productivity level – but I know many people who seem to love it! However, each of us is different!" [MUS04]. "The pandemic has changed the ability to connect in person through music. We are doing better now [after the lockdown is lifted], but everyone was suffering back then [during the lockdown]. Online performances will never replace in-person performances" [MUS15]. To sum up, the creative process determined by the restrictions resulting from the COVID-19 pandemic was assessed by music artists on the borderline of moderate negativity and neutrality (−0.29); details are presented in Figure 2.6.

Music artists' assessment of the impact of restrictions caused by the COVID-19 pandemic on music (i.e., with creators, audiences, institutions, sponsors, etc.) is moderately negative[3](−0.64). The most troublesome issues were the lack of live public performances of musical arts (27, −1.32), the limitation of real contact with other artists of music (31, −1.05), limiting real contacts with members of one's own band or music group (30, −0.84), and limitation of real contacts with creators of other arts (32, −0.79). Two aspects were assessed positively but

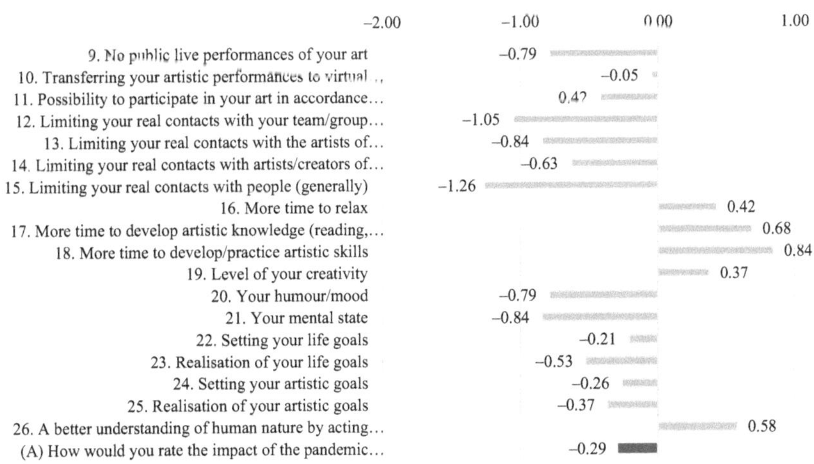

Figure 2.6 Assessment of the impact of the COVID-19 pandemic on music creators

Source: Author's own elaboration

minimally: transferring one's artistic creation to virtual reality (28, 0.11); and the possibility of participating in one's field of art according to the recipients' personal preferences regarding the duration of participation, length of participation, adjusting the volume of the sound, etc. (29, 0.05). "Although we have not been able to do much [during the restrictions], we could use the time to create content and offer small online appearances to audiences who otherwise would not be able to see and hear us in person" [MUS18]. These results are presented in Figure 2.7.

Changes in the creative attitude of music artists after the transition from traditional to digital methods of artistic activities were assessed negatively.[4] In summary, it can be said that with the transition from traditional to digital methods of artistic activities, music creators lose 15% of their creative potential. All the analysed parameters of the creative attitude lose quality after the transition from traditional to digital methods of artistic activities, and the loss varies between individual parameters. Ranking from the aspects that lose the most quality: contact with the audience (46, −27%), internal motivation to continue and end creative activity (36, −20%), creativity (42, −16%), inspiration to create (44, −16%), internal motivation to start creative activity (34, −14%), the possibility of delving into topics bothering society (48, −14%), and external motivation to start creative activity (38, −10%).

Two opinions emphasise the separateness and contrast between traditional and virtual methods: (1) "Live and virtual performance are completely different fields" [MUS19]; (2) "When it comes to interacting with the audience, I would say that virtual broadcasts of performances are more inconvenient for the audience than live participation. On the other hand, video clips are able to reach a wider audience if they are shared properly" [MUS18]. There were also voices strongly unfavourable to virtual activities: "I have reached the stage where I avoid all virtual activities if possible. I hate video calls and avoid them unless it's a necessary meeting I can't miss. It is difficult for me to establish relationships with people or talk freely in front of the camera" [MUS04]. Analytical results are presented in Figure 2.8.

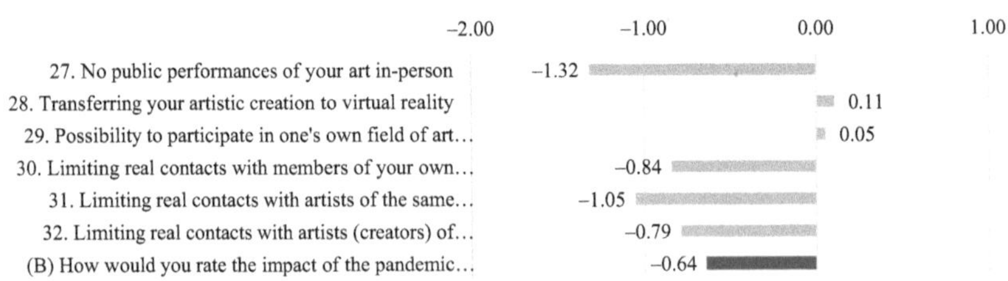

Figure 2.7 Impact of restrictions caused by the COVID-19 pandemic on the discipline of musical arts in the assessment of creators

Source: Author's own elaboration

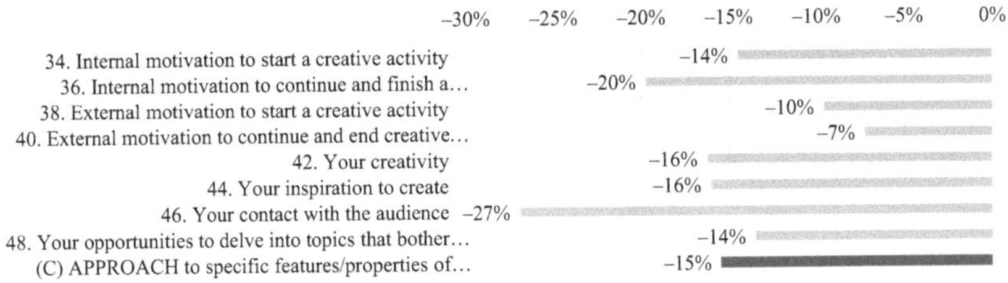

Figure 2.8 Changes in the creative attitude of music artists after the transition from traditional to digital methods of artistic activities

Source: Author's own elaboration

In the fourth group of questions, music artists referred to their own predictions of the situation in the field of musical arts after lifting the restrictions of the COVID-19 pandemic.[5] They concluded with moderate certainty that, sooner or later, everything would return to the state before the pandemic (question 49, 1.00), and real-time public performances would be simultaneously broadcast virtually (50, 0.63). Respondents moderately disagree with the statement that music artists will fall into two subcategories: those specialising in traditional live activities and those operating virtually (51, −0.32), which is emphasised by the following comment: "The creative process can have a double format because creation always happens in many different ways. When it comes to performances, I doubt anyone would be considered just a virtual performer or just a personal performer. The pandemic has become an opportunity for experimentation; now you need to know how to behave in front of the camera and how to behave in front of a live audience on stage. The same applies to exercise: good training today must include both video streaming and exposure to a real audience, resulting in more of a training experience" [MUS18]. Respondents emphasised the profound changes that the pandemic has made in their psyche and ways of functioning: "Nothing is and should not be as it was before the restrictions of the pandemic. Pushing the boundaries showed me new fields of expression and new ways of thinking creatively" [MUS9]. Figure 2.9 shows the graphical presentation of the results.

Assessment of the reception process in musical arts, in the context of traditional and digital forms of participation in the eyes of creators,[6] appears definitely negative in relation to digital and virtual forms (−1.39) and, thus, definitely positive in relation to traditional live forms. The strength of differences in two aspects, i.e. attracting the number of recipients (question 52, −0.79) and the contact of recipients with the work itself (57, −1.21), was assessed as moderate to the disadvantage of virtual forms. On the other hand, all other aspects were assessed strongly to the disadvantage of virtual forms, and these were: recipient satisfaction (53, −1.53), recipient gladness (54, −1.68), recipient engagement

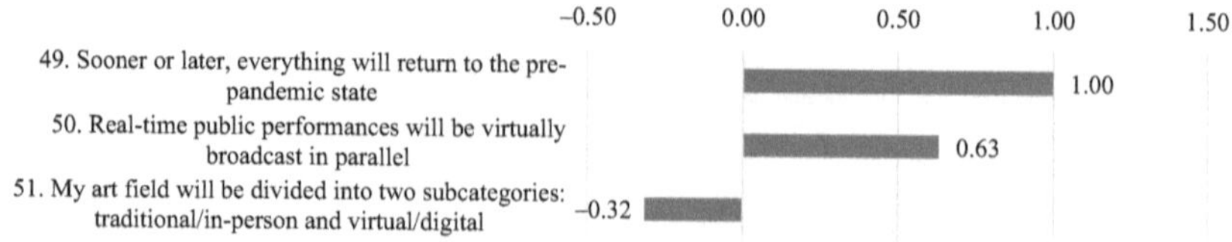

Figure 2.9 Evaluation of the future of musical arts in relation to traditional and digital methods of artistic activities in the opinion of creators

Source: Author's own elaboration

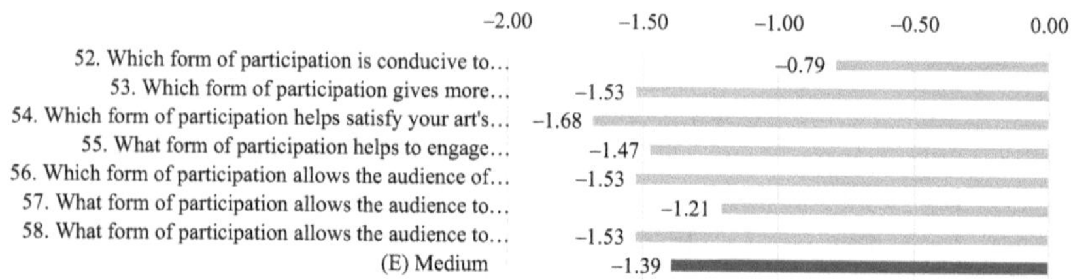

Figure 2.10 Evaluation of the reception process in musical arts in the context of traditional and virtual forms of participation in the opinion of the creators

Source: Author's own elaboration

(55, −1.47), the experience of catharsis by recipients (56, −1.53), contact of recipients with the creator/performer of art (58, −1.53). "I associate virtual media with a 'stand alone' receiver. There are moments when, in solitude, you connect deeply with the outer elements and can breed them at will. Personal events sometimes force the audience to see the same way for all audiences" [MUS18]. The synthetic results of this group of questions are presented in Figure 2.10.

The last group of questions concerned the issue of motives and inspirations in the creative process, the impact of awareness of the form of presenting a work (traditional or virtual) on the creative process, and the phenomenon of virtualisation of a given art discipline in the future. Musical artists responded as follows. Four people (21% of the creators of musical arts) stated that they did not see differences in their creative process in relation to the traditional and virtual form of the aesthetic situation [MUS02, MUS05, MUS17, MUS18] (question 59). One person said that the virtual form is more demanding [MUS16]. However, most respondents emphasised the differences between the two forms. The differences are shown in Table 2.1.

Eight (42%) of the music artists do not see differences in their creative process, taking into account their awareness that the work will be (or is) presented traditionally or virtually [MUS01, MUS02, MUS06, MUS11, MUS13, MUS14, MUS16, MUS17] (question 60). Eleven (58%) of music artists see smaller or larger

Table 2.1 Differences between traditional and virtual forms of the aesthetic situation in the eyes of music artists

Live	*Virtually*	*Respondent*
• emphasis on emotions and experiences	• emphasis on visual reception and image	MUS01
• "I try to get into the minds of the recipients and give them what they can expect from the need of the moment"		MUS07
• immediate response possible	• the possibility of a "delayed" reaction, e.g., in the form of a comment, which is also very important	MUS13
• fulfilment of one's vocation	• the need to maintain the audience's interest in me and my activities rather than a compulsion or an internal desire	MUS19
• listening to the audience present during the performance • "I like to react to changes in the atmosphere of the room"	• the virtual way is fine when the live way is not possible • there are also inspirations coming from me and from the musical material, and such inspirations are also possible in virtual formats	MUS03
• the sincerity of the heart poured into the lyrics and melody	• visual side • sound purity	MUS08
	• "I was surprised at how many people responded to virtual activities – posts came from all over the world"	MUS10
• "The world is tired of artificiality, of creating something that is virtual and therefore perhaps not real. Playing art live gives tangibility, uniqueness, individuality, and dependence on many factors, thanks to which you can enter into even greater interaction and understanding with recipients who need it"		MUS12
• "For me, performances are about communicating with the audience, and I feel that a performance needs a live audience to generate energy, a sense of uniqueness, drive, and excitement; it's hard for me to achieve this when creating in a virtual way"		MUS04
• "The audience can give a lot of energy, you cannot really feel it"		MUS06
• "Traditional contact with the audience leaves unforgettable memories and opens the door to self-criticism"		MUS09

Source: Author's own elaboration

differences in their creative process, taking into account their awareness that the work will be (or is) presented traditionally or virtually. These differences concern:

- the involvement of the creator and the recipient, the strength of survival, emotions, and satisfaction [MUS19];
- thought processes [MUS10], e.g.:
  - awareness that virtual recipients will receive the work much more negatively than live recipients [MUS07];
  - awareness that virtual recipients will perceive the work in a completely different way from live recipients[MUS09];
- new issues to be considered in virtual activities [MUS10], e.g.:
  - camera angles;
  - making things more concise;
  - means of expression: "There are elements that I will use for the music video, but I will not use them in a live concert. The same goes the other way around; in a live performance, there are things I will include that will not make sense for a music video where I would prioritise more layers and things I could not do on stage unless I clone myself" [MUS18];
- less freedom during virtual activities [MUS15];
- of the creative process: "Live art better accepts performance experiences generated by stress: obvious mistakes, diversity of interpretations, diversity of the visual presentation of the created art and performer, which cannot be said about the virtual 'live' presentation. A virtual performance prepared together with post-production provides comfort and the ability to control the whole, but also gives the work an artificiality" [MUS12];
- sources of inspiration: "Observing the audience during a traditional live performance is my main source of inspiration; I like to react to changes in the atmosphere in the room. On the other hand, there are also inspirations coming from within me and, for example, from musical material, and such inspirations are also possible in virtual formats" [MUS03].

Music artists are not entirely unanimous on the start or intensification of digitisation and virtualisation by the COVID-19 pandemic within their art discipline (question 61). Two out of 19 respondents (10.5%) believe that the COVID-19 pandemic has started the process of digitisation and virtualisation within their art discipline. According to 84%, the COVID-19 pandemic has only intensified the process of digitisation and virtualisation within their art discipline.

Literary arts

The analysis of the impact of restrictions resulting from the COVID-19 pandemic on the creative process from the perspective of the creator of literary arts is as follows.[7] Authors of literary arts considered the possibility of achieving their own life goals (question 23) and setting and achieving their own artistic goals (24, 25) as the negative effects of pandemic restrictions – all these aspects had a rather negative impact (rating: −0.33). Pandemic restrictions on relaxation time had the most negative impact (question 16, rating: −0.67). It seems that the limitations of mobility and the need to carry out all processes in a limited way and focus on the virtual space managed from their own home meant that the creators of literary arts devoted their free time to artistic work. The following were considered neutral: lack of public performances of one's work (9), limitation of one's real contacts with creators of other artistic disciplines (14), one's own mental state (21), and setting one's own life goals (22). On the other hand, the following were indicated as positive aspects: transferring one's artistic activities to virtual reality (10, 0.33); the possibility for recipients to participate in literary arts in accordance with their personal preferences, thus shaping the time and length of participation, regulating the parameters of the work, etc. (11, 0.33); limitation of real contacts with other literary authors (14, 0.33); limitation of real contacts with people (15, 0.33); more time to develop knowledge (17, 0.33) and artistic skills (18, 0.33); as well as one's mood (20, 0.33). The literary authors considered the following to be exceptionally positive: limiting real contact with their team and members of the creative group (12, 1.00), level of own creativity (19, 1, 00) and a better understanding of human nature manifested by acting in limited circumstances (26, 1.00). Let the following statement support the analytical results – showing the relationship between the creative personality and the individual's basic personality: "Given that I am an introvert by nature, bordering on misanthropy, the pandemic has not negatively affected my work, and maybe even helped me by being more lonely" [LIT1]. To sum up, literary artists assessed the creative process determined by the restrictions resulting from the COVID 19 pandemic on the borderline of neutrality and moderate positivity (0.20); details are presented in Figure 2.11.

The assessment by literary artists of the impact of restrictions caused by the COVID-19 pandemic on literary arts in general (i.e. together with authors, audiences, institutions, sponsors, etc.) is on the borderline between moderately negative and neutral (−0.22).[8] The most negative – although at a moderate level – was the limitation of real contact with members of one's team or creative group (30, −0.67). This further indicated: the possibility of participating in literary arts in accordance with the recipients' personal preferences as to the time of participation, length of participation, regulation of the parameters of the work, etc. (29, −0.33); limitation of real contacts with other literary artists (31, −0.33); and limitation of real contacts with authors of other art disciplines (32, −0.33). The lack of public performances of one's work was considered a neutral phenomenon (27, 0.00). Only transferring literary creativity to virtual reality was considered a moderately positive aspect (28, 0.33). The results are presented in Figure 2.12.

Changes in the creative attitude of literary artists after the transition from traditional to digital methods of artistic activities were assessed negatively.[9] In

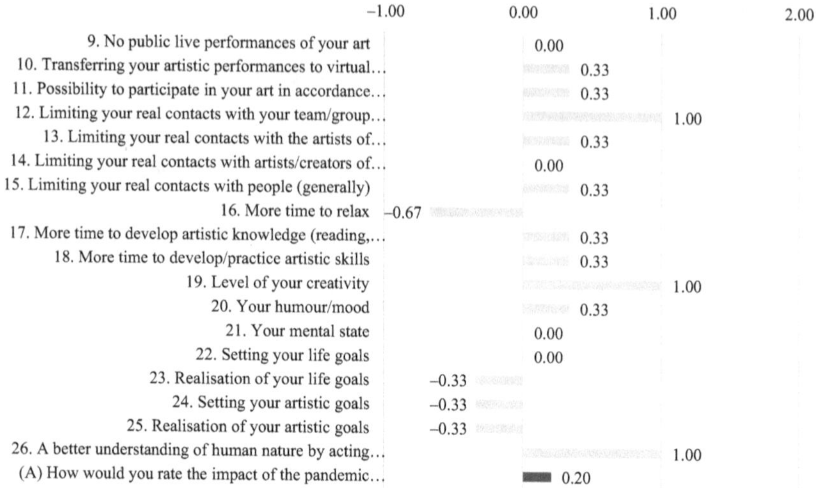

Figure 2.11 Assessment of the impact of the COVID-19 pandemic on literary artists

Source: Author's own elaboration

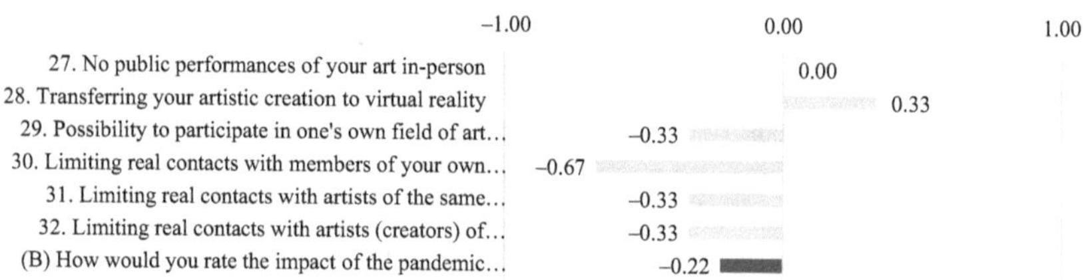

Figure 2.12 Impact of restrictions caused by the COVID-19 pandemic on the discipline of literary arts in the assessment of authors

Source: Author's own elaboration

total, it can be said that with the transition from traditional to digital methods of artistic activities, literary artists lose 19% of their creative potential. All the analysed parameters of the creative attitude lose quality after transitioning from traditional to digital methods of artistic activities, and the loss varies between individual parameters. Ranking from the aspects that lose the most quality: intrinsic motivation to start creative activity (34, −38%), inspiration to create (44, −23%), opportunities to delve into topics bothering society (48, −23%), extrinsic motivation to start creative activity (38, −18%), an internal motivation to continue and finish creative activity (36, −17%), creativity (42, −17%), an external motivation to continue and finish creative activity (40, −9%), and contact with the audience (46, −8%). The following statement represents one internal picture:

> For some strange reason, I have the irrational idea that an online conference or presentation is less meaningful than its offline counterpart. I'm also more nervous online because I am worried that I will run into any technical issues like a Wi-Fi signal outage.
>
> [LIT1]

The synthetic results are presented in Figure 2.13.

Authors of literary arts, referring to their predictions of the situation in the field of literary arts after lifting the restrictions of the COVID-19 pandemic,[10] decided with great certainty that real-time public events will be simultaneously broadcast virtually (50, 1.33). Furthermore, they were moderately confident that literary artists would be divided into two subcategories: those specialising in traditional live activities, and those working virtually (51, 0.33). However, they could not indicate the trend whether everything would return to the state sooner or later before the pandemic (49, 0.00). Figure 2.14 shows the graphical presentation of the results.

Evaluation of the reception process in literary arts in the context of traditional and digital forms of participation in the eyes of creators[11] looks ambiguous (0.10).

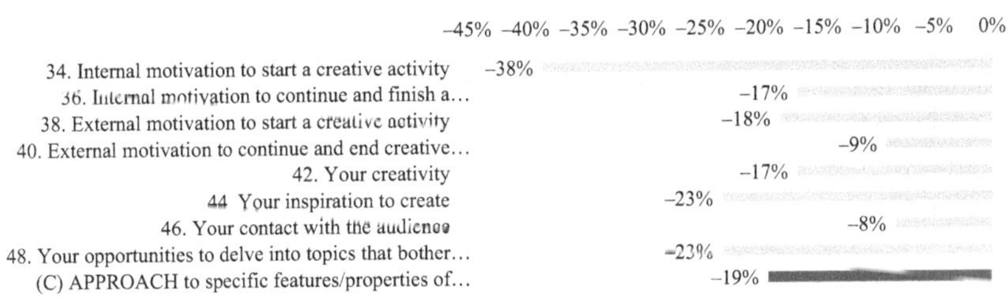

Figure 2.13 Changes in the creative attitude of literary artists after the transition from traditional to digital methods of artistic activities

Source: Author's own elaboration

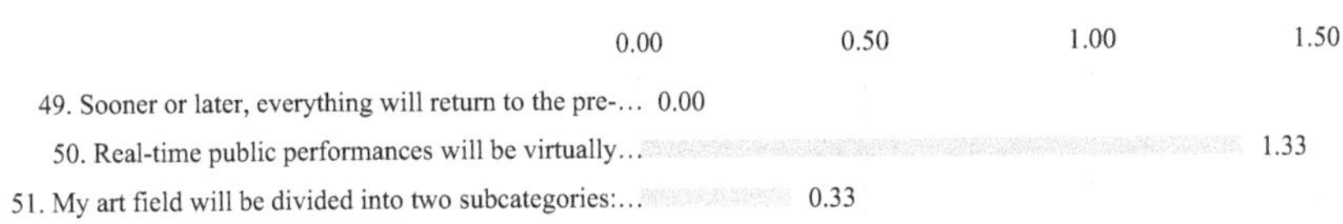

Figure 2.14 Assessment of the future of literary arts in relation to traditional and digital methods of artistic activities in the assessment of authors

Source: Author's own elaboration

Traditional forms have an advantage over digital ones in the following areas: audience engagement (55, −0.33), audience contact with the work itself (57, −0.33), and audience contact with the creator/performer (58, −1.00). In turn, the advantage of virtual over traditional forms concerns: the possibility of attracting more recipients (52, 1.00), obtaining greater recipient satisfaction (53, 0.67), obtaining greater recipient gladness (54, 0.33), and experiencing a state of catharsis by recipients (56, 0.33). "I believe an online conference is intellectually better because everything is much clearer (you can record the proceedings more easily, take screenshots of the presentation, etc.). On the other hand, the offline conference is probably better emotionally – at least for extroverts" [LIT1]. See Figure 2.15.

The creators of literary arts did not indicate differences in reasons, motives, or inspirations, distinguishing between the live and virtual aesthetic situations (59). The summary can be:

> The most important motives and inspirations for creating them in both forms is the ability to convey important messages and inspire people to think, act and get the best out of them. . . . I am driven mainly by my inner motivation and willingness to make changes.
>
> [LIT2]

When it comes to the differences in the creative process with the creator's awareness of the form of presenting the work (traditionally and virtually), the answers ranged across a whole spectrum of possibilities: from no differences [LIT2], to the greater demands of the traditional form [LIT3], to a preference for the virtual version, summed up by the statement "A live performance 'disappears' as soon as it happens" (question 60). The virtual form is problematic from an artistic point of view if the intention is to create a permanent record of the performance" [LIT1].

All literary artists unanimously confirmed that the COVID-19 pandemic had intensified the process of digitisation and virtualisation within their art discipline (question 61).

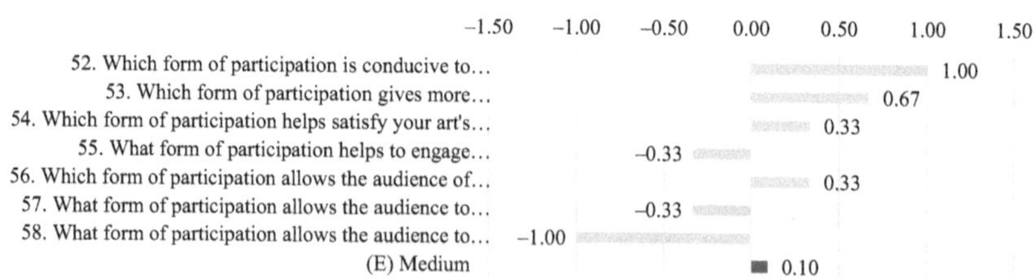

Figure 2.15 Evaluation of the reception process in literary arts in the context of traditional and virtual forms of participation in the assessment of authors

Source: Author's own elaboration

Visual arts

The analysis of the impact of restrictions resulting from the COVID-19 pandemic on the creative process from the perspective of a visual artist is as follows.[12] The following aspects had a rather negative impact: lack of live public performances of one's work (question 9, rating: −0.25), limitation of real contacts with own team/group members (12, −0.42), limitation of real contacts with other artists of the visual arts (13, −0.42), limitation of real contacts with creators of other art disciplines (14, −0.33), and limitation of real contacts with people in general (15, −0.42). Mood (20, −0.08) and mental state (21, −0.08) slightly affected the restrictions. The remark that "restrictions were replaced by very intensive, even excessive, online contact" [VIA02] may indicate that in traditional circumstances, the creator had more possibilities to regulate contacts; when switching to virtual mode, the freedom of contact was so much easier that their excessive number interfered with the implementation of basic activities. The creators considered the positive effects of the restrictions to be: transferring their artistic activities to virtual reality (10, 0.33), the possibility for recipients to participate in visual arts in accordance with their personal preferences in the form of shaping the time and length of participation or regulating the parameters of the work (11, 0.25), more time to relax (16, 0.75), developing artistic knowledge (17, 0.83), developing artistic skills (18, 1.00), and the level of one's creativity (19, 0.92). When it comes to issues related to goals and their implementation, the assessment is moderately positive and is as follows: the impact of pandemic restrictions on setting one's own life goals (22, 0.33) and their implementation (23, 0.25), and setting one's own artistic goals (24, 0.42) and achieving them (25, 0.25). Understanding human nature manifested by acting under constrained conditions was also moderately positive under pandemic constraints (26, 0.50). To sum up, visual artists assessed the creative process determined by the restrictions resulting from the COVID-19 pandemic on the borderline of neutrality and moderate positivity (0.21); details are presented in Figure 2.16.

Visual artists' assessment of the impact of restrictions caused by the COVID-19 pandemic on visual arts in general (i.e., with creators, audiences, institutions, and sponsors) is on the verge of being moderately negative and neutral[13] (−0.18). The restrictions had a moderately negative impact on the following issues: limiting real contact with members of your creative group (30, −0.50), with other visual artists (31, −0.50), and creators of other art disciplines (32, −0.33). The lack of live public performances of one's work (27, −0.08) and the possibility for recipients to participate in visual arts in accordance with their personal preferences as to the time of participation, length of participation, or regulation of the parameters of the work were considered neutral (29, 0.00). Only transferring one's artistic creation to virtual reality was rated moderately positive (28, 0.33). The results are presented in Figure 2.17.

Changes in the creative attitude of visual artists after the transition from traditional to digital methods of artistic activities were assessed negatively.[14] In

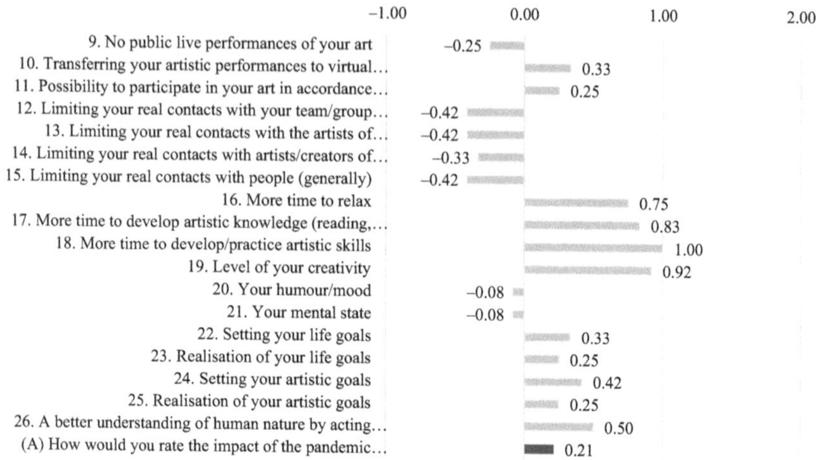

Figure 2.16 Assessment of the impact of the COVID-19 pandemic on visual artists

Source: Author's own elaboration

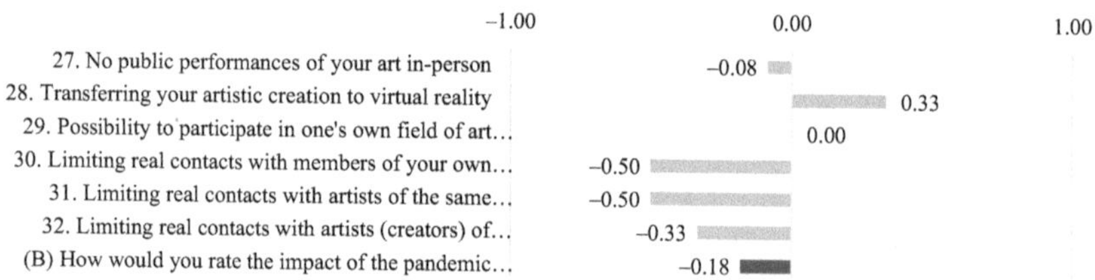

Figure 2.17 Impact of restrictions caused by the COVID-19 pandemic on the discipline of visual arts in the assessment of creators

Source: Author's own elaboration

summary, it can be said that with the transition from traditional to digital methods of artistic activities, visual artists lose only 5% of their creative potential. All the analysed parameters of the creative attitude lose quality after transitioning from traditional to digital methods of artistic activities, and the loss varies between individual parameters. Ranking the aspects from the most deteriorating in quality, we obtain the following list: contact with the audience (46, −15%), inspiration to create (44, −7%), external motivation to start creative activity (38, −5%), external motivation to continue and finish creative activity (40, −5%), the opportunity to delve into topics bothering society (48, −5%), creativity (42, −4%), and an internal motivation to start creative activity (34, −2%). Only the internal motivation to continue and finish creative activity does not change with the transition from traditional to digital methods of artistic activities in visual arts. The results are presented in Figure 2.18.

Visual artists, referring to their predictions of the situation in the field of visual arts after lifting the restrictions of the COVID-19 pandemic,[15] considered with moderate certainty that real-time public events will be simultaneously broadcast virtually (50, 0.50); literary artists will fall into two subcategories, those specialising in traditional live activities and those operating virtually (51, 0.33); and that sooner or later, everything will return to the way it was before the pandemic (49, 0.25). The graphical presentation of the results is shown in Figure 2.19.

Assessment of the reception process in visual arts in the context of traditional and virtual forms of participation in the eyes of artists[16] looks decidedly negative compared to digital and virtual forms and, thus, definitely positive compared to traditional live forms. The strength of differences in all aspects was assessed as moderate to the disadvantage of virtual forms, in terms of: audience satisfaction (53, −0.75), audience gladness (54, −0.67), audience engagement (55, −0.67), the possibility of experiencing a state of catharsis by the recipients (56, −1.08), the contact of the recipients with the work itself (57, −0.75), and the contact of the recipients with the creator/performer of the art (58, −1.00). Only the possibility of attracting more recipients was assessed moderately in favour of virtual forms (52, 0.25). A valuable commentary on this group of questions will be the following statement: "Although direct contact is the most important for the

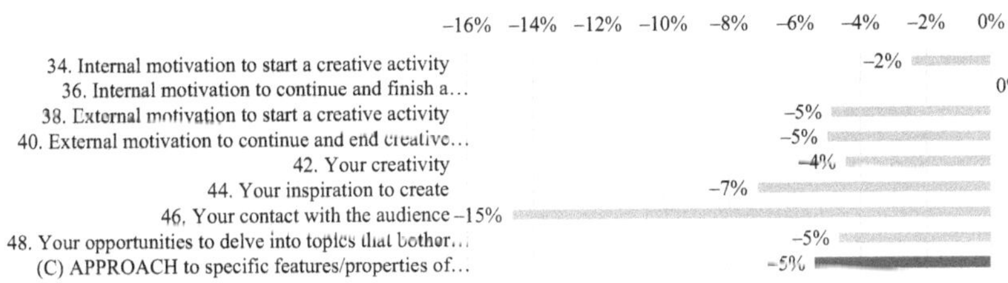

Figure 2.18 Changes in the creative attitude of visual artists after the transition from traditional to digital methods of artistic activities

Source: Author's own elaboration

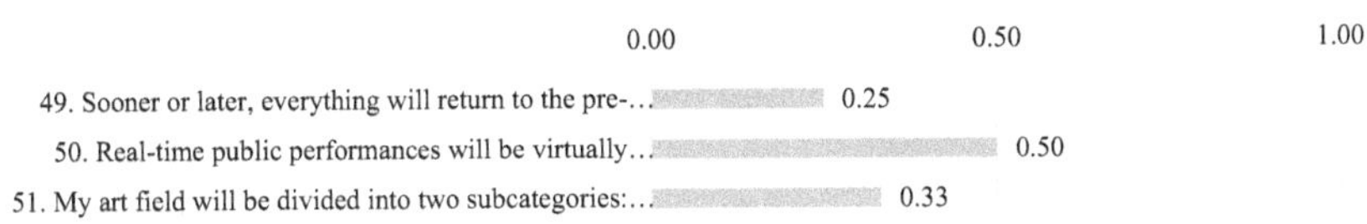

Figure 2.19 The future of visual arts compared to traditional and digital methods of artistic activities in the assessment of creators

Source: Author's own elaboration

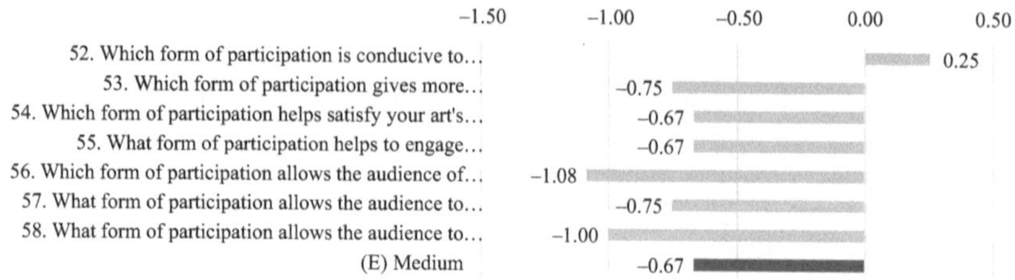

Figure 2.20 The process of reception in visual arts in the context of traditional and virtual forms of participation in the assessment of artists

Source: Author's own elaboration

artist, it is the visual arts recipients who relate well to virtual forms of presentation that allow for a wider reach. According to the creator, the work itself loses in such a reception, but I don't know if it disturbs the viewer" [VIA02]. The synthetic results of this group of questions are presented in Figure 2.20.

Two (17%) of the visual artists said that they saw no differences in their creative process compared to the traditional and virtual form of the aesthetic situation [VIA02, VIA08] (question 59): "Creating painting requires solitude – there is no difference between subsequent virtual or live presentation" [VIA02]. However, the vast majority of respondents (83%) emphasised the differences between the two forms, which concern:

- contact with the work, experiencing the creative process: "A work that will be presented virtually requires a different conceptualisation than that presented live. I try to make virtualisation add possibilities to the work that cannot be used in a traditional presentation" [VIA07];
- experiencing aesthetic experiences, and creative fulfilment: virtual forms are treated as a "compromise, transitional state, [method of obtaining] financial support and scholarships" [VIA01];
- contact with creative matter [VIA03];
- the recipient's contact with the work: "The most important thing is the mood and live contact of the recipient with the work" [VIA11];
- the possibility of conveying emotions: "more emotions can be conveyed live" [VIA12];
- treating activities in traditional forms as fundamental, which is reinforced by virtual activities, e.g., as a form of promotion [VIA10];
- virtual activity is more convenient [VIA05].

Three (25% out of 12) visual artists do not see differences in their creative process, knowing that the work will (or is) presented traditionally or virtually [VIA01, VIA07, VIA08] (question 60). Most creators, however, notice differences in their creative process: "I shape the visual message in a slightly different way – but this action is not fully conscious – I know that stronger and simpler messages work better on the Internet, so I choose intuitive ones for presentation there" [VIA02]. "If I have to do a job for the Internet, I have to have a separate idea for it" [VIA11]. Some doubts are also raised by the lack of influence on the fate of one's work presented virtually: "Live broadcasts are worse compared to traditional activities – they are unpredictable compared to living performances, and yet they are archived, e.g., on YouTube forever; no one seems to be removing live streaming services from YouTube" [VIA10].

All visual artists unanimously confirmed that the COVID-19 pandemic has intensified the process of digitisation and virtualisation within their art discipline (question 61).

2.3.3 Managing a cultural institution

In addition to self-management, managing the aesthetic situation, especially in terms of the creative process, but also taking into account the reception process, the creator may face the challenge of managing a cultural institution. Cultural institutions are managed either by professional managers, who are more or less familiar with the realities of the art world, or by artists who, due to their artistic achievements or position in the art world, have been recognised by the owner of the institution as a person able to implement the goals of the institution in an effective manner.

Both groups of managers have their own characteristics. Professional managers, unaware of the realities of the aesthetic situation, usually focus on organisational efficiency, process optimisation, and cost reduction, and are not particularly concerned with creative processes and perception processes. On the other hand, creators, without a managerial identity, forgetting or not being aware of the need to pay attention to the essence of organisational problems, focus on creating the best possible space for the development of creativity for artists and the process of perception for recipients, which in effect most often ends in financial problems for the institution (Morozova et al., 2016; Rius-Ulldemolins & Klein, 2021).

From the point of view of sources of financing, cultural institutions can be divided into subsidised and self-financing, and this distinction significantly determines the practice of managing them (Salcudean, 2015; Wnuczak & Osichuk, 2020). Institutions based on subsidies (the most common source of subsidies are local governments or the national government) are privileged because they can focus on fulfilling their mission, i.e., being a field for a multiplied aesthetic situation. Consequently, they can afford a kind of extravagance concerning self-financing institutions. This extravagance can be manifested in more ambitious activities that refer to the world of values more potently – without worrying about whether the recipient of art is willing to pay for the greater experience. In this case, the offered works may be more expressive in content and less "polite" towards the recipient. The second group of cultural institutions, which must consider the issue of self-financing alongside, and sometimes even before, artistic activity, is slightly more complex. Regardless of the chosen mission, which always concerns the aesthetic situation, they must consider both meeting the needs of art recipients and meeting the expectations of buyers of the offered product (a work of art as a good or a service). It is hard to expect that a cultural institution offering a very ambitious artistic program will have queues of viewers – it is impossible, for example, due to the shrinking group of recipients and the increase in the work's ambition level. The artistic program of self-financing cultural institutions confirms this state of affairs. Yes, we will find ambitious works in it, but they are in the minority; the dominant features of the programs always work to flatter more popular tastes. There is only one explanation: more viewers, more ticket revenue, and a greater chance for further activity.

The uniqueness of cultural institutions is characterised by the fact that some stakeholder groups (creators and recipients of works of art) operate in much broader contexts than other groups. It seems, therefore, that management of this type of organisation should be dealt with by artists-managers, i.e., individuals who have the identity of both art creators – who know the realities of the aesthetic situation – and managers – who can navigate in the organisational and financial world (more on this topic in Section 4.3.1, "Identity and self-perception of the artist-manager").

2.4 Conclusions

The quoted results of the study show how, in practice, the creator manages the creative process within the aesthetic situation. It must take into account many factors that together shape the quality of the aesthetic situation. The creative process, as seemingly ephemeral and seemingly impossible to capture by scientific models, can be – by means of an appropriate conceptual apparatus taken from aesthetics – broken down into many analytical elements, the single definition of which is not so difficult anymore. It is of course important how the quality parameters of the aesthetic situation are determined in order to be able to draw conclusions based on the results obtained. The methodology presented and used in this study can be successfully replicated in further research on the analysed problem.

The context of restrictions resulting from the COVID-19 pandemic, which strongly determined the aesthetic situation in each of the analysed art disciplines in a slightly different way, served only as a pretext for the dynamisation of phenomena in the researched area. Also, without factors as strong as the pandemic, the creator in the creative process must take into account the same parameters that synthetically allow him to manage the aesthetic situation from his own perspective in a conscious way.

2.5 Summary

The management factor is essential in fruitful artistic activity due to the achievements in organisation methods that can be successfully used to manage the real world and the aesthetic situation. By applying management models, of course, along with the necessary adjustments to the metaphysical world, we can expect an improvement in the efficiency of the creative process.

Management in art has three dimensions: self-management, aesthetic situation management, and cultural institution management. Different problems characterise each of these dimensions, but they also have common denominators in considering the metaphysical nature of the essence of the aesthetic situation.

Art can derive added value from management's achievements in terms of applying widely discussed organisational theories and paying attention to the efficiency factor. Management, understood as the implementation of goals in an effective manner, has a wide range of applications. Considering the achievements of the humanistic trend and self-management, applying this optic in artistic creativity should proceed in a way that does not raise objections or difficulties because both art and aesthetics, as well as humanistic management and self-management, are very close to each other.

Notes

1 Creativity management is discussed in greater detail in Chapter 5.
2 Five-point Likert scale: −2 = very negative impact, −1 = somewhat negative impact, 0 = neutral impact, +1 = somewhat positive impact, +2 = very positive impact.
3 Five-point Likert scale: −2 = very negative impact, −1 = somewhat negative impact, 0 = neutral impact, +1 = somewhat positive impact, +2 = very positive impact.
4 Five-point Likert scale: −2 = very negative impact, −1 = somewhat negative impact, 0 = neutral impact, 1 = somewhat positive impact, 2 = very positive impact
5 Five-point Likert scale: −2 = absolutely not, −1 = rather not, 0 = hard to say, 1 = rather yes, 2 = definitely yes.
6 Five-point Likert scale: −2 = definitely live, −1 = rather live, 0 = hard to tell, 1 = rather virtual, 2 = definitely virtual.
7 Five-point Likert scale: −2 = very negative impact, −1 = somewhat negative impact, 0 = neutral impact, +1 = somewhat positive impact, +2 = very positive impact.
8 Five-point Likert scale: −2 = very negative impact, −1 = somewhat negative impact, 0 = neutral impact, +1 = somewhat positive impact, +2 = very positive impact.
9 Five-point Likert scale: −2 = very negative impact, −1 = somewhat negative impact, 0 = neutral impact, +1 = somewhat positive impact, +2 = very positive impact.
10 Five-point Likert scale: −2 = absolutely not, −1 = rather not, 0 = hard to say, 1 = rather yes, 2 = definitely yes.
11 Five-point Likert scale: −2 = definitely live, −1 = rather live, 0 = hard to tell, 1 = rather virtual, 2 = definitely virtual.
12 Five-point Likert scale: −2 = very negative impact, −1 = somewhat negative impact, 0 = neutral impact, 1 = somewhat positive impact, 2 = very positive impact.
13 Five-point Likert scale: −2 = very negative impact, −1 = somewhat negative impact, 0 = neutral impact, 1 = somewhat positive impact, 2 = very positive impact.

14 Five-point Likert scale: −2 = very negative impact, −1 = somewhat negative impact, 0 = neutral impact, 1 = somewhat positive impact, 2 = very positive impact.
15 Five-point Likert scale: −2 = absolutely not, −1 = rather not, 0 = hard to say, 1 = rather yes, 2 = definitely yes.
16 Five-point Likert scale: −2 = definitely live, −1 = rather live, 0 = hard to tell, 1 = rather virtual, 2 = definitely virtual.

References

Arbuz-Spatari, O. (2019). Art – subject – object in artistic and plastic creativity of pupils and students in artistic education. *Review of Artistic Education, 18*(1), 233–240. https://doi.org/10.2478/rae-2019-0025

Artist. (2023a). In *Cambridge dictionary*. https://dictionary.cambridge.org/dictionary/english/artist

Artist. (2023b). In *Merriam-Webster*. www.merriam-webster.com/dictionary/artist

Beardsley, M. (1983). An aesthetic definition of art. In H. Curtler (Ed.), *What is art?* (pp. 15–29). Haven Publications.

Dai, D. Y., & Cheng, H. (2017). How to overcome the one-track mind: Teaching for creativity and wisdom. *Roeper Review, 39*(3), 174–177. https://doi.org/10.1080/02783193.2017.1318659

Danto, A. C. (1991). Dzieło sztuki a zwykłe przedmioty. In M. Gołaszewska (Ed.), *Estetyka w świecie: wybór tekstów: Tom III* (pp. 73–107). Uniwersytet Jagielloński.

Demiańczuk, J. (2022). Ostatni seans? *Polityka, 22*(3365), 14–16.

Dronsfield, J., Rancière, J., & Wright, S. (2008). An exchange with Jacques Rancière. *Art&Research, 2*(1), 1–11. www.artandresearch.org.uk/v2n1/jrexchange.html

Ekmekçi, A. K., Teraman, S. B. S., & Acar, P. (2014). Wisdom and management: A conceptual study on wisdom management. *Procedia – Social and Behavioral Sciences, 150*, 1199–1204. https://doi.org/10.1016/j.sbspro.2014.09.135

Gaut, B., & McIver Lopes, D. (2001). *The Routledge companion to aeshetics*. Routledge.

Ginsborg, J. (2018). "The brilliance of perfection" or "pointless finish"? What virtuosity means to musicians. *Musicae Scientiae, 22*(4), 454–473. https://doi.org/10.1177/1029864918776351

Gołaszewska, M. (1967). *Odbiorca sztuki jako krytyk*. Wydawnictwo Literackie.

Gołaszewska, M. (1984). *Zarys estetyki*. PWN.

Gołaszewska, M. (1986a). *Kim jest artysta?* Wydawnictwa Szkolne i Pedagogiczne.

Gołaszewska, M. (1986b). *O naturze wartości estetycznych*. Uniwersytet Jagielloński.

Gołaszewska, M. (2005). *Estetyka możliwości*. Wydawnictwo Uniwersytetu Jagiellońskiego.

Heredia-Carroza, J. (2019). Flamenco performer's perceived value: Development of a measurement index. *Scientific Annals of Economics and Business, 66*(Special issue), 59–71. https://doi.org/10.2478/saeb-2019-0017

Ingarden, R. (1970). *Studia z estetyki: Tom III*. Wydawnictwo Naukowe PWN.

Ingarden, R. (1981). *Wykłady i dyskusje z estetyki*. Państwowe Wydawnictwo Naukowe.

Jensen, E. F. (2012). *Schumann*. Oxford University Press.

Jung, C. G. (2014). *The spirit in man, art, and literature* (Vol. 15). https://doi.org/10.1515/9781400851010.791

Kaiser, J. (2018). Improvising technology, constructing virtuosity. *Cuadernos de Musica, Artes Visuales y Artes Escenicas, 13*(2), 87–96. https://doi.org/10.11144/javeriana.mavae13-2.itcv
Kostera, M. (2013). Helikon SA, czyli o sztuce, zarządzaniu i inspiracji. *Zarządzanie Kulturą, 6*(2), 46–53.
Kostera, M. (2014). *Occupy management! Inspirations and ideas for self-organization and self-management.* Routledge. https://doi.org/10.4324/9780203795033
Kostera, M., & Śliwa, M. (2012). *Zarządzanie w XXI wieku: Jakość, twórczość, kultura.* Wolters Kluwer Polska.
Leech-Wilkinson, D. (2018). The danger of virtuosity. *Musicae Scientiae, 22*(4), 558–561. https://doi.org/10.1177/1029864918790304
Leech-Wilkinson, D. (2020). *Challenging performance: Classical music performance norms and how to escape them.* https://challengingperformance.com/the-book-49/
Levinson, J. (2003). *The Oxford hanbook of aesthetics.* Oxford University Press.
Lind, R. (1992). The aesthetic essence of art. *Journal of Aesthetics and Art Criticism, 50,* 117–129.
Linstead, S., & Höpfl, H. J. (2000). *The aesthetics of organization.* SAGE Publications Ltd. https://uk.sagepub.com/en-gb/eur/the-aesthetics-of-organization/book205791#preview
Margolis, J. (1986). Dzieła sztuki jako byty ucieleśnione fizycznie i wyłonione kulturowo. In M. Gołaszewska (Ed.), *Estetyka w świecie: wybór tekstów: Tom II* (pp. 205–214). Uniwersytet Jagielloński.
Mendecka, G. (2010). *Oblicza twórczości.* Wydawnictwo Uniwersytetu Śląskiego.
Morozova, O., Nozdrenko, E., Zhukovskaya, L., & Kostylev, S. (2016). Management and art-management: Dimensions of conceptual interaction. *Economic Annals-XXI, 158*(3–4), 61–65. https://doi.org/10.21003/ea.V158-14
Nęcka, E. (2000). Twórczość. In J. Strelau (Ed.), *Psychologia: Podręcznik akademicki: Tom II: Psychologia ogólna.* Gdańskie Wydawnictwo Psychologiczne. www.scribd.com/doc/296833875/Psychologia-Tom-II-Jan-Strelau#
Nowak, A. (1986) Wprowadzenie do lektury Maxa Bensego: Twórcza zasada "stanu estetycznego". In M. Gołaszewska (Ed.), *Estetyka w świecie: wybór tekstów: Tom II* (pp. 119–124). Uniwersytet Jagielloński.
Nycz, R. (2000). *Dekonstrukcja w badaniach literackich.* Wydawnictwo Słowo Obraz Terytoria.
Ossowski, S. (1949). *U podstaw estetyki.* Spółdzielnia Wydawniczo-Oświatowa Czytelnik.
Ostrowicki, M. (1997). Teoria sytuacji estetycznej M. Gołaszewskiej jako fundament estetyki. http://www.sideymyoo.art.pl/old/Teoria_sytuacji_estetycznej.pdf
Rius-Ulldemolins, J., & Klein, R. (2021). From artistic direction to cultural management: Governance and management of Barcelona's artistic institutions in the twenty-first century. *International Journal of Public Sector Management, 34*(1), 33–49. https://doi.org/10.1108/IJPSM-03-2020-0082
Røyseng, S. (2008). Arts management and the autonomy of art. *International Journal of Cultural Policy, 14*(1), 37–48. https://doi.org/10.1080/10286630701856484
Salcudean, I. N. (2015). Creative industries – art and commerce; entrepreneurship and creativity. *Creativity, Innovation and Aesthetics, 1,* 10–25.

Schlesinger, G. (1979). Aesthetic experience and the definition of art. *British Journal of Aesthetics*, *19*, 167–176.

Shi, W., Ardelt, M., & Orwoll, L. (2017). Wisdom and creativity as two routes to satisfaction in later life: A personal traits model. *Innovation in Aging*, *1*(suppl_1), 72–72. https://doi.org/10.1093/geroni/igx004.298

Stachó, L. (2018). Mental virtuosity: A new theory of performers' attentional processes and strategies. *Musicae Scientiae*, *22*(4), 539–557. https://doi.org/10.1177/1029864918798415

Sternberg, R. J. (1985). Implicit theories of intelligence, creativity, and wisdom. *Journal of Personality and Social Psychology*, *49*(3), 607–627. https://doi.org/10.1037/0022-3514.49.3.607

Sternberg, R. J. (2003). *Wisdom, intelligence, and creativity synthesized*. Cambridge University Press. https://doi.org/10.1017/CBO9780511509612

Sztabiński, G. (2002). Artysta: definiowanie, redefiniowanie, oddefiniowanie. *Forum*, 158–180. www.asp.wroc.pl/dyskurs/Dyskurs2/GrzegorzSztabinski.pdf

Tarnopolski, A. (2017). Intelektualny wymiar kiczu: Mądrość i głupota: Sztuka i kicz. *Prace Naukowe Akademii Im. Jana Długosza w Częstochowie: Filozofia*, *XIV*, 215–227. https://doi.org/10.16926/fil.2017.14.09

Tatarkiewicz, W. (2015). *Historia estetyki: Tom I*. PWN.

Virtuosity. (2022). In *Cambridge dictionary*. https://dictionary.cambridge.org/pl/dictionary/english/virtuosity

Wnuczak, P., & Osiichuk, D. (2020). The impact of management control systems and managers' educational background on the effectiveness of public cultural institutions in a post-transition economy. *Economic Research-Ekonomska Istrazivanja*, *33*(1), 3166–3184. https://doi.org/10.1080/1331677X.2019.1691035

Woodward, J. B., & Funk, C. (2010). Developing the artist-leader. *Leadership*, *6*(3), 295–309. https://doi.org/10.1177/1742715010368768

Work of Art. (2023). In *Cambridge dictionary*. https://dictionary.cambridge.org/dictionary/english/work-of-art

3 Application of aesthetic theory in management

The key to the considerations contained in this chapter is the metaphor of the organisation as a work of art, which, based on the achievements of aesthetics, allows us to look at the manager as the creator and the stakeholders of the organisation as the recipients of this specific work of management art. Furthermore, these metaphorical references allow for arranging the entire narrative of the overlapping components of management and art based on the framework of the theory of the aesthetic situation. Thanks to this approach, managerial concepts gain additional contexts, and solutions borrowed from aesthetics bring a new quality to management theory and practice, especially in the virtuosity, artistry, and creativity of individuals (managers) and groups (organisations).

Similarly, if a meal can be considered a physical supply of nutrients to the body or an aesthetic tasting, or if music can be considered a sound background for various activities or an object of aesthetic listening, it is worth asking whether management may not have deeper dimensions apart from pragmatic efficiency in achieving goals. Can aestheticisation bring added value to management in the theoretical and practical dimensions? This chapter tries to answer these questions. First, however, the aestheticisation phenomenon was analysed to help understand and apply it in management in a conscious and possibly complete way.

3.1 Aestheticisation of management

The essence of aestheticisation is the search for meaning in seemingly disordered, chaotic, unstructured phenomena, and looking for relationships in a given system to humanise the routinised and mechanised reality. The key to aestheticisation is using aesthetic categories concerning something that has not been subject to these categories so far and thus was considered "beyond aesthetics" (Welsch, 2005). This search for meaning, however, does not have the character of giving it but of finding (reading) it, especially since the real world allows for various parallel approaches to explaining existing phenomena. It should be remembered, however, that aestheticisation seeking meaning is not about the

DOI: 10.4324/9781003458029-4

final explanation of the meaningfulness of existence, but about including an additional dimension to the analysed reality (Kociołek, 2020).

Depending on the types of phenomena subject to it, aestheticisation may concern (Gołaszewska, 1984a, pp. 163–232, 1984b, pp. 92–148):

1. ourselves (as an object of reflection) – our role in society and smaller groups; reasons (why) and teleology (what for) of existence; impact on reality, humanity, culture;
2. other people – their role in society and smaller groups; reasons (why) and teleology (what for) of existence; impact on reality, humanity, culture;
3. events – as a result of the arrangement of contexts, the effect of previous decisions, their poetics, and symmetry;
4. the natural world – the miracle of creation or the miracle of evolution; searching for meanings in a natural selection or survival of specific forms of an animate and inanimate nature;
5. the world of technology – as an emanation of the human intellect, ordering matter by human;
6. history – searching for meanings of particular events; putting them together.

Of course, these categories are mutually interpenetrating, so their separation was meant to explain the phenomenon of aestheticisation and not to seek its division (Gołaszewska, 1984a, pp. 163–232, 1984b, pp. 92–148).

There are two levels of aestheticisation: superficial and deep. *Superficial aestheticisation* refers to the outer layers of the perceived reality; therefore, the external appearance of cultural products and their internal appearance (buildings) are subject to it. The *aestheticisation of the depth* of reality refers to the essence and sometimes even the awareness of the perceived matter (Welsch, 2005). Therefore, this work refers to the aestheticisation of depth.

Aestheticisation of management can also be a source of inspiration in the search for ideas for new technologies, products, or structures by managers and other actors of the organisational theatre. Aesthetics, because it deals with abstract concepts, can be a dictionary of new concepts and new meanings for the previously used concepts in the management language. It seems that the issues of beauty, ugliness, or kitsch are not as far from the world of organisations as they might seem at first glance (Kostera, 2019, pp. 54–55).

Some voices see aestheticisation as a kind of field for anarchy, which clearly impacts management. However, *aesthetics as a path to critical management* seems much more convincing than ethical moralising or materialistic scientism. After all, art is an efficient vaccine against ideologising, which changes management into educating unified personnel, attitudes, and patterns (Guillet de Monthoux, 2014).

Referring to the division of beauty into four areas – (1) existing beauty, (2) the beauty of art, (3) beauty as a side product of human activities, (4) the beauty of events (more on this in Section 1.1.2, "Beauty and reality") – it can be said that the beauty of management is naturally associated with the last two categories. As a result of management, products that perform utilitarian functions (goods, devices, infrastructure) are created; some of these products are beautiful "by the way" of being useful. On the other hand, management also creates systems of processes taking place in reality, some of which can be attributed to aesthetic qualifications in the form of harmony and, thus, beauty. So, cannot the result (work) of management, which is the organisation, also be considered a category of the beauty of art? It seems that the affirmative answer is justified here; after all, the organisation is a product of deliberate human activity and simultaneously is a kind of the opposite of the existing beauty. If so, nothing stands in the way of seeing this purposeful human creation as beautiful as a work of art can be beautiful.

3.2 Metaphor of organisation as a work of art

Researchers have created many metaphors for the organisation, which is the essential field for processes and phenomena related to management (Sułkowski, 2011). Some metaphors also refer to the world of art, e.g., an organisation as an orchestra or jazz band (manager as conductor), an organisation as theatre (manager as an actor), or an organisation as history (Biehl-Missal, 2011). The shadow of the "organisation as a work of art" metaphor was outlined by the team of J. Reckhenrich, M. Kupp, and J. Anderson (Reckhenrich et al., 2009), while its full development with extensive use of the achievements of aesthetics – in the form of an organisation as a product of the "creator" (manager), which is created (modelled and managed) for the needs of "recipients" (stakeholders) according to specific "universal values" within the "real world" – was presented only in 2020 (Szostak & Sułkowski, 2020).

The assumptions of the theory of "aesthetic situation", which translates the theory of "axiological situation" into the field of aesthetics, have been discussed earlier (see Section 2.2, "Aesthetic situation"). To sum up its essence: the creator in the creative process creates a work of art; the recipient contemplates the work of art in the process of reception; and all these elements (creator, work, recipient) have connections and interactions with the world of universal values and take place in the real world, determining the type of art, but also creative methods and techniques. Although the most important from the point of view of aesthetics are universal values, and the most noticeable manifestation of creativity is the work itself, in the person of the creator (in consciousness and subconsciousness), there are fundamental processes that make up the phenomenon of creativity (Figure 3.1).

A manager in the context of an aesthetic situation can also be viewed through the prism of the interpersonal communication theory, which defines communication as the practice of exchanging information between individuals through a

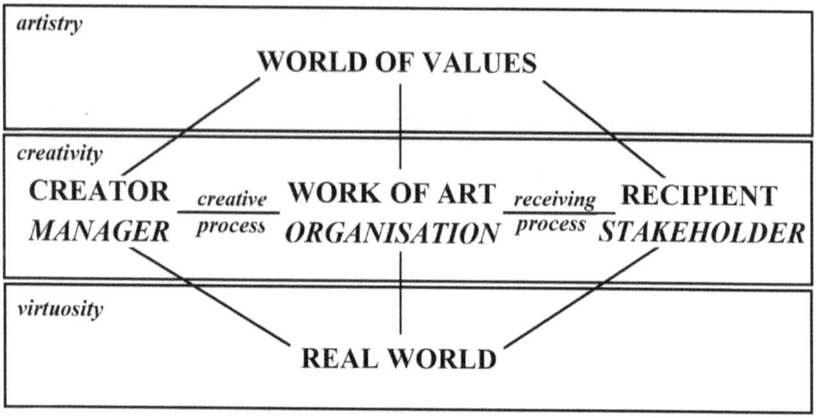

Figure 3.1 Application of M. Gołaszewska's theory of the aesthetic situation based on management, taking into account the competences of virtuosity, artistry, and creativity

Source: Author's own elaboration

standardised system of symbols, signs, and behaviours (Communication, 2022). Transferring this definition to the model of the aesthetic situation, the creator encodes the message in the work of art and places it in the channel; the receiver decodes the message to read (understand) what the sender wanted to say. There is a critical pitfall here: the recipient should be able to interpret the creator's message (work of art) in the proper sense; otherwise, an incorrectly decoded message will be received in the wrong way – not as intended by the creator. In addition, it should be remembered that the recipient is exposed to information noise, which disrupts and complicates the entire reception process (Abodunrin, 2017; Negus & Pickering, 2004).

3.2.1 Manager as creator

A *manager* is one of the fundamental roles in the management world, which is why the literature abounds with various definitions of this concept and descriptions of desirable features and competencies (Guranda & Nagy, 2011). A good manager is an effective organiser, effective in achieving economic and non-economic goals (Drucker, 2006a, 2006b); his actions are utilitarian. Based on the evolution of the classically understood role of a manager towards a multi-task agent and interpreter of reality, the ability to adapt the manager's role to the changing reality can be shown (Hracs, 2015). The manager may achieve goals imposed by the organisation's owner (separate ownership and management functions) or set goals independently (combined ownership and management functions); in the latter case, it is often referred to as a leader.

A *leader* can "influence psychological and institutional resources to motivate and trigger necessary actions" (Postuła & Majczyk, 2018). A good leader should adhere to the following commandments: have a vision, be focused and directed, be ready to take responsibility, know the area in which they operate, refer to universally recognised authorities, be motivating, be positive, learn from mistakes, have highly developed communication skills, and appreciate the cultural heritage. In addition, a good leader should use four types of power: delegated, associated, vested, and "rainmaker"; a leader without followers is a loner (Weingardt, 2000).

Some researchers point to an important fact related to leadership: the ability and willingness to follow a leader. This construct may be crucial to our analysis, as the visions and effects of creative thinking must be incorporated into the organisation by associates following these out-of-the-box ideas. Nevertheless, unfortunately, the modern world appreciates leaders, not followers; therefore, management education processes try to develop leadership qualities and competencies in everyone who wants them (Alvesson & Blom, 2015). However, unfortunately, not everyone can be a leader.

There are many juxtapositions and combinations of the qualities of a good leader in the management literature, but none of them explains how the desirable qualities of some "creators" produce a work of art and others do not. From the point of view of aesthetics, it is the *creative sense* that distinguishes selected people and predestines them to be the creators of a given situation and, therefore, to be leaders.

While both roles (manager and leader) have a long list of literature, it is difficult to find comprehensive comparisons in this field and differences in how co-workers perceive these roles (Postuła & Majczyk, 2018). What distinguishes both roles is the *art of exerting influence*. An analysis of leadership influence paths and types of leadership tactics shows that in today's leadership, the ability to influence is more valuable than authoritarianism (Nikolski, 2015).

It is impossible not to pay attention to many *mistakes made by leaders*, which, creating the *illusion phenomenon*, are the reasons for the failure of the leader's mission: (1) leader's narcissism; 2) moderate leader awareness; 3) too high an awareness of the leader. These mistakes lead to the following consequences: (1) undermining the courage of followers; (2) belief in one's infallibility and knowledge being more significant than it is in reality; (3) failure to verify own weak points by the leader; (4) relying on faulty knowledge, thinking, and paradigms; (5) detachment from reality; (6) underestimating the importance of commitment and wise advice from others; (7) underestimating listening skills; (8) listening to the wrong people; (9) not questioning own beliefs and plans by the leader; and (10) not paying attention to organisational dynamics. The literature also provides *solutions* which leaders should use to protect themselves from creating and operating in illusory conditions: (1) develop a leadership style that encourages open and honest communication; (2) encourage and solicit valuable feedback; (3) seek commitment, cooperation, and wise advice before making important decisions; (4) listen more, speak up, encourage open dialogue, and discern who can be trusted for honest and objective information; (5) verify assumptions before they are assimilated; (6) build and continuously develop an effective communication system; (7) plan ways to stay in touch with the environment, plan ways to engage the environment, and conduct regular reality checks; (8) build a system that provides the leader with up-to-date knowledge of reality and the possession of the necessary skills; (9) engage the environment to build a healthy and high-performance organisational culture; and (10) provide the organisation with the necessary training and consultancy (Warrick, 2019).

Scientists unanimously indicate that one of the basic features of an effective manager and leader is creativity in the approach to management and defining goals. To be a creative manager, one must abandon well-known patterns and old solutions and enter into active thinking. Three levels of creative thinking are crucial for an artist: *inspiration*, *intuition*, and *imagination*. The organisational processes are similar to the modelling of material by an artist creating a sculpture; it can be said that "creative sculpting" is a definition of management adequate to the challenges of the 21st century (Reckhenrich et al., 2009).

Although creativity and innovation as phenomena are difficult to observe as they occur, some research tools have already been developed, e.g., the "management innovation index", which allows for comparison of the level of creativity of an organisation (Kerle, 2010).

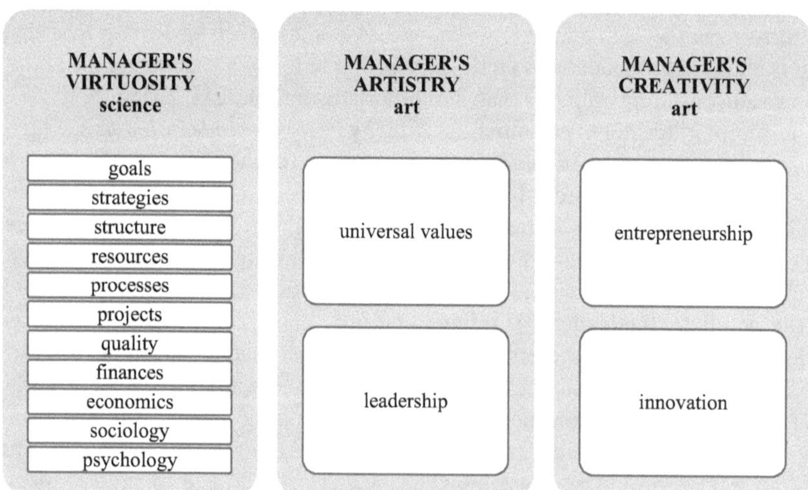

Figure 3.2 Components of science and art in management concerning aesthetic optics

Source: Author's own elaboration

The manager, considered a creator, is also responsible for the *organisation's atmosphere* – its creation and controlled evolution. On the one hand, the atmosphere is the result of many factors and the result of decisions; on the other hand, being a tool (means), it strongly impacts the effects of the individuals it affects, by analogy with the atmosphere in the spaces of everyday life created by the works of art placed there, but also the creative atmosphere affecting the activities created in these spaces (Biehl-Missal, 2015, pp. 165–166).

In order to structure further considerations regarding the view of the manager as a creator within the aesthetic situation, managerial activity should be divided into issues of virtuosity, artistry, and creativity. A synthetic approach to this division is presented in Figure 3.1, and this theory will be developed in the following subsections. Figure 3.2 depicts components of science and art of management through the optics of a manager's virtuosity, artistry, and creativity.

Manager virtuosity

Few publications address the issue of managerial virtuosity. Some try to place all aspects of artistic creativity under the cloak of virtuosity, including creativity or referring activity to universal values and virtues (Jackson, 2017). Some researchers find similarities between artistic virtuosity and management, including: (1) the pursuit of excellence in the face of fierce competition, (2) the need for discipline in acquiring and maintaining specific skills, and (3) the spirit of self-government and responsibility for oneself, and strong dependence on reputation (Jackson, 2017). Others, referring to the experience of orchestras, claim that virtuosity in their performances, extended by a reflective process, can be a means to improve the performance of the entire group (Marotto et al., 2007).

In the context of the analysed aesthetic situation, managerial virtuosity can be reduced to proficiency in using the components that were called measurable/hard in Chapter 1 (see Figure 1.3).

Manager creativity

It seems that the literature in the management field strives to describe the ideal model of a manager – which in itself is kitsch and, therefore, an action focused on effectiveness, not on learning the truth (Tarnopolski, 2017). Moreover, since the needs that management satisfies are different, it is reasonable to recognise that there are many types of managers; therefore, the search for an ideal model of a manager is unfounded.

The introduction of the differentiation of the dimensions of creativity and effectiveness allows showing the diversity of types of managers similar to the diversity of types of artists (Szostak & Sułkowski, 2020):

1. a visionary – a person with high creativity and low organisational efficiency; a visionary in the world of organisation will be a manager-theoretician

(e.g., an academic teacher in the field of management who has not worked in any organisation as a manager but is well-informed and creative in the field of management theory); a similar role in the artistic world will be played by a conceptualist, an artist creating a work, but not realising his idea in any artistic matter;
2. an imitator – low creativity and low organisational efficiency; the imitator in the organisational world will be an administrator or official who does not come up with any solutions but abides by the rules imposed by law or his superior; in the art world, an imitator is called a copyist;
3. a craftsman – low creativity and high organisational efficiency; an artisan in the organisational world can be a manager or a professional; in the art world, an artistic craftsman who specialises in certain forms of art (e.g., portraitist, landscape painter);
4. a creator – high creativity and high organisational efficiency; the creator in the organisational world will be a creative manager, a leader; in the artistic world – we find him a true artist.

In order to show the differences in the meanings of terms used in the managerial literature with the backbone of the artistic approach to the description of a manager, a graphic diagram was created that dichotomously differentiated the creativity and efficiency dimensions (Figure 3.3). Thanks to this model, it is easier to visualise roles from the world of art and the corresponding roles in the world of organisations.

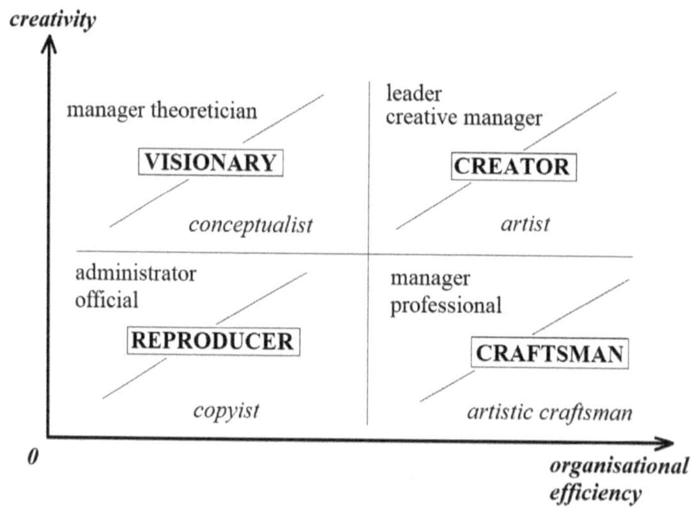

Figure 3.3 Types of managers and artists, taking into account different levels of creativity and organisational effectiveness

Source: Author's own elaboration based on Szostak and Sułkowski (2020)

Patterns of using the creative activities of artists in shaping and functioning of managers can be grouped according to the following approaches (Woodward & Funk, 2010):

1. trait approach – suggests that successful creators have developed and display certain personal qualities leading to above-average results; the general public notices leadership qualities;
2. behavioural approach – focuses on what a leader needs to do to show leadership; this approach analyses and codifies the skills and competencies of leaders achieving above-average results;
3. situational approach – recognises that context, problems, and people involved contribute to situations in which a leader emerges;
4. transformational approach – refers to leadership as a result of changes in followers who, seeing the leader's concern for the interests of the group as a whole, recognise him as a leader; this approach focuses on values and building trust.

Some researchers have pointed out that effective leaders combine intellect, creativity, and ethics (Gardner & Laskin, 2011). Based on this, leadership appears as a conglomerate of three optics/faces:

1. a manager (introducing financial, organisational, structural, and qualitative order);
2. an artist (introducing chaos through his work – both destructive and constructive);
3. a priest (a mediator between order and chaos, inspiring courage to accept the threatened creative potential of the organisation while alleviating the fears that arise during change).

In turn, the difference between the concept of a manager and the concept of a leader can be represented by the equation: leader = manager + artist + priest (Hatch et al., 2006).

The development of creative managerial skills is more effective using art-based education and training methods (Sutherland, 2013; Taylor & Ladkin, 2009) because it develops an element of creativity through timelessness, universality, and holism. Managers can learn from artists how to imitate the ability to design, feel, and inspire with the heart (as opposed to actions based on intellectual arguments), using techniques derived from theatre practice (skill transfer, projection technique, essence illustration, action), painting practice (framing, aestheticisation, and derutinisation of actions) or psychology of art (experiencing oneself and others, objectifying and associative work). In addition, learning improvisation techniques (results are based on research on theatre improvisation experiences) helps develop teachable leadership skills: creativity, resourcefulness, and dealing with uncertainty. Referring to the rules functioning in art historically, but often modified by subsequent epochs (e.g., perspective in painting, the omniscient narrator in fiction), researchers suggest perceiving organisations holistically and not only as a mechanism based on specific and unchanging principles; while the rules should be followed, their creative use and modification are desirable (Watkins & King, 2002). In other words, the principles and techniques of the phenomenon of creativity should also be treated creatively.

Manager artistry

It seems that an accurate distinction between the roles of a manager and those of an artist is the already-mentioned equation: leader = manager + artist + priest (Hatch et al., 2006). However, there is a noticeable need to correct and supplement the role of the artist in this equation in order to demythologise the popular understanding of the term "artist", which, according to colloquial usage, is closer to the term "visionary". It is the visionary who throws ideas around and does not implement them; it may seem chaotic and random. The artist has all the features of positively creative thinking and creating visions, but also has the ability to implement them consistently; it is difficult to deny the managerial skills of an opera director who, for many months, prepares dozens of singers, set designers, choreographers, and orchestra musicians, or a sculptor who consistently strives for the perfectly selected material and painstakingly implements his artistic idea in it. Every true artist is automatically a creative manager. However, not every director, sculptor, or musician is automatically an artist; if he does his work in a kitschy/reproductive/uncreative way, he is more of a craftsman, an uncreative manager.

As discussed earlier (see Section 2.2.1, "Creator"), "artist" is an ennobling concept also for people dealing with art. Artistry is creatively acting in a given field and rooted in universal values (not only efficiency) with minimal technical mastery (virtuosity). The stereotypical perception of artists as creative but chaotic people is reflected in management science; the literature does not confirm this cultural archetype. Disorganisation and chaos are based on character traits that belong to the individual's basic personality, which means that people with such traits can be found in every area of life. Management researchers who are not active artists use the concepts of art and artistic creativity in a theoretical way, not based on practice and experience. Some of their observations are insightful (Sztabiński, 2002).

Analysing the mutual relations between the concepts of artist and manager, it can be seen that both concepts have many common points and differences. The similarities include the fact that the artist and the manager start creative activities in the intangible sphere (concept phase) and then implement the ideas to realise goals in the material sphere. Another similarity is that both of them – without specialised education – can function well in their fields, proving the analogy between artistic and managerial talent. Among the differences, it should be noted that the manager may be satisfied with "slightly better" results; however, the artist always refers to the ideal and strives for it – he will consider his work immature if he does not see the work as a full reflection of the ideal. This kind of mixture of unattainable idealism and perfectionism is the cause of depression and frustration often found among artists – after all, few artists manage to materialise these ideals. Managerial utilitarianism is inherently incompatible with the artist's creative freedom, even though both pursue specific goals. Some artistic (musical) works live only in time, while organisations function in time and space. The classical work of art does not evolve (although contemporary works of art do: interactive works, installations); organisations evolve. Artists – with an artistic creation – rarely worry about the financial result of the entire artistic enterprise; they have administrative directors for this purpose (philharmonics, theatres, galleries); in turn, the manager usually has to consider the financial efficiency aspect of his work. An artist (writer, painter, musician) creates art individually, although his interpersonal and organisational skills (building/maintaining contacts with institutions/people) are not without significance; on the other hand, the manager works as a team – he is more of an orchestra conductor or a show director – and without interpersonal and organisational skills, he has little chance of success.

There is not always a need for the artistic thinking of a manager – hence, looking for similarities between a manager and an artist is not always necessary. However, a manager with high creativity and proficiency in his field can be successfully called a management artist. It will also be legitimate to call an artist a manager who, while realising his visions, knows how to organise reality according to his intentions – in contrast to conceptualists who do not deal with implementing their creative visions.

3.2.2 *Management as a creative process*

Interpretation of the creative process in the field of art (see Figure 2.5) in the context of the organisation management process is as follows: by transposing the issue of creative attitude to the management process, it can be concluded that the manager must have a *disposition*, which is a set of factors that may be the basis for undertaking the management process:

1. in terms of personality determinants, these will be personality traits, predispositions, interests;
2. in terms of social conditions, these will be cultural conditions, home conditions and circumstances of growing up and development, education, the influence of authorities, public opinion on management;
3. in terms of the richness of experience, these will be an experience of managing people and experience of managing organisations.

In order to start the creative process, apart from a *creative attitude* (managerial disposition), one also needs creativity, which appears when there are motives for undertaking a creative activity. In the case of a manager, the assigned motives will be: the desire to create an organisation that meets the goals set by the owner, the desire to create an organisation expressing the personality or values professed by the manager or the owner, the desire to create an organisation that creates a specific effect (product, service) with specific assumptions. The unassigned motives include: the need for the manager to obtain resources necessary for life, society's expectations towards a particular manager, and stereotypes concerning all managers.

In order for an organisation to be created, there must be a *direct impulse* to undertake the creative process, consisting of psychological activation through an external or internal stimulus:

1. lack of an organisation of a given type in the world, which will allow the fulfilment of certain assumptions, or which should be created (enrichment by the manager of reality with a new value based on the perceived imperfection of the world);
2. fascination with the world, reality (the manager can show admiration for the world);
3. an excess of own experience that the manager wants to use (wanting to present his experiences to others, looking for a way to use them in the organisation).

The sum of the previous components in the form of a creative attitude and an impulse leads to the *final decision* to undertake the creative process; this is when the real preparation for creative work and the first efforts take place. Creative work can be started immediately or require additional time, during which the following activities occur: formulation of artistic intention, formulation of artistic vision, and conceptualisation of the work. In an organisational context, immediate action may be in the case of a one-person business, where all work will be concentrated in the hands of one person (owner-manager); in the case of large organisations, the manager usually starts the conceptual process, formulates the mission and vision as well as the strategy of operation, and then organises and controls it. Like the art creator, the management artist is aware (Woodward & Funk, 2010).

The *realisation process* begins when the artist begins to objectify his intention, shaping the material of the work in such a way that it realises the intended aesthetic value and is equivalent to the artistic vision. In the example of an organisation, the implementation process will start when the business concept, mission, vision, and strategy are implemented: team building, organisation, and setting goals and tasks. At this point, it is worth paying attention to situations unforeseen in the previously planned concept of work, resulting from unforeseen coincidence or even an error at the implementation stage. Forcing an unintended result of the action (an actor's trip on the stage, a wrong sound made by a musician during improvisation) into a valuable and immanent part of the work of art requires a reflex, observation skills, and creativity of the artist. The same applies to the manager who notices the implementation of "accidents at work" and needs to transform them into healthy elements of work.

After the physical creative process is completed, there is a *post-implementation phase* consisting in verifying the value of the artist's work and gaining distance to the work by the artist. In the organisation context, the post-implementation phase occurs when the manager finishes working on a given project or ends cooperation with the organisation. Mainly, then, the manager can see the fullness of his work from a distance and assess whether he implemented his intentions or whether the values that guided the manager were/are visible in the organisation's activities.

3.2.3 Organisation as a work of art

Management analysis and research are sometimes compared to areas related to art theory: aesthetics, art history, and art criticism. By putting the manager at the centre of the analysis, each manager's decision is treated as a separate piece of work (Degot, 2007), significantly narrowing the optics. From the point of view of the essence of art, this is a mistake, because the work of art is the central component of the aesthetic situation; and just as the artist makes many decisions when working on his work, so the decisions of the manager are only single steps on the way to the creation and development of the organisation (work of art). If the work of an artist is only about the artist, then the work of the manager is about the manager. Of course, in both cases, the influence of the person setting the goal – the person commissioning the work of art, or the owner of the organisation – cannot be ruled out (Crick et al., 2021). A creative manager is an artist constantly creating/improving his work (like a composer who makes changes to the score after each public performance of the work) – the creative act is continuous here (Gołaszewska, 1984b). In the aesthetic context, the effects of the manager's work should be thoroughly assessed only after the "creative act" is completed because, during the creative process, the work is not considered finished.

It should be remembered that unconventional/creative methods of searching for solutions are recommended to organisations where the management system – usually based on logic and rational rules – is efficient. Otherwise, creativity can cause far-reaching organisational imbalance (Rear, 2016). Only well-managed organisations can successfully realise creative visions. On the other hand, a creative manager can find methods and solutions adequate to an unstable and/or illogical organisation – although such a situation should be treated as an exception and a temporary action, e.g., as part of change management (Edmonstone, 2018).

Transposing the differences between virtuosity, creativity, and artistry described earlier in the field of art into the theory of organisation (see Section 2.2.1, "Creator"), we can talk about the following *division of organisations* due to the dominance of one of these factors:

1. virtuoso organisations that are technically proficient in their field (e.g., in terms of the parameters of the product offered, the quality of sales techniques, and marketing);
2. creative organisations that operate creatively and innovatively (e.g., in terms of product, methods of operation, and communication);
3. artistic organisations[1] that are carriers of universal values (without forgetting about the effectiveness of their actions).

It should be noted that a virtuoso organisation does not have to be a creative or artistic organisation – it can perfect the technical side of activities that have been introduced to the market by competitors while not focusing its attention on values other than financial efficiency. A creative organisation does not have to be a virtuoso or artistic organisation – it can introduce new solutions to the market, but not care about their technical level or other values above financial efficiency. And, an artistic organisation does not have to be a creative or virtuoso organisation – focused on values, it may ignore the issue of introducing new solutions and concern for operational excellence. This classification of organisations has no reference to the company's performance: each of the listed types of organisations can achieve both positive and negative economic results.

With regard to this division of organisations and to the analysed metaphor in terms of the manager as a creator, it should be noted that – as with every creator in artistic activity – every manager uses his predispositions (and external circumstances) in one of the areas (virtuosity, creativity, artistry) and focuses his work in this direction. Therefore, it can be said with a high degree of probability that a strong correlation exists between the dominant manager's perspective (virtuosity, creativity, artistry) and the nature of the organisation (virtuosic, creative, artistic).

3.2.4 Organisation stakeholders as recipients

The recipients of the work of art are specific people (when the work was done to their order) or all potential viewers/listeners/participants who intentionally or accidentally came into contact with the work (Gołaszewska, 1984b). However, the concept of the recipient of a work of art is more complex in the case of an organisation because, in addition to customers who are the primary beneficiaries of the results generated by the organisation, this group – following the stakeholder theory – also includes other groups of entities (Weinberg et al., 2021).

The concept of stakeholders was introduced by the Stanford Research Institute in the 1960s, initially referring to a group of entities without whose support an organisation would cease to exist. In the following decades, the stakeholder theory was successively developed; the essence of the relationship between these entities was emphasised in the spirit of a systemic approach (Eskerod & Huemann, 2014), or the concept of stakeholders was expanded to include even all entities (organisations and individuals) participating in the functioning of the organisation or directly interested in its results (Freeman et al., 2018).

Stakeholders can be classified according to various criteria. The fundamental division reveals (1) *internal stakeholders* – employees, shareholders, and supervisory boards – and (2) *external stakeholders* – customers, suppliers, competitors, state authorities, special interest groups, financial institutions, media, trade unions, etc. Based on this division, the organisation's recipients as a work of art will be external stakeholders who, in a way, do not participate in creating the work by managers and internal stakeholders. On the other hand, just as the creator can perceive the work as a recipient (having distanced himself from work after the completion of the creative process), one can imagine that internal stakeholders – while maintaining analogous activities related to taking a distance from their organisation – can be in the field of influence of the organisation as a work of art.

Another criterion for dividing stakeholders is their *importance to the organisation* (Ayuso et al., 2011). Based on that, there are:

1. subconstituting stakeholders – without whom the company is unable to function (employees, owners);
2. contractual stakeholders – related to the organisation based on a more or less formal agreement (customers, suppliers, competitors, financial institutions);
3. contextual stakeholders – playing a fundamental role in achieving the organisation's reputation and social recognition for its activities (local administration, regional administration, national administration, and media).

Researchers have distinguished several types of stakeholder theories (Andriof & Waddock, 2017):

1. *descriptive (empirical, experimental) theories* – presenting the nature of the organisation's activities as a reflection of managerial behaviour (managerialism, organisational psychology/sociology) and organisational behaviour (organisation theory, decision theory);
2. *instrumental theories* – showing the results of the organisation in situations where managers adopt specific tactics; they refer to the behaviour of competitors on the market, relationships, and relational contracts (theories of social networks, the theory of transaction costs);
3. *normative theories* – establishing rules and standards of conduct for managers; assessments may concern rules centred around the system (theories of

utilitarianism, libertarianism, theories of social contracts) or rules focused on the organisation (the agency theory);

4. *metaphorical (narrative) theories* – creating metaphors related to the process of creating and exchanging values by stakeholders; in this case, the units of assessment are the participants of organisational processes.

In the spirit of this classification, the typical recipients of the organisation as a work of art will be contextual stakeholders. In contrast, the subconstituting and contractual stakeholders will play a double role: tools in the hands of the creative manager and recipients after appropriate distance to the organisation as a work of art.

Just as the recipients of the work can influence the creator in various ways (directly and indirectly), also the stakeholders can influence the organisation. Some researchers claim that the audience (recipients) of the artist-manager is the organisation (Atkinson, 2007). However, compared to the concept of an organisation as a work of art, this way of thinking has limitations and results from the assumption that a single manager's decision in the management process is a work of art. After all, we know that for a work to be created, its creator makes several decisions at the conceptual and implementation stage.

Indeed, the recipients are a source of feedback for the artist about the work and the values read from the work. Organisations use customer satisfaction verification tools (surveys, interviews) to revise their opinions and adjust organisational performance accordingly. In art, the artist, observing the reactions to his work, can compare his intentions with the actual reception and use this knowledge to implement it in new works or modify the already-created work.

3.2.5 Receiving process

The *receiving process* (also called the aesthetic process) consists of the sensual reception of the message in an artwork. The process of receiving a work of art begins with the phenomenon of ignorance (more on this subject in Section 6.4, "Ignorance in management") and ends with an interpretation (Woodward & Funk, 2010). In the case of the process of perception of the work being an organisation, the product/service – the purpose of which is to meet specific needs – is subject to sensory acceptance by customers. In this context, the process of perception of the organisation by recipients is multidimensional, e.g., the owner of the organisation compares the effect generated by the organisation with the goals of the organisation that he has set for it. In contrast, employees perceive the organisation by comparing their expectations towards the workplace with the organisational reality.

Tensions that occur between the recipient of the work and the creator of the work (see Section 2.2.4, "Recipient"), which may result from a misunderstanding of the work due to the incompetence of the recipient or the artist's incompetence or from a defect inherent in the work, can be translated into conflicts that occur between the stakeholders of the organisation (for the sake of simplicity, focusing only on employees for the moment) and the manager. The conflict causes a threat: the manager (creator) feels threatened in his right to decide on issues concerning the organisation (work), and employees (recipients) feel threatened in his right to understand the organisation (artwork) in which they function. This state is unfavourable for both sides: it inhibits the manager's actions (creator's development) and distracts employees from effective functioning (shaping the aesthetic sensitivity of recipients). Unresolved conflict can lead to the manager continuing politics and empowering employees to condemn the organisation. Entrenchment by both sides in their chosen positions further exacerbates the situation and moves away from solving the problem (Gołaszewska, 1967, pp. 20–21). This description is the field of *crisis management* activities.

The recipient's attitude towards modern art can be a metaphor for the attitude of stakeholders towards organisational change, i.e., the field of interest of *change management.* A work (organisation) that appears to be difficult, complicated, incomprehensible (especially in the absence of time to understand it), shockingly breaking with tradition, or using far-reaching simplifications requires time from the recipient (especially employees) to understand intentions and reflect on the legitimacy of solutions, expanding knowledge in new fields. Without the aforementioned possibilities, misunderstandings grow, and failure to eliminate the essence of the problem will not be replaced by symptomatic actions (directed at eliminating the effects). Among the reasons why the recipient of art is reluctant to modern art, the following should be mentioned (Gołaszewska, 1967, pp. 22–28):

1. slow adaptation to changes – technological development occurs at a logarithmic pace, while changes in human personality take more time, biological evolution (especially in terms of perception) does not keep up with fast changes in the environment caused by technology or new ideas,
2. the growing dynamics of change – with the delving into history, aesthetic trends and epochs lasted much longer; modern changes are happening faster and, usually, more abruptly, more by contrast and revolution than by natural evolution;
3. variety of news – they reach the recipient from all sides, so the recipient must make a permanent selection of information; lack of time for a deep analysis of all information causes the recipient usually to focus on easy art, which detaches from other information that may be much more important for understanding the essence of art;
4. democratisation – in place of the former elitism in the reception of art (art was interested in the educated strata of society), we are dealing with the dissemination of art; on the other hand, universality requires shallowing so that possibly an increasing part of society can participate in art consciously; one

should also add here the issue of the mobility of modern humans, and thus cultural differences between members of the same teams;

5. explanatory actions – they can lead to the recipient's release from the need to make an effort to understand the situation; the recipient waits for the art critic (training department, HR, change manager) to explain to him the meanings hidden in work and the techniques used to communicate; the recipient can take over the critic's opinions without more profound reflection, for "peace of mind", which – after the accumulation of such unprocessed layers of reality – can even cause the recipient's worldview to collapse.

3.2.6 Real world

Undoubtedly, the most extensively researched and described component of the aesthetic situation in management is the real world: organisations, their domains, and the dilemmas of the actions of organisations and their actors. It seems natural since these phenomena are tangible and, more or less, measurable. However, this does not change the fact that, as in the case of cold marble, it is the universal values with the help of the creator that give the sculpture life and meaning (Tatarkiewicz, 2015). In management, it is the goal and the way it is achieved that animates the organisation.

Each of the management areas in question (culture, documentation, enterprise, environment, finance, human resources, intellectual capital, knowledge, organisation, process, project, quality, real estate, relation, rights, risk, stress, time, value, etc.) requires from the manager theoretical knowledge and practical skills to navigate through its changing properties. The measure of this knowledge and skills is the manager's virtuosity in navigating the real world. Of course, the real world is evolving; however, despite this evolution, we see it as the primary environment for the functioning of the manager and the organisation's stakeholders and, therefore, a permanent affiliation to management issues.

3.2.7 World of values

The organisational culture, ethics, and corporate social responsibility theories develop the world of values in management science and practice. On the one hand, organisational culture – understood as a set of values, beliefs, behaviours, and attitudes that the organisation stands for and considers crucial in its operation – is a "secondary", subjective phenomenon resulting from these values, beliefs, behaviours, and attitudes. Nevertheless, on the other hand, managers treat business ethics and corporate social responsibility objectively as tools to achieve goals. The latter approach, being a practical action, i.e., in the spirit of managerial efficiency, can also be called an exclusive approach, a kind of easily applied "plaster on a bleeding wound", which allows the problem of values to be put aside in management (Saeidi et al., 2018).

The aestheticisation of management changes the perspective of the role of universal values in the entire management process; these values are not just an additional component but become equal to the creator, work, recipient, and the real-world spheres. Just as a work of art devoid of value becomes an artefact of kitsch, management devoid of values becomes a "feigning shell", which allows forgetting about good taste behind the € of efficiency and effectiveness in achieving goals (Moberg, 2010).

3.3 Summary

It is not possible to create one universal theory in the field of management, the use of which will satisfy everyone. However, one can describe the management phenomenon from different perspectives; we never know which perspective will reach our audience and help us better understand the manager's role in an organisation. The aestheticisation of management is not a homogeneous and objective phenomenon; it consists of many variable factors. However, the achievements of aesthetics can be a rich source of optics that can be successfully used to study management problems.

Crossing the boundaries between art and management allows us to conclude that the theory of aesthetics enables effective structuring and supports the understanding of the problems of management in the humanistic trend; if it does not reach someone in its entirety, it undoubtedly at least shows management in a new and coherently developed perspective. Considering the previous analyses regarding the aestheticisation of management, we definitely can consider management as an art and a manager as an artist of management (of course, this does not mean that all managers should be called artists per se – see Figure 3.3). In any case, the metaphor of the organisation as a work of art brings a new quality to the perception of organisational reality: a manager (creator) uses the tools in virtuosic, artistic, and creative ways; a manager (creator) influences the organisation (work of art), leaving his mark on it; an organisation (work of art) carries a specific message to its stakeholders (recipients); analysis of the organisation (constructive criticism – not to be confused with slandering or picking holes in – of a work of art) reveals the values according to which it is/was managed (created); stakeholders (recipients) receive the result designed by the manager (creator).

However, the application of aesthetic theory in the field of management has its limitations:

1. it should be moderate and cautious; because an organisation is usually a more complex and dynamic organism compared to a work of art, even minor changes within it may result in far-reaching and even irreversible consequences for stakeholders;
2. the metaphor of the organisation as a work of art applies primarily to senior/top managers (those whose decisions affect the entire organisation) and less to

operational managers; however – in the case of possibly autonomous actions of lower-level managers – taking into account a fragment of the organisation as a work of art in a specific time perspective (determined by the time of this particular lower-level manager's activity) – this metaphor can also be successfully applied here, e.g., an organisation department as a work of art of this manager department;

3. the aforementioned considerations should not be treated as a call for unconditionally strengthening the position of artists (who are experts in their artistic fields) in managerial positions; while art creators can bring positive results in terms of raising the level of creativity in an organisation, there is not necessarily a relationship between artistry in the arts and artistry in management; creativity in art transferred to the organisation will undoubtedly be revealing. However, the lack of managerial virtuosity (knowledge of the realities of a particular organisation, techniques and knowledge in the field of finance, etc.) can result in unforeseen problems and, as a result, cause more harm than good.

The following issues can be mentioned as *perspectives* for the application of aesthetic theory in the field of management:

1. development of management theory based on theories about art, roles, and characteristics of artistic creators can bring revealing results; since there are certain different types of creative personalities, it is worth examining whether the development of managers' creativity should take into account this typology, and whether the methods of developing managers' creativity should be differentiated according to this typology;
2. empirical research confirms that some managerial skills can be learned and taught (Woodward & Funk, 2010); however, similarly to the world of art, where not everyone, despite the same artistic education, becomes an artist, and not everyone, despite the same managerial education, becomes a manager; each individual has a unique set of personal features, and it is their arrangement that determines predispositions to act both in the world of art and the world of management;
3. broad understanding of the entire context, components, and relationships between them in terms of the metaphor of the organisation as a work of art increases the likelihood of successful implementation of this thinking by a manager seen as an artist of management because, similarly to the aesthetic situation, management must be holistically based on all entities and components of the management process with particular emphasis on values which affect the real world through the organisation; applying the theory of aesthetics in the process of management, artistry can be considered as a kind of higher level of management; the highest degree of gradation: administrator, manager, management artist.

Note

1 Not associating this concept with art only.

References

Abodunrin, J. A. (2017). Audience perception of effective communication in Nigerian paintings. *Harmonia: Journal of Arts Research and Education, 16*(2), 103. https://doi.org/10.15294/harmonia.v16i2.7824

Alvesson, M., & Blom, M. (2015). Less followership, less leadership? An inquiry into the basic but seemingly forgotten downsides of leadership. *M@n@gement, 18*(3), 266–282.

Andriof, J., & Waddock, S. (2017). Unfolding stakeholder engagement. In *Unfolding stakeholder thinking: Theory, responsibility and engagement* (pp. 19–42). https://doi.org/10.9774/gleaf.978-1-909493-28-5_3

Atkinson, D. M. (2007). *Thinking the art of management*. Palgrave Macmi llan. https://doi.org/10.1057/9780230589988

Ayuso, S., Ricart, J. E., & Rodríguez, M. A. (2011). Using stakeholder dialogue as a source for new ideas – a dynamic capability underlying sustainable innovation. *SSRN Electronic Jou rnal*. https://doi.org/10.2139/ssrn.918680

Biehl-Missal, B. (2011). *Wirtschaftsästhetik: Wie Unternehmen die Kunst als Inspiration und Werkzeug nutzen*. Gabler Verlag.

Biehl-Missal, B. (2015). Finding form: Gestalt as a development of aesthetic Approaches to organisation and management. *Dialogue and Universalism, 25*(4), 163–172. https://doi.org/10.5840/du201525492

Communication. (2022). In *Merriam-Web ster*. www.merriam-webster.com/dictionary/communication

Crick, J. M., Karamı, M., & Crick, D. (2021). The impact of the interaction between an entrepreneurial marketing orientation and coopetition on business performance. *International Journal of Entrepreneurial Behaviour and Research, 27*(6), 1423–1447. https://doi.org/10.1108/IJEBR-12-2020-0871

Degot, V. (2007). Portrait of the manager as an artist. *Aesthesis: International Journal of Art and Aesthetics in Management and Organizational Life, 1*(3), 6–42.

Drucker, P. F. (2006a). *The effective executive*. HarperCollins.

Drucker, P. F. (2006b). *The practice of management*. HarperCollins.

Edmonstone, J. (2018). Managing change, creativity and innovation. *Action Learning: Research and Practice, 15*(1), 69–72. https://doi.org/10.1080/14767333.2017.1414673

Eskerod, P., & Huemann, M. (2014). Advancing project stakeholder analysis by standing on the shoulders of giants. *Project Management Institute Research and Education Conference , 20*. www.pmi.org/learning/library/advancing-project-stakeholder-success-1912

Freeman, R. E., Harrison, J. S., & Zyglidopoulos, S. (2018). *Stakeholder theory – concepts and strategies*. Cambridge University Press.

Gardner, H., & Laskin, E. (2011). *Leading minds: An anatomy of leadership*. Basic Books.

Gołaszewska, M. (1967). *Odbiorca sztuki jako krytyk*. Wydawnictwo Literackie.

Gołaszewska, M. (1984a). *Estetyka rzeczywistości*. Instytut Wydawniczy PAX.

Gołaszewska, M. (1984b). *Zarys estetyki*. PWN.

Guillet de Monthoux, P. (2014). Terrorist/anarchist/artist: Why bother? *Ephemera: Theory & Politics in Organization*, *14*(4), 977–983. www.ephemerajournal.org/sites/default/files/pdfs/contribution/14-4guilletdemonthoux.pdf

Guranda, M., & Nagy, D. (2011, May 26–28). Educational management – art or science? *International Conference of Scientific Paper Afases 2011, Brasov*, 427–433.

Hatch, M. J., Kostera, M., & Koźmiński, A. K. (2006). The three faces of leadership: Manager, artist, priest. *Organizational Dynamics*, *35*(1), 49–68. https://doi.org/10.1016/j.orgdyn.2005.12.003

Hracs, B. J. (2015). Cultural intermediaries in the digital age: The case of independent musicians and managers in Toronto. *Regional Studies*, *49*(3), 461–475. https://doi.org/10.1080/00343404.2012.750425

Jackson, K. (2017). Music and virtuosity: A higher vision for business. *Humanistic Management Journal*, *2*(1), 15–36. https://doi.org/10.1007/s41463-017-0020-z

Kerle, R. (2010). How can creativity become a prime contributor to the strategic objective of the organization? *The Creative Leadership Forum*. http://thecreativeleadershipforum.academia.edu/RalphKerle/Papers/958193/Creativity_in_Organizations

Kociołek, K. (2020). Estetyzacja rzeczywistości – skutek dobrobytu czy upadek wartości? Analiza i krytyka poglądów Wolfganga Welscha dotyczących procesu estetyzacji. *Analiza i Egzystencja*, *52*, 37–54. https://doi.org/10.18276/AIE.2020.52-03

Kostera, M. (2019). *Organize ourselves! Inspirations and ideas for self-organization and self-management*. Mayfly Books. https://ruj.uj.edu.pl/xmlui/bitstream/handle/item/72058/kostera_organize_ourselves_2019.pdf?sequence=1&isAllowed=y

Marotto, M., Roos, J., & Victor, B. (2007). Collective virtuosity in organizations: A study of peak performance in an orchestra. *Journal of Management Studies*, *44*(3), 388–413. https://doi.org/10.1111/j.1467-6486.2007.00682.x

Moberg, D. J. (2010). The emergence of coherent taste. *Business Ethics Quarterly*, *20*(4), 750–751. http://search.proquest.com/docview/760026379?accountid=14549%5Cn http://hl5yy6xn2p.search.serialssolutions.com/?genre=article&sid=ProQ:&atitle=THE+EMERGENCE+OF+COHERENT+TASTE&title=Business+Ethics+Quarterly&issn=1052150X&date=2010-10-01&volume=20&issue=4&s

Negus, K., & Pickering, M. (2004). Creativity, communication and cultural value. In *Creativity, Communication and Cultural Value*. https://doi.org/10.4135/9781446220740

Nikolski, K. (2015). Leadership and management: Practice of the art of influence. *Annals of the "Constantin Brâncuşi" University of Târgu Jiu, Economy Series*, *2*(1), 31–39.

Postuła, A., & Majczyk, J. (2018). Managers and leaders in need of entrepreneurial competences. *Entrepreneurial Business and Economics Review*, *6*(1), 91–103. https://doi.org/10.15678/EBER.2018.060105

Rear, D. (2016). Reforming Japanese-style management: Destabilizing hegemony through discourse intervention. *Contemporary Japan*, *28*(2), 209–228. https://doi.org/10.1515/cj-2016-0011

Reckhenrich, J., Kupp, M., & Anderson, J. (2009). Understanding creativity: The manager as artist. *Business Strategy Review*, *20*(2), 68–73.

Saeidi, S. P., Othman, M. S. H., Štreimikienė, D., Saeidi, S. P., Mardani, A., & Stasiulis, N. (2018). The utilitarian aspect of the philosophy of ecology: The case of corporate social responsibility. *Filosofija, Sociologija*, *29*(1), 3 9–51. https://doi.org/10.6001/fil-soc.v29i1.3630

Sułkowski, Ł. (2011). Metafory, archetypy i paradoksy organizacji. *Organizacja i Kierowanie*, *145*(2), 55–70.

Sutherland, I. (2013). Arts-based methods in leadership development: Affording aesthetic workspaces, reflexivity and memories with momentum. *Management Learning*, *44*(1), 25–43. https://doi.org/10.1177/1350507612465063

Szostak, M., & Sułkowski, Ł. (2020). Manager as an artist: Creative endeavour in crossing the borders of art and organizational discourse. *Creativity Studies*, *13*(2), 351–368. https://doi.org/10.3846/cs.2020.11373

Sztabiński, G. (2002). Artysta: definiowanie, redefiniowanie, oddefiniowanie. *Forum*, 158–180. www.asp.wroc.pl/dyskurs/Dyskurs2/GrzegorzSztabinski.pdf

Tarnopolski, A. (2017). Intelektualny wymiar kiczu: Mądrość i głupota: Sztuka i kicz. *Prace Naukowe Akademii Im. Jana Długosza w Częstochowie. Filozofia*, *XIV*, 215–227. https://doi.org/10.16926/fil.2017.14.09

Tatarkiewicz, W. (2015). *Historia estetyki: Tom I*. PWN.

Taylor, S. S., & Ladkin, D. (2009). Understanding arts-based methods in managerial development. *Academy of Management Learning and Education*, *8*(1), 55–69. https://doi.org/10.5465/AMLE.2009.37012179

Warrick, D. D. (2019). Leadership illusions: Important implications for leaders and training and coaching leaders. *Organization Development Review*, *51*(2), 6–14. http://login.ezproxy.lib.umn.edu/login?url=http://search.ebscohost.com/login.aspx?direct=true&AuthType=ip,uid&db=aph&AN=135759018&site=ehost-live

Watkins, C., & King, I. W. (2002). Organizational performance: A view from the arts. *TAMARA: Journal of Critical Postmodern Organization Science*, *2*(1), 31–46.

Weinberg, C. B., Otten, C., Orbach, B., McKenzie, J., Gil, R., Chisholm, D. C., & Basuroy, S. (2021). Technological change and managerial challenges in the movie theater industry. *Journal of Cultural Economics*, *45*(2), 239–262. https://doi.org/10.1007/s10824-019-09374-z

Weingardt, R. G. (2000). Leaving a legacy. *Journal of Management in Engineering*, *16*(2), 42–47.

Welsch, W. (2005). Procesy estetyzacji: Zjawiska, rozróżnienia, perspektywy. In *Estetyka poza estetyką: o nową postać estetyki* (pp. 31–73). Universitas.

Woodward, J. B., & Funk, C. (2010). Developing the artist-leader. *Leadership*, *6*(3), 295–309. https://doi.org/10.1177/1742715010368768

4 Creative personality

Identity and perception

This chapter focuses on the problem of identity and the perception of these identities of creative individuals. The identities of creative personalities have been divided into simple (artist, creator in the sense of a creative person, manager, entrepreneur, and leader) and complex (artist-manager and artist-entrepreneur). The chapter aims to answer the following questions: (1) What role does identity play in an individual's artistic, managerial, and entrepreneurial activity? (2) What are the differences in the perception of a creative person and an artist? (3) What are the differences in the perception of a manager, entrepreneur, and leader? All the time, the analysis concerns management issues and, more precisely, self-management and self-organisation, seen through the prism of the aesthetic situation.

4.1 Identity and its perception

Personal *identity* is one of the critical elements that make up the individual. Although independent factors such as genetic makeup, social background, and chance events determine each person's fate, identity is the main driving force in private and professional life. Therefore, a research approach focusing on the identity of people who achieve above-average results in their activities is naturally able to correct educational and assistance programs to improve the quality of life of those individuals who experience identity problems or the consequences of identity problems.

In turn, *perception*, which is the process of sensory perception and interpretation of objects and events of the external world, answers the question of how a particular individual is perceived; perception also refers to a sense of awareness of the environment in which the individual functions. Although perception is of interest primarily to psychology, the importance of the phenomenon of perception in the context of the analysis of creative individuals from the point of view of aesthetics and management cannot be denied.

DOI: 10.4324/9781003458029-5

4.1.1 Identity and its types

Identity, which is a distinguishing character or personality of a person, emphasises elements of "who is" a given person (identity), as well as features that distinguish him from other people and groups – that is, "who he is not" (anti-identity). Because an individual has not only one identity but several, he develops different aspects of his identity in different environments (Antal et al., 2016); therefore, the individual and his discourses are subjected to contradictory pressures. Identity should be seen primarily as a process (becoming) rather than something that is characterised by absolutism (being). That "becoming" is a social process, because relationships with other individuals are needed to build one's identity. Identity is neither immutable nor final; it is a continuous process that stabilises periodically only under certain conditions (Bulei et al., 2014; Hay, 2014). The dynamics between identity and anti-identity are central to understanding identification challenges (Carroll & Levy, 2008). In turn, identification is essential for the effectiveness of achieving goals – both in self-management and in the context of managing the organisation.

Literature shows different types of identity. The fundamental distinction concerns individual identity, also known as personal identity (Cuganesan, 2017; Mochalova, 2020; Zambrell, 2016); and group identity, also known as collective identity (Khazraee & Novak, 2018; Vincent & Kouchaki, 2016; Zhang & Huxham, 2020). Adding sociological optics, we talk about social identity (McNeill & Venter, 2019; Sethi et al., 2012) and national identity (Grigoryan & Kotova, 2018; Saavedra Llamas & Grijalba de la Calle, 2020).

Scientists talk about identity on two levels (Brewer & Gardner, 1996): (1) independent (built on the principle of distinguishing from others), and (2) social (interactions perceived in terms of connections with others). Social identity was then divided into two dimensions: the relational dimension (bonds with specific other individuals) and the collective dimension (an individual's motivation acting in terms of the good of the collective). On this basis, three systems of self-awareness were established: independent (without references), relational (with references to specific other individuals), and collective (with references to a specific group). However, the concepts of the indicated self-awareness systems are not pure, which means that when the appropriate sources of activation are available, said mental units become activated depending on the circumstances. On this basis, the links between managers' professed values and self-concepts were then described (Lord & Brown, 2001).

By adding the optics of the organisation, we get the organisational identity (Erat et al., 2020), building the "I" of the individual based on the role played in the company or institution (the identity of the boss, leader, or manager and the identity of the operational employee). Also, identity integration (Tendayi Viki & Williams, 2014) can be observed, manifested in the transition from the state of incompatibility of one's "I" with the organisational role to their unity. Considering identity as an organisation's quality, we can discuss identity management strategies (Grigoryan & Kotova, 2018). Narrative identity is also distinguished (Gray et al., 2015; Sveningsson & Alvesson, 2003; Wolf, 2019), helping managers achieve specific goals. In addition, focusing on the area of professional activities of an individual reveals professional identity (Kunrath et al., 2020), where identification is based on professional work; strong professional identity is present among doctors, nursing staff, judges, police officers, military personnel, and teachers.

By adding an ethical perspective, one can define a moral identity in which the identification is based on the values professed or those against which the individual acts (Gerpott et al., 2019). However, one should not confuse moral identity with religious identity, which can be built on the appearance of rites and rituals without any reference to moral norms.

Taking into account the process approach, one can distinguish a developing identity (Yazar & Arifoglu, 2012). In specific circumstances, one speaks of an established identity (Erat et al., 2020), sustainable identity (McNeill & Venter, 2019), and identity work (Bennett & Hennekam, 2018; Hennekam & Bennett, 2016; Reedy, 2008). The aspect of the structure reveals the construction of identity (Watson, 2009; Zambrell, 2016), relational identity (Brewer & Gardner, 1996), identity regulation, or identity formation (Warhurst, 2011).

According to humanistic norms, an essentially autonomous, self-forming individual can choose an individualised identity, but the structuralist approach characterises identity as imposed from the outside by social influences that shape identity unconsciously. The poststructuralist position implies that identity is culturally conditioned. For example, managers can be seen as inactive and mindless puppets, but mainstream management discourses are far from such generalisations. Governance can be conceptualised regarding the tension between identity regulation and identity work (Alvesson & Willmott, 2002; Warhurst & Black, 2017; Watson, 2009). Work on identity implies a dialogue between internal ideas, wishes, and feelings and external metaphors and evaluations (Sveningsson & Alvesson, 2003).

Watson described the problem of dual control, where, on the one hand, managers are focused on self-management and, on the other, on managing the implementation of tasks by the organisation (Watson, 2001). Managers should treat the different dimensions of their identity as two sides of the same problem, not as conflicts with each other (Gotsi et al., 2010).

Finally, depending on the complexity, a simple (separate) identity can be distinguished, e.g., the manager's identity (Hallier, 2004; Watson, 2009), the artist's identity (Dahlsen, 2015), creative identity (Vincent & Kouchaki, 2016), and complex identity (David & Bar-Tal, 2009), called dialogic identity (Masso, 2010), such as the identity of an artist-manager or an artist-entrepreneur (Szostak & Sułkowski, 2021b). Management researchers have studied the problem of complex identities using the example of managers with an identity: designers (Kunrath et al., 2020), actors (Walter, 2015), artists (Degot, 2007; Szostak & Sułkowski, 2020a), individual national groups (Grigoryan & Kotova, 2018), people of mixed race (Tendayi Viki & Williams, 2014), or with the identity of creative individuals (Vincent & Kouchaki, 2016).

The preceding analysis shows that identity is a multidimensional issue. For this reason, its perception is neither simple nor unambiguous; differences in identity and identity perception lead to the conclusion that these issues may blur, and inference in this area should consider as many factors as possible.

4.1.2 Identity tensions and paradoxical thinking

In organisational contexts characterised by multiple logics ranging from compliance to innovation, individuals experience tensions between different identities; tensions between managerial and artistic identities are one such area (Adler, 2011, 2015a; Gotsi et al., 2010; Schein, 2001). Identity tensions intensify in a context of change and uncertainty (White, 1992). Managers who impose paradoxical requirements on employees resulting from their different identities will likely generate defence mechanisms among employees. In addition, separating the two poles of identity instead of integrating tensions makes it harder for employees to be creative (Antal et al., 2016; Voss et al., 2006). Artists and managers, using adaptive skills, can do their job anywhere because they have creative competence. This reasoning is confirmed by artists and managers working in all economic conditions and socio-political systems, perfectly adapting even to significant and rapid changes (Tchouikina, 2010). Artists do not feel tensions between their identities; therefore, they can be role models for managers who work in complex organisations full of internal oppositions and tensions (Adler, 2015a; Gangi, 2018; Schediwy et al., 2018).

Identity tensions in organisations need to be managed carefully because channelling identity tensions contributes to building employees' personal identities. Because there are differences in the interpretation of stress at different organisational levels, the responsibility of the top management team leader to approve stress levels for the appropriate lower-level managers becomes crucial. Researchers' interests in this area focus mainly on describing the identity of a manager who struggles with seemingly opposite problems, which is the reason for recognising identity tensions. The most frequently discussed identity tensions in the cultural and creative sectors are those between art and business, creativity and business, and artistic logic and economic logic (Kačerauskas, 2018; Saeidi et al., 2018; Schediwy et al., 2018).

The existing identity tensions must be used or relieved somehow; otherwise, they will lead to internal conflicts or burnout. The most common way of dealing with tensions is to defuse them by calming down one of the conflicting forces or by trying to find a compromise between these forces. Both of these solutions aim to calm the internal situation. Unfortunately, from the point of view of creativity, calming the inner conflict involves eliminating a vital source of creativity. Creativity feeds on tensions; the presence of tensions, i.e., the clash of seemingly opposing forces, generates creative potential; hence, activities aimed at finding the "golden mean" are activities against creativity. The opposite is the phenomenon of paradoxical thinking,

Paradoxical thinking is a process in which an individual identifies and defines the features of contrasting options to obtain positive results from implementing each option, despite their logical exclusion. The individual will be able to apply the positive aspects of their personal qualities to make more positive choices leading to effective outcomes (Antal et al., 2016). The paradox lies in the incoherent, universally exclusive elements that are present and functioning appropriately in the same period; e.g., a musician-performer must be focused on his public performance, but at the same time, the performer must be relaxed, because nervously tense muscles will not allow him to use his technical apparatus fully; the performer cannot strive for a compromised balance between muscle relaxation and muscle engagement, because accepting any level below the maximum will have a negative impact on the quality of performance; and the performer must work at the same time to maintain complete muscle relaxation and total focus on performance issues. Individuals who use their conflicting traits can outperform those who try to find peace and balance between these traits.

The theory of paradoxical thinking makes sense if there is an expression of the most positive aspect of basic personal qualities. Paradoxical problem-solving thinking requires thorough self-analysis to discover the most positive ways to express personal qualities. Referring to social identity theory is useful here: identity tensions between an individual's true self and the standards and expectations of the groups to which the individual belongs or wants to belong can be common among people in precarious professions (managers and artists can be seen as such professions). This statement underscores the requirement that individuals construct a self authenticated by others (Bennett & Hennekam, 2018; Fletcher & Olwyler, 1997; Knight & Paroutis, 2017).

4.1.3. Identity crisis

An *identity crisis* is a feeling of uncertainty about who or what a person is. An identity crisis can be caused by new situations in life, such as marriage, birth, death of a relative, and unemployment, but also migration, financial situation, injury, destruction of heritage, culture shock, or a pandemic. The destruction of one's cultural heritage reveals people's attachment to that cultural heritage, which reflects their daily rituals, memories, and community life and shows people's constructions of identity and understanding of intangible cultural heritage. The solution stems from the desire to rebuild a sense of identity (Harles & Rajbhandari, 2017). Building on the concepts of home, identity, and exodus, ideas such as integration, reception, and interdependence help to solve the crisis

(Sánchez-Escalonilla & García-Rico, 2019). Art can be healing due to the distance it creates from current socio-political issues (Rikou & Chaviara, 2016).

As vulnerable individuals, artists can be much more susceptible to all kinds of identity crises, although their ability to use paradoxical thinking in dealing with identity tensions is a helpful factor. The social self can be divided into two dimensions, relational and collective. On this basis, three self-awareness systems were distinguished depending on activation factors and circumstances: independent, relational, and collective (Brewer & Gardner, 1996). Given the aforementioned conceptions of identity, the impact of the COVID-19 pandemic on relationships between individuals (especially self-isolation and social distancing) may be an essential factor leading to identity crises.

A crisis situation brings to the fore an aspect of social experience in its inconsistency and complexity beyond individual control. The pandemic crisis may be paradoxically perceived as an opportunity for artists to present their work in new geographic zones or on different levels of perception. In times of crisis, art can broaden how people visualise their existence. Works of art created in times of crisis determine the recipients' reactions oscillating around attempts to maintain a state of detachment from the stream of crisis events (escapist function of art). Each work of art was created as a result of actions not only of an individual but also of the bonds of associations, which are crucial for overcoming an identity crisis. A variety of approaches can be used to build an identity. Creativity in managing identity references, rather than normative cultural patterns, is a prerequisite for identification. Identification choices are constructed based on perceptions of collective strategies offered by external factors: individual creativity and dialogue practices (Masso, 2010).

The literature offers many suggestions on how an artist can deal with psychological challenges after entering an identity crisis: by giving space to rest; using free time for non-creative activities; maintaining a commitment to one's art, but in a different way from before; working consistently on schedule; celebrating small victories; looking for other outlets for creativity; seeking support groups or therapy; or the final solution – removing from the realm of creativity entirely (Rasminsky, 2019).

Young creative professionals who enter the market using an entrepreneur identity indicate three ways to respond to the high degree of uncertainty when internalising their new role: (1) rejection of the new role, (2) adoption of the new role, and (3) conversion from the current role to the new one. In addition, they emphasise the importance of learning and internalising new standards of behaviour in their activities, especially in the field of entrepreneurship: self-promotion, accessibility, self-education, adaptation to market constraints, autonomy, and responsibility (Vivant, 2016). These conclusions can be applied to the theory of identity crises caused by external factors, such as the COVID-19 pandemic. Artists whose creative sources are based on environmental aesthetics require no financial constraints to create (Dahlsen, 2015). The varied and fragile career paths of such artists usually determine their downfall in difficult economic times and jeopardise their individualism in expressing creativity. History shows that art can survive even the most difficult times, and what is more, it can even be healing (there are many examples of individuals who, thanks to their creativity, survived extremely hostile conditions). Art can live, even if its creators suffer hunger and pain and lose the meaning of existence. Art can rise from the ashes, although artists pay the highest price in any creative process.

4.1.4 Perception and its process

Perception, also called reception, is a complex cognitive process resulting in an image of reality in the human mind (perception). It should be emphasised that perception is not a passive representation of reality; it is an active, even creative process of organising the material the senses provide (sight, smell, hearing, touch, and taste) into meaningful wholes. The processing of information received by the senses occurs at: (1) the sensory-motor level – then we talk about the perception of spatial-temporal wholes – and (2) the semantic-operational level – the perception of objects and signs. Internal patterns play a fundamental role in perception, representations, and cognitive schemes of reality, created based on previous experiences (Petrozolin-Skowrońska, 2017).

Psychology distinguishes the following *perception process stages* (Zimbardo & Gerrig, 2012, pp. 128–185): (1) perception of impressions through the senses; (2) perception of selected stimuli; and (3) identification and recognition. Since perception in a broad sense means capturing with the senses and registering in consciousness objects and events coming from the external environment, it will be legitimate to conclude that individuals can perceive even very stable phenomena in a very different way. After all, sensory reception, understanding, identification, determination, and preparation for reacting to stimuli are very individual issues and also determined by many factors.

In the example of the sense of sight, it is worth paying attention to the mechanisms of the human body that determine perceptual stability, understood as the ability to maintain an object's constant perception, despite its image's variability. The manifestations of this perceptual constancy are:

1. the shape constancy – perceiving the proper shape of an object despite changing the shape of its image on the retina;
2. the size constancy – perception of the true size of an object despite the change in the size of its image on the retina;
3. the brightness constancy – the tendency to perceive the whiteness, greyness, or blackness of objects as constant, with changing light intensity.

On the other hand, in the example of the sense of smell, the influence of smells on the perception of a place or a person is observed (Krzemińska, 2022). Even the concept of scent marketing has been distinguished, which uses the sense of smell to build impressions and influence perception (De Luca & Botelho, 2021; Grybś-Kabocik, 2018; Van Niekerk & Goldberg, 2021).

It is worth paying attention to the *types of cognitive structures*, i.e., those areas of identity that affect the process of perception. There are cognitive structures related to imagination, on the one hand, and related to intelligence, on the other. *Cognitive structures related to imagination* analyse sensory impressions determined by expectations, needs, feelings, defence mechanisms or contexts triggered by the subconscious. In turn, *cognitive structures related to intelligence* analyse sensory impressions corrected by sensations registered in the imagination but processed in a conscious, intellectual way.

Among the processes that organise perception, psychology distinguishes the following components (Zilnyk, 2011):

1. attention – understood as a state of concentration of awareness on a specific area of available information;
2. goal-oriented selection – understood as a factor determining the individual's choice for further processing of only part of the sensory stimuli; the choices made are a function of the individual's goals;
3. grasping by the stimulus – understood as the automatic attraction of the individual's attention by objects (or rather, the features of objects) in the environment, regardless of the individual's specific perceptual goals.

The impact of changing one factor on the perception of a set of factors allowed us to formulate the following *rules of organisation of perception* (Peterson & Berryhill, 2013):

1. the continuity rule – perceiving lines as continuous, even when they are broken lines;
2. the closure rule – based on the tendency to fill gaps in the experienced objects to create wholes;
3. the similarity rule – consisting in grouping elements that are most similar to each other;
4. the proximity rule – consisting in grouping the closest elements;
5. the common fate rule – the grouping of objects that seem to be moving in the same direction.

It should be borne in mind that having a creative identity and the ability to name and describe its features and references to the creative process are, unfortunately, two different issues. Despite their above-average creative achievements, many outstanding artists cannot talk about their works analytically; they cannot pass on their knowledge and skills to adepts or other artists. On the other hand, many average artists excel as theoreticians or educators in art.

4.2 Simple creative personalities

The subject of analysis in the identity of creative personalities and the perception of creative personalities will be artists, creators (in the sense of creative individuals not necessarily related to art), managers, entrepreneurs, and leaders. In order to distinguish these "single" creative identities from the "complex" creative personalities discussed in Section 4.3, these creative identities are referred to as simple; however, this term should not be associated with the simplicity or limited features of these identities.

4.2.1 Identity of simple creative personalities

The problem of simple creative identities will be discussed first in the form of a literature review and then illustrated with conclusions from my empirical research on the identity of an artist and a manager.

Research in the area of artist's identity and manager's identity shows that even people who have talent, personal qualities, and an established professional position in the aforementioned areas have problems with defining and distinguishing who an artist is in relation to a creative person (creator) and who is a manager in relation to a leader or an entrepreneur (Elstad & Jansson, 2020; Farmer et al., 2003). In addition, isolating the factor of creativity among people with one of the simple creative identities mentioned earlier shows that even people with highly developed abilities to describe their personal characteristics (high self-awareness, education, sensitivity) have difficulty distinguishing between a creative and a non-creative artist, a creative and a non-creative manager, a creative and a non-creative entrepreneur, or a creative and a non-creative leader. In order to verify these doubts, the literature on simple creative identities (artists, creators, managers, entrepreneurs, and leaders) was analysed, and the artist's and manager's self-perception of identity was empirically examined.

Artist identity was analysed in Section 2.2.1, "Creator".

The *identity of the creator*, i.e., a creative person (not only in the field of artistic activity), is mainly described in the context of individuals dealing with the following areas: classical arts (Ottery, 2006); new arts, such as a creator of anime (Reysen et al., 2020); social media, such as a social media creator (Arriagada & Ibáñez, 2020; Maynard, 2021; Mehta & Kaye, 2019) or a creator of fake news or rumours (Dong et al., 2019); founder of the business organisation (Fauchart & Gruber, 2011; Giacomin et al., 2007); and the founder of a religious institution (Jones & Massa, 2013).

Researchers of this problem emphasise the changing contexts and the creator's competence to adapt to these changes. Therefore, a deep analysis of creative identity is of interest to aesthetics, where one can find a detailed description of the creative personality against the background of the basic personality and types of creative personality (these problems are discussed in Section 2.2.1, "Creator") and the motives for undertaking creative activity (more on this subject in Section 5.2.2, "Creativity motives"). Among the particular characteristics of creators, researchers indicate having clear motives for undertaking creative activities (Gołaszewska, 1984, 1986), resistance to failures and failures (Leone & Schiavone, 2019), individualism (Ferguson, 2015; Lorenzo-Romero & Constantinides, 2019), courage (Davenport & Redman, 2020), and honesty (Thanh & Van Quang, 2019).[1]

Manager identity has been analysed in Section 3.2.1, "Manager as creator".

A common definition of entrepreneurship is the ability to start new business organisations and see new opportunities. However, management science mainly analyses the second element, assuming that the ability to establish new organisations results from noticing new opportunities (Nagy et al., 2020; Terán-Yépez & Guerrero-Mora, 2020). Entrepreneurship is more of an attitude than a skill. There are several types of entrepreneurship depending on the context: ethnic (Chaudhary, 2015), institutional (Almeida et al., 2014), cultural (Patriotta & Siegel, 2019), feminist (Lewis et al., 2016), millennial (Wilmoth, 2016), nascent (Kim et al., 2015), organisational (Moghaddam et al., 2015), business (Coppola et al., 2018), project-based (Ferriani et al., 2009), or social (Thompson, 2002). Context shapes what becomes entrepreneurial, and context should be the unit of analysis, not entrepreneurial units or outcomes. This perspective shifts the scale from individually to socially shaped entrepreneurship. Entrepreneurship seems to exist in many states independently of the observer and observation (Gaddefors & Anderson, 2017). A clear distinction should be made between the use of particular arts or artistic techniques (e.g., drawing) for the development of personal or organisational entrepreneurship (Clarke & Holt, 2019), concrete art (e.g., architecture) as a distinguishing element of sustainable development (Pinto et al., 2020), and the use of art theory (e.g., aesthetics) in the development of entrepreneurship as a process (Szostak & Sułkowski, 2020a).

The word "entrepreneur" – a person who organises, manages, and takes risks in a venture – has been used since at least the mid-nineteenth century; it was also used to describe a person undertaking dynamic actions. However, at the beginning of the 20th century, the word was applied to the individual owner of a business organisation, which brought its meaning closer to the concept of "entrepreneurial spirit".

The primary dichotomous division of entrepreneurship concerns entrepreneurial activities based on opportunities and entrepreneurial activities based on needs. Research shows that entrepreneurs dealing with art are guided by necessity due to limited employment opportunities in the long term (Albinsson, 2018), which is the current trend in the labour market, even for employees with less unique skills (Bilan et al., 2020). Nevertheless, risk-taking activities place new business founders among particular social identities (Fauchart & Gruber, 2011):

1. Darwinists – dominant in business and competitive situations;
2. communitarians – seeing their companies as social objects;
3. missionaries – seeing their businesses as politically conscious objects.

There is also the concept of entrepreneurial passion as consciously available, intense positive feelings experienced by engaging in entrepreneurial activities related to roles that are meaningful and relevant to one's identity (Cardon et al., 2009). However, the practice of artistic entrepreneurship is significantly different from the practice of business entrepreneurship (Honig & Samuelsson, 2021); first, due to the characteristics and goals of the artist, and secondly, due to the nature of the occasions, circumstances, and practices, mainly due to changes in the cultural and creative industries (Kačerauskas, 2018).

Research shows that a leader's level of identity positively affects vision communication with colleagues and subordinates (Venus et al., 2019); in turn, a narcissistic personality significantly impacts the integration of the leader's identity (Chen, 2018). Transformational leadership and procedural fairness positively and significantly affect trust in the leader, and the leader's trust positively affects creating a durable organisational identity (Erat et al., 2020). Arguments exist that a leader's values and approach to an organisation's identity impact organisational performance – including financial revenue (Voss et al., 2006). Leaders influence, encourage, provide vision for, motivate, inspire, and mobilise their followers; they influence employees, but the environment also inspires them; they most often influence people through their charisma (Jankurová et al., 2017).

The leader's identity must be strong enough to face the complex, dynamic, chaotic, highly subjective, interactive environment of modern organisations and contexts (Sutherland, 2013). Leadership motivation refers to comparing oneself to one's standards (Guillén et al., 2015). The intensity of surveillance moderates followers' reactions to leaders' actions (O'Donnell et al., 2010). A leader's effectiveness depends on the sharing of values between him and his followers and is negatively correlated with the pay gap between leader and followers (Steffens et al., 2020).

As with other identities, the leader's identity changes over time and with the results of identity work (Miscenko et al., 2017). The leader's moral identity and moral mindfulness as foundations for perceived ethical leadership and followers' moral identity and moral mindfulness as outcomes of ethical leadership were also examined (Ete et al., 2020; Zhu et al., 2016). The ethical approach and integrity of the leader were tested mainly based on the speed of decision-making (Van de Calseyde et al., 2020). The value of the leader's authenticity and high self-concept coherence are emphasised (Steffens et al., 2021; Zheng et al., 2020). Researchers describe the role of rationalism among leaders of environment-based politics (He & Feng, 2015), religiousness (Pascoe et al., 2019), or higher education institutions (Charteris et al., 2016).

In order to verify the simple creative identities of the artist and the manager, a qualitative study was conducted. The background for this study was the previous theoretical analysis applying aesthetic theories in management, i.e., the aesthetic situation and types of creative personality that complete the organisation metaphor as a work of art. The methodology used in this study is described in the

Introduction to this study (see "Research Methodology 3"), and the conclusions regarding the artist's identity are as follows.

Being an artist is seen as an innate and inalienable (permanent) phenomenon, but there is "a need for awareness and tools to express it; it is related to cognition, science, so to a large extent, professional artistry is instructive, although the imperative to create related to personality is inborn" [PL8].[2] Furthermore, "The desire to be creative, once discovered, is permanent and cannot be taken away, although practical opportunities to express it come and go with time" [UK1]. Therefore, it can be said that it is easy to identify as an artist, although the arguments for this are different.

In the context of the theory of independent and relational self-concepts (Luger, 2017), most respondents believe that there is no need to receive any external certifications (title, nomination, membership, awards) to be an artist. However, such marks are important factors in an artist's self-definition. "You don't need an organisation, title, or other acknowledgement to be an artist. However, being an artist is about more than just seeing yourself or defining yourself. You must be part of a community to practice and emerge as an artist" [US1]. "Having talent and skill (when practised) is permanent, but having resources (opportunities, time, audience) depends on external factors. One can be an artist only when both groups of factors are present" [UK2]. "From a substantive point of view, it is enough to have this divine spark, but there is a need to visualise its presence and the ability to use it creatively. External confirmation in the form of degrees in the field of art or recognition by trade organisations has been and is an important element of self-identification as an artist" [PL7]. "You need to know and work on expressing yourself – it usually involves professional and formal teaching. A professional title or nomination is only a consequence" [PL8]. Nevertheless, there is no safe area in self-perception when the person does not have an external certification: "I think sometimes I'm not taken seriously as a musician because I don't have a degree, or I'm not dedicated to music 100% of the time" [US3].

Most people pointed to a specific event or set of circumstances in their lives when they started to think of themselves as artists: "The time when I first sat down at the instrument" [PL4]; "From the moment when performing artistic activities began to be a 'natural' skill for me and ceased to cause technical difficulties" [PL7]; "The need to create has always accompanied me. But when it comes to the feeling of being a professional in the artistic field, it was the moment of graduating from an art university" [PL8, PL10, PL14]; "When I started teaching at the college level and started getting invited to perform in concerts" [US1]; "During the emigration from the Soviet Union, which lasted several months, I had no access to a piano. After my family, already in the US, came into possession of the spinet, I realised that I really miss music and started practising eagerly at that moment" [US3]; "In high school, around the age of 14–15; through self-analysis and contemplation" [UKR]; "At a very young age, when I started singing in several choirs" [UK2]; "since I started attending theatre classes" [PL13].

The manager identity results are as follows. Respondents had some problems self-defining themselves as managers. There are two main distinctions in the self-construction of the manager in the subjects surveyed: people management ("As the owner of an artist management agency, I am a manager and manage about 14 different artists" [BUL]) and managing things/processes/projects ("I consider myself a manager because of my job related to planning and decision-making, organising and leading" [PL1]). On the other hand, the number of people managed is emphasised in people management – the more subordinates, the stronger the self-definition as a manager.

It was essential to find out at what point or circumstance the person felt he was a manager. The first group of answers was related to the external determinant: "When I was hired as a manager" [PL9]; "When I started my own company and started organising events and employing people" [PL12]; "When I was promoted to team leader" [US3]. The second group of responses emphasised the process factor that relates to work on identity: "When management began to become natural for me, and difficulties in resolving conflicts began to disappear" [PL7]; "I didn't make such a decision at a specific moment, it was rather a process" [PL3].

The interviewees were also asked whether being a manager is a transferable (temporary) phenomenon or rather an inalienable (permanent) phenomenon. "I believe that some people are more successful managers than others, but I believe that managerial skills can be learned and transferred from an experienced manager to someone who wants to become a manager" [US1]. "I think being a manager is more of a transitional situation as the situation requires, although many would see being a manager as an end in itself" [UK1]. Some respondents stated that being a manager is transferable (temporary, temporary) [UKR, BUL, PL6], "it's just a position" [PL9], "a periodic phenomenon, limited to actions taken" [PL10], "In my opinion, negotiable. A person who has experienced professional burnout and will not find the strength to manage, will not effectively manage processes in the company, and because it is ineffective, it ceases to be a manager" [PL5]. Two respondents believed that being a manager is inalienable [US3, PL14], "it is a predisposition, a character trait" [PL11]. Some answers pointed to the transferability of some features and the inalienability of others: "It's a profession – so it's a negotiable phenomenon. The qualities that are desirable for a manager, and at the same time those that I consider permanent, are the qualities of a leader" [PL8].

Roughly half of the respondents cite management skills as learnable that should be "developed or built" [NIG]. Only three of them (13.6%) perceive them as innate [PL12, PL13, US2]. Both, learning or innate, were chosen by the rest (22.7%). "Skills can be learned, but some people are natural at being managers and leaders" [US3]. "Being a good people manager is innate through being sensitive to human nature, but techniques can be learned to help you deal with certain situations. They are only a supplement to natural management skills" [UK1]. "Innate qualities are essential. However, depending on the level of awareness and the ability to use them, they often have to be developed through various forms of education" [PL7]. "However, to be a good manager, you must have certain (permanent) personality traits" [PL8]. To summarise this area, there is a talent or some kind of aptitude for management, but the learning factor is also important.

External confirmation of being a manager (title, nomination, membership in an organisation) is necessary for 30% of respondents because: "a professional title is important to be taken seriously" [US3]; "good managers will find out for themselves whether they are successful, but accreditation is very helpful in developing in the business world" [UK1]; "you must at least hold a managerial position to be called a manager" [PL9]. For another 30%, self-assessment is enough because: "predispositions and experience are the most important" [PL8]; "more important is your intuition and real skills and achievements" [PL12].

The study's presented results confirm the characteristics and competencies of artists and managers in the literature on the subject. Extending the optics of identity with the issues of "becoming" and "being" allows us to see self-definition conditioning concerning various factors: experience, education, and external attributes in the form of an appointment or a diploma. Also, the issue of the ability to teach the competencies of an artist or a manager shows different views. It seems, therefore, that one should not strive to describe the ideal identity of an artist or a manager. As indicated earlier, there are different types of artistic creators and different types of managers – the awareness of managing the factors of virtuosity, artistry, and creativity, as well as different levels of organisational effectiveness, allow the creation of different categorisations in both cases (such as the categorisation proposed in Section 3.2.1, "Manager as creator").

The *similarities* between the identity of the artist and the identity of the manager include:

1. the fact that artists and managers start creative activities in the intangible sphere (conceptual phase) and then implement ideas/goals in the material sphere;
2. both – without specialist education – can function well in their fields;
3. some works of art and organisations function only in time (music, virtual organisations), while others function in both time and space (images, traditional organisations);
4. the artist (writer, painter, musician) creates art individually, which is analogous to self-management; in the case of creative team projects (orchestra, theatre performance), the artist, just like the organisation's manager, must have interpersonal and organisational skills.

Among the *differences* between the identity of the artist and the identity of the manager, it should be noted that:

1. the manager may be satisfied with "slightly better" results; the artist always refers to the ideal and strives for it;
2. the utilitarianism of the manager is inherently incompatible with the creative freedom of the artist, even though both pursue specific goals;
3. a classic work of art does not evolve; organisations evolve;
4. artists – in order to create good art – do not have to worry about the financial result of an artistic undertaking; they have administrative directors for this purpose (philharmonics, theatres, galleries); in turn, the manager usually has to take into account the aspect of financial efficiency of his activity.

The answers also show a tendency to combine artistic activity with creative activity (on principle: since I am an artist, I am also a creative person), and in the case of managerial activity, to combine it with leadership activity and, in a sense, also with entrepreneurship.

4.2.2 Perception of simple creative personalities

Analysis of the literature and the results of the original empirical study on the identity of simple creative personalities (see Section 4.2.1, "Identity of simple creative personalities") led to the conclusion that comparing a specific creative identity and its perception by society may reveal additional cognitive value. Researchers emphasise that there are some *determinants of the perception process*:

1. perceptual abilities of individuals (Wimschneider & Brem, 2019) – as mentioned earlier, individuals understand themselves in different ways and can talk about it in different ways; on the one hand, there is the problem of perception, and on the other hand, the problem of verbalisation of the results of the perception process; there is also no certainty that a person who is willing to share knowledge about his or her own identity has an above-average developed identity, while a person who is not willing to share does not necessarily have a poorly developed identity; the same applies to the perception of external phenomena;
2. the circumstances of the perception itself (Schielke, 2020) – the influence of circumstances and contexts on the perception of identity is intense; both the mood of the individual and the processes taking place around them determine the description of the analysed identity; the lack of permanent points of reference means that the specific content of the statement noticed by the researcher may be associated with both the real element of identity and the

change in the perception of this identity; the influence of other people's opinions can also be powerful;
3. cultural factors determining the way of perception (Saavedra Llamas & Grijalba de la Calle, 2020) – human as a social being is primarily determined by his own culture, which is especially noticeable when the environment changes; objectively, the same phenomena will be perceived differently depending on cultural conditions, such as attitudes, beliefs, or values.

Due to these determinants of the perception process and the complexity of the problem, it is generally impossible to obtain a simple answer to the question of how a particular identity is perceived. In trying to catalogue how researchers approach the problem of perceiving a particular identity, the following research strategies can be found:

1. they limit the issue of research from a general, broadly defined identity to a specific type of identity, e.g., the identity of the head of nursing staff (Baker et al., 2012) or the identity of the project manager (Lutas et al., 2020);
2. they carefully select a research group with a specific identity, e.g., teachers (Kasmaienezhadfard et al., 2015), designers (Kunrath et al., 2020), nursing staff (Kiran et al., 2019; Raso et al., 2020), consumers of individual products (Horn & Salvendy, 2009), or undergraduate students in business (Kohail et al., 2016);
3. they study the problem by comparing two research groups, e.g., artists and non-artists (Bhattacharya & Petsche, 2002).

In order to practically verify the results of the literature review and to supplement the material necessary to conclude the perception of simple creative identities, an original quantitative research methodology was developed, which is described in the Introduction to this work (see "Research Methodology 4"). Due to the research inquisitiveness in the field of learning, even the general distributions of the examined features, a pilot quantitative study was carried out according to the developed methodology. Detailed results of the study were published in separate articles, synthetically for the entire sample (Szostak & Sułkowski, 2021a), and taking into account the following sociological criteria: gender (Szostak, 2021c), national affiliation to communist and post-communist countries in relation to citizens of countries without a communist past (Szostak, 2021e), Polish citizens against citizens of other countries (Szostak, 2021b), having a creative identity versus individuals without a creative identity (Szostak & Sułkowski, 2020b), having the identity of an artist against non-artists (Szostak, 2023); having a manager's identity over non-managers (Szostak, 2022), having an entrepreneur's identity against non-entrepreneurs (Szostak, 2021a), and having a leader identity against non-leaders (Szostak, 2021d).

Being aware of the potential non-representativeness of the results of the study undertaken due to the small sample size, but still wanting to signal at least a general distribution of the examined properties, we can say that there are10 characteristics (out of 50 examined) describing each analysed creative identity (artist, creator, entrepreneur, leader, and manager) most unambiguously:

1. *artist*: the passion for action, creativity, talent, self-confidence, visualisation skills and imagination, originality, patience and perseverance in achieving goals, sensitivity to beauty, a tendency to be inspired, and the ability to observe;
2. *creator*: the passion for action, visualisation and imagination skills, self-confidence, talent, courage, patience and perseverance in achieving goals, innovation, ability to observe, originality, and the ability to set goals;
3. *entrepreneur*: seeking opportunities, patience and perseverance in achieving goals, the ability to set goals, responsibility, self-confidence, effectiveness, resistance to adversity and problems, organisation, courage, and focus on financial profit;
4. *leader*: charisma, ability to set goals, ability to solve conflicts, responsibility, patience and perseverance in achieving goals, self-confidence, courage, interpersonal skills (communication skills, reading emotions, sensitivity to others), resistance to adversity and problems, and personal qualities;
5. *manager*: efficiency, responsibility, ability to solve conflicts, ability to set goals, the tendency to plan, patience and perseverance in achieving goals, ability to analyse, leadership, self-confidence, interpersonal skills (communication skills, reading emotions, sensitivity to others).

The obtained results may confirm that the perception of the identity of the artist and that of the creator are very similar; the same features are considered significant in both cases, and the same features are considered irrelevant in both cases. In turn, the perception of the identity of a manager, entrepreneur, and leader – while maintaining some similarities – is more apparent.

The results of the research undertaken based on the developed methodology can be used by: (1) creative individuals (artists, creators, managers, entrepreneurs, leaders) for: (a) a better understanding of different layers of one's personality, and (b) comparing one's own identity with the general perception of a specific role by the environment; (2) scientists who want to study the similarities and differences between simple creative identities and their perception in the area of artistry, creativity, managerial skills, entrepreneurship, or leadership.

4.3 Complex creative personalities

Since the beginning of the 21st century, there has been an increase in the number of studies and publications on people with two (or more) creative identities.

Researchers searched for particular values, tensions, and paradoxes resulting from the coexistence of multiple identities. For example, managers who also performed the roles of architects (Cuganesan, 2017), artists (Hracs, 2015; Tchouikina, 2010; Zambrell, 2016), doctors (Netting & Williams, 1996), police officers (Ahuja et al., 2017), employees of the air traffic sector (Hallier, 2004), or specialists in various fields (Bulei et al., 2014) were examined.

This trend in research, conclusions from the my own, previously described research (see Section 4.2.1, "Identity of simple creative personalities", and Section 4.2.2, "Perception of simple creative personalities"), and especially those concerning the fuzzy and unsharp perception of individual simple creative identities, were the primary impulses for separating the complex creative identities of "artists-managers" and "artists-entrepreneurs". Another impulse was my experience – both practical and theoretical – in the field of art and management. In the practice of management, many artists manage various types of artistic organisations (Elstad & Jansson, 2020); there is also a group of individuals who are both professional artists and professional managers but in different environments, and with great success in both areas. It seems, therefore, that conducting research on the complex creative identities of an artist-manager and an artist-entrepreneur should reveal interesting conclusions in the area of creativity but also allow for a better understanding of such individuals' self-management and organisational activities.

4.3.1 *Identity and self-perception of the artist-manager*

The identity of the manager and the identity of the artist seem to contradict each other. The relatively poor literature on the subject tries to fight this stereotype, but the belief that these two worlds are separate seems to dominate the consciousness of individuals. Despite the apparent contradictions, these two identities can penetrate and complement each other. A "good" artist acts as a "good" manager; it is not the role/profession that determines personality traits, but it is the personality (creative, in particular) harnessed to artistic or managerial tasks that give the effect of "good" results (Szostak, 2020a; Szostak & Sułkowski, 2020a). In management practice, some artists manage various types of organisations, primarily cultural institutions, art schools, and organisations employing artists (Elstad & Jansson, 2020). There is also a group of people who are both professional artists and professional managers, operating with great success in both areas in the same or different environments. Research shows a common field of professional competencies of managers and artists (Adler, 2015b; Mietzner & Kamprath, 2013): creative skills, perseverance, commitment, and passion in action. It seems that comparing the identity of the artist and the manager's identity with the artist-manager's identity should reveal interesting conclusions.

The study aimed to find the characteristics of the identity of artists-managers using elements of their self-perception (self-construction). Using the aforementioned optics, it was necessary to introduce the concept of an "artist-manager", a professional artist working as a professional manager. It is essential to distinguish this identity to reveal new insights for the management area. Artists, with their predisposition to improvisation, can be a natural source of agile management practices (Morrow, 2018a, 2018b), e.g., through a well-designed process of improvisation skills development:

1. at the detailed level – the theory and practice of improvisation, e.g., fugue as a musical form, introduces the concept of a theme and its counterpoint realised in the same time scheme, in inversion, in augmentation;
2. at the general level – rules relating to specific musical forms (e.g., the already-mentioned form of fugue), which allow you to perceive the problem as a whole, even before starting the action (Szostak, 2019).

The analysis of the intrapsychic characteristics of the study participants, while having the researcher's knowledge and experience in the field under study, may be crucial to understanding the delicate psychological issues and optics as the subjects change their answers according to the theory of self-perception monitoring (Dufour et al., 2020; Kunrath et al., 2020). It should also be noted that the art of design can be an essential source of methods for management science. The discipline of design thinking, being an art in itself, offers methods (internal need for innovation and originality, constant search for creative solutions) that artists-managers can use in their practice (Hospers & Van Dalm, 2005; Martin et al., 2015).

In order to verify the theoretical assumptions, an empirical study was undertaken, the methodology of which is described in the Introduction to this work (see "Research methodology 5"). Detailed research results have been published in separate articles (Szostak & Sułkowski, 2021c, 2021d), while the study's conclusions relevant to this book's considerations are as follows.

The unique features of a person who is both a manager and an artist are: the ability to make decisions and be a leader, openness to understanding the other person [US1];[3] honesty and reliable work [US2]; better understanding of self and others by using both the right and left hemispheres of the brain [US3]; multitasking, universalism, flexibility [UKR]; the ability to make sound and informed decisions, be able to treat people at all levels with respect, and have a vision for the future [UK2]; interdisciplinarity [PL1]; the ability to maintain a healthy distance from problems [PL3]; greater sensitivity to impulses from the world, the ability to see more; rational behaviour due to not wasting resources, energy, and time on activities that will not bring the expected results; being more creative [PL7]; ingenuity, openness, and satisfaction due to having more than one sphere of professional satisfaction in life [PL8]; and versatility, strong ego [PL11].

As for the similarities between managerial and artistic activities, they are: honesty, integrity, attention to detail, being organised and persistent, strategic thinking, establishing excellent contact with the audience/organisation, recognising and responding to contexts appropriately, constantly taking into account the human factor, and being alone in final decisions. However, managerial and artistic activities also have some differences. "The artistic sphere allows time in a more peculiar world of thought than is possible in the managerial world" [US1]. "In management, you tend to place yourself and others under the controlled condition of a specific goal, whereas, in the arts, you infuse or combine your passion with creativity" [NIG]. "Paradoxically, artistic realities are more orderly and predictable [PL3]. "Management is more 'durable' (like tangible assets); the artistic sphere is more abstract (I versus ideas) even though these ideas are also realised in the real sphere; the influence of people on managerial activity is greater than in artistic activity; the manager must consider the human factor much more than the artistic one; in management, it is easier to recognise the situation; artistic realities are more tangible than noticeable – more experience is needed to navigate confidently" [PL7]. "Management activities are limited by many frameworks related to the need to consider many factors beyond our control in management. In artistic work, the only limitation is the artist himself" [PL8]. "Management activity is more focused on the external world, e.g., individual artists, and artistic activity – on the artist's inner world" [PL9].

Skills developed in artistic activity and used in managerial activities are considered to be patience, calmness, honesty, creativity, the tendency towards risk, irrationality, emotional sensitivity, ability to communicate expressively, self-control, simplicity, consistency in action, self-discipline, proper time management, punctuality responsibility, concentration, empathy, and generally all interpersonal skills. More elaborated responses were: "It is not easy to define because the characteristics of an artist are deeply internalised; are hard to choose. I think I can use the following features: creativity, non-standard approach to problems and reality, perseverance, although these are rather character traits" [PL7]. "All life experiences make up my whole picture. The only connection between these two areas is my person – including my emotions, changes, intellect – if they change, every area of my activity changes" [PL8].

Skills developed in managerial activity and used in artistic creation are: planning months in advance [US3]; being organised [PL1]; being pragmatic, using theory [UKR]; being able to appreciate structure and formality [UK1]; initiative, imagination, interpersonal skills [UK2]; self-discipline and teamwork [NIG]; attention to detail and overall impression [PL10]; and diplomatic skills, negotiations, self-presentation, stress, and emotion control [PL11]. Some answers were more complex. "Paradoxically, good work's basic and universal characteristics are important in both areas. An individual approach and character traits are important" [PL3]. "Both identities – being deeply internalised – interpenetrate, and it is difficult to distinguish which traits/skills come from which identity; may be due to character traits, and these character traits determine being an artist and a manager" [PL7]. "Acquiring certain management skills has no direct impact on the way I paint" [PL8]

Most respondents chose the artistic sphere as giving greater personal satisfaction because: "I can bring joy to myself and others through it, and this is a challenge for me" [US3]; "[In the artistic sphere] there is a much greater freedom of expression to which other people react naturally, which is fundamentally opposed to the formal structure and hierarchy in the managerial area" [UK1]; "[The artistic sphere gives more satisfaction because] it is more demanding" [PL10]; "Each time [when I engage in artistic activity] I feel spiritually renewed" [PL14]. On the other hand, one of the respondents chose the managerial sphere because "I am most satisfied with the satisfaction of customers who recommend us further" [PL5]. Both spheres were chosen [UKR] because they are "complementary" [PL11]. "Art is the most satisfying. Managerial work plays only a supplementary role, although it is a source of satisfying such needs as the need for success, appreciation, fulfilment of ambitions and contact with people" [PL8].

Respondents did not clearly indicate which of the spheres, artistic or managerial, is more demanding. The artistic sphere was chosen because: "[it] requires many hours of practice" [US3]; "about the constant need to develop and improve technique and fluency" [UK1]; "requires constant care, attention, maintenance, and development" [UK2]; "requires much higher competences and is a big challenge for me" [PL8]. The managerial sphere was chosen because of the "number of managed artists", "I have been in this profession for a short time, and each professional task requires me to expand my competencies" [PL9]. Two respondents chose both spheres as equally demanding, knowing that "each [sphere] requires a different effort and type of work" [PL7].

Respondents described the following situations in which they were perceived differently from the "classic" manager who is not an artist. "I'm considered the easiest person to get along with [in the company], which works to my advantage. They know that I won't get angry with them, and it will be easy to get along with me" [US1]. "I am asked for artistic input or advice, for example, in meetings as a manager" [UK2]. "Most often, it happens when an opinion on artistic activity is needed" [PL3]. "I often leave more freedom in how I express myself or present myself (e.g., in attire or less rigid means of communication), which I use to better communicate with my team or superiors. Sometimes, however, it carries the danger of treating me a bit disrespectfully – but this is more related to my gender [female] than to be an artist" [PL8]. "There are personal conversations, confessions. Sometimes I have the impression that I am a kind of psychologist" [PL14].

Respondents noticed situations in their lives in which they were perceived differently from a "classic" artist who is not a manager. "I haven't had many artistic situations when the environment noticed my non-artistic activity. If it happened (e.g., during announcements at concerts), it was rather in terms of curiosities that apart from art, I do something else (something more down-to-earth)" [PL7].

"I can be too pragmatic and harsh or direct" [UKR]. "Other artists will look up to me for direction or leadership" [UK2]. "My fellow artists notice my involvement in administrative and organisational matters" [PL3].

About half of the respondents do not experience paradoxical situations in their professional lives between the identity of an artist and that of a manager. "I believe that these two areas of my professional life influence each other. I believe my work uniquely shapes my managerial skills as a musician, and my approach as a manager is completely different from other editors and publishers in the company" [US1]. Those who experienced paradoxical situations said: "all the time; all I want to do is practice an instrument, but I also have to manage the details of many non-musical projects as a way to make money" [US3]; "most often when I perform the functions of a contractor and manager for myself" [PL4]. Two respondents from time to time experienced paradoxical situations: "when I can want something artistically, but I cannot allow it managerially (resources)" [UK2]; "I envy my colleagues who are just artists, that they are not aware of the administrative issues" [PL3].

When looking for a solution to a paradoxical situation in professional life, the dominant identities depend on the situation, place, and task: "the dominance of one of them cannot be explicitly supported", "these identities are interchangeable in different situations"; "It depends on the context and nature of the problem. Rather, it is about seeking a compromise between the suggestions of both identities. I don't change the optics of an artist to the optics of a manager, but I work with both optics in parallel". These answers convince that the identity of the artist-manager can be perceived as a coherent phenomenon.

Most artists-managers do not experience tensions between the artist's identity and the manager's identity in their professional lives or solve this problem unconsciously (intuitively). "I think I tried to make these two areas of my life compatible with each other. It seems that this was due to the need for multitasking and the need to act in both spheres at the same time. It seems to me that I can separate the two functions quite well, and I try to make them complement and support each other. I experience the parallel 'voices' of both optics, which I try to combine into one coherent message for myself and the environment." [PL7]. "I have no problem seeing myself as a manager and an artist at the same time; each of us works in different areas in our lives; I am one complete man who is responsible for everything he chooses as the field of his activity" [PL8].

Effective methods of avoiding the emergence of identity tensions between the identity of artist and manager include: "rest and relaxation" [US1], "using the gym" [US2], "postponing managerial activities and devoting time to [artistic] exercise" [US3], "playing chess or video games, watching TV, sleeping" [BUL], "doing intellectual analysis; rational approach to factors, their weighing and conscious decision-making" [PL7].

Referring to the question, "Is being an artist an added value to the role of a manager?", artists-managers emphasise many positive correlations in this respect: from multitasking, through greater sensitivity, to commitment, passion, and determination to work.

4.3.2 Identity and self-perception of the artist-entrepreneur

As noted earlier, identity is a delicate issue, but it determines an individual's life. While having more than one identity seems to provide more opportunities, it can also proportionally generate additional problems and challenges. Multiple-identity individuals face identity tensions exacerbated by change and uncertainty (White, 1992). In addition to internal factors, we observe external factors that trigger identity crises. However, it seems that people operating in the creative and artistic industries are less likely to experience the negative consequences of an identity crisis.

Wuhan, China, is where a new viral lung disease broke out in December 2019. Subsequent waves of the pandemic covered all continents. In March 2020, the World Health Organisation (WHO) announced the global scale of the spread of the COVID-19 virus (Kufel, 2020), which strongly affected the human population, economy, and trade. Governments have chosen different strategies to mitigate the devastating effects of the pandemic (Phelan et al., 2020; Liu et al., 2020; Sułkowski, 2020). With the outbreak of the pandemic, the situation has changed very profoundly. Scientists began to undertake research relatively soon after the beginning of this phenomenon despite the short time for in-depth research on the pandemic's impact on society. Several areas have become the subject of interest of scientists: entrepreneurship (Ratten, 2020a; Zahra, 2021), financial markets and the banking sector (Korzeb & Niedziółka, 2020; Pardal et al., 2020), sports entrepreneurship (Ratten, 2020b), technological innovations in small businesses (Akpan et al., 2020), digital deprivation (Kuc-Czarnecka, 2020), the impact of the pandemic on individual markets and the attitude of their customers (Marona & Tomal, 2020), and economic policy responding to the challenges of the pandemic in individual countries (Żak & Garncarz, 2020).

The COVID-19 pandemic can be considered one of the most significant global challenges since World War II, dramatically increasing the widespread sense of uncertainty. It can be assumed that the pandemic should positively increase creativity among people with creative personalities. Moreover, the dissonance between desires and reality limited by the pandemic should stimulate new creative solutions. However, a new problem emerged during the pandemic: significant and rapid changes in the essential elements of reality began to affect identity and cause negative consequences. Lockdown, social distancing, closed institutions, business troubles and their psychological consequences – all these elements led to identity crises.

Since the research problem addressed in this work focuses on crossing the boundaries of art and management, it seemed natural to examine the complex creative identity of artists-entrepreneurs in the context of the response to the

COVID-19 pandemic. My observations of artists' identities during the crisis led to the following tentative conclusions: (1) artists who work on permanent contracts with a guaranteed salary even when public performances are cancelled passively expect "normality", while neither their routine of private artistic practice nor their status changes compared to the time before the pandemic; (2) independent artists (entrepreneurs) have to look for new solutions themselves, because their sources of income immediately stopped, not to mention the prospect of future contracts.

Following Andy Warhol's statement that "being good at business is the most fascinating kind of art; making money is art, working is art, but good business is the best art" (Bureau & Zander, 2014), I argue that there is no clear consensus on the knowledge, skills, and abilities considered essential to the success of artistic entrepreneurs (Roberts, 2012). There is the entrepreneurial factor, but probably also the creativity factor. Most artists are self-employed, but relatively few art schools effectively develop their students' skills to create business ventures. It leads to the conclusion that the issue of crossing the boundaries between artistic and entrepreneurial creativity is not well understood. Conceptual and philosophical problems are encountered by art educators who claim that entrepreneurship is a crucial feature among the factors of professional success in the arts, i.e., creating new organisations, managing one's career, and having a higher willingness to take risks.

Analysing the phenomenon of the artist-entrepreneur, one should ask why artists became artists-entrepreneurs. Are they seeking greater freedom (independence from other people and organisations), new opportunities, and more or additional income (even if it involves more risk and uncertainty)? Or maybe entrepreneurship is an intrinsic part of the artist's identity, which appears in the face of problems? The artist-entrepreneur – firmly rooted in the aesthetic situation – subordinates the entrepreneur's identity to the world of universal values (Szostak & Sułkowski, 2020a). Therefore, when creating and developing business projects, many artists-entrepreneurs stop satisfying their basic existential needs and treat the business venture as facilitating artistic activity (Albinsson, 2018). Most enterprising artists do not sacrifice art to build a financial empire. Instead, their entrepreneurial activity is highly humanised and aestheticised, emphasising the importance of the world of universal values. Artists and arts organisations typically adopt entrepreneurial attitudes to improve works of art (Nytch, 2012; Szostak & Sułkowski, 2020a). Therefore, it can be said that artists-entrepreneurs are sustainable entrepreneurs with a highly developed sphere of organisational aesthetics, ethics, and social responsibility.

The *common components of the identity of artists and entrepreneurs* in the literature include intuition, creativity, imagination, obsession with their actions, the need to market their art/product, perfectionism, the desire to attract attention, striving to increase quantity but not at the expense of quality, targeted action to the goal, and the need to delegate organisational duties to be able to deal with creative activity. There are studies analysing three selected features attributed to entrepreneurs among artists (Poorsoltan, 2012): (1) ambiguity tolerance, (2) risk-taking, and (3) internal locus of control. As creative individuals, artists tolerate ambiguity and remain open to unstructured situations. There is a positive relationship between creativity and ambiguity tolerance. Artists take risks when creating because their environment is highly competitive and unsatisfactory. Risk-taking artists who experiment blur the boundaries of traditional disciplines. Artists have an internal locus of control because they are comfortable with ambiguity; they believe in themselves and often claim to be in control of their decisions and actions.

Analytical *levels of artistic entrepreneurship* have also been defined (Wyszomirski & Chang, 2015): (1) individual character traits, (2) goals, (3) strategies, (4) tactics, and (5) context. Thanks to this, a broad definition of "artistic entrepreneurship" was proposed as a management process through which cultural workers try to support their creativity and autonomy, develop adaptability, and create artistic, economic, and social values. Therefore, to identify arts entrepreneurs, we must focus on the imaginative combination of strategies, personal skills, and mindsets that work in and within the context of arts entrepreneurship.

The literature also describes *cultural entrepreneurship* based on (Albinsson, 2018): (1) economic wealth, (2) social transformation, (3) artistic innovations, and (4) institutional progress. This optic points to the dynamic development of intangible cultural features within and between societies but may be associated with the progress of infrastructure and organisation. These factors may define the artist's work as an entrepreneur. However, self-definition as an entrepreneur is not so apparent among artists.

Although the lion's share of artists see themselves as artists-entrepreneurs, people who started their careers in the 1960s and 1970s did not want to call themselves entrepreneurs. Most unenthusiastically recognise entrepreneurship as part of their artistic identity and consider it determined by necessity rather than a free choice. Some artists claim to be entrepreneurs who are not solely interested in maximising profit; they want to contribute to the development of culture and only obtain income sufficient to meet basic needs (Albinsson, 2018). Artist entrepreneurship has essential similarities with social entrepreneurship, but there is nevertheless a vital element of necessity-driven entrepreneurship among independent artists. Opportunity-based entrepreneurship refers to a higher degree of creativity, innovation, and novelty than necessity-based entrepreneurship (Andersson et al., 2011). Artists-entrepreneurs have the characteristics of entrepreneurship driven by necessity and opportunity.

Successful entrepreneurs – like engaged artists – are mostly passionate; however, the lack of proper entrepreneurship education among artists can lead to their identity crises, especially when entering the market, they do not see interest in their skills. Such a situation can give rise to internal rebellion. The phenomena of subversion and resistance in the art world are rarely explored in the context of entrepreneurship (Bureau & Zander, 2014), although the concept of "creative destruction" is commonly used (de Mateo Pérez, 2015; Poorsoltan, 2012). These perspectives should be added to the analysis of creativity because analysing these elements and seeing them through the prism of upheaval and resistance allow us to define new research areas regarding complex creative identities.

Creativity and entrepreneurship are not the same. Some creative people are highly entrepreneurial, and non-entrepreneurs are highly creative. We can also meet creative and entrepreneurial people (Bureau & Zander, 2014). Entrepreneurship and innovation are seen as phenomena that can end all crises, but those who repeat this statement perpetuate the misconception of creativity, innovation, and entrepreneurship (Borowiecki & Dahl, 2021). The entrepreneur moves in areas of opportunity identified by Drucker as unexpected, inappropriate, and innovative based on process needs, as well as changes in industry and market structure, diverse demographics, changes in perception, mood, and meaning, as well as new scientific and unscientific knowledge (de Mateo Pérez, 2015). An interdisciplinary analysis of the impact of creativity on the theory and practice of entrepreneurship by looking for the relationship between research creativity, motivation, updating, and innovation of entrepreneurial artists as owners or managers shows that: (1) randomness, uncertainty, and ambiguity must be perceived in broader business and social contexts; and (2) creativity is vital to successful entrepreneurial practice (Fillis & Rentschler, 2010). Thus, creativity is a critical factor in entrepreneurial decisions.

Entrepreneur traits or *entrepreneurial competencies* in the literature include: focus on possibilities and opportunities, ingenuity, imagination, openness to modifications, being motivated by one's individuality, functioning in a situation of scarcity of resources, using common knowledge, interacting, being guided by intuition, the ability to generate ideas (inventiveness), enthusiasm and vigour, using a network of contacts, analytical skills, common sense, strong willpower, aspirations, perseverance, fearlessness, dedication, determination, willingness to take risks, need for achievement, unlimited thinking, self-confidence, positive approach to change, flexibility, and internal locus of control. The intellectual abilities mentioned previously, which play an essential role in building an entrepreneur's identity and which can be learned, are situational personality traits that influence creativity (Bureau & Zander, 2014). It should be added that education positively impacts the development of skills and competencies in entrepreneurship (Solesvik, 2019).

Innovative entrepreneurship is emphasised as one of the general contemporary trends in art (Win, 2014). For example, we can cite the case of Ferran Adrià, a culinary artist, entrepreneur, and creator (DeFillippi et al., 2007). All three spheres of his activity are managed and developed separately through the creation of new enterprises (a consulting agency) in order to obtain profits for the development of creativity (laboratory research on new solutions in the field of taste) for use in artistic output (his own restaurant).

In order to verify the theoretical considerations, an *empirical study* was undertaken, the methodology of which is presented in the Introduction to this monograph (see "Research methodology 5"). Detailed conclusions from this study were published in a separate article (Szostak & Sułkowski, 2021b), while the general conclusions relevant to this monograph are as follows.

Individuals usually do not hesitate to define themselves as artists. An artist's identity refers to professional activity in various arts (music, painting, handicrafts) and education (formal and informal). Concerning the entrepreneurial identity, about half of the respondents believed they belonged to this group based on their professional activity (founding and running a company, organisation, or project) and responsibility for their financial stability and professional development. However, the other half of the respondents – those who do not run a business or an organisation – had difficulty calling themselves entrepreneurs, despite performing activities that fit into various definitions of entrepreneurship. Please note that no definition of entrepreneurship was provided during the study.

In the case of creativity, respondents were more explicit than in the case of entrepreneurship; almost all described themselves as possessors of creative identity and no doubt equated it with artistry, following the common-sense perception of creativity and artistry as the same phenomenon: "if I am an artist, I am also a creative person". However, according to research, being an artist does not equal being creative (Szostak & Sułkowski, 2020a).

The COVID-19 pandemic – and especially its social constraints – has caused profound structural changes in the lives of artists, both in the creative/artistic and financial/security areas. The situations described by the respondents can be recognised as identity crises: "nobody wants me", "nobody is interested in my art", and "people are afraid to participate in art because health is more important than art". Due to the turbulence caused by the pandemic and the ensuing waves of restrictions, most respondents focused on creative and entrepreneurial identities to find new options. Creative and entrepreneurial identities determined the effects of the external crisis and its impact on artistic identity. So, one can say that developing an entrepreneurial identity is a fundamental step towards healing the artist identity crisis caused by external factors (e.g., pandemic). All respondents highlighted a dramatic drop in demand for new artistic creations: ongoing projects were finalised (if possible) or frozen, but nothing new (in the traditional sense) was started, and no new projects emerged. In this situation, artists began to feel themselves as unnecessary and irrelevant elements of society. Moreover, or as a consequence, the issue of financial security arose: no job meant no money, i.e., no ability to pay the bills. The respondents also emphasised this factor.

The respondents had problems verbalising the differences between the optics of artistry, creativity, and entrepreneurship in their identity. Many respondents knew where to look for solutions, but not all started implementing their ideas. Another group tried to copy noticed ideas by starting new activities and projects (e.g., online performances, workshops, and competitions); unfortunately, without a creative approach or creative execution, their attempts failed, compounding the financial crisis. The type of follower of other people's ideas dominated here.

The problem of entrepreneurship and creativity among artists-entrepreneurs is also visible in the activities undertaken by professional artistic organisations – e.g., the American Guild of Organists from the United States and the Royal College of Organists from the United Kingdom. Immediately after the start of the pandemic and lockdown in Western countries (March 2020), these organisations began to develop virtual programs for their members, underlying the element of maintaining identity, giving a sense of practice, and seeking new opportunities for artistic development. However, after a few months of the pandemic, the efforts waned, and little remains of these ideas. This example embodies entrepreneurship without creativity: doing something without a creative analysis of the needs and capabilities of the participants or common sense. It can be stated that organisational entrepreneurship without a bit of creativity will fail in the medium to long term. On the other hand, even a small "amount" of creativity can achieve a "good" effect, e.g., online performances for particular groups of participants and online competitions explicitly designed for musicians-performers who suffered from pandemic restrictions (e.g., Sound Espressivo Global Contest). All kinds of activities that allow artists to practise their profession have been called healing about the artist's identity crisis. Even a brief moment of public online performance catalysed the need to prepare and the possibility of creative artistic activity and gave hope for the end of the crisis.

Applying the theory of aesthetics in the field of artistic creativity as a basis for analysing the phenomenon of entrepreneurial creativity opens up new potential areas in the analysis of entrepreneurs' creativity. Moreover, the novelty of this approach concerning the classical theory of entrepreneurship allows us to show a new perspective on the problem.

4.3.3 Conclusions

After analysing the results of both studies on the creative identities of the artist-manager and artist-entrepreneur, and the self-perception of the complex creative identities of the artist-manager and artist-entrepreneur, the conclusions can be grouped as follows:

1. a model for the development of individual creativity, which organises all issues of identity and identification around creativity, which is the key competence of an individual; this model can be applied to better understand and develop organisations and the creative society;
2. a detailed description of the identity of artists-managers, who are a separate group of managers among artists and artists among managers, and a list of challenges significant in understanding the identity of artists-managers;

3. a detailed description of the identity of artists-entrepreneurs, who are a separate group of entrepreneurs among artists and artists among entrepreneurs, and a list of challenges significant in understanding the identity of artists-entrepreneurs.

Individual creativity development model

After analysing the literature and the results of the conducted primary research, one can conclude that all the recurring key elements – i.e., identity, identification, identity tensions, and paradoxical thinking – can be combined into one coherent model in which the development of creativity is the main benefit and the primary catalyst. However, one condition for keeping these elements together is awareness of the ultimate goal (development of creativity) and perseverance in overcoming current problems. However, these issues are the natural environment for self-management.

Based on the analyses, a model of individual creativity development was created. In order to answer the fundamental question of what makes a person engage in creative activity, it was necessary to refer to the achievements of aesthetics, which developed the concept of "creative personality", which is a set of basic personality traits conditioning the start of creative activity, its continuation and shaping the final result (more on this topic in Section 2.2.1, "Creator"). Referring to the model, the creative personality must recognise at least two simple identities and start working on a complex identity in the form of identification. Different identities, work on the identification process, and the need to solve a creative problem create tensions between the opposite features and goals of simple identities. At this point, the individual should focus on the streams of emerging problems in an orderly and understandable (for him) way to avoid the destructive internal consequences of these tensions. To maintain and manage identity tensions, a process of paradoxical thinking needs to be triggered. Identity tensions should not be reduced, as they are the primary catalyst for creativity; the individual should learn to live with tensions and use them creatively (just as a musician does not struggle with the opposite goals of muscle flexibility and total concentration during a performance). To close the circle, creative activities can be said to develop by teaching the individual to understand their creative personality. With each cycle of the model, the individual's identity is more worked out and coherent, thanks to which the individual develops his creativity (Figure 4.1).

Identity of artists-managers

Research indicates a significant number of common features between the identity of the artist and the manager, which can be considered as a confirmation

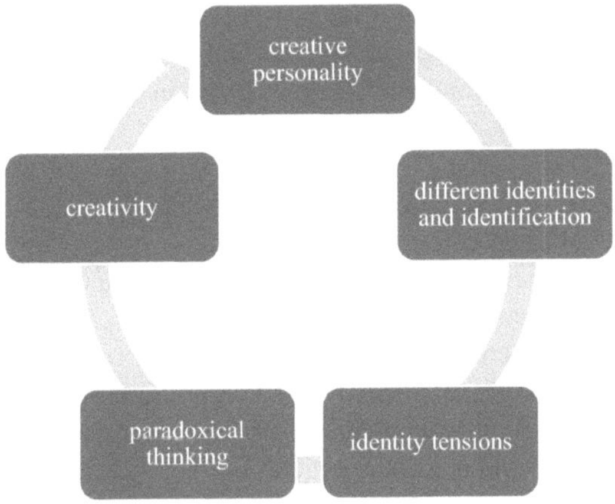

Figure 4.1 Creativity development model

Source: Author's own elaboration based on Szostak and Sułkowski (2021c)

that artists-managers have their own separate identities. The features of artists-managers are: self-discipline, imagination, extensive experience, dedication, perseverance in pursuing goals and multi-faceted activities, project work skills, discipline in achieving goals, ingenuity, commitment, passion, determination, creativity, excellent communication with the recipient, high-skill promotion and presentation (PR), dedication, patience, absolute diligence and total commitment, and consistency.

Although artists-managers experience discrepancies between the two identities, they do not perceive them as opposites or feel the pain of intrapsychic tensions between them. Instead, they use paradoxical thinking; being experts at using seemingly contradictory personal qualities, they achieve outstanding results. Working in paradoxical contexts and focusing on the positive aspects of seemingly contradictory personal characteristics, they find non-standard creative solutions. Understanding and implementing the identity construction of the artist-manager allows for the creative use of tensions and consequences of seemingly contradictory identities or goals at the organisational level.

The aforementioned components should help reduce the pain of inner psychic tensions and influence paradoxical thinking as a critical step towards developing creativity. Understanding and dealing with tensions and paradoxes in organisations can also improve group creativity and reduce negative consequences for individuals. It should be recognised that the artist's identity should be able to consciously control the process of a natural drift towards effective management, not to lose universal values; in turn, the manager's identity can perfectly support uninhibited creativity through effective management. In this context, the identity of the artist-manager should be a desirable resource of contemporary organisations because it opens up several possibilities for its use and further development in many contexts, e.g., creative industry.

The novelty of the conducted research is in the following *practical implications*:

1. the stereotypical perception of the identity of the artist and the manager as highly different has no empirical confirmation;
2. there is a synergy between the identities of the artist and the manager;
3. understanding the nature and attributes of artistic creativity, aesthetic theories, and the phenomenon of artist-manager identity can be a valuable contribution to the practice of management and organisational life;
4. artistic identity does not negatively affect the performance of the manager's tasks – it should be considered an additional benefit, not a conflicting competence; it is a question of the level of role internalisation – if one or both roles are not deeply internalised, the individual will experience tensions that interfere with role performance.

While struggling to identify artists-managers, the following challenges were found:

1. varying degrees of self-knowledge – even if a person is a great professional in one or both fields, it does not mean that they can describe their identity; self-knowledge is another skill that needs to be developed to enable the artist-manager (and not only the artist-manager) to talk about his complex identity;
2. reluctance to share personal states – especially when it comes to aspects that show the individual in a negative light;
3. denial and modelling mechanisms – individuals use these psychologically defined mechanisms to change the way they perceive their identity;
4. social validation mechanism – used by individuals to confirm their identity with recipients; if the research concerns sensitive elements of personality, it should be taken into account that this mechanism will influence the responses;
5. the respondent's trust in the researcher (or lack of it) – telling the naked truth about deeply hidden personal characteristics and motives is not an easy task;
6. inability to use quantitative research – since being an artist-manager is not a common phenomenon, research can be conducted primarily with the use of qualitative methodology; it is also a fact that artists-managers are more personalities than just "ordinary" people, and it is challenging to make averages here;
7. a different combination of simple creative personalities in a complex creative identity (in the scale of an artist and a manager) – different strengths of the identity of the artist and the identity of the manager imply different identities of the artist-manager: more artist and less manager, etc.;

8. the identity of the artist-manager should not be imitated by individuals seeking such an identity, because each artist-manager is different; at most, one should read the description of such a phenomenon and undertake work on one's complex creative identity.

Studying the intrapsychic characteristics of the respondents while having the researcher's knowledge and experience in the analysed field was crucial to understanding the delicate psychological issues and optics, as individuals transform their answers according to self-perception monitoring (Brown, 1990).

Among the study's *limitations*, it should be noted that there are not many artists-managers among artists and managers, which is why the research area is small. Nevertheless, this group can contribute to the study of creativity. The sample included mainly representatives of the musical arts (82%); representatives of other arts may have different characteristics. All respondents were managers and artists during the study – a more extended period of functioning in one of the roles surveyed may change the outlook and imply different answers. Different self-awareness of identity by the respondents and different levels of knowledge in the identity field certainly determine the ability to express opinions on this subject.

Among the *perspectives*, there is a need for detailed research on the differences between identity and self-perception by artists-managers; the results can significantly contribute to the model of individual creativity development presented earlier. Quantitative studies of the perceptions of artists, managers, and artists-managers may also reveal new horizons in understanding the differences between the perception of artists-managers by different social groups and the identity of artists-managers; a larger sample could show the distribution of responses defined in this study. Finally, another perspective may be quantitative research in perceiving artists and managers by people of different cultures, nationalities, and age groups – they could show potential areas of identity crises in defined groups.

Identity of artists-entrepreneurs

To summarise the interviews and autoethnographic analysis, a matrix was created that combines three vital creative competencies of the artist-entrepreneur: artistry, creativity, and entrepreneurship (Figure 4.2). On this basis, four types of complex identities of artists-entrepreneurs have been described, characterised by the following set of competencies:

1. artistry and creativity, but without entrepreneurship – this arrangement characterises a creative art creator who does not show interest in undertaking entrepreneurial activity; it focuses on creative artistic activity, considering

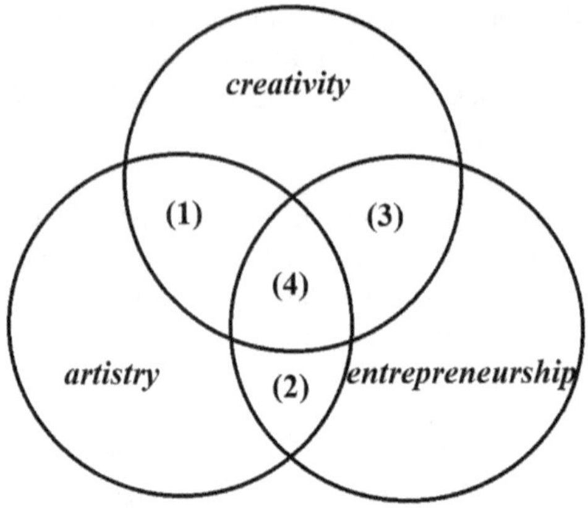

Figure 4.2 A matrix of components of the artist-entrepreneur's complex creative identity

Source: Author's own elaboration based on Szostak and Sułkowski (2021b)

the need to undertake entrepreneurial activity as uninteresting, derogatory, or difficult; this arrangement may also occur when the entity has reserves of funds or their inflow from external sources;

2. artistry and entrepreneurship, but without creativity – this arrangement characterises an individual operating in the optics of monetising his art; works of art do not have the features of creativity, but they retain an appropriate level of artistry to qualify them as artistic activity; when artistry gives way to virtuosity, one can speak of an enterprising craftsman of art;
3. creativity and entrepreneurship, but without artistry – this arrangement characterises an individual who can develop and monetise his area of activity in the field of creativity, however, losing the immanent feature of art, i.e., artistry (the world of values); this arrangement is characteristic of a kitsch producer;
4. artistry, creativity, and entrepreneurship – this system characterises an individual who does not lose artistry in his creative activity, is creative, and at the same time monetises his results.

The analysis of the results indicates that an external crisis (such as the COVID-19 pandemic) swings the pendulum between the critical competencies of simple creative identities towards the entrepreneurial identity with the fundamental role of the creativity factor, and the need to maintain artistry to maintain the appropriate level of works of art without slipping towards depreciation (that is, into the embrace of kitsch). There is a high probability that when the influence of the external factor subsides, the pendulum moving between simple identities will return to its natural, neutral position.

Using aesthetic theories of artistic creation, it can be said that artists-entrepreneurs may experience an identity crisis for external reasons (like the COVID-19 pandemic) because they lose the social context and sense of the natural order of things. Artists-entrepreneurs (1) use the sociological theory of creativity (consisting in meeting the needs of social groups), (2) apply the cultural approach (being a function of the state of culture with different artistic ideals at a given level of development), and (3) create works of art according to the order of nature. In contrast, artists-entrepreneurs who use other theories of creativity (inner inspiration, discovering timeless ideas, imitating divine creativity, inner need, ideology), or using a psychological approach, are more resistant to external crises and their impact on a complex creative identity.

The COVID-19 pandemic strongly impacted the identity of artists, and the analysis of the internal situation of creative individuals fulfils most of the characteristics of an identity crisis. Artists with an entrepreneurial identity cope with the crisis better than those without an entrepreneurial identity. The term "better" means they can search and find solutions without feeling deep inner pain because their second identity gives an additional opportunity in the change process. Creative artists-entrepreneurs are looking for new forms of activity in times of crisis. The study confirms that combining and self-managing different creative identities is helpful in situations of change and uncertainty.

Among the limitations of the study, it should be emphasised that: (1) the study was conducted in the initial phase of the COVID-19 pandemic, when the development of the crisis and any prospect of its completion was unknown; (2) in the event of an external crisis, art and other more culturally advanced areas of human life lose their importance for the majority of recipients who focus on meeting basic needs, which could have influenced the answers given by the respondents; and (3) the respondents were not distinguished due to their personal characteristics (age, sex, education) because the qualitative nature of the study made it impossible to draw more detailed conclusions.

The test results can be used by:

1. people (entrepreneurs, managers, artists) with complex identities to better understand the crisis, its impact, and opportunities coming from different layers of human personality, emphasising the competence of creativity;
2. business and marketers in the search for new types of customers and understanding market participants with more complex identities and needs;
3. scientists who want to research the following issues:

    a. perception of complex identities (e.g., artists-entrepreneurs),
    b. features distinguishing artistry, creativity, and entrepreneurship among individuals with a complex creative identity,

c. the impact of personal characteristics of artists-entrepreneurs on their own identities (there is a high probability that personal characteristics and not external factors are the dominant determinants in artistry, creativity, and entrepreneurship).

Potential hypotheses for further research in this regard may be as follows: (1) the majority of society does not recognise the difference between creativity and artistry; (2) a shift towards remote methods of participation in art and artistic communication should be expected (even if it is a qualitatively inferior way of participating in classical arts, it still allows for an easier, faster and safer way to maintain bonds between creators and audiences); (3) a turn towards a marketing approach in an aesthetic situation should be expected – in order to feel needed, and thus generate the creators' means of subsistence, art will be more willing to meet the needs of the recipients, instead of being a tool of mission and education (a turn towards kitsch); or even on the contrary (4) as a result of solid experiences in connection with crises (e.g., a pandemic).

4.4 Summary

The role of identity in creative activities is crucial. Compliance between the social role and identity allows for achieving the assumed goals effectively – without losing resources for activities that do not consider the characteristics of specific identities. As it has been shown, in addition to simple creative identities, there are also complex creative identities. Like any identity, a complex creative identity also arises through the process of "becoming" and is not given as a resource ("being"). Identity – especially creative identity – is dynamic. This dynamism implies internal friction, which can burden the individual if not optimally managed. In order to avoid the clash of identities, creative individuals use the phenomenon of paradoxical thinking, which allows for combining seemingly irreconcilable phenomena.

From the management point of view, the presented model of individual creativity development is crucial in two dimensions. First, as a self-managing unit, the manager can consciously direct the development of his creativity. Secondly, the manager can consciously direct the development of creativity of the organisation he manages. He must bear in mind that creative teams are not the sum of their components, and a team with more creative units will not always be more creative than a team with fewer creative units. In managing such teams, the manager must demonstrate both virtuosity (knowledge about psychology, motivation, and organisation) and artistry (how to use the possessed virtuosity to influence the team in the intended way).

Due to its vital importance – both in the managerial and organisational dimensions – the phenomenon of creativity is the subject of detailed analysis in the next chapter.

Notes

1 More on the phenomenon of creativity is in Chapter 5.
2 The characteristics of the study participants are presented in Table 0.3.
3 The codes refer to individual respondents, and their detailed characteristics are presented in Table 0.3.

References

Adler, N. J. (2011). Leading beautifully: The creative economy and beyond. *Journal of Management Inquiry*, *20*(3), 208–221. https://doi.org/10.1177/1056492602111007

Adler, N. J. (2015a). Finding beauty in a fractured world: Art inspires leaders-leaders change the world. *Academy of Management Review*, *40*(3), 480–494. https://doi.org/10.5465/amr.2015.0044

Adler, N. J. (2015b). The artistry of global leadership: Going beyond the dehydrated strategies of management, economics, and politics. *Journal of Leadership Studies*, *9*(1), 4 8–51. https://doi.org/10.1002/jls

Ahuja, S., Nikolova, N., & Clegg, S. (2017). Paradoxical identity: The changing nature of architectural work and its relation to architects' identity. *Journal of Professions and Organization*, *4*(3), 2–19. https://doi.org/10.1093/jpo/jow013

Akpan, I. J., Soopramanien, D., & Kwak, D. H. (2020). Cutting-edge technologies for small business and innovation in the era of COVID-19 global health pandemic. *Journal of Small Business and Entrepreneurship*, *0*(0), 1–11. https://doi.org/10.1080/08276331.2020.1799294

Albinsson, S. (2018). Musicians as entrepreneurs or entrepreneurs as musicians? *Creativity and Innovation Management*, *27*(3), 348–357. https://doi.org/10.1111/caim.12254

Almeida, F., de Paula, N., & Pessali, H. (2014). Institutional entrepreneurship in building the Brazilian market of functional yogurts. *British Food Journal*, *116*(1), 2–15. https://doi.org/10.1108/BFJ-02-2012-0028

Alvesson, M., & Willmott, H. (2002). Identity regulation as organizational control: Producing the appropriate individual. *Journal of Management Studies*, *39*(5), 619–644. https://doi.org/10.1111/1467-6486.00305

Andersson, M., Braunerhjelm, P., & Thulin, P. (2011). Creative destruction and productivity: Entrepreneurship by type, sector and sequence. *Journal of Entrepreneurship and Public Policy*, *1*(2), 125–146. https://doi.org/10.1108/20452101211261417

Antal, A. B., Debucquet, G., & Fremeaux, S. (2016). Addressing identity tensions through paradoxical thinking: Lessons from artistic interventions in organizations. *Management International*, *21*(1), 25–40. https://doi.org/10.7202/1052495ar

Arriagada, A., & Ibáñez, F. (2020). "You need at least one picture daily, if not, you're dead": Content creators and platform evolution in the social media ecology. *Social Media and Society*, *6*(3), 1–12. https://doi.org/10.1177/2056305120944624

Baker, S., Marshburn, D. M., Crickmore, K. D., Rose, S. B., Dutton, K., & Hudson, P. C. (2012). What do you do? Perception of nurse manager responsibilities. *Nursing Management*, *43*(12), 24–29. https://doi.org/10.1097/01.NUMA.0000422890.99334.21

Bennett, D., & Hennekam, S. (2018). Self-authorship and creative industries workers' career decision-making. *Human Relations*, *71*(11), 1454–1477. https://doi.org/10.1177/0018726717747369

Bhattacharya, J., & Petsche, H. (2002). Shadows of artistry: Cortical synchrony during perception and imagery of visual art. *Cognitive Brain Research*, *13*(2), 179–186. https://doi.org/10.1016/S0926-6410(01)00110-0

Bilan, Y., Mishchuk, H., Roshchyk, I., & Joshi, O. (2020). Hiring and retaining skilled employees in smes: Problems in human resource practices and links with organizational success. *Business: Theory and Practice*, *21*(2), 780–791. https://doi.org/10.3846/btp.2020.12750

Borowiecki, K. J., & Dahl, C. M. (2021). What makes an artist? The evolution and clustering of creative activity in the US since 1850. *Regional Science and Urban Economics*, *86*, 1–23. https://doi.org/10.1016/j.regsciurbeco.2020.103614

Brewer, M. B., & Gardner, W. (1996). Who is this "we"? Levels of collective identity and self representations. *Journal of Personality and Social Psychology*, *71*(1), 83–93. https://doi.org/10.1037/0022-3514.71.1.83

Brown, J. D. (1990). Evaluating one's abilities: Shortcuts and stumbling blocks on the road to self-knowledge. *Journal of Experimental Social Psychology*, *26*(2), 149–167. https://doi.org/10.1016/0022-1031(90)90073-U

Bulei, I., Mihalcioiu, V., & Tucmeanu, A. (2014). The professional vs. the manager – identity issues and key features. *Valahian Journal of Economic Studies*, *5*(3), 31–36.

Bureau, S., & Zander, I. (2014). Entrepreneurship as an art of subversion. *Scandinavian Journal of Management*, *30*(1), 124–133. https://doi.org/10.1016/j.scaman.2013.12.002

Cardon, M. S., Wincent, J., Singh, J., & Drnovsek, M. (2009). The nature and experience of entrepreneurial passion. *Academy of Management Review*, *34*(3), 511–532. https://doi.org/10.5465/AMR.2009.40633190

Carroll, B., & Levy, L. (2008). Defaulting to management: Leadership defined by what it is not. *Organization*, *15*(1), 75–96. https://doi.org/10.1177/1350508407084486

Charteris, J., Smardon, D., & Nelson, E. (2016). Innovative learning environments and discourses of leadership: Is physical change out of step with pedagogical development? *Journal of Educational Leadership, Policy and Practice*, *31*(1/2), 33–47. http://search.ebscohost.com/login.aspx?direct=true%7B&%7Ddb=a9h%7B&%7DAN=121772163%7B&%7Dsite=ehost-live

Chaudhary, A. R. (2015). Racialized incorporation: The effects of race and generational status on self-employment and industry-sector prestige in the United States. *International Migration Review*, *49*(2), 318–354. https://doi.org/10.1111/imre.12087

Chen, L. (2018). Thinking paradoxically: How and when female narcissistic leaders integrate gender–leader identities. *Social Behavior and Personality*, *46*(2), 339–352. https://doi.org/10.2224/sbp.6910

Clarke, J. S., & Holt, R. (2019, June). Images of entrepreneurship: Using drawing to explore entrepreneurial experience. *Journal of Business Venturing Insights*, *11*, 2019–2021. https://doi.org/10.1016/j.jbvi.2019.e00129

Coppola, A., Ianuario, S., Chinnici, G., Di Vita, G., & Pappalardo, G. (2018). Endogenous and exogenous determinants of agricultural productivity: What is the most relevant for the competitivenessof the Italian agricultural systems? *Agris On-Line Papers in Economics and Informatics*, *10*(2), 33–47. https://doi.org/10.7160/aol.2018.100204.Introduction

Cuganesan, S. (2017). Identity paradoxes: How senior managers and employees negotiate similarity and distinctiveness tensions over time. *Organization Studies*, *38*(3–4), 489–511. https://doi.org/10.1177/0170840616655482

Dahlsen, J. (2015). An environmental artist and PhD candidate's observations of globalism's post GFC aftermath: Is there economic viability, for marginalised artists creating the culture of environmental sustainability? *Developmental Observer*, *8*(1), 97–131. https://doi.org/10.14434/do.v8i1.27785

Davenport, T. H., & Redman, T. C. (2020). Digital transformation comes down to talent in 4 key areas. *Harvard Business Review*, 2–6. https://hbr.org/2020/05/digital-transformation-comes-down-to-talent-in-4-key-areas

David, O., & Bar-Tal, D. (2009). A sociopsychological conception of collective identity: The case of national identity as an example. *Personality and Social Psychology Review*, *13*(4), 354–379. https://doi.org/10.1177/1088868309344412

De Luca, R., & Botelho, D. (2021). The unconscious perception of smells as a driver of consumer responses: A framework integrating the emotion-cognition approach to scent marketing. *AMS Review*, *11*(1–2), 145–161. https://doi.org/10.1007/s13162-019-00154-8

de Mateo Pérez, R. (2015). Cultural and communication industries: Myth and logic of the terms creativity and entrepreneurial innovation. *Revista Latina de Comunicacion Social*, *70*, 813–832. https://doi.org/10.4185/RLCS-2015-1073

DeFillippi, R., Grabher, G., & Jones, C. (2007). Introduction to paradoxes of creativity: Managerial and organizational challenges in the cultural economy. *Journal of Organizational Behavior*, *28*, 511–521. https://doi.org/10.1002/job

Degot, V. (2007). Portrait of the manager as an artist. *Aesthesis: International Journal of Art and Aesthetics in Management and Organizational Life*, *1*(3), 6–42.

Dong, X., Liu, Y., Wu, C., Lian, Y., & Tang, D. (2019). A double-identity rumor spreading model. *Physica A: Statistical Mechanics and Its Applications*, *528*. https://doi.org/10.1016/j.physa.2019.121479

Dufour, L., Maoret, M., & Montani, F. (2020). Coupling high self-perceived creativity and successful newcomer adjustment in organizations: The role of supervisor trust and support for authentic self-expression. *Journal of Management Studies*, *57*(8), 1531–1555. https://doi.org/10.1111/joms.12547

Elstad, B., & Jansson, D. (2020). From artist to manager – working conditions, career satisfaction, and professional identity among graduated arts management students. *Journal of Arts Management Law and Society*, *50*(3), 184–198. https://doi.org/10.1080/10632921.2020.1746717

Erat, S., Kitapçi, H., & Akçin, K. (2020). Managerial perception and organizational identity: A comparative analysis. *Sustainability*, *12*(6), 1–16. https://doi.org/10.3390/su12062278

Ete, Z., Sosik, J. J., Cheong, M., Chun, J. U., Zhu, W., Arenas, F. J., & Scherer, J. A. (2020). Leader honesty/humility and subordinate organizational citizenship behavior: A case of too-much-of-a-good-thing? *Journal of Managerial Psychology*, *35*(5), 391–404. https://doi.org/10.1108/JMP-10-2019-0557

Farmer, S. M., Tierney, P., & Kung-Mcintyre, K. (2003). Employee creativity in Taiwan: An application of role identity theory. *Academy of Management Journal*, *46*(5), 618–630. https://doi.org/10.2307/30040653

Fauchart, E., & Gruber, M. (2011). Darwinians, communitarians, and missionaries: The role of founder identity in entrepreneurship. *Academy of Management Journal*, *54*(5), 935–957. https://doi.org/10.5465/amj.2009.0211

Ferguson, B. (2015). Professional creators unveiled: Screenwriters' experiences collaborating in motion picture development teams. *Dissertation Abstracts International: Section B: The Sciences and Engineering*, *75*(7-B (E)). http://search.ebscohost.com/login.aspx?direct=true&db=psyh&AN=2015-99020-484&login.asp&site=ehost-live&scope=site

Ferriani, S., Cattani, G., & Baden-Fuller, C. (2009). The relational antecedents of project-entrepreneurship: Network centrality, team composition and project performance. *Research Policy*, *38*(10), 1545–1558. https://doi.org/10.1016/j.respol.2009.09.001

Fillis, I., & Rentschler, R. (2010). The role of creativity in entrepreneurship. *Journal of Enterprising Culture*, *18*(1), 49–81. https://doi.org/10.1142/s0218495810000501

Fletcher, J., & Olwyler, K. (1997). How to profit from your reputation. *Forbes*, 1–3. www.forbes.com/sites/michakaufman/2012/12/12/how-to-profit-from-your-reputation/

Gaddefors, J., & Anderson, A. R. (2017). Entrepreneursheep and context: When entrepreneurship is greater than entrepreneurs. *International Journal of Entrepreneurial Behavior & Research*, *23*(2), 267–278. https://doi.org/10.1108/IJEBR-01-2016-0040

Gangi, J. (2018). Classical guitar study as creativity training: Potential benefits for managers and entrepreneurs. *Journal of Open Innovation: Technology, Market, and Complexity*, *4*(45), 1–10. https://doi.org/10.3390/joitmc4040045

Gerpott, F. H., Van Quaquebeke, N., Schlamp, S., & Voelpel, S. C. (2019). An identity perspective on ethical leadership to explain organizational citizenship behavior: The interplay of follower moral identity and leader group prototypicality. *Journal of Business Ethics*, *156*(4), 1063–1078. https://doi.org/10.1007/s10551-017-3625-0

Giacomin, O., Guyot, J.-L., Janssen, F., & Lohest, O. (2007). Novice creators: Personal identity and push pull dynamics. *CRECIS Working Paper*, *10*(2007), 1–30.

Gołaszewska, M. (1984). *Zarys estetyki*. PWN.

Gołaszewska, M. (1986). *Kim jest artysta?* Wydawnictwa Szkolne i Pedagogiczne.

Gotsi, M., Andriopoulos, C., Lewis, M. W., & Ingram, A. E. (2010). Managing creatives: Paradoxical approaches to identity regulation. *Human Relations*, *63*(6), 781–805. https://doi.org/10.1177/0018726709342929

Gray, D. E., Gabriel, Y., & Goregaokar, H. (2015). Coaching unemployed managers and professionals through the trauma of unemployment: Derailed or undaunted? *Management Learning*, *46*(3), 299–316. https://doi.org/10.1177/1350507614532752

Grigoryan, L. K., & Kotova, M. V. (2018). National identity management strategies: Do they help or hinder adoption of multiculturalism in Russia? *Psychology in Russia: State of the Art*, *11*(3), 18–35. https://doi.org/10.11621/pir.2018.0302

Grybś-Kabocik, M. (2018). The scent marketing: Consumers perception. *The Business and Management Review*, *9*(4), 9–10.

Guillén, L., Mayo, M., & Korotov, K. (2015). Is leadership a part of me? A leader identity approach to understanding the motivation to lead. *Leadership Quarterly*, *26*(5), 802–820. https://doi.org/10.1016/j.leaqua.2015.05.001

Hallier, J. (2004). Embellishing the past: Middle manager identity and informality in the implementaion of new technology. *New Technology, Work and Employment*, *19*(1), 4 3–62. https://doi.org/10.1111/j.1468-005X.2004.00127.x

Harles, M., & Rajbhandari, S. (2017). Contemporary artists' response to heritage in times of crisis: 12 Baishakh and Photo Kathmandu. *Material Religion*, *13*(3), 387–390. https://doi.org/10.1080/17432200.2017.1335058

Hay, A. (2014). "I don't know what I am doing!": Surfacing struggles of managerial identity work. *Management Learning*, *45*(5), 509–524. https://doi.org/10.1177/1350507613483421

He, K., & Feng, H. (2015). Transcending rationalism and constructivism: Chinese leaders' operational codes, socialization processes, and multilateralism after the Cold War. *European Political Science Review*, *7*(3), 401–426. https://doi.org/10.1017/S1755773914000241

Hennekam, S., & Bennett, D. (2016). Self-management of work in the creative industries in the Netherlands. *International Journal of Arts Management*, *19*(1), 31–41.

Honig, B., & Samuelsson, M. (2021). Business planning by intrapreneurs and entrepreneurs under environmental uncertainty and institutional pressure. *Technovation*, *99*, 10 2124. https://doi.org/10.1016/j.technovation.2020.102124

Horn, D., & Salvendy, G. (2009). Measuring consumer perception of product creativity: Impact on satisfaction and purchasability. *Human Factors and Ergonomics in Manufacturing*, *19*(3), 223–240. https://doi.org/10.1002/hfm.20150

Hospers, G. J., & Van Dalm, R. (2005). How to create a creative city? The viewpoints of Richard Florida and Jane Jacobs. *Foresight*, *7*(4), 8–12. https://doi.org/10.1108/14636680510611796

Hracs, B. J. (2015). Cultural intermediaries in the digital age: The case of independent musicians and managers in Toronto. *Regional Studies*, *49*(3), 461–475. https://doi.org/10.1080/00343404.2012.750425

Jankurová, A., Ljudvigová, I., & Gubová, K. (2017). Research of the nature of leadership activities. *Economics and Sociology*, *10*(1), 135–151. https://doi.org/10.14254/2071-789X.2017/10-1/10

Jones, C., & Massa, F. G. (2013). From novel practice to consecrated exemplar: Unity temple as a case of institutional evangelizing. *Organization Studies*, *34*(8), 1099–1136. https://doi.org/10.1177/0170840613492073

Kačerauskas, T. (2018). Indices of creative economy: Critique of R. Florida's creativity indices. *Economics and Sociology*, *11*(4), 280–288. https://doi.org/10.14254/2071-789X.2018/11-4/18

Kasmaienezhadfard, S., Talebloo, B., Roustae, R., & Pourrajab, M. (2015). Students' learning through teaching creativity: Teachers' perception. *Journal of Educational, Health and Community Psychology*, *4*(1), 1–13. https://doi.org/10.12928/jehcp.v4i1.3699

Khazraee, E., & Novak, A. N. (2018). Digitally mediated protest: Social media affordances for collective identity construction. *Social Media and Society*, *4*(1), 1–14. https://doi.org/10.1177/2056305118765740

Kim, P. H., Longest, K. C., & Lippmann, S. (2015). The tortoise versus the hare: Progress and business viability differences between conventional and leisure-based founders. *Journal of Business Venturing*, *30*(2), 185–204. https://doi.org/10.1016/j.jbusvent.2014.02.005

Kiran, N., Afzal, M., Hussain, M., & Gilani, S. A. (2019). Initials impact of nursing manager perception of empowerment and years of experience on resistance to change in practice. *Journal of Health, Medicine and Nursing*, *62*, 8 2–89. https://doi.org/10.7176/jhmn/62-11

Knight, E., & Paroutis, S. (2017). Becoming salient: The TMT leader's role in shaping the interpretive context of paradoxical tensions. *Organization Studies*, *38*(3–4), 403–432. https://doi.org/10.1177/0170840616640844

Kohail, Y., Saida, Y., Obad, J., & Soulhi, A. (2016). The qualities of a good manager . . . what does it means? Lessons learned from the undergraduate business students' perception in kingdom of Morocco. *International Journal of Business and Management, 11*(8), 86–96. https://doi.org/10.5539/ijbm.v11n8p86

Korzeb, Z., & Niedziółka, P. (2020). Resistance of commercial banks to the crisis caused by the COVID-19 pandemic: The case of Poland. *Equilibrium, 15*(2), 205–234. https://doi.org/10.24136/eq.2020.010

Krzemińska, A. (2022). Zapach przeszłości. *Polityka, 34*(3377), 61–63.

Kuc-Czarnecka, M. (2020). COVID-19 and digital deprivation in Poland. *Oeconomia Copernicana, 11*(3), 415–431. https://doi.org/10.24136/OC.2020.017

Kufel, T. (2020). ARIMA-based forecasting of the dynamics of confirmed Covid-19 cases for selected European countries. *Equilibrium. Quarterly Journal of Economics and Economic Policy, 15*(2), 181–204. https://doi.org/10.24136/eq.2020.009

Kunrath, K., Cash, P., & Kleinsmann, M. (2020). Social- and self-perception of designers' professional identity. *Journal of Engineering Design, 31*(2), 100–126. https://doi.org/10.1080/09544828.2019.1676883

Leone, D., & Schiavone, F. (2019). Innovation and knowledge sharing in crowdfunding: How social dynamics affect project success. *Technology Analysis and Strategic Management, 31*(7), 803–816. https://doi.org/10.1080/09537325.2018.1554858

Lewis, K. V., Ho, M., Harris, C., & Morrison, R. (2016). Becoming an entrepreneur: Opportunities and identity transitions. *International Journal of Gender and Entrepreneurship, 8*(2), 1–6. https://doi.org/10.1108/IJGE-02-2015-0006

Liu, Y., Gayle, A. A., Wilder-Smith, A., & Rocklöv, J. (2020). The reproductive number of COVID-19 is higher compared to SARS coronavirus. *Journal of Travel Medicine, 27*(2), 1–4. https://doi.org/10.1093/jtm/taaa021

Lord, R. G., & Brown, D. J. (2001). Leadership, values, and subordinate self-concepts. *The Leadership Quarterly, 12*, 133–152.

Lorenzo-Romero, C., & Constantinides, E. (2019). On-line crowdsourcing: Motives of customers to participate in online collaborative innovation processes. *Sustainability, 11*(12), 3479. https://doi.org/10.3390/su11123479

Luger, J. D. (2017). But I'm just an artist!? Intersections, identity, meaning, and context. *Antipode, 49*(5), 1329–1348. https://doi.org/10.1111/anti.12327

Lutas, M., Nistor, R., Radu, M., & Beleiu, I. (2020). Perceptions regarding the profile of an ideal project manager. *Amfiteatru Economic, 22*(54), 608–622. https://doi.org/10.24818/EA/2020/54/608

Marona, B., & Tomal, M. (2020). The COVID-19 pandemic impact upon housing brokers' workflow and their clients' attitude: Real estate market in Krakow. *Entrepreneurial Business and Economics Review, 8*(4), 221–232. https://doi.org/10.15678/eber.2020.080412

Martin, R., Florida, R., Pogue, M., & Mellander, C. (2015). Creativity, clusters and the competitive advantage of cities. *Competitiveness Review, 25*(5), 482–496. https://doi.org/10.1108/CR-07-2015-0069

Masso, A. (2010). Geographical perspective on identity construction: Identification strategies of Russian youth in Estonia. *International Journal of Interdisciplinary Social Sciences, 5*(6), 5 1–62. https://doi.org/10.18848/1833-1882/CGP/v05i06/51763

Maynard, A. D. (2021). How to succeed as an academic on YouTube. *Frontiers in Communicatio n, 5*. https://doi.org/10.3389/fcomm.2020.572181

McNeill, L., & Venter, B. (2019). Identity, self-concept and young women's engagement with collaborative, sustainable fashion consumption models. *International Journal of Consumer Studies*, *43*(4), 368–378. https://doi.org/10.1111/ijcs.12516

Mehta, S., & Kaye, D. B. V. (2019). Pushing the next level: Investigating digital content creation in India. *Television and New Media*. https://doi.org/10.1177/1527476419861698

Mietzner, D., & Kamprath, M. (2013). A competence portfolio for professionals in the creative industries. *Creativity and Innovation Management*, *22*(3), 280–294. https://doi.org/10.1111/caim.12026

Miscenko, D., Guenter, H., & Day, D. V. (2017). Am I a leader? Examining leader identity development over time. *Leadership Quarterly*, *28*(5), 605–620. https://doi.org/10.1016/j.leaqua.2017.01.004

Mochalova, N. Y. (2020). Personal identity of the artist as a condition and result of creativity in art. *Ethnic Culture*, *2*(3), 62–67. https://doi.org/10.31483/r-74987

Moghaddam, J. Y., Khorakian, A., & Maharati, Y. (2015). Organizational entrepreneurship and its impact on the performance of governmental organizations in the city of Mashhad. *Procedia – Social and Behavioral Sciences*, *169*, 75–87. https://doi.org/10.1016/j.sbspro.2015.01.288

Morrow, G. (2018a). Artist management: Agility in the creative and cultural industries. In *Artist management: Agility in the creative and cultural industries*. Routledge. https://doi.org/10.4324/9781315520896

Morrow, G. (2018b). Distributed agility: Artist co-management in the music attention economy. *International Journal of Arts Management*, *20*(3), 38–48.

Nagy, J., Jámbor, Z., & Freund, A. (2020). Digitalisation in the food industry – case studies on the effects of IT and technological development on companies. *Agris On-Line Papers in Economics and Informatics*, *12*(4), 77–92. https://doi.org/10.7160/AOL.2020.120406

Netting, F. E., & Williams, F. G. (1996). Case manager-physician collaboration: Implications for professional identity, roles, and relationships. *Health and Social Work*, *21*(3), 216–224. https://doi.org/10.1093/hsw/21.3.216

Nytch, J. (2012) The Case of the Pittsburgh New Music Ensemble : An Illustration of Entrepreneurial Theory in an Artistic Setting. *Artivate*, *1*(1), 25–34. www.jstor.org/stable/10.34053/artivate.1.1.0025

O'Donnell, A. T., Jetten, J., & Ryan, M. K. (2010). Watching over your own: How surveillance moderates the impact of shared identity on perceptions of leaders and follower behaviour. *European Journal of Social Psychology*, *40*(6), 1046–1061. https://doi.org/10.1002/ejsp.701

Ottery, J. R. (2006). Who are they and what do they have to do with what i want to be? "The writing of multicultural identity and college success stories for first-year writers". In *Identity papers: Literacy and power in higher education* (pp. 122–137). Utah State University Press.

Pardal, P., Dias, R., Šuleř, P., Teixeira, N., & Krulický, T. (2020). Integration in Central European capital markets in the context of the global COVID-19 pandemic. *Equilibrium*, *15*(4), 627–650. https://doi.org/10.24136/eq.2020.027

Pascoe, S., Brincat, S., & Croucher, A. (2019). The discourses of climate change science: Scientific reporting, climate negotiations and the case of Papua New Guinea. *Global Environmental Change*, *54*, 78–87. https://doi.org/10.1016/j.gloenvcha.2018.11.010

Patriotta, G., & Siegel, D. (2019). The context of entrepreneurship. *Journal of Management Studies*, *56*(6), 1194–1196. https://doi.org/10.1111/joms.12440

Peterson, D. J., & Berryhill, M. E. (2013). The gestalt principle of similarity benefits visual working memory. *Psychonomic Bulletin and Review*, *20*(6), 1282–1289. https://doi.org/10.3758/s13423-013-0460-x

Petrozolin-Skowrońska, B. (2017). Percepcja. In *Nowa encyklopedia powszechna PWN: Tom 4*. Wydawnictwo Naukowe PWN.

Phelan, A. L., Katz, R., & Gostin, L. O. (2020). The novel coronavirus originating in Wuhan, China: Challenges for global health governance. *JAMA – Journal of the American Medical Association*, *323*(8), 709–710. https://doi.org/10.1001/jama.2020.1097

Pinto, M. R., Viola, S., Onesti, A., & Ciampa, F. (2020). Artists residencies, challenges and opportunities for communities' empowerment and heritage regeneration. *Sustainability (Switzerland)*, *12*(22), 1–20. https://doi.org/10.3390/su12229651

Poorsoltan, K. (2012). Artists as entrepreneurs. *International Journal of Entrepreneurship*, *16*, 77–94. www.researchgate.net/publication/286390088_Artists_as_Entrepreneurs

Rasminsky, A. (2019). When injury leads to an identity crisis. *Dance Magazine*, *93*(7), 32–35. www.dancemagazine.com/injury-depression-2638932468.html

Raso, R., Fitzpatrick, J. J., & Masick, K. (2020). Clinical nurses' perceptions of authentic nurse leadership and healthy work environment. *Journal of Nursing Administration*, *50*(9), 489–494. https://doi.org/10.1097/NNA.0000000000000921

Ratten, V. (2020a). Coronavirus (Covid-19) and entrepreneurship: Changing life and work landscape. *Journal of Small Business and Entrepreneurship*, *32*(5), 1–14. https://doi.org/10.1080/08276331.2020.1790167

Ratten, V. (2020b). Coronavirus disease (Covid-19) and sport entrepreneurship. *International Journal of Entrepreneurial Behaviour and Research*, *26*(6), 1379–1388. https://doi.org/10.1108/IJEBR-06-2020-0387

Reedy, P. (2008). Mirror, mirror, on the wall: Reflecting on the ethics and effects of a collective critical management studies identity project. *Management Learning*, *39*(1), 57–72. https://doi.org/10.1177/1350507607085978

Reysen, S., Katzarska-Miller, I., Plante, C. N., Roberts, S. E., Gerbasi, K. C., Brooks, T. R., & Tague, A. M. (2020). Anime and global citizenship identification. *The Phoenix Papers*, *4*(2), 48–61. https://doi.org/10.17605/OSF.IO/JXPTQ

Rikou, E., & Chaviara, I. (2016). "Crisis" as art: Young artists envisage mutating Greece. *Visual Anthropology Review*, *32*(1), 47–60. https://doi.org/10.1111/var.12092

Roberts, J. S. (2012). Infusing entrepreneurship within non-business disciplines: Preparing artists and others for self-employment and entrepreneurship. *Artivate: A Journal of Entrepreneurship in the Arts*, *1*(2), 53–63. www.jstor.org/stable/10.34053/artivate.1.2.0053

Saavedra Llamas, M., & Grijalba de la Calle, N. (2020). The creative cinematographic process at the service of national identity: Pedro Almodóvar and the promotion of Spanish stereotypes. *Creativity Studies*, *13*(2), 369–386. https://doi.org/10.3846/cs.2020.8563

Saeidi, S. P., Othman, M. S. H., Štreimikienė, D., Saeidi, S. P., Mardani, A., & Stasiulis, N. (2018). The utilitarian aspect of the philosophy of ecology: The case of corporate social responsibility. *Filosofija, Sociologija*, *29*(1), 39–51. https://doi.org/10.6001/fil-soc.v29i1.3630

Sánchez-Escalonilla García-Rico, A. (2019). La crisis del sueño europeo: Hogar y éxodo en el nuevo cine sobre migrantes y refugiados (2005–2018). *Revista de Comunicación*, *18*(1), 277–297. https://doi.org/10.26441/rc18.1-2019-a14

Schediwy, L., Bhansing, P. V., & Loots, E. (2018). Young musicians' career identities: do bohemian and entrepreneurial career identities compete or cohere? *Creative Industries Journal, 11*(2), 174–196. https://doi.org/10.1080/17510694.2018.1489197

Schein, E. H. (2001). The role of art and the artist. *Reflections: The SoL Journal, 2*(4), 8 1–83. https://doi.org/10.1162/152417301750385495

Schielke, T. (2020). Interpreting art with light: Museum lighting between objectivity and hyperrealism. *LEUKOS – Journal of Illuminating Engineering Society of North America, 16*(1), 7–24. https://doi.org/10.1080/15502724.2018.1530123

Sethi, A., Mishra, N., & Dash, M. (2012). Social identity crisis amongst employees in mergers & acquisitions. *SSRN Electronic Journal*, 244–263. https://doi.org/10.2139/ssrn.1588565

Solesvik, M. (2019). Entrepreneurial competencies and intentions: The influence of enterprise education. *ICERI2019 Proceedings, 1*, 11321–11321. https://doi.org/10.21125/iceri.2019.2810

Steffens, N. K., Haslam, S. A., Peters, K., & Quiggin, J. (2020). Identity economics meets identity leadership: Exploring the consequences of elevated CEO pay. *Leadership Quarterly, 31*(3). https://doi.org/10.1016/j.leaqua.2018.10.001

Steffens, N. K., Wolyniec, N., Okimoto, T. G., Mols, F., Haslam, S. A., & Kay, A. A. (2021). Knowing me, knowing us: Personal and collective self-awareness enhances authentic leadership and leader endorsement. *Leadership Quart erly*. https://doi.org/10.1016/j.leaqua.2021.101498

Sułkowski, Ł. (2020). Covid-19 pandemic; recession, virtual revolution leading to deglobalization? *Journal of Intercultural Management, 12*(1), 1–11. https://doi.org/10.2478/joim-2020-0029

Sutherland, I. (2013). Arts-based methods in leadership development: Affording aesthetic workspaces, reflexivity and memories with momentum. *Management Learning, 44*(1), 25–43. https://doi.org/10.1177/1350507612465063

Sveningsson, S., & Alvesson, M. (2003). Managing managerial identities: Organizational fragmentation, discourse and identity struggle. *Human Relations, 56*(10), 1163–1193. https://doi.org/10.1177/00187267035610001

Szostak, M. (2019). The art of stylish organ improvisation. *The Organ, 390*, 20–27. https://depot.ceon.pl/handle/123456789/17687

Szostak, M. (2020a). Creativity and artistry in organ music. *The Organ, 391*, 24 31. https://depot.ceon.pl/handle/123456789/19170

Szostak, M. (2020b). Does creativity influence the perception of creative identities? *European Research Studies Journal, 23*(4), 312–333. https://doi.org/10.35808/ersj/2444

Szostak, M. (2021a). Does entrepreneurial factor influence creative identities perception? *Entrepreneurship and Sustainability Issues, 9*(1), 150–175. https://doi.org/10.9770/jesi.2021.9.1(9)

Szostak, M. (2021c). Impact of gender differences in perception of creative identities of artist, creator, manager, entrepreneur and leader on sustainability. *Entrepreneurship and Sustainability Issues, 9*(2), 1 0–36. https://doi.org/10.9770/jesi.2021.9.2(1)

Szostak, M. (2021d). Perception of creative identities by leaders and non-leaders: Consequences for theory and practice of management. *European Research Studies Journal, XXIV*(4), 211–232.

Szostak, M. (2021e). Post-communist burden influence on the perception of creative identities: Consequences for managers and leaders. *European Research Studies Journal, 24*(3), 282–302. https://doi.org/10.35808/ersj/2354

Szostak, M. (2022). Perception of creative identities by managers and non-managers: Does a manager see more? *Entrepreneurship and Sustainability Issues*, *9*(3), 2 4–49. https://doi.org/10.9770/jesi.2022.9.3(2)

Szostak, M. (2023). Perception of creative identities by artistic and non-artistic individuals: Consequences for management. *Creativity Studies*, *16*(1), 1–25. https://doi.org/10.3846/cs.2023.15081

Szostak, M., & Sułkowski, Ł. (2020a). Manager as an artist: Creative endeavour in crossing the borders of art and organizational discourse. *Creativity Studies*, *13*(2), 351–368. https://doi.org/10.3846/cs.2020.11373

Szostak, M., & Sułkowski, Ł. (2020b, April 1–2). Kitsch in management: Characteristic forms, carriers and propagators. *Education Excellence and Innovation Management: A 2025 Vision to Sustain Economic Development during Global Challenges: Proceedings of the 35th International Business Information Management Association Conference (IBIMA)*, 7584–7598. https://depot.ceon.pl/handle/123456789/19173

Szostak, M., & Sułkowski, Ł. (2021a). Artist, creator, manager, entrepreneur, leader: How society perceive these identities? *Economics and Sociology*, *14*(2), 209–221. https://doi.org/10.14254/2071-789X.2021/14-2/11

Szostak, M., & Sułkowski, Ł. (2021b). Identity crisis of artists during the COVID-19 pandemic and shift towards entrepreneurship. *Entrepreneurial Business and Economics Review*, *9*(3), 87–102. https://doi.org/doi.org/10.15678/EBER.2021.090306

Szostak, M., & Sułkowski, Ł. (2021c). The challenges in identification of artists-managers: Consequences for creativity. *Creativity Studies*, *14*(1), 112–124. https://doi.org/10.3846/cs.2021.13822

Szostak, M., & Sułkowski, Ł. (2021d). The identity and self-perception of artists-managers. *Problems and Perspectives in Management*, *19*(1), 372–386. https://doi.org/10.21511/ppm.19(1).2021.32

Tchouikina, S. (2010). The crisis in Russian cultural management: Western influences and the formation of new professional identities in the 1990s-2000s. *Journal of Arts Management Law and Society*, *40*(1), 76–91. https://doi.org/10.1080/10632921003603950

Tendayi Viki, G., & Williams, M. L. J. (2014). The role of identity integration in enhancing creativity among mixed-race individuals. *Journal of Creative Behavior*, *48*(3), 198–208. https://doi.org/10.1002/jocb.48

Terán-Yépez, E., & Guerrero-Mora, A. (2020). Determining factors of international opportunity recognition: A conceptual approach. *International Entrepreneurship Review*, *6*(4), 6 5–80. https://doi.org/10.15678/ier.2020.0604.05

Thanh, N. H., & Van Quang, N. (2019). Ethical leadership in the digital era: Requirements for developing ethical leaderships in Vietnam. *The International Journal of Business & Management*, *7*(7). https://doi.org/10.24940/theijbm/2019/v7/i7/bm1907-028

Thompson, J. L. (2002). The world of the social entrepreneur. *International Journal of Public Sector Management*, *15*(4–5), 412–431. https://doi.org/10.1108/09513550210435746

Van de Calseyde, P. P. F. M., Evans, A. M., & Demerouti, E. (2020). Leader decision speed as a signal of honesty. *Leadership Quart erly*. https://doi.org/10.1016/j.leaqua.2020.101442

Van Niekerk, C., & Goldberg, R. (2021). The influence of scent marketing on consumers' approach and avoidance behaviour in the high-end fashion industry. *Mediterranean Journal of Social Sciences*, *12*(4) , 12. https://doi.org/10.36941/mjss-2021-0024

Venus, M., Johnson, R. E., Zhang, S., Wang, X. H. (Frank), & Lanaj, K. (2019). Seeing the big picture: A within-person examination of leader construal level and vision communication. *Journal of Management*, *45*(7), 2666–2684. https://doi.org/10.1177/0149206318761576

Vincent, L. C., & Kouchaki, M. (2016). Creative, rare, entitled, and dishonest: How commonality of creativity in one's group decreases an individual's entitlement and dishonesty. *Academy of Management Journal*, *59*(4), 1451–1473. https://doi.org/10.5465/amj.2014.1109

Vivant, E. (2016). Rejection, adoption or conversion. The three ways of being a young graduate auto-entrepreneur. *Work Organisation, Labour & Globalisation*, *10*(2), 68–83. https://hal-enpc.archives-ouvertes.fr/hal-01408579

Voss, Z. G., Cable, D. M., & Voss, G. B. (2006). Organizational identity and firm performance: What happens when leaders disagree about "who we are?" *Organization Science*, *17*(6), 741–755. https://doi.org/10.1287/orsc.1060.0218

Walter, H. M. (2015). *Artist, professional, gentleman: Designing the body of the actor-manager, 1870–1900*. Royal College of Art.

Warhurst, R. (2011). Managers' practice and managers' learning as identity formation: Reassessing the mba contribution. *Management Learning*, *42*(3), 261–278. https://doi.org/10.1177/1350507610387567

Warhurst, R., & Black, K. (2017). What do managers know? Wisdom and manager identity in later career. *Management Learning*, *48*(4), 416–430. https://doi.org/10.1177/1350507616679346

Watson, T. J. (2001). *In search of management: Culture, chaos and control in managerial work* (1st ed.). Cengage Learning EMEA.

Watson, T. J. (2009). Narrative, life story and manager identity: A case study in autobiographical identity work. *Human Relations*, *62*(3), 425–452. https://doi.org/10.1177/0018726708101044

White, H. (1992). *Identity and control: A structural theory of social action*. Princeton University Press.

Wilmoth, D. (2016). The missing millennial entrepreneurs. *Small Business Administration Office of Advocacy: Economic Research Series*, *2015*, 2–7. https://cdn.advocacy.sba.gov/wp-content/uploads/2016/02/07133439/Millenial_IB.pdf

Wimschneider, C., & Brem, A. (2019). The perception of creativity through multicultural experience-results from an empirical analysis. *International Journal of Innovation Management*, *23*(7). https://doi.org/10.1142/S1363919619500658

Win, T. S. (2014). Marketing the entrepreneurial artist in the innovation age: Aesthetic labor, artistic subjectivity, and the creative industries. *Anthropology of Work Review*, *35*(1), 2–13. https://doi.org/10.1111/awr.12026

Wolf, C. (2019). Not lost in translation: Managerial career narratives and the construction of protean identities. *Human Relations*, *72*(3), 505–533. https://doi.org/10.1177/0018726718778094

Wyszomirski, M., & Chang, W. J. (2015). What is arts entrepreneurship? Tracking the development of its definition in scholarly journals. *Artivate: A Journal of Entrepreneurship in the Arts*, *4*(2), 11–31. http://barnettcenter.osu.edu/sites/default/files/2019-08/what_is_arts_entrepreneurship.pdf

Yazar, T., & Arifoglu, G. (2012). A research of audio visual educational aids on the creativity levels of 4–14 year old children as a process in primary education. *Procedia – Social and Behavioral Sciences*, *51*, 301–306. https://doi.org/10.1016/j.sbspro.2012.08.163

Zahra, S. A. (2021). International entrepreneurship in the post Covid world. *Journal of World Business*, *56*(1). https://doi.org/10.1016/j.jwb.2020.101143

Żak, M., & Garncarz, J. (2020). Economic policy towards the challenges of the COVID-19 pandemic in selected European Union countries. *International Entrepreneurship Review*, *6*(4), 21–34.

Zambrell, K. (2016). Managers' identity construction at work: Artistic interventions as triggers for identity work. *Organizational Aesthetics*, *5*(2), 34–67.

Zhang, Y., & Huxham, C. (2020). Collective identity construction in international collaborations. *Journal of General Management*, *45*(3). https://doi.org/10.1177/0306307019886181

Zheng, M. X., Yuan, Y., van Dijke, M., De Cremer, D., & Van Hiel, A. (2020). The interactive effect of a leader's sense of uniqueness and sense of belongingness on followers' perceptions of leader authenticity. *Journal of Business Ethics*, *164*(3), 515–533. https://doi.org/10.1007/s10551-018-4070-4

Zhu, W., Trevinõ, L. K., & Zheng, X. (2016). Ethical leaders and their followers: The transmission of moral identity and moral attentiveness. *Business Ethics Quarterly*, *26*(1), 95–115. https://doi.org/10.1017/beq.2016.11

Zilnyk, A. (2011). A brief introduction to perception. *Perspectives in Public Health*, *131*(6), 248–249. https://doi.org/10.1177/1757913911425736

Zimbardo, P. G., & Gerrig, R. J. (2012). *Psychologia i życie*. Wydawnictwo Naukowe PWN. https://libra.ibuk.pl/reader/psychologia-i-zycie-philip-g-zimbardo-richard-j-43918

5 Creativity in artistic and managerial activities – source, motive, inspiration, improvisation

Placing management issues on the map of the theory of artistic creativity may help in a fresh look at the phenomenon of creativity of both the manager himself and the organisation he manages. This double perspective determines the complex role of a modern manager, who is expected, on the one hand, to be creative in order to find a way to the future of the organisation in a changing environment yet follow the expectations of stakeholders and maintaining specific standards; and, on the other hand, to build and maintain the creative potential of the organisation.

In Chapters 2 and 3, the primary levels of consideration in art and management were virtuosity and, in parallel, artistry and creativity. On this basis, it can be said that in order to be an artist (of art or management), it is enough to be proficient in one's field (virtuosity) and to apply and deepen this virtuosity with the reviving universal values (art), so that the recipient feels something more than just the experience of technically well-done work. It should be noted that creativity was discussed in the contexts just mentioned – next to virtuosity and artistry – as an optional but desirable factor.

This chapter will discuss the role of creativity in artistic and managerial activities, which is a unique and desirable feature both in the arts and the world of organisation. Presentation of the essence of creativity from the point of view of management aesthetics requires the introduction and analysis of issues related to the sources of creativity, motives for undertaking creative activities and sources of inspiration, with particular emphasis on contextual inspiration. As a result, engaged creativity will be developed, in which truth and effective management play an essential role. In addition, the phenomenon of improvised creative activities based on artistic improvisation will be analysed, which can be an essential source for analysing improvised managerial behaviour.

This chapter aims to answer the following questions: (1) How can aesthetic theory broaden our understanding of creativity and help us manage creativity efficiently? 2) What can artistic improvisation contribute to understanding the essence of creativity, and how can it help effectively manage creativity? (3)

DOI: 10.4324/9781003458029-6

How can the creator manage the process of engaged artistic creation in order to achieve the set of goals effectively? (4) How do recipients of particular art disciplines evaluate various forms of participation in an aesthetic situation?

5.1 Art of creativity

The dictionary definition of *creativity* refers to the ability to create or use original and unusual ideas or to create something new or imaginative (Creativity, 2023a). The synonyms of creativity are ingenuity, innovation, inventiveness, and originality (Creativity, 2023b). The essence of creativity is a set of qualitative features of the thought process (divergence and convergence; smoothness, flexibility, originality; breadth of categorisation; sensitivity to the problem; abstraction, synthesis, rearrangement of ideas), as well as the imagination, fantasy, and individual personality characteristics (dynamism, focus on creative searches, creative well-being and independence), implemented in a person's creative activity (Kochereva, 2019).

Creativity is one of an individual's most valuable contemporary competencies and one of the most sought-after resources in modern organisations. Therefore, the phenomenon of creativity is of interest to many scientific disciplines:

1. psychology – individual creativity (Lebuda & Csikszentmihalyi, 2020; Mochalova, 2020; Szostak & Sułkowski, 2021d, 2021c, 2021b; Tendayi Viki & Williams, 2014);
2. sociology – group creativity (Literat, 2012; W. Liu et al., 2018; Stolarick & Florida, 2006; Szostak, 2021e, 2021d, 2023a; Szostak & Sułkowski, 2021a; Vincent & Kouchaki, 2016);
3. management – creativity of organisational actors, such as managers, leaders, and entrepreneurs, the creativity of organisations or teams (Reiter-Palmon, 2017; Szostak, 2021b, 2022c; Tang et al., 2020);
4. aesthetics – creativity of creative individuals (Gołaszewska, 1984, 1986, 2005);
5. ethics – ethical issues and limitations conditioning creative activity (Bigo, 2018; García-González, 2021; Närvänen et al., 2018);
6. cultural studies – culturally conditioned creativity (Larso & Saphiranti, 2016; Major et al., 1998; Skoldberg Johansson et al., 2015; Szostak, 2021c, 2022b);
7. gender studies – gender-based creativity (Ahmad & Zadeh, 2016; Born & Devine, 2016; Lebuda & Csikszentmihalyi, 2020; Szostak, 2021d, 2023b);
8. behavioural economics – creativity conditioned by a combination of psychological, social, cognitive, and emotional factors (Dash, 2019; Neto et al., 2019; Scheuer, 2018; Szostak, 2023b).

Also, the phenomenon of *artistic creativity* is of interest to many scientific fields, i.e.:

1. psychology – the work of composers, performers, and writers (Grace et al., 2019; Nagy, 2015; Pavlova, 2018; Simonton, 1994; Tanggaard, 2014);

2. sociology – creativity of orchestras, bands, and choirs (Grote, 2014; Marra, 2019);
3. management – creativity of organisations and artistic teams (Duconseille & Saner, 2020);
4. aesthetics – creativity in an aesthetic situation, especially in the creative process and creativity located in a work of art (Daniel, 2021; Gołaszewska, 1984; Hocking, 2019; Jung, 2014; Szostak, 2021a; Szostak & Sułkowski, 2020).

Although the individual creative process is of interest primarily to the psychology of creativity, one must not forget that groups can also be creative. It seems, therefore, that a fuller understanding of the phenomenon of creativity requires an interdisciplinary approach involving research methods of social sciences and humanities (Nęcka, 2000).

Since studying creativity is not easy, most researchers focus on selected areas or aspects of creativity: gender differences (Ungureanu & Vasile, 2016) or stimulating creativity (Ceylan et al., 2008). Thanks to this research, we know that the gender of the manager does not affect the organisation's creative potential (Ahmad & Zadeh, 2016), and we know how to stimulate creative activity. It is also known that there is a positive correlation between the creativity of the leader and the creativity of the team, and this correlation is strengthened by the complexity of the tasks but weakened by the empowerment of the leader; leadership style is not essential in this field; and highly creative leaders apply original ideas in research, development, and management activities.

While it is relatively easy to describe the phenomenon from the theoretical point of view, being a "creativity virtuoso" or "artist of creativity" is not so easy. The problem of managing creativity appears to be highly complex in practice in the context of the essence of creativity.

5.1.1 Creativity concepts

Many components and stages of the creative process have been distinguished, the analysis and management of which allow for creative activities in various circumstances. It has been found that every child is born creative, but educational and socialisation processes that impose many restrictions suppress their innate creativity (Gloton & Clero, 1988, pp. 54, 75–92). In this context, the process of recreating or "digging out" to the natural deposits of creativity becomes crucial (Dahlberg, 2007).

Psychological concepts of creativity can be divided into *general* concepts of the creative process (classical and contemporary) and *systemic* concepts of creativity.

According to the *classical theory of the creative process* by Graham Wallas, the creative process consists of four successive stages (Nęcka, 2000):

1. preparation – performing the initial activities of collecting the necessary data and formulating the problem that needs to be solved;

2. incubation – spontaneous, unconscious maturation (incubation) of an idea, regardless of the intentional work on this idea;
3. illumination – glare associated with a sudden solution to the problem as a consequence of the appearance of the so-called moment of insight (i.e., an unexpected change in the perception of the problem, leading to a fresh and fuller understanding of the essence of the problem);
4. verification – checking the suitability of the created solution.

According to Robert Weisberg's *classic incremental theory*, the creative process is simply the tedious solving of a specific problem, which – taking place step by step – is essentially devoid of spectacular insights, intellectual breakthroughs, or moments of insight (Weisberg, 2006). *Contemporary concepts of the creative process* – e.g., the concept of creative interaction (Nęcka, 2000) and the genploration model focusing on the mechanisms of generating and exploring pre-inventive structures, e.g., mental images (see Figure 5.1; Ward et al., 1992) – break with the classic scheme of successive stages. From the point of view of modern theories, the creative process is not orderly, repetitive, and schematic as classical theories saw it and is characterised by both returning to earlier moments and thinking ahead. In other words, these concepts focus on the result and not on methodical processing according to the usual scheme of stages.

A characteristic feature of *systemic concepts of creativity* is that they distinguish many independent components of creativity: psychological, social, and cultural. Creativity is assumed to be a dynamic system within these concepts, and the individual components mutually and constantly interact. The final effect

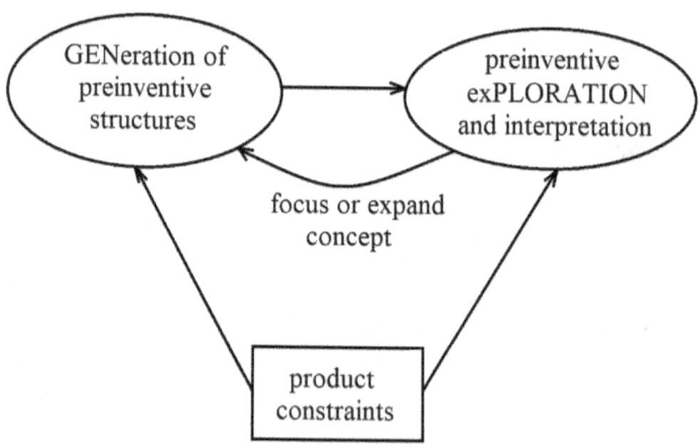

Figure 5.1 Creativity according to the genploration model

Source: Author's own elaboration based on Ward et al. (1992)

is more than the simple sum of the actions of its components, so there is a synergy process (Nęcka, 2000). Systemic concepts of creativity include:

1. investment concept – this refers to the metaphor of buying cheap and selling more expensive stocks, taking into account the role of the strategy of investing by culture creators in their work, which is, to a large extent, a matter of decisions (Sternberg & Lubart, 1991);
2. the concept of transgression – J. Kozielecki assumes that an individual intentionally goes beyond what he is and what he has, and by going beyond the typical limits of action, that individual shapes new structures or destroys what has been stabilised so far (Kułaga & Trzcionka, 2019);
3. the concept of creativity as the result of three-way human interaction – this interaction occurs with the field of knowledge and the field that determines this field of knowledge (Csikszentmihalyi, 2014) – see Figure 5.2.

Some concepts confirm the aesthetic theory of creative personality (see Section 2.2.1, "Creator") – stating that creativity is a skill available to everyone, characterised by creating new connections and generating new ideas. Differentiated thinking and the ability to go beyond the beaten track can catalyse the potential to produce original and valuable results. In order for the aforementioned potentials to occur, certain dispositions are needed, which include: personal characteristics, affective process, cognitive abilities, expertise and proficiency in a given field, motivation, intellectual abilities, and support from the cultural environment, as well as imagination and the ability to evaluate ideas and implementation activities. In addition to the existence of these dispositions,

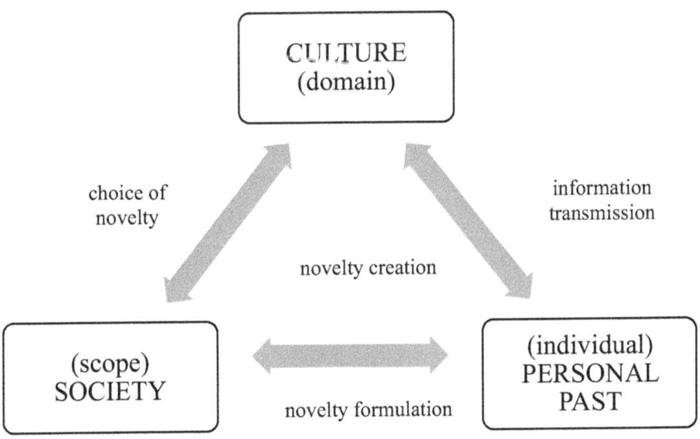

Figure 5.2 Creativity as a result of three-way human interaction

Source: Author's own elaboration based on Csikszentmihalyi (2014)

the interrelationships between all dispositions are also important (Ferrari et al., 2009). This theory is presented graphically in Figure 5.3.

In the spirit of dialectics, creativity can be analysed in comparison with its opposite, i.e., *fixation*, consisting in clinging to one way of acting despite changing circumstances. The long-term impact of restrictions, which eventually become habits, can lead to fixation (Crilly, 2019; Crilly & Cardoso, 2017).

The importance of *identity* for all creative endeavours, discussed extensively in Chapter 4, is fundamental (Elstad & Jansson, 2020). Psychology has developed a distinction between simple identities and complex identities (Collver & Weitkamp, 2018; David & Bar-Tal, 2009; Noonan, 2019; Shpak & Pchelkina, 2020; Zamaraeva & Koptseva, 2020). Identity tensions, ways of using these tensions (e.g., through paradoxical thinking), and deliberate and unintentional *changes in identity* can be an excellent form of catalysing creativity. Internal or external circumstances may determine changes in complex identities seeking new directions in their activities (Szostak & Sułkowski, 2021b).

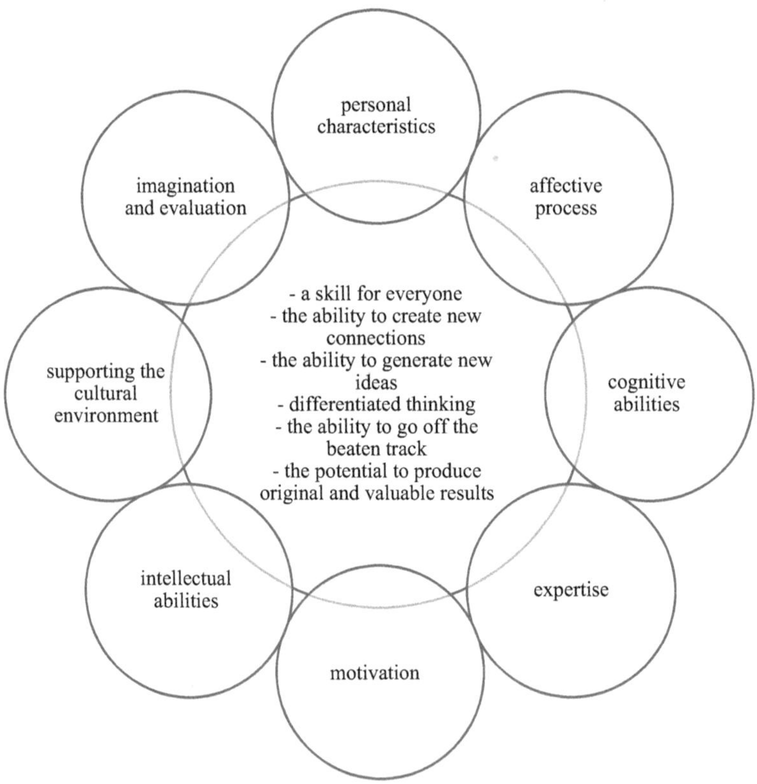

Figure 5.3 What is creativity?

Source: Author's own elaboration based on Ferrari et al. (2009)

The social role of individuals also influences creativity, but not in the same way for everyone. In this context, the perception of roles is an essential factor in perceiving the phenomenon of creativity (Szostak & Sułkowski, 2021b, 2021c, 2021d). However, research shows no fundamental statistical differences in the perception of creative identities (such as artists, managers, creators, leaders, and entrepreneurs) between men and women (Szostak, 2021d), people with and without creative factors (Szostak, 2020b), people with or without entrepreneurial factors (Szostak, 2021b), societies with and without communist history (Szostak, 2021c, 2021e). Also, an individual's identity crisis can positively and negatively affect creativity (Szostak & Sułkowski, 2021b). As one of the identity factors, self-definition affects creative individuals (Szostak & Sułkowski, 2021c, 2021a), highlighting the links between identity and creativity. On this basis, the description of creative identities based on different levels of creativity and organisational effectiveness is justified (see the subsection "Manager creativity" in Section 3.2.1).

5.1.2 Limits of creativity

In the context of constraints, creativity can be considered from a subjectivist and an objectivist perspective. The *subjectivist aspect* draws attention to the process of perception of creative activity: the same action in the same circumstances may be perceived differently by individuals – as creative or non-creative. The *objectivist aspect* emphasises that creativity is not unlimited and may be limited by factors internal and external to the creative individual (Acar et al., 2019; Baer, 2012; Craft, 2003).

Internal factors limiting creativity include fatigue, loss and weakening of motivation, and loss of inspiration. Creative activity is exhausting (How Thinking Hard Makes the Brain Tired, 2022); hence the need to maintain a long-term creative state can lead to many adverse effects in the form of burnout, depression, and even loss of mind (Brieger et al., 2020; Bulei et al., 2014; Cullum et al., 2020; Rasminsky, 2019; Schielke, 2020; Schreiner et al., 2018). Individuals who maintain a high level of creativity for a long time, at the end of the creative process, may perceive their lives and the environment as colourless, negative, and uninspiring, and in extreme situations may even lose the sense of their existence. This thesis can be confirmed by the mental problems of creative individuals, which led them to socially acceptable limits, and even to self-mutilation (Vincent van Gogh) or taking their own lives. It should be assumed that exhaustion after a complicated and productive creative process is natural. Therefore, the inner post-creative emptiness should be seen as a natural periodic state, not as the individual's permanent wear and tear. The following arguments support this reasoning: (1) every living being needs rest after doing work, regardless of the type of activity; (2) the creative process undertaken and carried out using the full capabilities of the individual consumes available energy resources. Therefore, the inner emptiness shows that creativity needs a proper ignition in the form of inspiration and fuel that is a source of creative energy in the form of motifs (Szostak, 2021b). A convincingly creative individual should act "despite" constraints, not "up to" the level of constraints. According to the principle that once resources are used up, they must be replenished, the same should be done with creative potential.

External factors limiting creativity include changes in contexts (organisational, social, cultural), changes in domains, changes in systems (legal, social), changes in rules, changes in relationships, and changes in resources (Acar et al., 2019; Baer, 2012). In addition, the lack of psychological interventions aimed at getting out of the alleys of fixation in human behaviour (physical, emotional, intellectual, spiritual) should be considered the following limit of creativity (Craft, 2003; Gross et al., 2019).

5.1.3 Role of involvement

According to dictionary definitions, *involvement* is an attitude of conviction about the rightness of specific actions or goals, supported by a relentless desire to achieve them while devoting time, strength, and resources (Żmigrodzki, 2022). Involvement includes participation in a specific process or event and emotional involvement in an experience or activity in which the person involved finds meaning, happiness, interest, or a sense of value flow. Involvement can apply to creating or enjoying art, work, leisure activities, and all areas of life. Following the aforementioned characteristics and considering the achievements of aesthetics, commitment can be called a *function of the benefits from achieving goals, motives for action and inspiration* (see Figure 5.4). Without these factors, achieving a sustained commitment to the creative activity will be difficult.

Research highlights the crucial role of engaging individuals and groups in the creative process (Dahlberg, 2007). Since imagination without knowledge will not be productive, knowledge without imagination will not help to live in a world full of changes. However, without the ability to synthesise, evaluate, and develop ideas, achieving effective creativity is impossible (Parnes, 1972). However, the question remains how to generate and maintain commitment so that the individuals and the managed units do not lose their desire for creative activities. Based on the study of the knowledge absorption process in the organisation, scientists have proven that individuals engage through (Sjödin et al., 2019):

1. appreciating the potential of the area by working through validation of available incentives and feasibility verification, which together constitute a recognition of value;
2. affirming the value of their area by ensuring legitimacy and demonstrating a shared understanding of the business value of the goal they pursue;
3. supporting the integration of the area by employing support and securing resources to integrate and obtain benefits for the organisation.

It seems that the management has developed quite a broad track record in the field of *motivation*, aiming to engage employees. The question remains whether

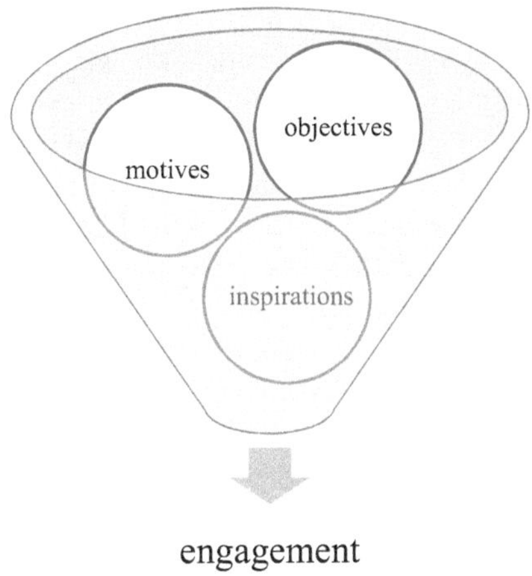

Figure 5.4 Engagement as a function

Source: Author's own elaboration

external methods of motivation (wage and non-wage) are sufficient to generate and maintain a commitment to creative activity. Creativity is not a mechanical activity that one can force someone to do. Creativity is primarily the result of internal circumstances and, to a lesser extent, external circumstances to the individual. Therefore, external methods of motivation will not be effective against internal circumstances (Gloton & Clero, 1988, pp. 71–72). Referring to the model of involvement as a function of the benefits of achieving goals, motives, and inspiration, in order to catalyse creative activity, one should focus on managing each of these elements. Classic motivational activities are enough to obtain benefits from achieving the achieved goals. In order to recognise what motivates a given individual to creative activity and the sources of inspiration to which a given individual is sensitive, in creative activity, one should refer to the theory of aesthetics – especially the creative process within the aesthetic situation (see Section 2.2.1, "Creator", and Section 2.2.2, "Creative process").

5.2 Management of creativity

Management, understood as a way to achieve goals efficiently, also applies to creativity, emphasising managerial functions that allow planning, organising, implementing, and controlling creative activity. Conscious creativity (artistic or managerial) allows it to be managed in many aspects: making decisions to undertake creative activities in specific contexts and undertaking, maintaining, developing, and finalising creative activities. After all, from the point of view of aesthetics, an unfinished creative process does not generate a work of art; a work of art must be completed to speak of its full impact as intended by the creator.

The fundamental research problem of this part will be the art of individual creativity, combining a mixture of professional knowledge, professional experience, intuition (based on knowledge and experience), and the creator's identity (Szostak & Sułkowski, 2021d, 2021b). Knowledge and work experience can be measured, organised, and developed. If intuition is based on professional knowledge and experience, this is their function, and it seems to be a manageable problem (Stierand & Dörfler, 2014). The creator's identity can be organised and developed, although this requires high self-management skills, especially in the context of external impulses (Szostak & Sułkowski, 2021b, 2021d). Because artistic creativity determines the stages of undertaking, implementing, and finishing artistic activities, and because these phases are formally divided, a managerial approach consisting of planning, organising, and controlling in order to achieve a specific goal can be successfully applied here (Szostak, 2021a; Szostak & Sułkowski, 2020).

Based on aesthetic theory, artistic creation is not the only feature of identity. By being aware of the three types of pure creative personality, one can discover different types of creative personality that affect the creative process in different ways (see Section 2.2.1, "Creator"). The personal characteristics of the creator play an essential role in individual creativity; however, the role of the creative environment is also crucial (Kochereva, 2019). From a psychological point of view, creativity, curiosity, and schizotypy (eccentric behaviour and bizarre beliefs accompanied by symptoms of social withdrawal) are similar phenomena; the only difference here is the perception of the factor driving these three types of behaviour (Gross et al., 2019).

The theory of a *creative approach to problem-solving* distinguishes the following stages: (1) finding the problem, (2) solving the problem, and (3) implementing solutions. Within these steps, the following steps should be taken (Basadur & DeGroote, 1995):

1. finding the problem – i.e., the main field for further activities; the problem may be noticed by the entity or be pointed out from the outside;
2. finding facts – i.e., the main determinants affecting the essence of the problem as well as the perception of the phenomenon that seems to be a problem;
3. defining the problem – the reliability of this stage determines the success of further actions; an incorrect definition of the problem will lead to solving a different problem from the one noticed in the first stage;
4. finding solutions – depending on the definition of the problem, the solutions may concern repairing the situation or preventing the occurrence of similar situations in the future;
5. evaluation and selection of options – the main criteria should be the effectiveness of alternatives and the possibility of their implementation; a common mistake is the analysis of alternatives based on the wrong criteria or too few of them;
6. action planning – the successful implementation of the selected option and solving the essence of the problem depend on this stage;

7. gaining acceptance – a critical stage when the previous stages are dealt with by people other than those who approve plans for implementation; acceptance may also relate to the issue of providing funds for the implementation of corrective actions;
8. taking action – sticking to the action plan is essential here, but also the quality of the actions taken; the quality of the plan and its implementation are entirely different.

A deeper understanding of the essence of the problem of creativity management requires the analysis of additional issues: the sources and the motives of creativity (Crilly & Cardoso, 2017; Molero-Jurado et al., 2020; Penaluna & Penaluna, 2020; Szostak, 2021b) and the introduction of the concepts of "contextual inspiration" and "engaged creativity" (Formica & Edmondson, 2020; Szostak, 2020a, 2021a; Szostak & Sułkowski, 2020). Not without significance will also be individual and group creativity (Liu et al., 2018; Vincent & Kouchaki, 2016) and awareness of the limits of creativity discussed earlier (Craft, 2003; Gross et al., 2019). The whole spectrum of components related to creativity management is visualised on Figure 5.5.

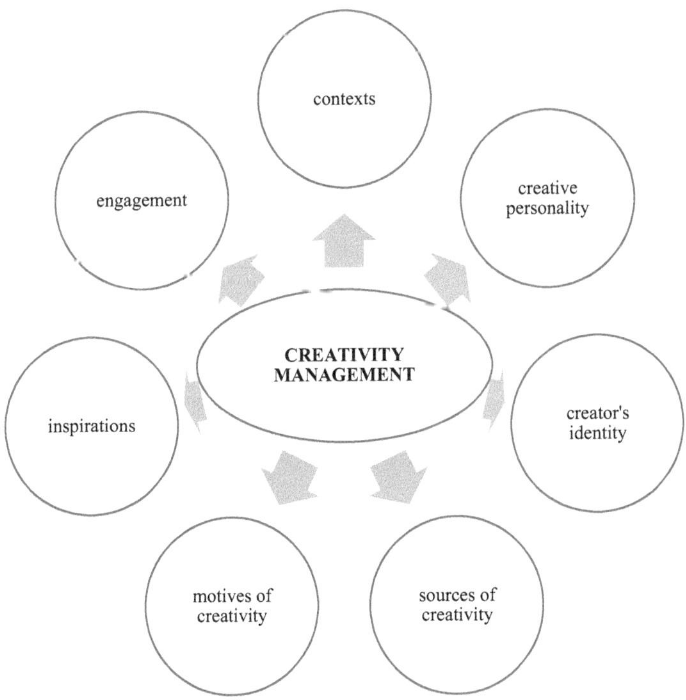

Figure 5.5 Creativity management components

Source: Author's own elaboration

5.2.1 Sources of creativity

Attention was paid to the essence of the sources of creativity from the beginning of philosophical thought and reflection on the search for the meaning of existence. Individual epochs interchangeably recognised divine or human supernatural powers as the primary sources of this unusual activity. According to Nietzsche, the sources of artistic creativity were nature, its forces and powers, the will of individual human growth, and culture as a game of traditional conventions with inventions (Kostyszak, 2020). Synthesising the achievements of the theory of aesthetics in this area, one can say that they are the *sources of artistic creation* (Arbuz-Spatari, 2019; Calic & Hélie, 2018; Gołaszewska, 1984; Hongisto & Pape, 2015; Jung, 2014; Meshkova & Enikolopov, 2017):

1. willingness to express the personality of the creator – creation as a way of expression and communication;
2. egoism and narcissism – creation as a confirmation or denial of egoism or narcissism; these factors are decisive due to their inexhaustible deposits and the fact that they can inspire negatively (egoism and narcissism as belittling others) and positively (egoism and narcissism as self-lifting);
3. fascination with the world – creating in the image of nature; creation modelled on the beauty, ugliness, or aggression of nature;
4. ideology – creation as a response to an ideological imperative;
5. material necessity – creation as a means of obtaining funds for living;
6. excess of creative energy – creation as the use of energy remaining after the implementation of current daily tasks;
7. imitation of divine creativity – creation as a sense of extraordinary possibilities or as a phenomenon in itself;
8. discovering timeless ideas – creation as referring to universal values;
9. perception of the imperfection of the world – creation as a response to the existing situation;
10. cultural development – creation as constant growth in the area beyond nature;
11. contradictions – creation against something, creation as an answer;
12. meeting the needs of the group – creation as a response to social expectations.

It should be borne in mind that the sources of creativity, despite their analytical presentation, in reality, most often function in a synthetic form, and their combination depends on factors both internal and external to the individual. Sources of creativity may relate to individual and group artistic creation, thus revealing the space for *artistic creativity management*. Awareness of the presence of many sources of creativity and the possibility of their stimulation and compilation opens up for the manager an area that strongly determines the creativity of the individual and the group. Of course, knowing about the potential sources of artistic creativity is not enough to efficiently manage the creative process. Therefore, after internalising the sources of artistic creation, it is necessary to focus on issues of motives and inspirations in context taking creative actions (Crilly & Cardoso, 2017; Molero-Jurado et al., 2020; Penaluna & Penaluna, 2020; Szostak, 2021b).

5.2.2 Creativity motives

Because the role of motives in undertaking creative activity is fundamental (Foxon, 2008; Moulard et al., 2014), awareness of the presence and the typology of motifs helps to manage the creative artistic process. On the other hand, the perception of the motives of artistic creativity is not apparent and uniform among individuals (Zhou et al., 2017).

From the point of view of aesthetics, the *motives for creative activity* can fall into two categories (Gołaszewska, 1984, 1986, pp. 29–34):

1. assigned – directly affecting the modelling of the work and implemented with the participation of creative work:
    a. considering oneself as a creator, i.e., the need to form a work that collects and expresses the creator's expectations;
    b. taking into account the work, i.e., attention focused on the perfection of the work, realising the high aesthetic value;
    c. consideration towards the recipient, i.e., the tendency to provide others with the experience that a work of art can bring;
2. unassigned – marked indirectly in work and possible to be also implemented with the use of other activities, additionally activating creative forces, e.g.:
    a. economic considerations;
    b. social coercion;
    c. compliance with stereotypes.

For a manager who has a managerial attitude,[1] the assigned motives include: (1) the desire to create an organisation that would meet the goals set by the owner; (2) the desire to create an organisation that expresses the personality of the manager or expresses the values professed by the manager; and (3) the willingness to create an organisation creating an effect (product, service) with specific assumptions. Furthermore, among the unassigned motives of the manager's activity, the following can be mentioned: (1) the need for the manager to obtain resources necessary for life, and (2) meeting society's expectations towards a particular manager.

The following phenomena may supplement the aforementioned classification of motives significant for artistically creative behaviour: challenge, coping, sense of duty, pleasure, expression, need for recognition, and pro-social activity. Moreover, the motifs' meaning varies from play to play; for example, visual arts, literature, and music are most motivated by expression and coping motives, while crafts are most motivated by pro-social and discretionary motives (Benedek et al., 2020). Literature also emphasises entrepreneurship as one of the critical motives of artistic creation (Robinson & Novak-Leonard, 2021; Szostak, 2020b; Szostak & Sułkowski, 2021b). It should not be forgotten that negative motives and unethical behaviours can also lead to dark creativity (Li et al., 2018; Liu et al., 2012; Palmer et al., 2020).

In order for a work to be created, there should be a direct *impulse (inspiration) to undertake the creative process*, i.e., psychological activation through an external or internal stimulus (Adler & Ippolito, 2018; Biehl-Missal, 2011; Norliana & Fakhrul Anwar, 2019; Penaluna & Penaluna, 2020; Szostak, 2018, 2021b): (1) the lack of perception in the world that allows or requires fulfilment (seeing the inadequacy, the artist decides to extend reality with a new value); (2) interest in the world and reality (the artist wants to show his admiration for the world and save this state from oblivion); (3) the excess of his own experiences, from which the artist wants to free himself (wanting to present them to others, looking for a manner to express them in an artistic form).

Since the type of fuel determines the duration of the fire, some fuels burn out quickly; others need more time to be fully consumed. Each fuel has different consequences, such as heat levels, waste, or environmental impact. The same analogies can be applied to the motives of artistic creation.

5.2.3 Contextual inspiration

To stay within the scope of the metaphor "theme as fuel and inspiration as ignition", it is evident that the correct type of ignition is required for each type of fuel. Therefore, after describing the motives of artistic creation, it is necessary to focus on inspiration (Calic & Hélie, 2018; Zedelius et al., 2021). An art creator who wants to be effective should search, be open to, and be fluent in various sources of inspiration. He needs to know what inspires him and what de-inspires him; he must be able to look for new sources of inspiration and effectively use known sources of inspiration.

The most straightforward distinction between the *sources of inspiration* divides them into external (objective) and internal (subjective) towards the creator. Following the example of musical arts, external sources of inspiration for a musician-instrumentalist include, among others: the instrument itself, the acoustics of the interior, the audience (their number, the potential level of perceiving the work of art), circumstances, interior architecture, history of the place and people associated with the place, epoch, style, musical theme or form. Internal sources of inspiration include technical skills (virtuosity), musicality, imagination, sensitivity, mood (inner state) at the time of the creative process, religiousness, and spiritual experiences (Szostak, 2021f, pp. 365–385).

In general, the direct impulses (inspirations) to undertake the creative process described in the literature can be divided into the following categories (Adler & Ippolito, 2018; Biehl-Missal, 2011; Norliana & Fakhrul Anwar, 2019; Penaluna & Penaluna, 2020; Szostak, 2018):

1. lack of perception in the world which allows or requires fulfilment,
2. interest in the world and reality,
3. an excess of one's experiences from which the artist wants to free himself.

Because art makers need to be adaptive (Goldberg-Miller & Xiao, 2018), they should observe contexts and act creatively. Adaptation includes goal setting, strategy building, and performance evaluation. From today's perspective, many historical artists seem exceptional and autonomous, while their works were created by adaptation in terms of goals, circumstances, and environments (Szostak, 2021a).

Nevertheless, while retaining the main problem of effective artistic creation and being persuasive simultaneously, there is a need to add the adjective "contextual" to the noun "inspiration". Its essential meaning lies in the community of values, thoughts, feelings, knowledge, and spirituality between the creator and the recipient (Huang & Liu, 2019; Puente-Díaz et al., 2021; Rani Satyam et al., 2022). On the contrary, inspiration drawn from an area unknown to the recipient may be valuable for the creator and the artistic quality of the work, but it may not be understandable and engaging for the recipient.

Bearing that recipients prefer to participate in more friendly art disciplines and contemplate more familiar works of art within their preferred disciplines, my observation as a musician-improviser and conscious music recipient can be valuable here. Audiences prefer improvisations built around familiar themes; such improvisations are more understandable, easier to perceive, and give greater pleasure and satisfaction to the recipients. Improvisations of this kind are perceived more warmly, trigger more substantial contact between the recipient and the improviser, and catalyse more profound and lasting relationships.

5.2.4 Individual and group creativity

Aesthetic theories related to creativity based on the organisation as a work of art metaphor can be applied to management directly and indirectly. First, the theory of basic and creative personalities can be applied to the behaviour of organisational actors: managers and employees. Secondly, the types of creative personalities (intuitive, reflective, behavioural) are found in organisational actors who, being creative individuals, represent various mixtures of these pure forms. Thirdly, the themes of creativity (fascination with the world, perception of the world's imperfections, excess of creative energy, egoism and narcissism, and material necessity) can also be applied to managers who are artists in the organisational world.

Individual creativity, considered an art in itself, must combine an appropriate level of substantive knowledge, practical experience, intuition built based on knowledge and experience, and a strong identity of the creator. On the other hand, individual creativity is the basis of group creativity, and while the effect of creativity is the same in both cases, the overall approach from a creativity management perspective is different. Due to the complexity of the problems faced by today's organisations and the fact that a single person cannot solve them independently due to their limitations and specialisations, the role of group search for creative and innovative solutions is crucial (Reiter-Palmon, 2017).

The role of managers in organising an optimal environment for developing group creativity is fundamental (Alsuwaidi & Omar, 2020; W. Liu et al., 2018). For this purpose, different techniques are used with different effects in different areas (Sik, 2016). It has also been revealed that group creativity development techniques can reduce the creativity of individuals (Vincent & Kouchaki, 2016), and paradoxically, lower individual creativity can increase group creativity. It is because group creativity is not the sum of the individual creativity of group members. Instead, group creativity should be treated as a function of individual group members' creativity. When group members inspire and catalyse each other's creative abilities, group creativity will be greater than the sum of individual group members' creativity. On the other hand, when individuals do not cooperate with each other or their creative personalities are not compatible, group creativity will be less than the sum of individual creativity of individual group members.

Analysing group creativity following the aesthetic situation theory and in the spirit of the organisation metaphor as a work of art, one sees that a person who conducts a creative process intending to achieve a set goal should be treated as a creator. All the consequences of the aesthetic situation should be applied analogously here.

Creativity can be assigned several functions in management: positive – seeking a competitive advantage (Acar et al., 2019; Martin et al., 2015; Müller & Ulrich, 2013; Ripoll et al., 2019), team integration (Che Ibrahim et al., 2018; Lemoine & Blum, 2021; Li & Yue, 2019; Zhang & Kwan, 2019), and increase in social capital (Sözbilir, 2018; Szczepaniak, 2018; Szostak, 2021c); or negative – decrease in team effectiveness (Li et al., 2018), which, paradoxically, may reduce social capital as a side effect (Kačerauskas, 2018; Sözbilir, 2018; Szostak, 2022b). Therefore, it must be a constant theme and trigger in the form of contextual inspiration to fulfil these functions.

Group creativity management should take into account the autonomy of the group members. Individuals within a group may be responsible for individual stages of the creative process (in the spirit of general theories of creativity) or for individual components of the creative process (in the spirit of systemic theories of creativity). Managing a creative group may also involve watching over the creative spontaneity of individuals by directing emerging conflicts (when they have creative potential) or disarming them (when they do not have creative potential). The manager of the creative group should be a creative artist himself and create with a creative team; the classic organisation of this area will not be effective.

5.2.5 Creativity involved

As opposed to (disengaged) selfless creativity, the concept of "engaged creativity" can be implemented (Fricdman et al., 2015; Palhares et al., 2021; Vuscan & Feng, 2018). Furthermore, since the essence of creativity is a set of qualitative features of the thought process, as well as imagination, fantasy, and individual personality traits implemented in the creative activity of a person (Kochereva, 2019), we can talk about the creator's awareness of the purposefulness of creative activities. On this basis, creative activities can be divided into non-engaged and engaged.

Based on the concept of the aesthetic situation, an essential component of engaged creativity is universal values, and the most noticeable sign of engaged creativity is the work of art itself. Moreover, essential processes in the creator's personality make up the phenomenon of engaged creativity (Szostak, 2021a). Therefore, the role of the basic and creative personality and the strength of the creator's identity (Szostak, 2023a; Szostak & Sułkowski, 2021d, 2021b, 2021c) are of fundamental importance for engaged creativity because they determine the human approach to creative activities, which in turn can be appropriately directed to meet specific contexts and circumstances (Elstad & Jansson, 2020).

The circumstances in which people with different identities function determine different results of the actions taken. The research presented so far defines the complex identities of artists-managers and artists-entrepreneurs and shows that they develop their engaged creativity by using paradoxical thinking, catalysing identity tensions, and trying to combine conflicting factors (DeFillippi et al., 2007; Szostak & Sułkowski, 2021c). Self-determination, as one of the crucial factors determining identity, affects the engaged creativity of an individual (Szostak & Sułkowski, 2021c, 2021a). Feeling unsafe will not develop a full palette of convincingly creative activities. On the other hand, uncertainty can catalyse creativity in the search for non-standard solutions to reduce negative feelings – the creator is less likely to be persuasive when feeling insecure. It is not easy to define the optimal circumstances or environments for convincingly creative activities (Ripoll et al., 2019). Therefore, identity can be seen as the basic level of considerations about engaged creativity: by low/weak self-definition as a creator and weak legitimacy of the right to create, lower engaged creativity will occur.

Based on the preceding, one can conclude that the identity and type of creative personality are decisive in terms of the resistance of an individual's creative attitude to the external influence of the popularity of other creators. It is because popular creators are naturally perceived as perfect in their field and convincing to the audience. Hence, the conclusion is that creators must be able to distinguish between popularity and quality (the truth factor), as well as their real creativity from following current trends.

5.3 Artistic improvisation

Although the dictionary definition of *improvisation* as spontaneous composing of a work on the spot, under the influence of emotions and without any preparation (Kopaliński, 1989), refers only to artistic activity, the phenomenon of improvisation has occurred and still occurs to varying degrees in every field of human activity, including management. Artistic improvisation, as an activity combining elements of creativity and reproduction (performance) in a spontaneous, one-time, and unique process (Oleszkiewicz, 1997, p. 7), can play an essential role in analysing management problems. The key here is that improvisation involves a tension between the objectivity of a set model (form) and the subjectivity of spontaneous production (Dahlhaus & Eggebrecht, 1978). Although from the point of view of aesthetics, all art disciplines have many common features, the performing arts – musical performance, acting, visual performance – can bring particularly revealing and valuable conclusions for managers.

Spontaneous artistic activity was the fundamental source from which art was born. Due to its ephemerality and lack of physical form,[2] music is considered one of the highest forms of art (Dutton, 2019, p. 354). Before the artists of ancient Greece (dealing with the so-called triple chorea, i.e., a synthetic artistic activity combining poetry, music, and dance) began to compose their repetitive works (mimesis), improvised performances were used to entertain and worship the deities commonly and naturally. Thus, it can be said that improvisation is an immanent and fundamental feature of artistic creation (Tatarkiewicz, 2015, pp. 21–31). In the sense of experimentation, musical improvisation, especially in monophonic cultures (Gregorian chant), was a phenomenon preceding the materialisation of the first pieces of music: first tried, then memorised and transmitted verbally, and then written down. Improvisation is also recognised as the source of the development of polyphony and new musical forms in the following centuries (Chodkowski, 1995). The evolution and refinement of keyboard instruments were conducive to improvisation, resulting in organists remaining the leading improvisers among all instrumentalists today (Improvisation, 2000, p. 126).

There are three types of creativity in improvised music from the formal side (Chodkowski, 1995): (1) creativity based on a specific musical theme in close communication with a specific form (in the example of musical arts, it will be, among others, a fugue, partita, variation), or by adding some of its elements to existing work (e.g., instrumental or vocal part or basso continuo); (2) creativity involving the introduction of an additional part to existing work (e.g., cadenza in an instrumental concerto); and (3) creativity resulting in a wholly new and autonomous work (e.g., free fantasy, impression). Since the formal side of artistic improvisation is limited to the issues described here, the creator-performer's creative attitude should focus primarily on the content rather than on the form. It does not mean, however, that one should not undertake creative activities in the field of forms.

Generating a musical work "here and now" is often seen as a knowledge-based process from which the improviser draws (Wilson, 2021). Although improvisation can be perceived as random activities, its process is well organised and based on deep knowledge of the substantive area (music, dance, acting), on experience, on intuition resulting from knowledge and experience, and on a creative identity that allows one to undertake appropriate artistic activities with adequate self-confidence; without a strong sense of doing the right thing, improvisation will be weak in expression and devoid of an artistic message (Palhares et al., 2021; Szostak, 2020a, 2021a).

The quintessence of a good artist – that is, focusing on universal values and ideas that are understandable and relevant to humanity, regardless of the era (Szostak, 2020a) – also refers to a good improviser. On this basis, a good improviser should be equipped with the following features: creativity, intuition, sensitivity, "losing yourself" in the creative process by putting everything into the creative process (from the conceptual phase to the implementation phase), the ability to set and achieve goals, the ability to observe the world perseverance, consistency in hard work on one's skills, mental toughness, openness, perceptiveness, responsibility, self-discipline, self-analysis, and self-correction. In addition, the improviser must present a minimally acceptable level of virtuosity and experience in his field (Gołaszewska, 1984; Szostak, 2022c; Szostak & Sułkowski, 2021d). Referring to the previously discussed combination of key competencies of an artistic creator, it can be said that because the artist conveys values and the virtuoso is fluent in his field, only the combination of the artistry of creativity and virtuosity of creativity will reveal the craftsmanship of a perfect improviser (Szostak, 2021a).

The most important *goals of an improviser* include: bringing the recipient to a state of catharsis, giving the recipient satisfaction and pleasure, materialising ideas, conveying universal values, and transforming ugliness (the world) into beauty (art).

In the context of improvisation, interference between the creator and the recipient of the same work is basically impossible due to the ephemeral nature of improvised production. Only including the possibility of preserving the work (recording) in this process allows the improviser to become a recipient of his work. It takes time for the improviser to be able to perceive his improvisation as a recipient. I had many situations when listening to a recording of my improvisations on the same day gave me the impression of a bad result: I heard (or maybe even felt) all the nuances remembered from the creative-performing process. Nevertheless, the same recording appeared very good, passionate, and convincing after a few days, weeks, or months.

This example also confirms that an improviser can be considered a "tool in the hands of many factors", which he is unaware of and does not fully understand during the creative process. Many accounts preserved in art history about the destruction of their works by artists (e.g., Francis Bacon, Johannes Brahms, Fryderyk Chopin, Paul Ducas, Claude Monet) only confirm this thesis.

Artistic improvisation brings a number of essential issues to management because it is a particular form of creative activity. It requires one to be proficient in virtuosity, artistry, and creativity while maintaining constant attention to a specific goal, actively considering contexts, and monitoring these issues in real time by one person. By analogy, it can be said that the improviser makes all the manager's and the organisation's decisions independently in one creative process. Of course, this does not mean that all these decisions are made only with thought and intellectual work; many decisions result from intuition or subconsciousness. In contrast, neither intuition nor the subconscious are innate, so they are shaped in such a way that they effectively serve the improviser,

The improviser can be analysed as a *manager of the improvisational process*. Each improvisation takes place in a specific environment and contexts resulting from it; for improvisation to be persuasive, engaged, and grounded, the improviser should consider the circumstances in which he or she will be improvising. An improviser has specific features of a basic personality and a creative personality shaped on its basis – awareness of personality typology, their impact on the creative process and ways to use them is another competence to master. An improviser without the creator's identity will not be convincing; the improviser must feel confident in what he does; improvisation is a work through which he communicates with the audience, and therefore the improviser must know what he wants to convey, how to do it effectively, and, finally, carry out the process itself from start to finish. The improviser must understand the sources of his creativity, the motives for undertaking creative activities, and the sources of inspiration. Without these elements, it is difficult to talk about involvement in the process of improvisational creativity. Artistic improvisation is not an automatic activity. An improviser must consider the aforementioned components to be called an improvisational process manager (Figure 5.6).

The process of artistic improvisation described in this section can be used as a source of analysis for *managerial improvisation*, e.g., in the field of *improvised managerial decisions* (Kochereva, 2019). Of course, there is a fundamental difference between improvised and random decisions. Every managerial decision occurs in a specific environment and context (Hargreaves, 2012; Kochereva, 2019). For an improvised decision to be persuasive, engaging, and embedded in these contexts, the manager should consider the circumstances in which he or

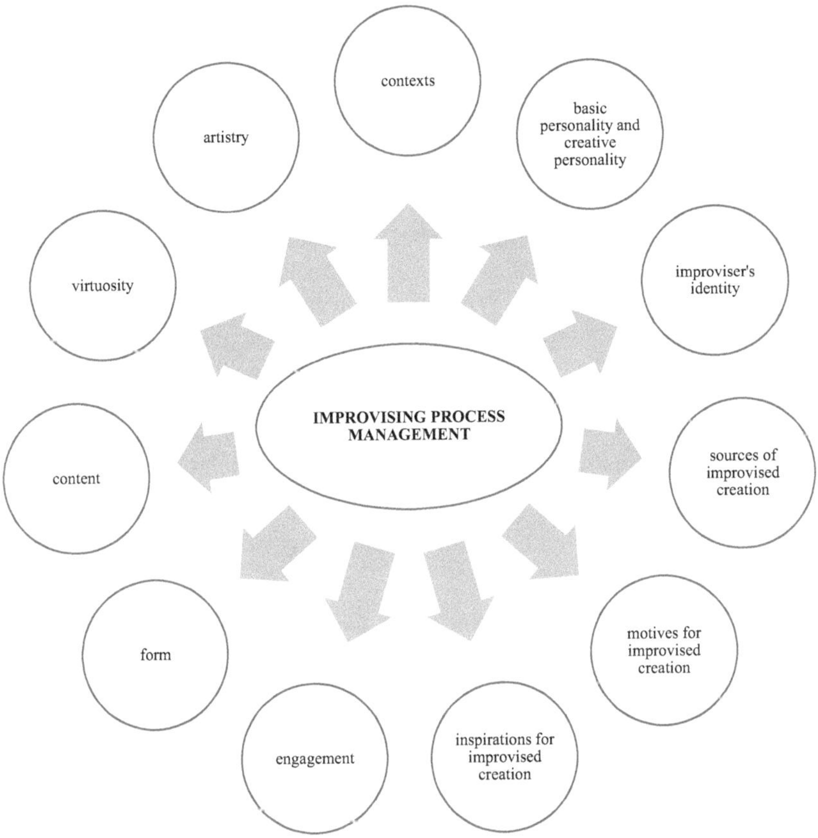

Figure 5.6 Components of improvisation process management

Source: Author's own elaboration

she will have to make decisions in an improvised manner. A manager, like every individual, has certain basic personality traits and a creative personality shaped on their basis; he should be aware of these personality typologies, their impact on the creative process, and the ways of using them. If a manager has a reflective or behavioural type of creative personality, then he or she should be extraordinarily prudent in making improvised decisions. A manager without a creative identity will not be confident. A manager should understand the sources from which his creativity stems, the motives for taking his actions and the sources that inspire him, i.e. what influences his behaviour. Without awareness of these elements, it is difficult to talk about involvement in the process of improvisational creativity. Improvised managerial decisions are not made automatically. The manager must consider the aforementioned components to be able to make improvised decisions instead of random decisions – even though the processes will look identical to the observer.

Another analogy between improvisation activity and organisational issues can be found in the area of project management according to the agile methodology. A comparison of the features of the improvised activity management process and the features of the project work process according to the agile methodology shows many common features in the form of taking into account: the environment and contexts, own capabilities and competencies (type of creative personality), and commitment as a function of goals, motives, and inspirations, as well as factors of permanent self-verification and autocorrect. Of course, project management according to the agile methodology applies to teams and also has differences from the improvisation process (for example, the time factor and separating the conceptual phase from the implementation phase); however, it is nothing more than the implementation of the philosophy of the improvisation process described in this section based on teamwork on complex projects.

5.4 Form of participation in art and level of artistry and creativity

Living in the 21st century, we participate in various areas of human activity through ever-new ways and methods, even without any particular awareness of the changes. However, the form of participation shapes the content of participation and consequently changes our inputs and outputs (Karayilanoğlu & Arabacioğlu, 2020). Global shifts towards the intensification of digital transformation affect most activities, ranging from the health, education, and social care sectors, through the information and technology sectors, to manufacturing, commerce, and arts and media (Bradley et al., 2020; Lei & Tan, 2021). In the field of culture and art, technological progress is transforming social interactions, aesthetic experiences, and forms of expression (Kröner et al., 2021). The COVID-19 pandemic, according to the common opinion of researchers, has caused a multi-sectoral acceleration of digitisation and computerisation processes (Kudyba, 2020; Tregua et al., 2021). Significant changes affect small, medium, and large organisations in the private and public sectors. Changes towards virtualisation, teleworking, remote management, and interactive network communication have been visible for many decades, but both the pace and scale of these activities accelerated significantly in 2020–2021, which was the result of the pandemic.

Considering participation in art from the perspective of the aesthetic situation, we consider this phenomenon from two different perspectives: the optics of the creator, and the optics of the recipient. Therefore, the metamodel of these considerations can be described as a function of combining "aesthetic situation" and "digital technologies" to obtain results regarding possible changes in the levels of creativity and artistry depending on the type of participation. In other words, it is about the impact of virtualisation on individual elements of the aesthetic situation in terms of changes in the level of creativity and artistry.

In order to empirically verify the creativity management process, a complex primary study was planned, divided into two stages:

1. creator-work (creative process) – the results of this stage are presented in Section 2.3.2, "Management of the aesthetic situation";
2. work-recipient (receipt process) – this stage will be presented now.

The objectives of the second stage were: (1) to assess the impact of digital technologies on the perception of each type of art (negative or positive); (2) assessment of the scale of the impact of digital technologies on the perception of each type of art; and (3) assessment of the scale of loss/gain of creativity and artistry due to the use of digital technologies in each type of art. In order to achieve these goals, the following research hypotheses were formulated:

H1. The form of participation (real or digital) in art determines the level of quality of audience participation in an aesthetic situation.
H2. The form of participation in art shapes the level of quality of participation in the aesthetic situation of recipients of each type of art in a different way.

It should be emphasised that the study focuses on the real and digital process of receiving works of art by the recipient and not on using digital tools to talk about art and works of art.

5.4.1 Creator's perspective

The analysis of the artist's perspective towards the aesthetic situation taking place traditionally or virtually is described in Chapter 2 from the epistemological, empirical, and application sides. The methodology of the undertaken study is presented in the Introduction of the monograph (see "Research methodology 1"), while detailed results and conclusions are included in Section 2.3.2, "Management of the aesthetic situation".

5.4.2 Recipient's perspective

From the point of view of the aesthetic situation, the creator creates his work, taking into account the real world and the world of universal values, and then leaves this finished result (work of art) to the recipient. The recipient may choose the method of participation in the collection process per his will, possibilities, and circumstances. On the other hand, from a practical point of view, a wrong decision about the form of perception can deeply determine the content and process of reception because each form of participation has advantages and disadvantages. It should also be noted that more experienced audiences can use a less effective form of participation more fluently without losing too much of the artistic content. However, even the most effective participation form may not be enough to deliver all the content to a less experienced recipient.

Art has made a sharp turn thanks to advanced IT tools, digitisation, social media, and business skills (Handa, 2020). The performing arts, in particular, have undergone a radical change in the digital age as ephemeral performances can now be replayed and relived (Dunne-Howrie, 2020). The increase in digitisation in art was faster, broader, and deeper from year to year. In addition, the COVID-19 pandemic has added new impetus to this process: travel bans and the need to maintain social distancing. At this point in the still-unfinished COVID-19 pandemic, it will not be easy to assess which factors were the causes and which were the effects of the virtualisation of art (Habelsberger & Bhansing, 2021; Zahra, 2021). At the same time, however, we see that, apart from the digital transformation of participation, new trends are emerging among creators, such as a turn towards entrepreneurship (Szostak & Sułkowski, 2021b) or even problems with self-identification (Szostak & Sułkowski, 2021c, 2021d) that were previously rare or even unknown.

The combination of digitisation and casual work through outsourcing by corporations, NGOs, and governments creates completely new working conditions (Hermes et al., 2017). Therefore, more attention should be paid to the cognitive and affective dimensions of participation in art, going beyond the usual patterns of approaches to art. In the new digital environment, employees and art lovers stimulate inclusivity and active participation in the arts (Huang, 2015). Participation in art requires the senses. However, the digitisation of art is limited by the technology of transferring the experiences of the analogue senses into virtual dimensions (Mao & Jiang, 2021). It is, therefore, legitimate for digital participation in the arts to be called "digital mediation"; this concept defines the role of digital technology in a precise position, i.e., "between" the work of art and the recipient (Jarrier & Bourgeon-Renault, 2019). The senses enable physical, emotional (Buravenkova et al., 2018), intellectual, and spiritual (Rivas-Carmona, 2020; Wu, 2020) participation in the arts; the analysis of the acceptance process at all these levels reveals the degree of complexity of the examined problem.

There is also a fundamental question to be solved: is the digitisation and virtualisation of the aesthetic situation an evolution or a revolution concerning the essence of art? We can find arguments for both approaches. Digital technologies allow for the transformation of the environment and change the historical approach to many issues. It can be said that today's culture is somehow structured by digitisation (Roberge & Chantepie, 2017). Bearing that the digital revolution influences and is shaped differently by individual cultures, it also extends spirituality from its authentic context in the socio-cultural interpretation of the natural world to contemporary, digitally mediated environments (Sosnowska,

2015). The mediatisation of cultural practices changes the mechanisms of cultural memory formation, and online communication skills have become the basis for education that balances tradition and modernisation (Arkhangelsky & Novikova, 2021). Participating in the arts through digital tools also has new applications, i.e., a form of advanced treatment for ageing and demented patients suffering from apathy and lack of interest and enthusiasm that can accompany memory and cognitive decline (Tao et al., 2020). The concept of online art crowdsourcing is understood as the practice of using the Internet as a participatory platform to directly engage the public in the creation of works of art; this approach aims to show the relationship between the collective imagination and the individual artistic sensitivity of its participants (Literat, 2012). Digitisation of the aesthetic experience (using digital participation tools) should also be considered in the context of increasing or losing creativity.

Digitisation opens horizons for a broader range of art recipients but also triggers other issues. First, the approach of mass audiences to the quality of a work of art: higher artistry of the work may mean perceptual difficulties and fewer recipients; lower artistry of the work and greater ease of perception will attract more recipients. Secondly, digital exclusion limits participation in the reception process: in addition to the desire to participate in art, the recipient must have appropriate digital tools (hardware, software, Internet access). Thirdly, the digitisation of art can be used to develop the service role of art to make it more understandable and customer-centric (Pöppel et al., 2018). A significant problem, however, is the relationship between value and quality by means of which a person evaluates and compares various objects, including art, with which he comes into contact (Fortuna & Modliński, 2021).

Concerning musical arts, when receiving a concert in real form, the recipient comes face to face with a work of art in the shape desired by the artist; no volume control – the artist strictly designs dynamics; no pauses on request – the form of the work is clear and unchanging regardless of the opinion of the listeners, the viewer avoids leaving the audience seat, and pauses in the opera performance are marked and designed by the composer. In turn, the digital form of participation in musical arts allows for these corrections and – if it is made randomly – the work of art affects the recipient differently from the desires of the creator. Notably, electronic music, computer music, and digital sound art have their creative practices and historical processes separated from the so-called classical music (Born & Devine, 2016); the electronic environment and the digital way of participation are natural for this kind of music. In performing arts, perceived traditionally, the recipient is also a kind of prisoner of the work of art; he must follow the rules of the work (its length, breaks, volume, visibility). Contemporary performing arts reinforce intermediality, hybridisation, and dialogue between different media and languages. With the development of digital technology, the performing arts experience new possibilities that shape their ontology (Zorita-Aguirre, 2020).

Of all the arts, the performing arts are most affected by digitisation, showing how different interaction methods determine the user experience (Dube & İnce, 2019). Social media can be used as a marketing tool and a form of digital staging that helps engage audiences with the development and outcomes of theatre performances. Nevertheless, social media platforms can be used in unusual ways to hybridise the digital/physical space between performer and audience, resulting in an original co-produced performance. The blurring of this border causes marketing to become a co-created interaction while inviting viewers to participate in the performance (Miles, 2018).

Theoretically, the literary arts should not be deeply affected by the form of participation; however, the questions posed by interactive technologies have their predecessors in pre-electronic artistic traditions (Ryan, 2020). Digitisation makes literary collections accessible at a fingertip, but books are increasingly changing from "physical repositories" to "access portals" to their content. We can say that people who are attracted to printing artefacts (books, magazines) often find that digital substitutes lack feeling. Digitised texts retain the linguistic content of printed works but contain few significant physical features that fundamentally shape interpretation and contain valuable historical traces and reading interactions (Stauffer, 2012). Changing physical interactions with a work of art can also change its meaning (Forlini et al., 2018).

Audiovisual arts are, by their very nature, consistent with a digital form of participation. However, being the recipient of an audiovisual work (e.g., a movie) in a real cinema or digitally at home, we can imagine significant differences between these forms (Demiańczuk, 2022). For example, the recipient cannot stop or change the volume of a movie in a theatre; at home, yes, it is possible. Moreover, in the cinema, the viewer is influenced by the audience's reaction; he is alone at home. Therefore, the use of visual image technology based on the user interface (UI) and virtual reality (VR) technology in art allows for the development of digital media art (Mao & Jiang, 2021).

The form of the reception process of visual arts also significantly determines the shape of the reception process: the image is determined by its content, but also by its form (size), the environment (in which it appears to the recipient), and the emotions it evokes. The picture's frame cuts off the outside world from the world of painting, but the outside world also determines the feelings around and towards the picture. On this basis, digital collaboration in art, digital marketing, and digital performance can differentiate and include audiences as authentic co-producers of art (Fortuna & Modliński, 2021).

Following this, it seems interesting to examine how the recipients of art perceive the works created in this process – as created by machines or people, as created by the artists themselves, only by the recipients, or by both sides together. However, the effectiveness and durability of digitalising the aesthetic situation have not yet been proven (Nawa & Sirayi, 2014). On this basis, management – understood as the effective achievement of goals – consists of selecting and moderating the optimal type of participation in each type of art, taking into account the acceptable loss/gain of creativity and artistry for creators and/or recipients of art. Art makers are working "harder" by professionalising and "smarter" in the digital environment, shifting specialisation and getting help with creative and non-creative duties from collaborators and performers. In this new organisational model, managers play an essential intermediary role in connecting, coordinating, and overseeing these processes (Hracs, 2015) to connect values and the real world on the wave of the global digitisation trend, significantly accelerated during the COVID-19 pandemic (Lei & Tan, 2021).

In order to verify the theoretical considerations and recognise the phenomenon on empirical grounds, a pilot study was undertaken, the methodological details of which are described in the Introduction to this monograph (see "Research methodology 2"). Since the research sample can be considered unrepresentative for an extensive range of occurrences of the examined features, detailed results of this study are not presented in this book. However, they were published in independent articles due to their significant cognitive value. The structure of the study allowed for the presentation of the results in a synthetic form (Szostak & Sułkowski, 2023) and taking into account the following sociological criteria of the examined entities: gender (Szostak, 2023b), originating from communist and post-communist countries in opposition to countries without a communist history (Szostak, 2022b), and having and not having Polish citizenship (Szostak, 2022a). After a thorough analysis of the accelerated digitisation and virtualisation of the aesthetic situation forced by the COVID-19 pandemic – from the perspective of both creators and recipients in every art discipline – the synthetic conclusions from this area are as follows.

From the artist's perspective, the virtualisation of the creative process within the aesthetic situation is an unfavourable phenomenon, and the level of loss of the quality of the aesthetic situation depends on individual art disciplines. Therefore, the creators try to rationalise the need to adapt the creative process to forced virtualisation and the impact of this situation on the management of the aesthetic situation. However, they strongly advocate the preference for traditional forms of participation in art, both in terms of their perspective and the perception of the audience by the creators.

The virtual form of participation in an aesthetic situation generally reduces the level of quality of participation according to the audience. Here, too, the level of loss of quality of the aesthetic situation varies across art disciplines: the quality of traditional (live) participation in the musical, performing, literary, and visual arts is higher in the eyes of the audience than in the case of virtual participation; only in the audiovisual arts is the quality of participation in a traditional way (allowing for live interactions) rated lower than fully virtual participation.

The form of participation (live or virtual) in art has a slightly different effect on the level of quality of participation in an aesthetic situation in the opinion of Polish and foreign audiences. Cultural differences between Poles and citizens of other countries are also visible between participation in particular types of art and between particular forms of participation in particular types of art. Extrapolating the results, it can be concluded that these differences are based on basic cultural dimensions, including individualism-collectivism or uncertainty avoidance resulting strictly from historical conditions. Probably proportionally to the time that elapses from the beginning of the journey from communism to capitalism, these differences will decrease even after the post-communist traumas have healed.

The results of this study may be valuable for: (1) art creators, looking for optimal methods of distributing works of art among different categories of recipients; (2) art managers and marketers, who want to understand better the perspectives of different categories of art recipients and their preferences regarding participation in art in traditional or virtual form; and (3) art recipients, in order to compare their own opinion on the ways of participating in art with the preferences of various categories of art recipients.

5.5 Summary

The theory of aesthetics contributes a lot to describing the phenomenon of creativity of the manager as a self-managing unit and the person responsible for the creativity of the organisation he manages. Learning the theories about creativity, both in terms of the stages of the creative process (in classical theories) and its components and their mutual interactions (in system theories) allows us to look at the phenomenon of creativity more consciously. This awareness is an excellent basis for managing individual and organisational creative activity. The awareness of the existence of both personalities (basic and creative) in each individual causes that the creative potential lies dormant in each of them. The key, however, is to discover a way to find a creative personality and develop it skilfully; this development is time-consuming and demanding. The manager must also consider that creative activity is exhausting, so creativity has its limits, which he should be aware of – especially if it requires creativity from the team he manages. Optimal results in stimulating creativity can be achieved by addressing the issue of engagement; because creativity is determined primarily by factors internal to the individual, classic mechanisms of motivation (which refer to factors controlled externally by the individual) are not enough; here, it is necessary to reach for the issues that stimulate the individual's involvement in creative activity. The manager can successfully model his team's creative process by viewing engagement as a function of goals, motives, and inspirations. On the other hand, being a convincing creator requires having a solid and conscious motive and the right trigger in the form of inspiration driven by the current context and the significant role of the environment. A convincing artist cannot forget about the universal values that should be present in his works to preserve true art's main features.

Artistic improvisation – because it combines the need for parallel coordination of virtuosity, artistry, and creativity, considering time management and contextual references to the goal accompanying a given creative activity – can contribute greatly to understanding the essence of creativity and thus help manage creativity effectively. All the processes mentioned in this chapter occur in the improviser's mind in parallel, and a change in one of them determines immediate adjustments in the other processes. The improviser is, therefore, an emanation of the artist of self-management. Understanding all the components of the improvisation process and how to coordinate them can help managers deal with the challenges of multitasking and creativity.

Awareness of the components of the aesthetic situation and their mutual relations and interactions is the basis for the artist to manage the process of engaged artistic creation in terms of efficiency in achieving the set goals. The fact that each art discipline uses the human senses in a different combination means that the artist working in each discipline must adjust how to manage the creative process within a specific aesthetic situation. Furthermore, the multiplicity and depth of changes taking place in reality (with particular emphasis on the struggle with the COVID-19 pandemic) means that the process of managing the aesthetic situation must consider new contexts that have not existed so far. Such a context, which fundamentally changes the artist's perspective in each art discipline differently, is the issue of digitalisation and virtualisation of the aesthetic situation. This issue causes the creator to face hitherto-unknown problems that he must solve if he still wants to "be on the wave". The presented results of my empirical research in the field of managing the creative process in an aesthetic situation taking place in a traditional (live) and virtual way show which components and their relationships must be modified so that the work can continue to affect the recipient in the way intended by the creator.

The contexts mentioned in this chapter also affect the recipient and his process of receiving a work of art within the aesthetic situation in a traditional (live) and virtual way. The discussed results of their empirical research show the creators how the recipients evaluate various components and their relationships within the aesthetic situation that plays out in two ways. Despite the fact that both studies concern metaphysical phenomena, the research tools used allow for objectifying the subjective feelings of the research participants. They can indicate to the creators the issues that should be addressed in a virtualised aesthetic situation.

Notes

1 This is an analogy to the creative attitude in the theory of aesthetics – see Figure 2.4.

2 The score is not a physical dimension of a musical work, but only a record of actions that must be taken to make a given work exist.

References

Acar, O. A., Tarakci, M., & van Knippenberg, D. (2019). Creativity and innovation under constraints: A cross-disciplinary integrative review. *Journal of Management*, *45*(1), 96–121. https://doi.org/10.1177/0149206318805832

Adler, N. J., & Ippolito, L. M. (2018). Musical leadership and societal transformation: Inspiration and courage in action. *Kwartalnik Ekonomistów i Menedżerów*, *50*(4), 41–65. https://doi.org/10.5604/01.3001.0013.0629

Ahmad, S. M., & Zadeh, Z. F. (2016). Gender differences on the variables of emotional intelligence, creative-potential and job satisfaction in managers. *Pakistan Journal of Psychology*, *47*(2), 61–77.

Alsuwaidi, K. A. K. Y., & Omar, A. J. (2020). Structural model of principals' innovative leadership attributes on managerial creativity. *International Journal of Sustainable Construction Engineering and Technology*, *11*(2), 150–156. https://doi.org/10.30880/ijscet.2020.11.02.017

Arbuz-Spatari, O. (2019). Art – subject – object in artistic and plastic creativity of pupils and students in artistic education. *Review of Artistic Education*, *18*(1), 233–240. https://doi.org/10.2478/rae-2019-0025

Arkhangelsky, A. N., & Novikova, A. A. (2021). A transmedia turn in educational strategies: Storytelling in teaching literature to school students. *Voprosy Obrazovaniya*, *2021*(2), 63–81. https://doi.org/10.17323/1814-9545-2021-2-63-81

Baer, J. (2012). Domain specificity and the limits of creativity theory. *Journal of Creative Behavior*, *46*(1), 16–29. https://doi.org/10.1002/jocb.002

Basadur, M., & DeGroote, M. G. (1995). Optimal ideation-evaluation ratios. *Creativity Research Journal*, *8*(1), 63–75. https://doi.org/10.1207/s15326934crj0801_5

Benedek, M., Bruckdorfer, R., & Jauk, E. (2020). Motives for creativity: Exploring the what and why of everyday creativity. *Journal of Creative Behavior*, *54*(3), 610–625. https://doi.org/10.1002/jocb.396

Biehl-Missal, B. (2011). *Wirtschaftsästhetik: Wie Unternehmen die Kunst als Inspiration und Werkzeug nutzen*. Gabler Verlag.

Bigo, V. (2018). On silence, creativity and ethics in organization studies. *Organization Studies*, *39*(1), 121–133. https://doi.org/10.1177/0170840617717553

Born, G., & Devine, K. (2016). Gender, creativity and education in digital musics and sound art. *Contemporary Music Review*, *35*(1), 1–20. https://doi.org/10.1080/07494467.2016.1177255

Bradley, C., Hirt, M., Hudson, S., Northcote, N., & Smit, S. (2020, July). The great acceleration. *McKinsey & Company*, 1–7.

Brieger, S. A., De Clercq, D., & Meynhardt, T. (2020). Doing good, feeling good? Entrepreneurs' social value creation beliefs and work-related well-being. *Journal of Business Ethics*. https://doi.org/10.1007/s10551-020-04512-6

Bulei, I., Mihalcioiu, V., & Tucmeanu, A. (2014). The professional vs. the manager – identity issues and key Features. *Valahian Journal of Economic Studies*, *5*(3), 31–36.

Buravenkova, Y., Yakupov, R., Samsonovich, A. V., & Stepanskaya, E. (2018). Toward a virtual composer assistant. *Procedia Computer Science*, *123*, 553–561. https://doi.org/10.1016/j.procs.2018.01.084

Calic, G., & Hélie, S. (2018, August). Creative sparks or paralysis traps? The effects of contradictions on creative processing and creative products. *Frontiers in Psychology*, *9*, 1–17. https://doi.org/10.3389/fpsyg.2018.01489

Ceylan, C., Dul, J., & Aytac, S. (2008). Can the office environment stimulate a manager's creativity? *Human Factors and Ergonomics in Manufacturing*, *18*(6), 589–602. https://doi.org/10.1002/hfm.20128

Che Ibrahim, C. K. I., Costello, S. B., & Wilkinson, S. (2018). Making sense of team integration practice through the "lived experience" of alliance project teams. *Engineering, Construction and Architectural Management*, *25*(5), 598–622. https://doi.org/10.1108/ECAM-09-2016-0208

Chodkowski, A. (1995). Improwizacja. In *Encyklopedia muzyki* (p. 382). Wydawnictwo naukowe PWN.

Collver, J., & Weitkamp, E. (2018). Alter egos: An exploration of the perspectives and identities of science comic creators. *Journal of Science Communication*, *17*(1). https://doi.org/10.22323/2.17010201

Craft, A. (2003). The limits to creativity in education: Dilemmas for the educator. *British Journal of Educational Studies*, *51*(2), 113–127. https://doi.org/10.1111/j.1467-8527.2003.00229.x

Creativity. (2023a). In *Cambridge dictionary*. https://dictionary.cambridge.org/dictionary/english/creativity

Creativity. (2023b). In *Merriam-Webster*. www.merriam-webster.com/dictionary/creativity

Crilly, N. (2019). Creativity and fixation in the real world: A literature review of case study research. *Design Studies*, *64*, 154–168. https://doi.org/10.1016/j.destud.2019.07.002

Crilly, N., & Cardoso, C. (2017). Where next for research on fixation, inspiration and creativity in design? *Design Studies*, *50*, 1–38. https://doi.org/10.1016/j.destud.2017.02.001

Csikszentmihalyi, M. (2014). Flow and the foundations of positive psychology: The collected works of Mihaly Csikszentmihalyi. In *Flow and the Foundations of Positive Psychology: The Collected Works of Mihaly Csikszentmihalyi*. https://doi.org/10.1007/978-94-017-9088-8

Cullum, R. J., Shaughnessy, A., Mayat, N. Y., & Brown, M. E. (2020). Identity in lockdown: Supporting primary care professional identity development in the COVID-19 generation. *Education for Primary Care*, *31*(4), 200–204. https://doi.org/10.1080/14739879.2020.1779616

Dahlberg, S. T. (2007). Creative engagement. *Supporting Creative Acts beyond Dissemination: Creativity & Cognition 2007*, 1–5. https://doi.org/10.1145/3106548.3106599

Dahlhaus, C., & Eggebrecht, H. H. (1978). Improvisation. In *Brockhaus Riemann Musiklexikon* (Vol. I, p. 580). B. Schott's Söhne.

Daniel, R. (2021). Exploring creativity through artists' reflections. *Creativity Studies*, *14*(1), 1–17. https://doi.org/10.3846/cs.2021.11207

Dash, P. (2019). Creativity and innovation: Addressing entrepreneurship commitments. *International Journal of Psychosocial Rehabilitation*, *23*(6), 148–154. https://doi.org/10.37200/IJPR/V23I6/PR190750

David, O., & Bar-Tal, D. (2009). A sociopsychological conception of collective identity: The case of national identity as an example. *Personality and Social Psychology Review*, *13*(4), 354–379. https://doi.org/10.1177/1088868309344412

DeFillippi, R., Grabher, G., & Jones, C. (2007). Introduction to paradoxes of creativity: Managerial and organizational challenges in the cultural economy. *Journal of Organizational Behavior*, *28*, 511–521. https://doi.org/10.1002/job

Demiańczuk, J. (2022). Ostatni seans? *Polityka*, *22*(3365), 14–16.

Dube, T. J., & İnce, G. (2019). A novel interface for generating choreography based on augmented reality. *International Journal of Human Computer Studies*, *132*, 12–24. https://doi.org/10.1016/j.ijhcs.2019.07.005

Duconseille, F., & Saner, R. (2020). Creative placemaking for inclusive urban landscapes. *Journal of Arts Management Law and Society*, *50*(3), 137–154. https://doi.org/10.1080/10632921.2020.1754985

Dunne-Howrie, J. (2020). Documenting performance: The contexts & processes of digital curation and archiving. *International Journal of Performance Arts and Digital Media*, *16*(2), 217–218. https://doi.org/10.1080/14794713.2020.1778840

Dutton, D. (2019). *Instynkt sztuki*. Copernicus Cener Press.

The Economist. (2022). How thinking hard makes the brain tired. *The Economist*. www.economist.com/science-and-technology/2022/08/11/how-thinking-hard-makes-the-brain-tired

Elstad, B., & Jansson, D. (2020). From artist to manager – working conditions, career satisfaction, and professional identity among graduated arts management students. *Journal of Arts Management Law and Society*, *50*(3), 184–198. https://doi.org/10.1080/10632921.2020.1746717

Ferrari, A., Cachia, R., & Yves, P. (2009). Innovation and creativity in education and training in the EU member states: Fostering creative learning and supporting innovative teaching. In *JRC Technical Notes*. www.jrc.ec.europa.eu/%0Awww.researchgate.net/publication/265996963_Innovation_and_Creativity_in_Education_and_Training_in_the_EU_Member_States_Fostering_Creative_Learning_and_Supporting_Innovative_Teaching_Literature_review_on_Innovation_an

Forlini, S., Hinrichs, U., & Brosz, J. (2018). Mining the material archive: Balancing sensate experience and sense-making in digitized print collections. *Open Library of Humanities*, *4*(2), 1–36. https://doi.org/10.16995/olh.282

Formica, P., & Edmondson, J. (2020). Innovation and the arts: The value of humanities studies for business. In *Innovation and the arts: The value of humanities studies for business*. Emerald Publishing Limited. https://doi.org/10.1108/9781789738858

Fortuna, P., & Modliński, A. (2021). A(I)rtist or counterfeiter? Artificial intelligence as (D)Evaluating factor on the art market. *Journal of Arts Management Law and Society*, *51*(3), 188–201. https://doi.org/10.1080/10632921.2021.1887032

Foxon, M. (2008). The influence of motivation to transfer, action planning, and manager support on the transfer process. *Performance Improvement Quarterly*, *10*(2), 42–63. https://doi.org/10.1111/j.1937-8327.1997.tb00048.x

Friedman, H. H., Leverton, C., & Friedman, L. W. (2015). To foster creativity and success, remove intentional and unintentional discrimination. *SSRN Electronic Journal*. https://doi.org/10.2139/ssrn.2649712

García-González, D. E. (2021). Ethics, creativity and imagination: Essential elements for building cultures of peace. *Araucaria*, *48*, 303–324. https://doi.org/10.12795/araucaria.2021.i48.14

Gloton, R., & Clero, C. (1988). *Twórcza aktywność dziecka*. Wydawnictwa Szkolne i Pedagogiczne.

Gołaszewska, M. (1984). *Zarys estetyki*. PWN.
Gołaszewska, M. (1986). *Kim jest artysta?* Wydawnictwa Szkolne i Pedagogiczne.
Gołaszewska, M. (2005). *Estetyka możliwości*. Wydawnictwo Uniwersytetu Jagiellońskiego.
Goldberg-Miller, S. B. D., & Xiao, Y. (2018). Arts entrepreneurship and cultural policy innovation in Beijing. *Artivate: A Journal of Entrepreneurship in the Arts*, *7*(1), 23–47. https://artivate.org/artivate/article/view/77/66
Grace, V., Huberth, M., & Fujioka, T. (2019). Effects of extramusical information and human presence on perceived emotion intensity in electronic music. *Psychomusicology: Music, Mind, and Brain*, *29*(2–3), 117–127. https://doi.org/10.1037/pmu0000223
Gross, M. E., Araujo, D. B., Zedelius, C. M., & Schooler, J. W. (2019). Is perception the missing link between creativity, curiosity and schizotypy? Evidence from spontaneous eye-movements and responses to auditory oddball stimuli. *NeuroImage*, *202*. https://doi.org/10.1016/j.neuroimage.2019.116125
Grote, F. (2014). Jamming with machines social technologies in musical creativity. *Conference of the European Research Network Sociology of the Arts*, 1–4. https://fgrote.files.wordpress.com/2014/09/esa-arts_2014_grote_-jamming_with_machines.pdf
Habelsberger, B. E. M., & Bhansing, P. V. (2021). Art galleries in transformation: Is COVID-19 driving digitisation? *Arts*, *10*(48), 1–23. https://doi.org/10.3390/arts10030048
Handa, J. (2020). Impact of social media and digitalization on the growth of fashion designers. *International Journal of Textile and Fashion Technology (IJTFT)*, *10*(1), 1–12. www.tjprc.org/view-archives.php?keyword=&from_date=&to_date=&id=&type=2&journal=29&page=11
Hargreaves, D. J. (2012). Musical imagination: Perception and production, beauty and creativity. *Psychology of Music*, *40*(5), 539–557. https://doi.org/10.1177/0305735612444893
Hermes, J., Koch, K., Bakhuisen, N., & Borghuis, P. (2017). This is my life: The stories of independent workers in the creative industries in the Netherlands. *Javnost*, *24*(1), 87–101. https://doi.org/10.1080/13183222.2017.1280892
Hocking, I. (2019, February). Portrait of an artist as collaborator: An interpretative phenomenological analysis of an artist. *Frontiers in Psychology*, *10*, 1–10. https://doi.org/10.3389/fpsyg.2019.00251
Hongisto, I., & Pape, T. (2015). Unexpected artivism: The fabulatory function in Kumaré. *Studies in Documentary Film*, *9*(1), 69–83. https://doi.org/10.1080/17503280.2014.1002252
Hracs, B. J. (2015). Cultural intermediaries in the digital age: The case of independent musicians and managers in Toronto. *Regional Studies*, *49*(3), 461–475. https://doi.org/10.1080/00343404.2012.750425
Huang, C. E., & Liu, C. H. (2019). Impacts of social capital and knowledge acquisition on service innovation: An integrated empirical analysis of the role of shared values. *Journal of Hospitality Marketing and Management*, *28*(5), 645–664. https://doi.org/10.1080/19368623.2019.1540957
Huang, Y. (2015). Review of "audience engagement and the role of arts talk in the digital era", by Lynne Conner. *Journal of Arts Management, Law, and Society*, *45*(4), 269–270. https://doi.org/10.1080/10632921.2015.1065537
Improvisation. (2000). In *Encyclopædia Britannica: Edycja polska* (Vol. 17). Wydawnictwo Kurpisz.

Jarrier, E., & Bourgeon-Renault, D. (2019). The role of digital mediation devices in the satisfaction of art museum audiences. *Le Rôle Des Dispositifs Numériques de Médiation Dans La Satisfaction Des Publics de Musée d'art*, *5*(3), 67–84. https://search.ebscohost.com/login.aspx?direct=true&db=bth&AN=146420604&lang=es&site=ehost-live

Jung, C. G. (2014). *The spirit in man, art, and literature* (Vol. 15). https://doi.org/10.1515/9781400851010.791

Kačerauskas, T. (2018). Indices of creative economy: Critique of R. Florida's creativity indices. *Economics and Sociology*, *11*(4), 280–288. https://doi.org/10.14254/2071-789X.2018/11-4/18

Karayilanoğlu, G., & Arabacioğlu, B. C. (2020). Digital interactive experiences in contemporary art museums. *Turkish Online Journal of Design Art and Communication*, *10*(4), 423–440. https://doi.org/10.7456/11004100/007

Kochereva, D. (2019). Phenomenon of creativity: Contents, essence, features of development. *HUMANITARIUM*, *43*(1), 85–92. https://doi.org/10.31470/2308-5126-2019-43-1-85–92

Kopaliński, W. (1989). Improwizacja. In *Słownik wyrazów obcych i zwrotów obcojęzycznych* (Wydanie XV, pp. 781–782). Wiedza Powszechna.

Kostyszak, M. (2020). Nietzscheańska koncepcja źródeł twórczości artystycznej. *Grotowski.Net*. https://grotowski.net/performer/performer-20/nietzscheanska-koncepcja-zrodel-tworczosci-artystycznej

Kröner, S., Christ, A., & Penthin, M. (2021). Digitalization in aesthetics, arts and cultural education – a scoping review. *Zeitschrift Fur Erziehungswissenschaft*, *24*(1), 9–39. https://doi.org/10.1007/s11618-021-00989-7

Kudyba, S. (2020). COVID-19 and the acceleration of digital transformation and the future of work. *Information Systems Management*, *37*(4), 284–287. https://doi.org/10.1080/10580530.2020.1818903

Kułaga, M., & Trzcionka, M. (2019). Granice wyobrażone i rzeczywiste – ewolucja i transgresja. *Politeja*, *16*(1(58)), 465–491. https://doi.org/10.12797/politeja.16.2019.58.25

Larso, D., & Saphiranti, D. (2016). The role of creative courses in entrepreneurship education: A case study in Indonesia. *International Journal of Business*, *21*(3), 216–225.

Lebuda, I., & Csikszentmihalyi, M. (2020). All you need is love: The importance of partner and family relations to highly creative individuals' well-being and success. *Journal of Creative Behavior*, *54*(1), 100–114. https://doi.org/10.1002/jocb.348

Lei, P., & Tan, E. B. (2021). Applying digital arts experience to strengthen the organizational culture in higher education during the pandemic. *International Journal for Innovation Education and Research*, *9*(5), 169–173. https://doi.org/10.31686/ijier.vol9.iss5.3080

Lemoine, G. J., & Blum, T. C. (2021). Servant leadership, leader gender, and team gender role: Testing a female advantage in a cascading model of performance. *Personnel Psychology*, *74*(1), 3–28. https://doi.org/10.1111/peps.12379

Li, G., Liu, H., & Luo, Y. (2018). Directive versus participative leadership: Dispositional antecedents and team consequences. *Journal of Occupational and Organizational Psychology*, *91*(3), 645–664. https://doi.org/10.1111/joop.12213

Li, T., & Yue, C. (2019). Working with creative leaders: An examination of the relationship between leader and team creativity. *Social Behavior and Personality*, *47*(6). https://doi.org/10.2224/sbp.8084

Literat, I. (2012). The work of art in the age of mediated participation: Crowdsourced art and collective creativity. *International Journal of Communication*, *6*, 2962–2984.

Liu, D., Liao, H., & Loi, R. (2012). The dark side of leadership: A three-level investigation of the cascading effect of abusive supervision on employee creativity. *Academy of Management Journal*, *55*(5), 1187–1212. https://doi.org/10.5465/amj.2010.0400

Liu, W., Fang, Y., Shi, J., & Mo, S. (2018). The impact of supervisor's creativity expectation on team creativity. *Acta Psychologica Sinica*, *50*(6), 667–677. https://doi.org/10.3724/SP.J.1041.2018.00667

Major, S., Zealand, N., & Connell, A. (1998). From arts management to creative industries. *Media*, 1–6.

Mao, T., & Jiang, X. (2021). The use of digital media art using UI and visual sensing image technology. *Journal of Sensors*, *2021*. https://doi.org/10.1155/2021/9280945

Marra, C. (2019). The relationship between large ensemble participation and the social identity of high-performing secondary band, orchestra, and choir students. *Sustainability*, *11*(1), 1–14. http://scioteca.caf.com/bitstream/handle/123456789/1091/RED2017-Eng-8ene.pdf?sequence=12&isAllowed=y%0A/10.1016/j.regsciurbeco.2008.06.005%0Awww.researchgate.net/publication/305320484_SISTEM_PEMBETUNGAN_TERPUSAT_STRATEGI_MELESTARI

Martin, R., Florida, R., Pogue, M., & Mellander, C. (2015). Creativity, clusters and the competitive advantage of cities. *Competitiveness Review*, *25*(5), 482–496. https://doi.org/10.1108/CR-07-2015-0069

Meshkova, N. V., & Enikolopov, S. N. (2017). Negative creativity in education: Features, threats and research perspectives. *Psychological Science and Education*, *22*(5), 67–76. https://doi.org/10.17759/pse.2017220508

Miles, S. (2018). "Do we have lift-off?" Social media marketing and digital performance at a British arts festival. *Journal of Arts Management Law and Society*, *48*(5), 305–320. https://doi.org/10.1080/10632921.2017.1366379

Mochalova, N. Y. (2020). Personal identity of the artist as a condition and result of creativity in art. *Ethnic Culture*, *2*(3), 62–67. https://doi.org/10.31483/r-74987

Molero-Jurado, M. del M., Pérez-Fuentes, M. del C., Soriano, J. G., Tortosa, B. M., Oropesa, N. F., Simón-Márquez, M. del M., & Gázquez-Linares, J. J. (2020). Personality and job creativity in relation to engagement in nursing. *Anales de Psicologia*, *36*(3), 533–542. https://doi.org/10.6018/analesps.405391

Moulard, J. G., Rice, D. H., Garrity, C. P., & Mangus, S. M. (2014). Artist authenticity: How artists' passion and commitment shape consumers' perceptions and behavioral intentions across genders. *Psychology and Marketing*, *31*(8), 576–590. https://doi.org/10.1002/mar.20719

Müller, S. D., & Ulrich, F. (2013). Creativity and information systems in a hypercompetitive environment: A literature review. *Communications of the Association for Information Systems*, *32*(1), 175–200. https://doi.org/10.17705/1cais.03207

Nagy, Z. (2015). The apperception of musical creativity: Performance as ritual, composition as self-realization. *Creativity Research Journal*, *27*(1), 68–75. https://doi.org/10.1080/10400419.2014.961784

Närvänen, E., Mesiranta, N., Sutinen, U. M., & Mattila, M. (2018). Creativity, aesthetics and ethics of food waste in social media campaigns. *Journal of Cleaner Production*, *195*, 102–110. https://doi.org/10.1016/j.jclepro.2018.05.202

Nawa, L. L., & Sirayi, M. (2014). Digital technology and cultural heritage sites in the city of Tshwane. *Journal of Arts Management Law and Society*, *44*(4), 246–257. https://doi.org/10.1080/10632921.2014.964384

Nęcka, E. (2000). Twórczość. In J. Strelau (Ed.), *Psychologia: Podręcznik akademicki: Tom II: Psychologia ogólna*. Gdańskie Wydawnictwo Psychologiczne. www.scribd.com/doc/296833875/Psychologia-Tom-II-Jan-Strelau#

Neto, J. C., Filipe, J. A., & Caleiro, A. B. (2019). Creativity and innovation: A contribution of behavioral economics. *International Journal of Innovation Studies*, *3*(1), 12–21. https://doi.org/10.1016/j.ijis.2019.06.003

Noonan, H. (2019). Personal identity: The simple and complex views revisited. *Disputatio*, *11*(52), 9–22. https://doi.org/10.2478/disp-2019-0001

Norliana, A. M., & Fakhrul Anwar, Z. (2019). Entrepreneurship education: Inspiration from the greatest entrepreneur. *Journal of Science and Management Research*, *1*(2600–738X), 17–25. www.researchgate.net/publication/330854557_Entrepreneurship_Education_Inspiration_from_the_Greatest_Entrepreneur

Oleszkiewicz, J. (1997). *I ty możesz improwizować*. Centrum Edukacji Artystycznej.

Palhares, P. T., Branco, D., & Gonçalves, Ó. F. (2021). Mind wandering and musical creativity in jazz improvisation. *Psychology of Music*. https://doi.org/10.1177/03057356211033346

Palmer, C., Kraus, S., & Ribeiro-Soriano, D. (2020). Exploring dark creativity: The role of power in an unethical marketing task. *Economic Research-Ekonomska Istrazivanja*, *33*(1), 145–159. https://doi.org/10.1080/1331677X.2019.1660907

Parnes, S. J. (1972). *Creativity: Unlocking human potential*. Creative Education Foundation.

Pavlova, E. M. (2018). Model of connections between self-esteem of creativity and intelligence, tolerance of uncertainty and creativity. *Psychology, Journal of the Higher School of Economics*, *15*(1), 69–78. https://doi.org/10.17323/1813-8918-2018-1-69-78

Penaluna, A., & Penaluna, K. (2020). In search of entrepreneurial competencies: Peripheral vision and multidisciplinary inspiration. *Industry and Higher Education*, *20*(10), 1–14. https://doi.org/10.1177/0950422220963796

Pöppel, J., Finsterwalder, J., & Laycock, R. A. (2018). Developing a film-based service experience blueprinting technique. *Journal of Business Research*, *85*, 459–466. https://doi.org/10.1016/j.jbusres.2017.10.024

Puente-Díaz, R., Cavazos-Arroyo, J., & Vargas-Barrera, F. (2021). Metacognitive feelings as a source of information in the evaluation and selection of creative ideas. *Thinking Skills and Creativity*, *39*. https://doi.org/10.1016/j.tsc.2020.100767

Rani Satyam, V., Savić, M., Cilli-Turner, E., El Turkey, H., & Karakok, G. (2022). Exploring the role of students' views of creativity on feeling creative. *International Journal of Mathematical Education in Science and Technology*, *53*(1), 151–164. https://doi.org/10.1080/0020739X.2021.1961032

Rasminsky, A. (2019). When injury leads to an identity crisis. *Dance Magazine*, *93*(7), 32–35. www.dancemagazine.com/injury-depression-2638932468.html

Reiter-Palmon, R. (2017). Team creativity and innovation. In *Team Creativity and Innovation*. https://doi.org/10.1093/oso/9780190222093.001.0001

Ripoll, R. R., Pesantez, L. B. T., & Dominguez, J. M. (2019). *Happiness management: A lighthouse for social wellbeing, creativity and sustainability*. Peter Lang. https://doi.org/10.3726/b15813

Rivas-Carmona, M. del M. (2020). The power of (Re)creation and social transformation of binomial "art-technology" in times of crisis: Musical poetic narrative in Rozalén's "lyric video" "aves enjauladas". *Cultura: International Journal of Philosophy of Culture and Axiology*, *17*(2), 217–231.

Roberge, J., & Chantepie, P. (2017). The promised land of comparative digital cultural policy studies. *Journal of Arts Management Law and Society*, *47*(5), 295–299. https://doi.org/10.1080/10632921.2017.1398584

Robinson, M., & Novak-Leonard, J. (2021). Refining understandings of entrepreneurial artists. *Artivate: A Journal of Entrepreneurship in the Arts*, *10*(1). https://doi.org/10.34053/artivate.10.1.135

Ryan, M.-L. (2020). *Narrative as virtual reality 2*. Johns Hopkins University Press. https://doi.org/10.1353/book.72246

Scheuer, T. (2018). Computational agents, design and innovative behaviour: Hetero economicus. *Economic Thought*, *7*(2), 82–96.

Schielke, T. (2020). Interpreting art with light: Museum lighting between objectivity and hyperrealism. *LEUKOS – Journal of Illuminating Engineering Society of North America*, *16*(1), 7–24. https://doi.org/10.1080/15502724.2018.1530123

Schreiner, E., Trent, S. B., Prange, K. A., & Allen, J. A. (2018). Leading volunteers: Investigating volunteers' perceptions of leaders' behavior and gender. *Nonprofit Management and Leadership*, *29*(2), 241–260. https://doi.org/10.1002/nml.21331

Shpak, A. A., & Pchelkina, D. S. (2020). Methodology for the study of complex identity. *Journal of Siberian Federal University – Humanities and Social Sciences*, *13*(5), 752–761. https://doi.org/10.17516/1997-1370-0604

Sik, A. (2016). Creativity in cross-domain collaborations: Searching factors to increase efficiency. *Management Research Review*, *39*(2), 144–166. https://doi.org/10.1108/MRR-11-2015-0273

Simonton, D. K. (1994). Computer content analysis of melodic structure: Classical composers and their compositions. *Psychology of Music*, *22*(1), 31–43. https://doi.org/10.1177/0305735694221003

Sjödin, D., Frishammar, J., & Thorgren, S. (2019). How individuals engage in the absorption of new external knowledge: A process model of absorptive capacity. *Journal of Product Innovation Management*, *36*(3), 356–380. https://doi.org/10.1111/jpim.12482

Skoldberg Johansson, U., Woodilla, J., & Antal Berthoin, A. (2015). *Artistic interventions in organizations research, theory and practice*. Routledge. www.routledge.com/Artistic-Interventions-in-Organizations-Research-Theory-and-Practice/Skoldberg-Woodilla-Antal/p/book/9781138497436%0A

Sosnowska, E. (2015). Touch, look and listen: The multisensory experience in digital art of Japan. *Journal of Science and Technology of the Arts*, *7*(1), 63. https://doi.org/10.7559/citarj.v7i1.147

Sözbilir, F. (2018). The interaction between social capital, creativity and efficiency in organizations. *Thinking Skills and Creativity*, *27*, 92–100. https://doi.org/10.1016/j.tsc.2017.12.006

Stauffer, A. (2012). The nineteenth-century archive in the digital age. *European Romantic Review*, *23*(3), 335–341. https://doi.org/10.1080/10509585.2012.674264

Sternberg, R. J., & Lubart, T. I. (1991). An investment theory of creativity and its development. *Human Development*, *34*(1), 1–31. https://doi.org/10.1159/000277029

Stierand, M., & Dörfler, V. (2014). Researching intuition in personal creativity. In *Handbook of Research Methods on Intuition* (pp. 249–263). https://doi.org/10.4337/9781782545996.00030

Stolarick, K., & Florida, R. (2006). Creativity, connections and innovation: A study of linkages in the Montréal Region. *Environment and Planning A*, *38*(10), 1799–1817. https://doi.org/10.1068/a3874

Szczepaniak, K. (2018). Arts for business: Creative co-operation for innovation and sustainable development of the company as a brand and community. *Kwartalnik Ekonomistów i Menedżerów*, *50*(4), 127–141. https://doi.org/10.5604/01.3001.0013.0639

Szostak, M. (2018). The French symphonic organs – instrument as inspiration for the performer. *The Organ*, *386*, 6–27. https://depot.ceon.pl/handle/123456789/19172

Szostak, M. (2020a). Creativity and artistry in organ music. *The Organ*, *391*, 24–31. https://depot.ceon.pl/handle/123456789/19170

Szostak, M. (2020b). Does creativity influence the perception of creative identities? *European Research Studies Journal*, *23*(4), 312–333. https://doi.org/10.35808/ersj/2444

Szostak, M. (2021a). Artistry, management, and creativity: Links and common denominators. *Discourses on Culture*, *16*(1), 23–54. https://doi.org/10.36145/DoC2021.08

Szostak, M. (2021b). Does entrepreneurial factor influence creative identities perception? *Entrepreneurship and Sustainability Issues*, *9*(1), 150–175. https://doi.org/10.9770/jesi.2021.9.1(9)

Szostak, M. (2021c). Does Polish post-communist cultural Burden influence the perception of creative identities? *Journal of Intercultural Management*, *13*(2), 29–58. https://doi.org/10.2478/joim-2021-0060

Szostak, M. (2021d). Impact of gender differences in perception of creative identities of artist, creator, manager, entrepreneur and leader on sustainability. *Entrepreneurship and Sustainability Issues*, *9*(2), 10–36. https://doi.org/10.9770/jesi.2021.9.2(1)

Szostak, M. (2021e). Post-communist burden influence on the perception of creative identities: Consequences for managers and leaders. *European Research Studies Journal*, *24*(3), 282–302. https://doi.org/10.35808/ersj/2354

Szostak, M. (2021f). *The organ as a source of inspiration: The rebirth of a giant (Paris – Vatican – Licheń)*. SINDRUK-DIMK.

Szostak, M. (2022a). Peculiarities of art management in a digital context – a case study of Poland. *Entrepreneurship and Sustainability Issues*, *9*(4), 10–44. https://doi.org/10.9770/jesi.2022.9.4(1)

Szostak, M. (2022b). Peculiarities of values transfer among countries via arts digitalization. *Entrepreneurship and Sustainability Issues*, *10*(1), 10–49. https://doi.org/10.9770/jesi.2022.10.1(1)

Szostak, M. (2022c). Perception of creative identities by managers and non-managers: Does a manager see more? *Entrepreneurship and Sustainability Issues*, *9*(3), 24–49. https://doi.org/10.9770/jesi.2022.9.3(2)

Szostak, M. (2023a). Perception of creative identities by artistic and non-artistic individuals: Consequences for management. *Creativity Studies*, *16*(1), 1–25. https://doi.org/10.3846/cs.2023.15081

Szostak, M. (2023b). Gender differences regarding participation form in the arts receiving process: Consequences for aesthetic situation management. *International Journal of Contemporary Management*, *59*(1), 26–56. https://doi.org/10.2478/ijcm-2022-0010

Szostak, M., & Sułkowski, Ł. (2020). Manager as an artist: Creative endeavour in crossing the borders of art and organizational discourse. *Creativity Studies*, *13*(2), 351–368. https://doi.org/10.3846/cs.2020.11373

Szostak, M., & Sułkowski, Ł. (2021a). Artist, creator, manager, entrepreneur, leader: How society perceive these identities? *Economics and Sociology*, *14*(2), 209–221. https://doi.org/10.14254/2071-789X.2021/14-2/11

Szostak, M., & Sułkowski, Ł. (2021b). Identity crisis of artists during the COVID-19 pandemic and shift towards entrepreneurship. *Entrepreneurial Business and Economics Review*, *9*(3), 87–102. https://doi.org/doi.org/10.15678/EBER.2021.090306

Szostak, M., & Sułkowski, Ł. (2021c). The challenges in identification of artists-man agers: Consequences for creativity. *Creativity Studies*, *14*(1), 112–124. https://doi.org/10.3846/cs.2021.13822

Szostak, M., & Sułkowski, Ł. (2021d). The identity and self-perception of artists-managers. *Problems and Perspectives in Management*, *19*(1), 372–386. https://doi.org/10.21511/ppm.19(1).2021.32

Szostak, M., & Sułkowski, Ł. (2023). How to manage the aesthetical situation regarding the in-real or digital form of participation in arts? Art receivers' perspective. *Creativity Studies, TBA*.

Tang, C., Zhang, Y., & Reiter-Palmon, R. (2020). Network centrality, knowledge searching and creativity: The role of domain. *Creativity and Innovation Management*. https://doi.org/10.1111/caim.12351

Tanggaard, L. (2014). *Fooling around: Creative learning pathways* (1st ed.). Information Age Publishing. http://www.infoagepub.com/products/Fooling-Around

Tao, T., Sato, R., Matsuda, Y., Takata, J., Kim, F., Daikubara, Y., Fujita, K., Hanamoto, K., Kinoshita, F., Colman, R., & Koshiba, M. (2020). Elderly body movement alteration at 2nd experience of digital art installation with cognitive and motivation scores. *Multidisciplinary Scientific Journal*, *3*(2), 138–150. https://doi.org/10.3390/j3020012

Tatarkiewicz, W. (2015). *Historia estetyki: Tom I*. PWN.

Tendayi Viki, G., & Williams, M. L. J. (2014). The role of identity integration in enhancing creativity among mixed-race individuals. *Journal of Creative Behavior*, *48*(3), 198–208. https://doi.org/10.1002/jocb.48

Tregua, M., Mele, C., Russo Spena, T., Marzullo, M. L., & Carotenuto, A. (2021). Digital transformation in the era of Covid-19. *Lecture Notes in Networks and Systems*, *266*, 97–105. https://doi.org/10.1007/978-3-030-80840-2_10

Ungureanu, A., & Vasile, A. (2016). Romanian business women: Managers or leaders? Empirical study. *SEA – Practical Application of Science*, *IV*(2(11)), 327–333.

Vincent, L. C., & Kouchaki, M. (2016). Creative, rare, entitled, and dishonest: How commonality of creativity in one's group decreases an individual's entitlement and dishonesty. *Academy of Management Journal*, *59*(4), 1451–1473. https://doi.org/10.5465/amj.2014.1109

Vuscan, I. S., & Feng, S. (2018). The inspirational value of unintentional design occurrences: Freeing aesthetic. *IOP Conference Series: Materials Science and Engineering*, *399*(1), 1–13. https://doi.org/10.1088/1757-899X/399/1/012052

Ward, T. B., Saunders, K. N., & Dodds, R. A. (1992). Creative cognition in gifted adolescents. *Roeper Review*, *21*(4), 189–212. https://doi.org/10.1080/02783199909553973

Weisberg, R. W. (2006). *Creativity: Understanding innovation in problem solving, science, invention, and the arts*. John Wiley.

Wilson, A. (2021). Improvisation and authenticity in early 20th century western music. In *The Routledge handbook of philosophy and improvisation in the arts* (pp. 355–373). Routledge. https://doi.org/10.4324/9781003179443-29

Wu, J. C. (2020). From physical to spiritual: Defining the practice of embodied sonic meditation. *Organised Sound*, *25*(3), 307–320. https://doi.org/10.1017/S1355771820000266

Zahra, S. A. (2021). International entrepreneurship in the post Covid world. *Journal of World Business*, *56*(1). https://doi.org/10.1016/j.jwb.2020.101143

Zamaraeva, Y. S., & Koptseva, N. P. (2020). History of complex identity research. *Journal of Siberian Federal University – Humanities and Social Sciences*, *13*(7), 1216–1229. https://doi.org/10.17516/1997-1370-0637

Zedelius, C. M., Protzko, J., Broadway, J. M., & Schooler, J. W. (2021). What types of daydreaming predict creativity? Laboratory and experience sampling evidence. *Psychology of Aesthetics, Creativity, and the Arts*, *15*(4), 596–611. https://doi.org/10.1037/aca0000342

Zhang, X., & Kwan, H. K. (2019). Team behavioral integration links team interdependence with team performance: An empirical investigation in R&D teams. *Frontiers of Business Research in China*, *13*(1). https://doi.org/10.1186/s11782-019-0054-1

Zhou, J., Wang, X. M., Song, L. J., & Wu, J. (2017). Is it new? Personal and contextual influences on perceptions of novelty and creativity. *Journal of Applied Psychology*, *102*(2), 180–202. https://doi.org/10.1037/apl0000166

Żmigrodzki, P. (2022). Zaangażowanie. In *Wielki Słownik Języka Polskiego*. Instytut Języka Polskiego PAN. https://wsjp.pl/haslo/podglad/42185/zaangazowanie

Zorita-Aguirre, I. (2020). Mutations in performing arts space in the digital age. *Arte, Individuo y Sociedad*, *32*(2), 503–518. https://doi.org/10.5209/aris.65437

6 Kitsch and ignorance in management

After a detailed analysis of the artistic and managerial activity in terms of virtuosity, artistry, and creativity, it is worth focusing now on attitudes as opposed to the discussed aestheticisation of management. An individual who considers the aestheticisation of management to be an unnecessary phenomenon or, for various reasons, difficult to apply has the following attitudes to choose from: (1) an approach opposite to the aestheticisation of management, i.e., a turn towards kitsch behaviour; (2) an apparently neutral approach to the aestheticisation of management, i.e., a conscious disregard for this phenomenon; and (3) a genuinely neutral approach, resulting from the lack of awareness of the phenomenon of the aestheticisation of management. The last two attitudes concern the phenomenon of ignorance.

This chapter aims to answer the following questions: (1) Can the theory of aesthetic kitsch be applied to management? (2) Can ignorance and kitsch in management, based on dialectics, help understand the essence and meaning of the aestheticisation of management? (3) How does one counteract ignorance regarding the aestheticisation of management?

6.1 Kitsch in aesthetics

Due to commodification, kitsch focuses on the problems inherent in capitalism. If art becomes an extension of everyday life, it loses itself and automatically becomes a commodity among other commodities, i.e., kitsch (Rosenberg, 1959). Kitsch lies at the opposite pole of the scale to purely artistic creation, which is why every artist, consciously or unconsciously, moves between these poles of ideal states. Although kitsch has always existed in art, kitsch was not named until the Munich School of Painting at the end of the 19th century, and the development of the scientific analysis of this phenomenon started from this period. This development went hand in hand with the practical intensification of kitsch in the art of the 19th and 20th centuries when the emphasis was placed on satisfying the taste of the mass audience through cheap and quick quasi-artistic production in place of full-fledged works of art (Calinescu, 1987;

DOI: 10.4324/9781003458029-7

Greenberg, 1985). Kitsch was and still is a way to increase the financial profits of artists who, putting aside the issue of fidelity to the ideals of art, focus on producing artefacts that find large audiences and thus enable them to earn a living more effectively. The kitsch phenomenon is a kind of victory of quantity over quality. The beginnings of kitsch lie in a romantic, degraded form emphasising dramatic effects, pathos, and sentimentality in a clichéd way (Broch, 1969b; Calinescu, 1987). Some scholars question its romantic origins and point to the poor aesthetic taste of Roman merchants of the classical period as the source. Undoubtedly, however, universal access to kitsch and its spread were possible thanks to the economic development and mass culture of 19th-century industrialism.

Dictionary definitions of kitsch focus mainly on the meaning of the kitsch artefact rather than the kitsch phenomenon as a whole. A kitsch artefact means something appealing to popular or low taste, often being of poor quality, considered by many to be ugly, lacking in style, or false, but liked by others, if only for its fun. The synonyms of kitsch are nonsense, rubble, waste, sewage, garbage, scrap, and slag. Since it is not easy to define what kitsch is, aesthetic theorists prefer the method of reviewing the characteristics of a kitsch artefact (Banach, 1968; Wilkoszewska, 2007), which include:

1. fundamentality – understood as unambiguity and non-acceptance of nuances;
2. imitativeness – i.e., copying and imitating solutions that have proven successful and popular with recipients so far;
3. exaggeration – exaggerating and emphasising the catchy features of the work, as well as the lack of nuance;
4. hysteria – as a means of easily gaining interest and strong emotions.

In turn, the most popular themes of aesthetic kitsch include patriotism, religion, eroticism, and politics. These areas are popular subjects of kitsch because each person has an attitude towards his homeland and the best ways of expressing his feelings towards it; an attitude towards faith, often confused with apparent rituals, which he likes to defend because thus he defends his own identity; an attitude towards sexuality from the side of his preferences and curiosity towards the preferences of other people; and political views that he can engage in any discourse and thus strongly polarise it. For each of these areas, the individual has strong feelings and identifies with his vision, recognising that the visions of others are, by definition, wrong or at least worse than his visions. From this point of view, it can be said that kitsch likes primal instincts, which also require primal fulfilment because kitsch responds to the eternal human need for emotion. Kitsch is similar to window putty, which fills cavities with an easily adhering mass. Therefore, it can be said that the essence of kitsch is an exceptional quality that evokes emotions surely and easily, visible in human creativity and having stereotypical features while quickly filling the gaps in culture.

Theodor Adorno (1903–1969) saw kitsch as a cultural industry in which art is controlled and formulated by the market's needs and passed on to a passive population that accepts it uncritically. What is easily marketable is not challenging art but usually formally incoherent content, filling the audience's free time and providing them with straightforward acceptable content. Art is subjective, demanding, and oriented towards the oppressiveness of the surrounding structures; kitsch is a parody of catharsis and aesthetic consciousness (Adorno, 2002, pp. 360–364).

An essential contribution to defining kitsch was the addition of ethical discourse, i.e. the introduction of norms defining what is good and what is not (Samier, 2008). Good, as one of the three elements of the Platonic triad, is strongly associated with truth and, consequently, with beauty. However, kitsch wants to act based on prettiness and pleasing, and not – like art – based on truth. Kitsch is created due to giving up the truth in favour of prettiness. Kitsch is not bad art; kitsch is sometimes called evil in art, creating its reference system. Based on this approach, it is impossible to use the scale mentioned at the beginning of this section, where there is art on the one hand and kitsch on the other; in this case, art and kitsch should be seen as different levels and opposing phenomena (Broch, 1969a).

The theory of aesthetics created the concept of kitsch, which means the phenomenon of departing from artistic values in favour of kitsch features. As an aesthetic defence against reality, kitsch seemingly normalises painful episodes of history, neutralising, trivialising, commercialising, and exploiting them, as in the case of transforming Nazism into a contemporary consumer commodity (Saltzman, 2001). This kitsch consists of sentimentalised and unreflective manipulation of emotions, distortion of perception, limiting rationality and understanding, and avoiding or suppressing unpleasant or disturbing aspects of reality. Unreflective and uncritical kitsch easily succumbs to propaganda and group thinking. It is mistaken for entertainment, attractiveness, or fame, masks personal flaws, and serves to cajole. Moreover, kitsch as dogma diverts attention from essential issues underlying reality, especially those contradictory and conflicting, preferring compliance and maintaining the status quo (Kulka, 1996; Solomon, 1997).

Kitsch is usually figurative, drawing on conventions (e.g., 19th-century Romanticism or socialist realism) rather than abstract styles. One of its most characteristic features is the use of standard and tried-and-tested canons of representation rather than esoteric, idiosyncratic, original, or innovative styles (Kulka, 1996). All this is to achieve unquestionable and easy identification of the object by the recipients. The aesthetic conservatism of kitsch, though stylistically reactionary, implies its accessibility and comprehensibility by the recipients. Its expressiveness and one-dimensionality (lack of ambiguity, nuances, uncertainties, or hidden meanings) usually allow only one interpretation, emphasising its fundamentality and dogmatism. As "art" pre-digested and presented to the viewer, kitsch saves his effort, providing instant pleasure without having to go to the trouble of interpretation, which is an immanent feature of art. Kitsch, being mechanical, works by formulas; being a vicarious experience and a feign of sensation, it changes according to fashion, although, in essence, it always remains the same (Greenberg, 1985).

Kitsch is the epitome of falsehood because, pretending to be valuable, it demands money from its consumers. However, on the other hand, money – measuring the relative value of objects – reduces people's artistic activity to the margin of alienation. As a result, works of art are increasingly evolving towards a closed world, with fewer and fewer points where the subjective viewer can develop his will, reflection, and feelings in a multi-level process of contemplation. In this way, economic modes of interaction replace socially rooted ones, transforming every aspect of life to fit the logic of market exchange through commodification.

Based on the theory of the aesthetic situation, the problem of the "experience of kitsch" can be presented, showing its opposition to the "aesthetic experience". To distinguish it from a work of art, a kitsch product will be called a "kitsch artefact" and a kitsch maker a "kitsch producer". A synthesis of the discussed phenomena is presented in Table 6.1.

Table 6.1 Differences between aesthetic experience and kitsch experience

Component	*Aesthetic experience*	*Kitsch experience*
Creator/Producer	focus on universal values	targeting a mass audience
	creative inventiveness	duplication, copying
	open to criticism and discussion	open to criticism and discussion
Work/Artefact	an advantage over the recipient	dominated by the desires and needs of the recipient (most often patriotic, religious, sexual, or political)
	extending the recipient's existence	confirms the recipient's habits
	cohesion	pretentiousness
	filling the future based on the past	fulfilling the present
Recipient	submission to a work of art	willingness to interact with the artefact
	exclusiveness	egalitarianism, mass scale
	willingness to contemplate the work from all sides/ dimensions	selection of elements to be considered from the desires of the recipient
	participation of thought, consciousness, and will	avoidance of thought, awareness, and will (lack of thought, credulity, irrationality)

Component	*Aesthetic experience*	*Kitsch experience*
	deep emotions, feelings	shallow and fleeting experience, sentimentalism
	inner contemplation	external experience
	the need for solitude	the need for community
World of values	dominant: true	dominant: prettiness and pleasure
Real world	source of creative inspiration	source of impulses to satisfy

Source. Author's own elaboration based on Adorno (2002); Banach (1968); Broch (1933); Gołaszewska (1984a, 1984b, 1986)

A reliable *art creator*, emphasising universal values, is open to criticism and discussion about his work because, thanks to them, he can see what the recipient (and a critic who is a specific form of recipient) notices in his work and what moves him in it. On the other hand, the *producer of kitsch* – imitating his own or someone else's ideas and patterns – focuses on the mass audience, avoiding criticism, which he treats as an attack on his autonomy. Critical analysis of kitsch suddenly reveals a void in values, thus justifying the reluctance to criticism and discussion. One of the motivations of the manufacturer of kitsch is to create the appearance and impression resulting in the desire to make something look more valuable than it is. Thus, kitsch is, in essence, a deceptive and camouflaged forgery under the guise of art (Calinescu, 1987). The *work of art* is coherent, has an advantage over the recipient, and, by filling the future based on the past, extends the recipient's present.[1]

The *kitsch artefact* is often dominated by the recipient's patriotic, religious, sexual, or political desires and needs; it confirms the recipient's habits and fills the present only with the glitter of its pretentiousness. The *recipient of art* is submissive towards the contemplated work, which gives it exclusivity and, at the same time, allows the work to be considered from all sides and in all aspects. The recipient of art must use reason, awareness, and will to contemplate the values, deep emotions, and feelings placed in the work. The kitsch artefact lacks the essential criteria of aesthetic values – unity, balance, or harmony, which consists of the internal logic of structure and style, complexity, multidimensionality, fullness, a combination of heterogeneous forms, and the elaboration of structures and details. The kitsch artefact also lacks the artistic value of a creative and innovative contribution to art history, i.e., opening up new possibilities and suggesting solutions to current artistic problems (Kulka, 1996). The artefact of kitsch – presenting a seemingly original concept – does not enrich the recipient's associations with objects or themes but is somewhat parasitic, because it does not create intrinsic beauty. Essentially, a kitsch artefact, while imitative, has no provenance – it is detached from the essence of the original and lacks consideration of the contexts of the original.

The *kitsch consumer* wants to interfere with the artefact of kitsch through a sense of egalitarianism on a massive scale, chooses things to consider from his desires, avoiding his thoughts, consciousness, and will, focusing attention on external, fleeting, and sentimental experiences, preferably in a community of people in the same situation. The consumer understands kitsch quickly. Kitsch does not question the socio-political reality or particular interests, does not require great intellectual effort, and avoids unpleasant conflicts. It promises a happy ending but reinforces prejudice. The attractiveness of kitsch for the consumer does not lie in the manufacturer of kitsch, its origin, its contribution to the development of art, or even social status. Kitsch is absorbed as an end because it immediately satisfies the desire and does not interfere with the consumer's feelings and beliefs. It also aims at universal rather than individual emotions, relying on the "most common" denominator possible (Samier, 2008); it is moving but empty, serving primarily as a distraction. Kitsch, unlike art, does not accept the nature of things in light of their critical or revealing attributes, only to the extent that they cover and protect, or relieve and comfort (Gregotti, 1969). Kitsch does not directly question the basic metaphysical and moral assumptions of human existence, the meaning of human effort, the adopted moral code, or the meaning of life – it simply does not refer to these phenomena in the sense of disregarding them (Broch, 1969a; Kulka, 1996). Considering the *world of values*, the aesthetic experience is dominated by truth and beauty, and the kitsch experience by pleasure and prettiness. The *real world* is a source of creative inspiration for aesthetic experiences and a source of impulses to be satisfied in a kitsch experience.

The development of the theory of kitsch in aesthetics has been creatively taken over by theories of various fields of human activity, always maintaining a common kitsch denominator.

6.2 Non-aesthetic kitsch

Populism and the preference for quantity over quality occur in every area of life. According to the law of supply and demand, if there is a demand, people will always be willing to satisfy it by supplying the expected product. Similarly, the existing supply facilitates the possibility of satisfying the needs with products of lower quality, thus eliminating the demand for higher-quality products.

Based on the analysis of the phenomenon of aesthetic kitsch, an analysis of the main spheres of reality – i.e., intellectual activity, education, politics, social relations, and religion – will now be carried out in terms of the presence of kitsch features in them.

6.2.1 Intellectual kitsch

The mental abilities of human beings, which, apart from biological factors, are also determined by culture, can be considered a foundation of extra-aesthetic kitsch. Usually, the positive possibilities of the human intellect are analysed, although it is hard to hide that the intellect is also susceptible to the phenomenon of kitsch (Grimsted, 1991). Based on the philosophy of wisdom and focusing on *Aristotle's system of virtues*, a wise human being should possess the following set of virtues (Tarnopolski, 2017):

1. adequate scope of knowledge:
   a. instrumental – relating to the use of tools,
   b. scientific – concerning what can be learned about reality employing scientific cognition,
   c. practical – responsible for the ability to practically implement instrumental and scientific knowledge;
2. intelligence – the ability to use these types of knowledge;
3. auxiliary intellectual virtues:
   a. ingenuity – the ability to think creatively and create concepts,
   b. sharpness – the ability to perceive and react promptly,
   c. prudence – the ability to act thoughtfully, without rashness,
   d. cleverness – the ability to quickly and practically deal with difficult situations.

Intellectual kitsch is based on simplification. However, it is necessary to distinguish between scientific simplification for research purposes and simplification based on reducing everything to a common denominator, if only because of the reluctance to discover the truth or the assumption of one's superiority. Intellectual kitsch can be defined based on the mechanism of using knowledge: possessed knowledge does not guarantee wisdom. For this, one still needs reliable intellectual work, scientific verification of hypotheses and sound judgement. If any of these elements are missing (intellect with extensive knowledge, or knowledge with an efficient intellect), you will notice the abyss of intellectual kitsch. An evaluation of the described situations will reveal that the first case is more dangerous. The second case is theoretically less hopeless because knowledge can be supplemented. However, what if the lack of will to broaden knowledge prevails, and the intellectual kitsch finds a group of recipients, financial patrons, and clappers? In today's globalised society, strongly networked and quickly communicating via social media, such a situation is only a matter of time.

Intellectual kitsch, touching only on the most superficial aspects of reality, is visible, e.g., in the contemporary approach to teaching, the aim is to make learning pleasant and trouble-free, promising a painless and conflict-free path of improvement. An example of this is "homegrown" theology using lots of clichés, demanding scientific respect, and offering nothing but soppy stories in return. Likewise, defining scapegoats, whether in the form of individuals or entire social groups, and blaming them for all the evil in the world is also intellectual kitsch.

On the occasion of intellectual kitsch, the question arises of considering stupidity and ignorance (more about it in Section 6.4) in the context of kitschiness concerning wisdom. Philosophy has grappled with the question of stupidity since ancient times; these considerations were also familiar to thinkers of all subsequent epochs. One of the broader *taxonomies of stupidity* was proposed by J. Stelmach, who talked about stupidity being the result (Brożek et al., 2021, pp. 11–60):

1. ignorance or disregard for the basic rules of language communication,
2. persistent distancing from factual knowledge,
3. cognitive minimalism,
4. inability to understand and interpret complex cases,
5. ease of succumbing to negative emotions,
6. no sense of humour,
7. tendency to take excessive risks,
8. searching for objects of substitute interest.

6.2.2 Educational kitsch

In a consumer society based on immediate gratification (Firat et al., 2013) – the expectation of success without hard work, without difficulties, and without the need to resolve conflicts – educational institutions are transformed into an administration that consoles and reassures but does not educate. The same principles that underlie the commercialisation of education have weakened scientific institutions' autonomous, collegial management and based science development mainly on the whims of the commercialised intellectual market (Lugg, 1999). The artefacts of kitsch in education are books for dummies, YouTube tutorials, blogs, and channels on even the most challenging subjects, which provide simple guidance, reduce the necessary qualifications to an average level achievable by everyone, and glorify superficial vocational workshops that reduce complex theory to simplified rules.

Intellectual kitsch driving educational kitsch produces total or comprehensive kitsch. Such principles are present in many teaching approaches, including "learning organisation" models that promise a straight path to unspecified kitsch "success". For example, teaching politics or strategy is replaced by anecdotes and war stories devoid of theory and analysis, eliminating fundamental theory and rigorous analysis of empirical research. Without a scientific foundation, anecdotes do not require deep knowledge or effort to understand the merits and do not teach criticism or analysis (Andreski, 2002; Bourdieu, 1985).

Educational kitsch will be: (1) reforms of the superficial (formal-only) side of education, without looking at the truth of the content of educational processes;[2]

(2) changes in school obligatory reading lists; and (3) tracking down unrighteous behaviour of teachers, considered sources of youth demoralisation when students and teachers struggle with the lack of support in systemic solutions to real problems. Instead of undertaking a thorough analysis of problems and incurring the effort of repair work, which is unpopular in elections, the carriers of educational kitsch propose substitute topics in the form of looking for enemies and subversives who want to harm the actions of kitschists. Kitsch activity in education gives the impression of making groundbreaking moves and the exhausting struggle for the common good. Such actions are explained with simple and populist arguments, which makes it easier to gain widespread public applause, even though, in reality, none of the fundamental problems is solved. Distraction-feigned actions and stubborn ignorance of facts both meet the marks of intellectual kitsch, and since they take place in the sphere of education, they are also educational kitsch.

6.2.3 Political kitsch

The primary goal of political kitsch is to create and consolidate ideologies and power structures for the exercise of power, and not for solving real problems of society or its groups. Kitsch in politics is visible in the officially approved ways of understanding reality (e.g., the party's "message of the day"), the forcible elimination of irony and any criticism – even if it is fully justified.

In an ideological context, kitsch assumes the status of dogma. The preference for kitsch in politics – especially in authoritarian regimes and top-down management styles – is to explore comfort topics and use propaganda uncritically. The political symbols of kitsch are easy to understand; they call for unreflective emotional reactions, they treat the values of a political regime or ideological system as a closed, coherent whole endowed with apparent beauty and harmony, and they lead to the stylisation of "beauty" that intercepts mythical patterns (Friedländer, 1990). The kitsch political leadership strives to provide society with psychological comfort without referring to real problems; it affirms mythologies, values predictability, and redefines history, culture, and all of reality – essentially a lie wrapped up in appearances.

Kitsch can be found in all types of political systems. Socialist realism not only sanctioned but even imposed kitsch, creating a "perfect world" of spectacular military parades, organised rallies, gala party conventions, unions of various social groups and exemplary enterprises, which, artificially kept alive, played the role of propaganda for success (Kostera, 1997). Capitalism also uses kitsch, exemplified by advertising using social class distinctions or status symbols, to create artificial needs and illusions to support the ideology of the consumer society (Freidin, 2000). The artefacts of capitalist kitsch are houses imitating the style of ancient Greece or buildings in gambling resorts (Las Vegas, Atlantic City) modelled on the Taj Mahal or the Pyramid of Cheops (Kulka, 1996).

Although politicians should be carriers of ideals, political kitsch reduces them to the role of pawns and voting machines. Political symbols – often a manifestation of kitsch – allow them to perform a mobilising function in regimes. Contemporary politics is commonly considered a muddy field; however, representatives of today's political "elites" seem to participate in a race for the title of political kitsch master. Flattering the basest instincts and tastes to get a better result in elections and win more voters to one's side is the norm today, not the exception. Lack of any value system (not even mentioning the values of truth, goodness, and beauty), intentional distortion of the meaning of words and concepts, and announcing one's successes at every opportunity, regardless of the facts, denies human dignity and decency. "Journalism" on commission, public television, an open propaganda mouthpiece, claims to be the only pluralistic and objective broadcaster.

Treating people from other groups as traitors, taking away their humanity or the right to national affiliation, accusing them – all this seems like the worst nightmare, and yet it is the essence of the modern political scene with "God, honour, and homeland" on its lips. This includes sacrificing the common good, the economic condition of the country, treaties and international cooperation, peace, bending or even falsifying facts (statistics, rules), openly violating the law, creating apparent solutions to stay in power for another political season, nepotism, cronyism, and other particular benefits. An authority that protects itself from citizens behind police cordons loses its mandate to hold office. Society is not for power; power is for society.

In addition, there is the phenomenon of fanfaronade manifested in defining all of one's own initiatives as national – even if they crumble to dust in a few moments or were not implemented – and the expansion of the administration not to solve problems but to create well-paid positions that can be filled with its supporters without paying attention to the substantive competence.

6.2.4 Social kitsch

We also find kitsch in social policy. In the United States, for example, public policy was used by liberals in the 1950s and 1960s to recruit art to support the freedom and superiority of the American way of life (Howard, 2004). Similarly, the public arts policy of cities results in easily digestible artefacts disguised as art. Public "art" is usually regarded by residents as unproblematic and unprovocative; kitsch introduces "user-friendly" installations, which are unnoticeable elements of the urban environment, designed to cover, protect, relieve, and comfort (Hall, 1989). Such a spatial policy aims to beautify and embellish rather than aestheticise reality and challenge active contemplation. The preference for kitsch – especially evident in totalitarian regimes, authoritarian regimes, and top-down management styles – consists in quickly assimilating one's themes and, unlike art, quickly succumbing to propaganda (Greenberg, 1985).

Another case of social kitsch, mainly used by politics, is reducing any otherness of social minorities to the category of "worse and dangerous". An example here may be representatives of the LGBTQ+ community, whom opponents reduce only to people who have sex differently, as if this particular activity determines the value of an individual (Linstead, 2002), or refugees whose humanity gives way to questions of origin and ethnicity.

Thus, transposing the phenomenon of kitsch into the social dimension, we can conclude that a society that adheres to kitsch is based on four principles (Ritzer, 1996):

1. efficiency – the fastest and cheapest way to meet needs;
2. calculability – emphasis on the quantitative aspects of products, and thus their simplification;
3. predictability – widespread standardisation of products and services resulting in routinisation of thoughts and actions;
4. control – all over all: those exercising power over society and society over those exercising power; according to this philosophy, a person without control immediately begins to act unethically.

Kitsch is also visible in globalisation: mass products travel the world, displacing local cultures and creating a universal culture in its place (Greenberg, 1985; Micklethwait & Wooldridge, 2000b). Celebrities – famous for being famous – as experts on everything (pop star and horticulture graduate as virus vaccine expert, boxer as social commentator), playback singers liked for being physically attractive, hypocritical marketing praising everything, regardless of its true value – such phenomena are all manifestations of social kitsch.

6.2.5 Religious kitsch

Religion, as a manifestation of man's spiritual life, is also not free from the phenomenon of kitsch. Benoit Mathot (Mathot, 2015), drawing on the philosophical and aesthetic concepts of Broch, Kundera, and Žižek, describes religious kitsch as pointing to a dead-end road to external manifestations of sacraments or liturgical rituals, which – without understanding their meaning based on the logic of faith – are a collection of empty gestures that do not lead to the truth (Pawek, 1969). Kitsch religion provides spirituality without the requirement of orthodox faith and real – not only verbal – action following the truths of faith (Klinghoffer, 1996).

One can mention here the billboard campaign of religious kitsch circles against communion given in the hand in the Catholic Church as the most critical problem to be resolved during the raging pandemic of the deadly coronavirus, which the bishops considered a manifestation of insufficient adult catechesis. Excluding and depreciating everything else, this also includes radicalism regarding protecting the unborn while keeping silent about the profound deficits of systemic care for seriously ill people who are living. The same applies to the so-called national Catholic religiosity (Western and Eastern). Does not Christianity presuppose equality and fraternity? Can anyone be excluded under this banner based on nationality?

Religious hierarchs who impose unattainable standards on their followers while living in contradiction to themselves, or who whitewash their "sins" by highlighting the shortcomings of others, are nothing but carriers of kitsch. Fat "clerics" talking from their palaces about poverty and penance against the background of dripping gold candlesticks at desks bending under the weight of Italian marbles, precious stones, and their pride, are also carriers. Hierarchs involved in the cover-up of paedophilia, avoiding responsibility before the statutory law, which they so willingly want to use to stigmatise sinners, generously forgive those who dare to draw attention to the problem.

Stuffing ideological and ethical issues into the system of secular statutory law de facto involves admitting that the entire catechisation does not bring positive results, since it requires a system of physical punishment. "Catholic" radio stations, supported by intellectually kitschy "professionals" who breathe open hatred towards Jews, freemasons, leftists, refugees, the cruel "gender monster",[3] and "LGBTQ+ rainbow hydra" without even being able to define the phenomenon they passionately talk about. The "faithful" who spit on others because their vision of the world is "the only right one" is also a perfect example of recipients but also carriers of religious kitsch.

A manifestation of religious kitsch will also be monuments (of dead people), which become more important than the rights of living people and legal instruments of defence against offending religious feelings. In this case, kitsch equates faith with fleeting feelings and emotions instead of considering it an intellectual and spiritual construct. The result, therefore, is religious kitsch, which must be defended by force (demanding that the "guilty" be put in prison) because there is no other way to justify such a pretence. Also, in religious kitsch, one can see striving for feigned and substantive activities.

6.3 Organisational kitsch

The growing pace of life and the widespread belief that running a profitable business is one of the most important goals of every person can be considered as the source of kitsch in management. The fast pace of modern life requires quick decisions; managers have less and less time for reliable analyses; hence the search for universal and simple rules becomes a natural solution. Often far from the truth, these rules act as a remedy for problems, filling the hallmarks of kitsch.

Nonsense is inevitable when circumstances require someone to speak without understanding the subject; businesspeople, politicians, PR specialists, and consultants, forced to speak on every subject, not wanting to show their incompetence by not speaking, will tell nonsense. Concepts, or rather tips and spells, of various provenances of "gurus" of management are primarily nonsense or charismatic obviousness; they offer a "philosopher's stone" of business, the purpose of which is primarily to flatter the egos of managers and financial profit from the distribution of their own "magic books". The sources of bullshit management expansion are attempts to comment on every issue, repeating the same fashionable concepts and lack of critical thinking (Spicer, 2013; Sułkowski, 2019). Instead of dealing with efficiency and rational administration, management is seen as having an increasingly strong desire to enchant the consumer with magic and the fantastic. The methods of resistance to organisational kitsch are their scientific demystification and substantive opposition (Sułkowski, 2019).

6.3.1 Forms of organisational kitsch

Characteristic forms of kitsch in management are: (1) one-best-way (seeing only one universal formula for solving each problem); (2) oversimplification; (3) grandiosity; (4) corpo-language; (5) organisational cynicism; (6) functional stupidity; (7) unnecessary jobs (bullshit jobs); and (8) seeming management.

The area of management is increasingly dominated by the rules of the "mass intellectual goods" market. There was a demand for recipes for quick market success. Management gurus, consulting companies, and publishing house managers promote the ideas of management aimed at achieving only the highest possible sales of their "products". "Management shamans", rejecting the theoretical achievements of the discipline, use simple and colloquial categories, which allows them to attract crowds of followers; they ideally find their place and publicity thanks to a simple diagnosis of all organisational problems (Micklethwait & Wooldridge, 2000a). Therefore, commercial criteria begin to prevail over cognitive values. Due to these circumstances, *one-best-way* and *oversimplification* are the dominating approaches. It does not mean that outstanding managers or advisors do not create managerial achievements; only that they lose their scientific character, becoming an area of mass culture (scientific truth gives way to superficial "prettiness" and easiness). When analysing the problem of commercialisation of ideas for management, it is worth paying attention to the issue of popularising knowledge about management. Dissemination of science is the process by which researchers deliver complex theories and discoveries so that they become available and somehow accessible to the public. The market for mass goods created conditions in which the "production" of simplified ideas became a substitute for scientific knowledge. Management guides are popular in the publishing market and cyberspace. Their authors focus more on self-promotion than on providing reliable knowledge. They break with the tradition of true masters of management (Drucker, Kotler, Ansoff), who skilfully combined popularisation with reliable theory.

Fanfaronade refers to delusions of grandeur, characteristic of people with disorders of their characteristics and meaning and can be seen in the obsession of dictators and leaders with building monuments to themselves and their legacy during their lifetime. *Grandiosity* combines narcissism and the desire to increase self-esteem. Organisations imbued with an ethos of greatness are susceptible to being led by narcissistic leaders. The inflation of size labels is widespread: a group of employees becomes an "emergency executive team", rationalisation and improvement are called "business process engineering", and management training takes the form of "executive development programs".[4] This newspeak could be passed over daily if it motivated entities to act more effectively. What will remain if all standard concepts are replaced by concepts infected with delusions of grandeur and importance? They will be devalued, and the next phase of searching for manifestations of greatness in the language of the organisation will take place. A new vocabulary of euphemisms (*corpo-language*) has emerged, fuelled by guru activity and disseminated through educational programs where simple tasks are elevated to heroic status and mundane calculations are turned into great undertakings. Corpo-language combined with grandiosity is about presenting phenomena to make them seem as attractive and unusual as possible without seeing them as apparent (Alvesson, 2018; Alvesson & Gabriel, 2015).

Organisational cynicism has emerged as a new paradigm of employer-employee relationships and arises when employees lack trust in the organisation and feel that the organisation cannot be trusted (Durrah et al., 2019). Unfortunately, many employees are highly cynical about their organisations, feeling disappointed and angry.

Stupidity is often associated with low intelligence, but there is no clear link between IQ level and actual human thinking and action in the social context. Intelligent people can do stupid things. *Functional stupidity* is associated with narrow thinking in which fixed frameworks are accepted uncritically. Managers and subordinates follow templates, ignoring assumptions and beliefs. In the context of kitsch, the main aspects of functional stupidity are lack of reflection, reluctance to look for reasons, and lack of substantive justification. In the context of organisational kitsch manifested in functional stupidity, one should also mention bureaucracy consisting of the uncritical implementation of regulations and procedures, regardless of whether they make sense. Unlike bureaucracy, which is a full-fledged method of rule-based management to eliminate individual discretion, bureaucratism is a perversion of the essence of bureaucracy. In bureaucratism, it is not the goal of the process that is important, but the process itself.

Bullshit jobs are tasks whose disappearance would cause no noticeable environmental change and would be received with indifference. There are five types of bullshit jobs: (1) making someone (customer, boss) feel important: assistants, porters, elevator operators; (2) ruthless pursuit of the interests of clients: lobbyists, lawyers, PR/marketing specialists; (3) solving problems that could be avoided with a better organisation; (4) generation of documents, procedures, and rituals instead of actual, needed actions; and (5) managing people who do not need management, or assigning additional responsibilities that do not make sense (Graeber, 2019).

When the manager does not set goals or plans for the future, and the organisation operates at its own pace and direction, we talk about *seeming management.* The kitsch manager artificially maintains his position. Apparent management, most often associated with the manager's narcissistic personality, is a hazardous phenomenon for the organisation due to the creation of illusions.

6.3.2 Carriers and promoters of organisational kitsch

Among the carriers and promoters of organisational kitsch, the following figures from the world of organisations can be distinguished: management gurus, narcissistic managers, hypocritical managers, and employees subjecting themselves to organisational kitsch (corporate people doing unnecessary jobs).

A *guru* is a spiritual master who gives advice. Management is susceptible to gurus for several reasons: (1) it applies, in the vast majority, to organisations focused on financial profit, so gurus' "prescriptions" are an easily accessible investment with a potentially high rate of return; (2) it is common, as everyone struggles with problems in the managed area, so simple solutions are desirable and therefore enjoy much interest; and (3) verification of the guru's theses is not easy. It is enough that the guru has above-average wealth, which justifies his role and the theories he proposes; in this case, scientific justifications are not required, and even the more complicated they are, the worse for them, because according to the law of Copernicus that bad money drives out good, easily, although erroneous, a prescription will always find more supporters than a logically complex, but accurate explanation. On the other hand, a consulting sector has emerged between business sectors and other organisations and business schools that use scientific achievements and research to a small extent, deepening the gap between management theory and practice. Moreover, the concepts promoted in consulting are – for marketing purposes – presented uncritically, which limits the authority of management sciences in the long run.

The proliferation of management guru concepts is usually not scientific. On the contrary, they are characterised by tautological construction, oversimplification of reality, and the impossibility of verification, which resemble pseudoscience concepts such as astrology (Wilson, 2000). Furthermore, management gurus often use utopian motives, referring to the vision of an ideal organisation leading to a perfect social order; as an example, we can use the concept of a "learning organisation", described as the basis of a "knowledge-oriented society".

The management guru focuses on the process of intuitive cognition, which is supposed to cause changes. Managerial culture is based on socially produced power that reflects power structures. Some influential executives take the position of gurus instead of reflective and critical researchers. Gurus are, therefore, the "heroes" and the most important exponents of an oppressive culture and management ideology. The gurus producing the most widespread guides and simple and "practical" management concepts focus on a clear, "contagious" idea combined with effective marketing. Gurus' works are eagerly read because their concepts seduce, and they seduce because they (1) do not require deeper reflection, (2) are easy to understand and remember, (3) have an element of "shocking" news, and (4) they are taught in simple, easy-to-understand wording.

Contrary to appearances, gurus are not rebels against the existing power structures; on the contrary, they support them, acting as the "entertainment industry" in management. They create media interest in management concepts and structures, sanctioning the obviousness and naturalness of this order. They torment their minds with specific "memes" of contagious concepts while postponing reflection on issues fundamental to the organisation, such as power or justice. Gurus try to "program the minds" of managers according to the interests of those in power. The "culture industry" guru is supported by mass advertising, PR, and marketing activities leading to building the position of "idols" for managers. Gurus are specially treated in management because their publications, which do not meet scientific rigours, are of a popularising nature, and therefore, being outside the circle of interest of scientists, they are relatively rarely constructively criticised on the merits.

Since relations with practice and consulting are an inseparable feature of management understood as a practical scientific discipline, creating publications addressed to practitioners is valuable. Some management gurus from the past (Drucker, Kotler, Ansoff) also popularised them by creating valuable scientific achievements, which sometimes formed the foundations for entire management subdisciplines. Undoubtedly, there is a need to translate science understandably for the inexperienced reader; otherwise, this field will continue to be naturally filled by managerial kitsch (Pinnington, 2001).

The second group of organisational kitschists are *narcissistic managers* who build egocentric constructs. They focus on the superficiality of actions and creating their role in the organisation. In this case, the organisation becomes a means to build and drive its myth, not a tool to achieve business goals. What is new is the generalised culture of narcissism that pervades late capitalism, where people are obsessed with trying to build a positive self-image, often through the consumption of objects, experiences, and brands. The consequences of narcissistic attitudes on managers can be different: from deteriorating organisational performance, through demotivating employees, to creating fiction and artificial reality that can dull the vigilance and credibility of the organisation.

The third group of carriers and promoters of organisational kitsch are *hypocritical managers and owners* who, pretending to create and implement the organisation's mission, focus solely on maximising their financial profits. Of course, efficiency (profitability) is the natural goal of every organisation, but in this case, the element of building a false mission is emphasised, using simple deception and resignation from the truth in favour of pretending external "prettiness". The presence of professional ethics can be an essential distinguishing factor here (Szostak and Sułkowski, 2020).

The fourth group of carriers of organisational kitsch consists of *unreflective employees* who – consciously or unconsciously – uphold corporatism, perform unnecessary work following the principle "if they pay me for it, I can do unnecessary activities for anyone", and maintain the fanfaronade of their superiors or the status quo of apparent management. On the one hand, in the spirit of conformism, one can understand such behaviour. However, on the other hand, since the essence of management is the effective implementation of the goals set for the organisation, any actions inconsistent or contradictory to this approach fulfil the hallmarks of organisational kitsch.

The organisational kitsch theory applies to companies focused on financial profit, non-profit organisations, and all areas where people work in groups – communities, political systems, or religious organisations. The phenomenon of organisational kitsch affects all spheres of human activity.

6.4 Ignorance in management

Considering the reluctance to aestheticise the world dominated by efficiency and fast pace in the race for material wealth, two extreme conclusions can be drawn:

1. elitist conclusion: the aestheticisation of reality (including management) will never be the dominant approach due to the need to equip the individual with the resources of sensitivity, perception, and intellect, allowing for abstract reasoning, which in the context of economic efficiency is a luxury; this does not mean, however, that aestheticisation should not be pursued;
2. egalitarian conclusion: everyone aestheticises reality to some extent, although reaching a certain degree of complexity, he makes a conscious or unconscious decision to stop further processing; so, there is development potential here.

These conclusions lead to a phenomenon lying at the intersection of (1) ignoring (in the sense of intentional omission), (2) disregard and arrogance (as premeditated actions and against raised objections), and (3) unawareness (lack of knowledge, i.e., ignorance).

For further considerations, the critical problem will be the conscious ignoring of the aestheticisation of management and an attempt to find potential arguments behind such a purposeful attitude. Before that, however, one should analyse the nature of ignorance and its functions.

6.4.1 The theory of ignorance

The theory of ignorance will be presented based on analysing the essence of ignorance, its sources and functions, and the problem of managing ignorance in the context of the essence of ignorance and the organisational context.

The essence of ignorance

The dictionary definition of the noun "ignorance" means lack of knowledge, education, or awareness in a given field (Ignorance, 2022), and its synonym is unawareness. However, the verb "to ignore" has a slightly different meaning, i.e., consciously not reacting to some behaviour, event, or phenomenon (Ignore, 2023). From this verb comes the noun "ignore", meaning deliberately not noticing or not considering, synonymous with disregard and neglect (Ignorowanie, 2023). It is worth noting here that the colloquial meaning of the noun "ignorance" is coloured negatively (probably by taking over the meaning from the noun "ignoring", as from conscious disregard), although the noun "ignorance" has a more neutral character in the dictionary (Mesjasz, 2017). Furthermore, ignorance may concern a fragment of knowledge in a specific field (here, the term "error" is used) or the entire field (here, the term "meta-ignorance" is used) (Smithson, 1989, p. 6).

The literature on ignorance is not extensive. Although the first references to ignorance date back to ancient times, the discourse was dominated by the view of certainty in knowledge or approaching this state with the most significant possible probability. Even the great encyclopaedias of philosophy avoided this subject (Smithson, 1989, pp. 1–2). The heyday of scientific interest in ignorance falls in the last two decades of the 20th century. New terms for the scientific interest in ignorance also began to be introduced: agnotology (Proctor & Schiebinger, 2008), or the sociology of ignorance (McGoey, 2012).

Attempts to define ignorance were accompanied by attempts to classify this phenomenon in terms of the attitude to knowledge and ignorance. One of the first dichotomous typologies of ignorance was proposed by M. Smithson (Smithson, 1989, p. 7):

1. passive ignorance – regarding the future, includes issues of which the given subject is unaware;
2. active ignorance – concerning issues that are ignored by a given entity: (a) the unknowns resulting from passive ignorance are defined as "error", and (b) the issues resulting from active ignorance are defined as "inadequacy".

Smithson divided each of these two categories of active ignorance into successive levels, presenting a rather intricate process though the logical structure of concepts denoting other categories of ignorance (Figure 6.1).

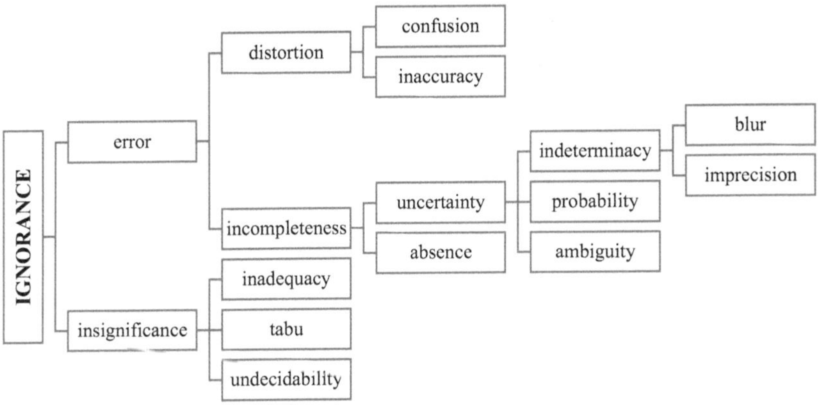

Figure 6.1 M. Smithson's classification of active ignorance

Source: Author's own elaboration based on Mesjasz (2017); Smithson (1989, p. 18)

Another dichotomous classification of ignorance was proposed by M. Gross (2007):

1. ignorance as known unknowns – relating to knowing what is known about the limits of knowledge; there are some phenomena we know we do not know about; we know the question, but we do not know the answer – we are aware of our ignorance;
2. ignorance as unknown unknowns – referring to a complete lack of knowledge to the point that the individual is unaware of his ignorance; these unknown unknowns are entirely beyond the foresight of the individual.

Capturing the dynamic nature of ignorance and knowledge, Gross argues that these different kinds of knowledge about the unknown interact over time (recursion), transforming these unknowns, developing new knowledge, and defining new frontiers of knowledge (Roberts, 2009).

Congleton (2001, pp. 39–41) likewise distinguishes between two types of ignorance:

1. natural ignorance – referring to the fact that every individual is born in a state of natural ignorance, but over time their natural ignorance shrinks, and knowledge is accumulated and developed;
2. rational ignorance – referring to the fact that rational ignorance gradually increases as awareness of one's ignorance increases (although natural ignorance remains dominant); the individual is not able to know everything (if only because of the limitations of the information processing capacity), so he must make choices in terms of knowledge and ignorance; hence, rational ignorance is a way of dealing with these limitations.

Rational ignorance from Congleton's typology can be seen as the result of bounded rationality and refer to known unknowns from M. Gross's typology, while natural ignorance can refer to unknown unknowns.

Proctor and Schiebinger (2008, p. 3) – assuming that the state of ignorance can be caused by myopia, secrecy, suppression, neglect, disappearance or forgetfulness – distinguished three types of ignorance:

1. ignorance as a native state (resource) – ignorance caused by myopia, suppression, neglect, disappearance, forgetfulness, or being the result of secrecy;
2. ignorance as a lost sphere (selective choice) – ignorance resulting from focusing attention on one problem while neglecting other problems;
3. ignorance as a deliberate and actively created and maintained construction – ignorance resulting from focusing on seemingly true knowledge built by someone consciously and premeditatedly.

Based on the concepts of the opposite of knowledge, a categorisation of knowledge was developed (Gross, 2007, p. 751):

1. knowledge – belief in what has been scientifically substantiated as true and is accepted by a group of individuals;
2. ignorance – knowledge about the limitations of knowledge in a specific area; it increases with the next stage of new knowledge;
3. non-knowledge – knowledge of what is unknown but taken into account in planning the future;
4. negative knowledge – knowledge of what is unknown but considered irrelevant or dangerous; it can lead to non-knowledge;
5. extended knowledge – based on planning and/or research in the field of non-knowledge; it can lead to non-knowledge by discovering the limits of newly learned knowledge;
6. nescience – lack of knowledge; it is a prerequisite for complete surprise beyond any conjecture, but it belongs to a different epistemological class than all of the other categories.

Perhaps the most universal and holistic classification of ignorance can be described by the following four states of knowledge or lack thereof (Mesjasz, 2017):

1. I know that I know – seemingly unrelated to ignorance; however, knowing what we know (only) does not mean knowing what we do not know;
2. I know that I do not know – includes "I know that I know" (1), but also the awareness of not knowing more than what is known;
3. I do not know that I know – unawareness (indefiniteness) of the possessed knowledge or inability to realise the applied practical skills and solutions;
4. I do not know that I do not know – unawareness of what I do not know; it can be compared to a double circle of ignorance: (a) ignorance about something that exists, and (b) ignorance about not knowing that something exists.

The relationship between these four types of ignorance is presented graphically in Figure 6.2: the first three types of ignorance – (1) I know that I know, (2) I know that I do not know, (3) I do not know that I know –d are immersed in the fourth type, I do not know that I do not know, because it is from the fourth type that the road to awareness begins.

Synthesising all the aforementioned typologies of ignorance based on the indicated quadruple typology, it can be said that a person is born with ignorance of the "I do not know that I do not know" type (4), which we refer non-pejoratively to unconsciousness, and even to innocence. In socialisation and education, a person expands knowledge, realising another type of ignorance, "I know that I know" (1). Reaching the ignorance of the "I know that I know" type (1) may take place through the realisation of the "I do not know that I know" type (3) in the case of naming the knowledge that, for some reason, he has used so far. The last type of ignorance, "I know that I do not know" (2), may be considered desirable because it means awareness of the unconscious; this awareness of what is unknown eliminates the state of ignorance. This process of transformation of ignorance is presented in Figure 6.3.

In connection with the statement that ignorance is always associated with knowledge creation (Janich et al., 2017, p. 95), it can be expected that

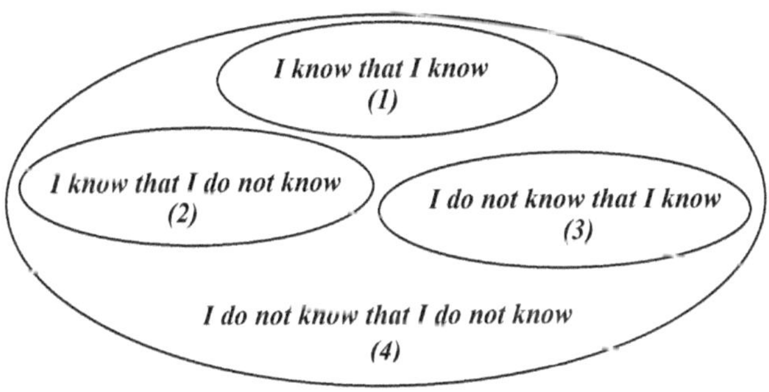

Figure 6.2 Ocean of ignorance

Source: Author's own elaboration

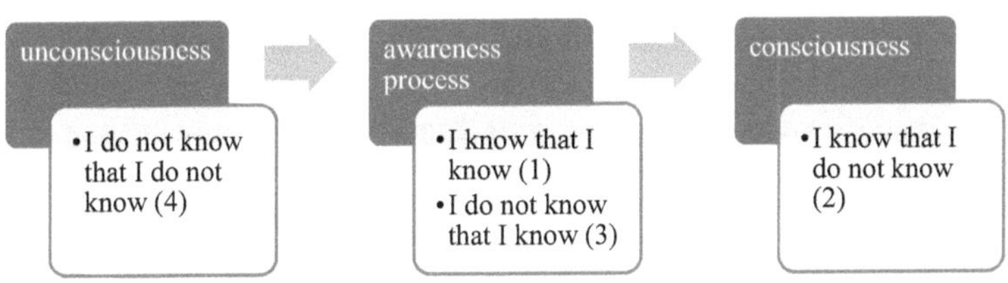

Figure 6.3 The process of transforming ignorance

Source: Author's own elaboration

increasing the stock of knowledge should lead to decreasing the stock of ignorance. However, the opposite is true: knowledge and ignorance are not symmetrical because increasing knowledge about a topic does not reduce ignorance about the same topic. Instead, it is because new knowledge usually leads to identifying new areas of ignorance that were not realised before discovering this knowledge.

Sources and functions of ignorance

The following phenomena are considered to be the key sources of ignorance (Roberts, 2012, p. 219):

1. lack of knowledge: unknown unknown and known unknown;
2. existing knowledge: knowable known unknown, unknown known, and errors;
3. suppression and limitation of knowledge: privacy, taboos, secrets, denials.

Knowing the definitions and typologies of ignorance, it is now necessary to focus on the reasons for using conscious ignorance. In the mid-20th century, Moore and Tumin (1949) distinguished the social functions of ignorance:

1. maintaining a privileged position;
2. upholding traditional values;
3. maintaining competition;
4. maintaining stereotypes.

In addition to the social functions of ignorance, which show why groups use this phenomenon, for the sake of completeness, individual functions of ignorance must be distinguished, which will answer the question of why individuals resort to conscious ignorance:

1. survival and protection of identity in the face of an overwhelming mass of information and stimuli – modernity is characterised by an excess of information and stimuli reaching the individual; their enormity should first be sorted into valuable and invaluable; the valuable ones should be ordered in terms of importance and then assimilated; because the average person is not able to select and organise all the information and stimuli reaching him, one of the logical solutions is to ignore; the primary purpose of this ignoring is to protect one's own identity and the will from surviving, allowing one to focus on one's activities; being cut off from the flow of information and stimuli can lead to a life of ignorance and apathy (Osiemo, 2012);
2. showing affection to someone or something – in a situation where the possibility of verbal communication is not possible, a form of ignorance can be

a strong carrier of feelings (usually negative ones); the strength of this solution is very high; this type of ostracism is considered mobbing (Rasool et al., 2020; Rudert et al., 2021; Vui-Yee & Yen-Hwa, 2020);
3. ego exposure – showing one's importance can take various forms: both active (concerning taking action) and passive (regarding not taking action) (Siddique et al., 2021).

Ignorance management and organisational ignorance

Efforts to incorporate ignorance into organisational understanding focus on eliminating ignorance through improved knowledge management practices (Roberts, 2012). However, looking at ignorance from a systems perspective, one can say that it is the opposite of knowledge management. Since the amount of knowledge in the organisation is growing faster and faster, managing ignorance – i.e., the area of ignorance – seems to be the right and logical approach (Roberts, 2009). Some voices managing ignorance is a phenomenon that can bring more benefits than focusing only on managing knowledge, i.e., what is known (Zack, 1999). Following this lead, one can say that ignorance management should determine the areas where knowledge management should be developed. After all, it is impossible to have complete knowledge of everything.

Organisational ignorance is defined in terms of the following knowledge-processing problems (Zack, 1999):

1. uncertainty – lack of sufficient information;
2. complexity – having to process more information than the organisation can control or understand;
3. ambiguity – lack of a conceptual framework to interpret the information held;
4. ambiguity – having competing or conflicting conceptual frameworks to interpret the possessed information.

At the turn of the millennium, it was argued that each of these four problems could be mitigated by the development of an appropriate knowledge management infrastructure (IT technology) and the development of a coherent framework (strategy) for describing and managing organisational ignorance (Zack, 1999). Nevertheless, a quarter of a century later, we may doubt whether the indicated methods are adequate for today's world's problems.

Based on the assumption that organisational ignorance emerges from political processes, four types of organisational ignorance have been identified (Harvey et al., 2001, pp. 452–458):

1. pluralistic ignorance – refers to situations in which an individual has false opinions about others; evaluation leads to this type of ignorance;

2. populist ignorance – related to an ignorance shared socially and resulting from false knowledge received from the environment; interpretation leads to this type of ignorance;
3. probabilistic ignorance – results from an individual's inability to learn from general experience; individuals tend to think linearly rather than non-linearly; inquiry leads to this type of ignorance;
4. pragmatic ignorance – occurs in constantly changing environments when knowledge cannot be acquired in time to make a quality decision; negotiation leads to this type of ignorance.

Based on the social functions of ignorance (Moore & Tumin, 1949), the following references to managing ignorance in organisations have been proposed (Roberts, 2009):

1. ignorance as a preserver of a privileged position – concerning competitors or employees; by keeping employees ignorant, managers can differentiate teams in this way, maintaining pay differentials, and eliminating jealousy; ignorance in the form of a secret can also be used concerning organisational strategies and new product development; confidentiality may be necessary from a security point of view (organisations involved in the production of toxic or dangerous products such as nuclear fuel production or defence equipment suppliers);
2. ignorance as reinforcement of traditional values – isolation to preserve existing practices; not knowing other options can help to maintain stability in organisations, e.g., not knowing pay and working conditions in other organisations can prevent demands for better working conditions and higher pay and help retain staff;
3. ignorance as a preservative of fair competition – for a competitive market to be sustainable, competitors must be unaware of some of the policies and decisions of other competitors; full knowledge would undermine the basis of competition;
4. ignorance as a preservative of stereotypes – supporting ruling positions; reducing the amount of information processed by decision makers; in large organisations, employees are reduced to members of stereotypical groups (sales, marketing, finance); stereotypes are a shorthand (at the same time imperfect and problematic) way of classifying people according to their role in a group (organisation); in the absence of knowledge, managers make decisions based on knowledge of stereotypes, not knowledge of individuals.

In business organisations, organisational ignorance can be used for (Roberts, 2009): (1) maintaining stability, norms of behaviour, and working practices; (2) supporting organisational culture and authorities; (3) motivating employees; and (4) stimulating innovation. In turn, focusing on improving the learning organisation and knowledge management, the following ways of mitigating organisational ignorance are indicated (Harvey et al., 2001): (1) information identification and classification; (2) classification of knowledge; (3) unlearning knowledge that interferes with proper functioning; (3) recognition of discontinuous situations and data; and (4) developing a pluralistic philosophy (perspective) of management.

As seen here, the management literature sees organisational ignorance as something that needs to be mitigated through better knowledge management and organisational learning (Harvey et al., 2001; Zack, 1999). Ignorance is then seen as a lack of knowledge and something that needs to be addressed by the discovery or acquisition of new knowledge or the application of new and improved knowledge management techniques, practices, and systems. In this sense, managing ignorance becomes synonymous with managing knowledge. However, in an organisational context, ignorance is more than a lack of knowledge, as ignorance can be strategic to the operation and success of an organisation. Therefore, other aspects of organisational ignorance need to be considered. Managing ignorance productively is not always about erasing it by applying the proper knowledge. Despite the existing contributions in this section, there is no systematic approach to understanding ignorance management.

Many implications and conclusions emerge from research on organisational ignorance (Roberts, 2009, 2012):

1. ignorance management is more than just the flip side of knowledge management; although knowledge management and ignorance management are closely related, there are elements of ignorance in organisations that should be treated as distinct from knowledge and knowledge management;
2. the development of organisational systems that overcome the individual's ability to possess and process knowledge contributes to the ignorance of the members of the organisation; complex systems of organisational hierarchy, creating a detailed division of labour, imply the distribution of ignorance and knowledge among organisational actors;
3. awareness of ignorance and active management of ignorance can improve an organisation's ability to compete in rapidly changing markets – since ignorance can be used strategically;
4. the emphasis on knowledge management to reduce ignorance through the dissemination and creation of knowledge can result in neglect and even the creation of ignorance; it diverts attention from the need to commit resources to manage ignorance within the organisation and the wider business environment;
5. the exercise of power is one of the functions of ignorance in a social organisation – in a business organisation, power results from differences in ignorance or knowledge between managers and employees, the organisation, and its stakeholders;

6. ignorance can play an essential role in the creative process – because ignorance stimulates curiosity and the search for knowledge and promotes new ways of thinking that challenge existing paradigms and thus help push the boundaries of knowledge.

6.4.2 Ignorance in an aesthetic situation

In the context of the purposes of this chapter, the active or deliberate type of ignorance will be relevant, the nature of which is better described by the word "disregard" and, in some extreme cases, even "arrogance." It is about omitting specific aspects of the components of the aesthetic situation or the relationship between them in a conscious (premeditated) way. Ignorance in the aesthetic situation should be considered from two perspectives, the creator and the recipient, and each of these perspectives may concern three levels.

Ignorance of the creator may concern:

1. real world – not paying attention to the level of virtuosity, both from the point of view of (lack of) preparation in the workshop and the role of virtuosity in the level of quality of the aesthetic situation;
2. works of art – ignoring the factor of creativity; it is not always necessary, but it cannot be dismissed entirely from consideration;
3. world of values – not paying attention to the level of artistry; it is both a problem of the creator's contribution to the work and the potential that this work will present to the recipient.

Recipient ignorance may concern:

1. real world – inability to recognise the level of an artist's virtuosity; often accompanied by a preference for perceptually accessible performances;
2. works of art – not paying attention to the factor of creativity; perception of the work limited only to the content layer, without taking into account the creativity of the form, or perception of the work limited only to the form layer, without taking into account the creativity in terms of content;
3. world of values – not paying attention to the level of artistry; focusing on virtuosity and/or creativity without aesthetic references.

6.4.3 Ignorance towards management aesthetics

The fundamental issue for the entire chapter is the question of how to counteract ignorance towards the aesthetics of management. It seems that the vital remedy here is the education of both managers and all specialists who, over time, take managerial positions in their organisations, but also general education in the field of aesthetics, paying attention to the comprehensive benefits of participation in art. Of course, this process is long-term, arduous, and expensive; however, since the aestheticisation of reality points to additional dimensions, the aestheticisation of management can naturally become the same way to humanise management.

Managers should implement humanistic management; however, managed persons have the full right to demand compliance with the organisation's values. It is not an easy or quick process: it requires changes in the mentality of managers and organisation owners. On the lines of owners-managers and managers-employees, there is a permanent clash of optics and expectations. The realisation is usually a compromise between these optics. Including the world of universal values in this discourse is not unusual.

The problem of difficulties in implementing the humanistic approach in management can also be viewed from the perspective of design thinking and value-based economy (Klamer, 2017). What will remain in the functioning of a business organisation after removing the optics of financial profit? What is essential for a human being if we put aside the contents of his wallet? What, apart from the level of wealth, is vital for society? Of course, universal values will probably remain – the essential issue is precisely how many of these universal values exist and in what condition they are there. Of course, it depends on many factors, including education, level of economic development, wealth, status, and the level of satisfaction with various needs. However, on the other hand, one should realise that values do not depend on the aforementioned material factors because they are ideal and immutable entities: one can act beautifully without being wealthy, one can be rich and not act reasonably, and one can act in accordance with the truth, regardless of one's possessions.

In the analysed problem, one cannot forget about communication as a constitutive of an organisation (CCO), which – constituting the axis of theoretical development within the framework of organisational communication studies – is based on the idea that an organisation appears and is sustained and transformed just through communication (Kuhn, 2021; Schoeneborn et al., 2014). In this spirit, it can be concluded that the very appearance of universal values in the organisational discourse may be a breakthrough in expanding the organisational reality; then, there are the stages of reaching a compromise and implementing the results.

6.5 Summary

Due to its universality, the theory of aesthetic kitsch can be successfully applied in management because it refers to the universal values of truth and beauty, and these are immanent categories of the aestheticisation of management. Undoubtedly, the theory of aesthetic kitsch transposed to the world of management can help organisational actors better perceive organisational behaviours that bear the hallmarks of kitsch.

In addition to kitsch, which can be called active negative action on the grounds of the aestheticisation of management, there is also the phenomenon of ignorance. Both concepts of ignorance and kitsch in management can, based on dialectics, successfully help in understanding the essence and meaning of the aestheticisation of management. These phenomena are difficult to explain directly, but they can be easier to understand by describing the opposites. Understanding the essence of ignorance is crucial in eliminating ignorance concerning the aestheticisation of management, because in order to be able to fight a phenomenon effectively, one must first understand its cause and then act on its effects. One should bear in mind that ignorance does not always result from the deliberate action of an ignorant person – it can be primary ignorance, or unconsciousness, which can be overcome in the process of awareness. More complex cases are those when an ignorant person consciously and deliberately disregards a specific phenomenon.

Counteracting ignorance towards the aestheticisation of management requires knowledge in the field of the aestheticisation of management and examples of its practical application in order to be effective. Due to the complex nature of the phenomenon of ignorance and the different faces of ignorance, much depends on getting to know this phenomenon from the theoretical point of view as fully as possible. Furthermore, because the aestheticisation of management has been present in the literature for a relatively short time, and even shorter in practice, there is a particular need to describe this phenomenon from a scientific point of view and to show its practical applications. Thanks to this, using real examples, one can hope to inspire others to make an effort to make management more aesthetically pleasing.

Notes

1 Being filled with his past experiences, a recipient approaches artwork and shapes his future through the receiving process.
2 A process like that was undertaken in the 2000s and 2010s in Poland; one government changed the last years of primary schools to lower secondary schools, but a few years later, the next government returned to the previous state.
3 A "gender monster" is a rhetoric figure used by right-wing politicians and journalists in Poland in the and 2020s when describing all issues related to gender and LGBTQ+ issues in opposition to "normality" described and required by the traditionalistic Roman Catholic Church.
4 This linguistic process is highly visible in non-English-speaking countries, where English-speaking corporations implement their corporate vocabulary into local divisions. In conclusion, local language became a hybrid of local grammar with English nouns and names.

References

Adorno, T. W. (2002). *Essays on music*. University of California Press.
Alvesson, M. (2018). Grandiosity, and functional stupidity. *The Psychologist*, *31*, 50–53. https://espace.library.uq.edu.au/view/UQ:42a53ac

Alvesson, M., & Gabriel, Y. (2015). Grandiosity in contemporary management and education. *Management Learning*, *47*(4), 464–473. https://doi.org/10.1177/1350507615618321

Andreski, S. (2002). *Czarnoksięstwo w naukach społecznych*. Oficyna Naukowa.

Banach, A. (1968). *O kiczu*. Wydawnictwo Literackie.

Bourdieu, P. (1985). *Les intellectuels et les pouvoir: Michel Foucault, une histoire de la vérité*. Syros.

Broch, H. (1933). *Das Böse in dem Wertsystem der Kunst*. S. Fischer. https://doi.org/10.1515/9783111502489-168

Broch, H. (1969a). Evil in the system of artistic values. In G. Dorfles (Ed.), *Kitsch: The world of bad taste* (pp. 68–76). Universe Books.

Broch, H. (1969b). Notes on the problem of kitsch. In G. Dorfles (Ed.), *Kitsch: The world of bad taste* (pp. 49–67). Universe Books.

Brożek, B., Stelmach, J., & Heller, M. (2021). *Szkice z filofozii głupoty*. Copernicus Cener Press.

Calinescu, M. (1987). *Five faces of modernity: Modernism, avant-garde, decadence, kitsch, postmodernism*. Duke University Press.

Congleton, R. (2001). Rational ignorance, rational voter expectations, and public policy: A discrete informational foundation for fiscal illusion. *Public Choice*, *107*(1). https://doi.org/10.1023/A:1010337412291

Durrah, O., Chaudhary, M., & Gharib, M. (2019). Organizational cynicism and its impact on organizational pride in industrial organizations. *International Journal of Environmental Research and Public Health*, *16*(7), 1–16. https://doi.org/10.3390/ijerph16071203

Firat, A., Kutucuo, K., & Saltik, A. (2013). Consumption, consumer culture and consumer society. *Journal of Community Positive Practces*, *XIII*(1), 182–203.

Freidin, G. (2000). Transfiguration of kitsch: Timur Kibirov's sentiments. In M. Balina, N. Condee, & E. Dobrenko (Eds.), *Endquote: Sots-art literature and soviet grand style*. Northwestern University Press.

Friedländer, S. (1990). Preface to a symposium: Kitsch and the apocalyptic imagination. *Salmagundi*, *85–86*, 201–206.

Gołaszewska, M. (1984a). *Estetyka rzeczywistości*. Instytut Wydawniczy PAX.

Gołaszewska, M. (1984b). *Zarys estetyki*. PWN.

Gołaszewska, M. (1986). *O naturze wartości estetycznych*. Uniwersytet Jagielloński.

Graeber, D. (2019). *Bullshit jobs: The rise of pointless work, and what we can do about it*. Penguin Books.

Greenberg, C. (1985). Avant-garde and kitsch. In F. Frascina (Ed.), *Pollock and after: The critical debate*. Harper and Row.

Gregotti, V. (1969). Kitsch and architecture. In G. Dorfles (Ed.), *Kitsch: The world of bad taste*. Universe Books.

Grimsted, D. (1991). The purple rose of popular culture theory: An exploration of intellectual kitsch. *American Quarterly*, *43*(4), 541. https://doi.org/10.2307/2713081

Gross, M. (2007). The unknown in process: Dynamic connections of ignorance, non-knowledge and related concepts. *Current Sociology*, *55*(5), 742–759. https://doi.org/10.1177/0011392107079928

Hall, M. (1989). Forward in an aftermath: Public art goes kitsch. In A. Raven (Ed.), *Art in the public interest*. UMI Press.

Harvey, M. G., Novicevic, M. M., Buckley, M. R., & Ferris, G. R. (2001). A historic perspective on organizational ignorance. *Journal of Managerial Psychology*, *16*(6), 449–468. https://doi.org/10.1108/EUM0000000005774

Howard, D. (2004). Between avant-garde and kitsch: Pragmatic liberalism, public arts funding, and the cold war in the United States. *Canadian Review of American Studies*, *34*(3), 291–303.

Ignorance. (2022). In *Merriam-Webster*. www.merriam-webster.com/dictionary/ignorance

Ignore. (2023). In *Merriam-Webster*. www.merriam-webster.com/dictionary/ignore

Ignorowanie. (2023). *Słownik języka polskiego PWN*. Wydawnictwo Naukowe PWN. https://sjp.pwn.pl/slowniki/ignorowanie.html

Janich, N., Rhein, L., & Simmerling, A. (2017). "Do I know what I don't know?" The communication of non-knowledge and uncertain knowledge in science. *Fachsprache*, *32*(3–4), 86–99. https://doi.org/10.24989/fs.v32i3-4.1392

Klamer, A. (2017). *Doing the right thing: A value based economy*. Ubiquity Press. https://doi.org/10.5334/bbb

Klinghoffer, D. (1996). Kitsch religion. In K. Washburn & J. Thornton (Eds.), *Dumbing down: Essays on the strip mining of American culture*. W. W. Norton.

Kostera, M. (1997). The kitsch-organisation. *Studies in Cultures, Organizations, and Societies*, *3*(2), 163–177. https://doi.org/10.1080/10245289708523494

Kuhn, T. (2021). (Re)moving blinders: Communication-as-constitutive theorizing as provocation to practice-based organization scholarship. *Management Learning*, *52*(1), 109–121. https://doi.org/10.1177/1350507620931508

Kulka, T. (1996). *Kitsch and art*. Pennsylvania State University Press.

Linstead, S. (2002). Organizational kitsch: The aesthetic turn in management. *Organization*, *9*(4), 657–682. https://doi.org/10.4324/9781351147965-4

Lugg, C. (1999). *Pedagogy and popular culture*. Routledge.

Mathot, B. (2015). Religious kitsch and dynamics of faith. *Etudes Theologiques et Religieuses*, *90*(1), 67–83. https://doi.org/10.3917/etr.0901.0067

McGoey, L. (2012). Strategic unknowns: Towards a sociology of ignorance. *Economy and Society*, *41*(1), 1–16. https://doi.org/10.1080/03085147.2011.637330

Mesjasz, C. (2017). Ignorancja i wiedza z zarządzaniu. *Przegląd Organizacji*, *7*(7), 3–10. https://doi.org/10.33141/po.2017.07.01

Micklethwait, J., & Wooldridge, A. (2000a). *Szamani zarządzania*. Zysk i s-ka.

Micklethwait, J., & Wooldridge, A. (2000b). *The world tomorrow: The essentials of globalization*. Times Books.

Moore, W. E., & Tumin, M. M. (1949). Some social functions of ignorance. *American Sociological Review*, *14*(6), 787–895. https://doi.org/10.2307/2086681

Osiemo, L. B. (2012). Developing responsible leaders: The university at the service of the person. *Journal of Business Ethics*, *108*(2), 131–143. https://doi.org/10.1007/s10551-011-1087-3

Pawek, K. (1969). Christian Kitsch. In G. Dorfles (Ed.), *Kitsch: The world of bad taste*. Universe Books.

Pinnington, A. (2001). Charles Handy: The exemplary guru. *Philosophy of Management*, *1*(3), 47–55.

Proctor, R. N., & Schiebinger, L. (2008). Agnotology: The making and unmaking of ignorance. In *The making and unmaking of differences*. Stanford University Press. https://doi.org/10.1515/9783839404263

Rasool, S. F., Wang, M., Zhang, Y., & Samma, M. (2020). Sustainable work performance: The roles of workplace violence and occupational stress. *International Journal of Environmental Research and Public Health, 17*(3). https://doi.org/10.3390/ijerph17030912

Ritzer, G. (1996). *The McDonaldization of society: An investigation into the changing character of contemporary social life*. Pine Forge Press.

Roberts, J. (2009, April 26–28). From knowledge management to ignorance management. *International Conference on Organizational Learning, Knowledge and Capabilities (OLKC), Amsterdam, The Netherlands.*

Roberts, J. (2012). Organizational ignorance: Towards a managerial perspective on the unknown. *Management Learning, 44*(3), 215–236. https://doi.org/10.1177/1350507612443208

Rosenberg, H. (1959). *Tradition of the new*. Hachette Books.

Rudert, S. C., Janke, S., & Greifeneder, R. (2021). Ostracism breeds depression: Longitudinal associations between ostracism and depression over a three-year-period. *Journal of Affective Disorders Reports, 4*. https://doi.org/10.1016/j.jadr.2021.100118

Saltzman, L. (2001). Avante-garde and kitsch revisited: On the ethics of representation. In N. Kleeblatt (Ed.), *Mirroring evil*. Rutgers University Press.

Samier, E. (2008). On the kitschification of educational administration: An aesthetic critique of theory and practice in the field. *International Studies in Educational Achievement, 36*(3), 3–18. https://doi.org/10.1016/b978-0-08-037268-6.50001-7

Schoeneborn, D., Blaschke, S., Cooren, F., McPhee, R. D., Seidl, D., & Taylor, J. R. (2014). The three schools of CCO thinking: Interactive dialogue and systematic comparison. *Management Communication Quarterly, 28*(2), 285–316. https://doi.org/10.1177/0893318914527000

Siddique, Z., Pasha, S. A., & Ali, S. (2021). Analyzing hidden elements in Disney movies and effects on children. *Global Sociological Review, VI*(II), 76–87. https://doi.org/10.31703/gsr.2021(vi-ii).10

Smithson, M. (1989). *Ignorance and uncertainty: Emerging paradigms*. Springer-Verlag. https://doi.org/10.1007/978-1-4612-3628-3

Solomon, R. (1997). Kitsch. In D. Goldblatt & L. Brown (Eds.), *Aesthetics: A reader in philosophy of the arts*. Prentice Hall.

Spicer, A. (2013). Shooting the shit: The role of bullshit in organisations. *Management (France), 16*(5), 653–666. https://doi.org/10.3917/mana.165.0653

Sułkowski, Ł. (2019). Bullshit management – the critical management studies perspective. *Economics and Sociology, 12*(1), 302–312. https://doi.org/10.14254/2071-789X.2019/12-1/18

Szostak, M., & Sułkowski, Ł. (2020). Kitsch in management: Characteristic forms, carriers and propagators. *Education Excellence and Innovation Management: A 2025 Vision to Sustain Economic Development during Global Challenges: Proceedings of the 35th International Business Information Management Association Conference (IBIMA)*, 7584–7598. https://depot.ceon.pl/handle/123456789/19173

Tarnopolski, A. (2017). Intelektualny wymiar kiczu: Mądrość i głupota: Sztuka i kicz. *Prace Naukowe Akademii Im. Jana Długosza w Częstochowie: Filozofia, XIV*, 215–227. https://doi.org/10.16926/fil.2017.14.09

Vui-Yee, K., & Yen-Hwa, T. (2020). When does ostracism lead to turnover intention? The moderated mediation model of job stress and job autonomy. *IIMB Management Review, 32*(3), 238–248. https://doi.org/10.1016/j.iimb.2019.10.007

Wilkoszewska, K. (2007). *Wizje i re-wizje: Wielka księga estetyki w Polsce*. Towarzystwo Autorów i Wydawców Prac Naukowych Universitas.

Wilson, F. (2000). *The logic and methodology of science and pseudoscience*. Canadian Scholars Press. https://philpapers.org/rec/WILTLA-11

Zack, M. H. (1999). Managing organizational ignorance. *Knowledge Directions*, *1*(Summer). http://web.cba.neu.edu/~mzack/articles/orgig/orgig.htm

Conclusion

After an in-depth analysis of the research area, referring to the theses whose verification was the purpose of the analyses undertaken, we can conclude that: (T1) aesthetic theory and artistic practice have great potential to enrich the theory and practice of management with qualitative components, primarily through deep immersion in the world of values; and (T2) management theory and practice have the potential to enrich the theory of aesthetics and artistic practice with efficiency components. In order to substantiate these statements in greater detail, individual working hypotheses require references.

(H1A) Analysing the duality in the definitions of management in referring to the factors of art and science, it should be stated that art is no less critical in effective management than science. Chapter 1 proves that, apart from the broadly described factor of science, the factor of art is not only a capacious concept with which phenomena that do not fall within the empirical scientific framework should be associated. The factor of art in management, thanks to the achievements of aesthetics, has been shown as no less structured and with no less conceptual, semantic, and practical scope than management theory. Combining these two factors (art and science) gives a complete picture of the definition of management as a synthesis of art and science.

(H1B) The management factor is important in productive artistic activity due to the achievements in the field of organisation methods that can be successfully used not only to manage the real world but also to self-manage, manage the aesthetic situation, and manage a cultural institution. Of course, this requires transposition and necessary adjustments to navigate the world of metaphysical phenomena; however, the creative process's effectiveness increases with appropriate management methods.

(H2A) Management can derive added value from art by applying aesthetic theory, which primarily pays special attention to universal values and extends the organisational reality with additional dimensions. Thanks to such optics, management appears as an activity with a deeper and broader meaning than just organisational effectiveness concerning achieving the owners' financial goals.[1]

DOI: 10.4324/9781003458029-8

(H2B) Art can derive added value from the achievements of management in terms of applications widely discussed in the literature of organisation theory and paying attention to the efficiency factor. Management understood in this work as implementing goals efficiently has many applications. Taking into account the achievements of the humanistic trend and self-management, the application of this optic in the field of artistic creativity should proceed in a way that does not raise objections or difficulties, because both art and aesthetics, as well as humanistic management and self-management, are essentially very close to each other.

(H3) Aestheticisation can bring added value to management in the theoretical dimension in terms of paying attention to universal values and a human being as a living and feeling being, which should be reflected in the practical dimension of management in the form of extending the approach to the organisation to the issue of a set of individual units, and not just a mechanical machine designed to pursue the goals of its owners ruthlessly. The aestheticisation of management flows directly from the trend of the aestheticisation of reality described in the literature, and the aestheticisation of reality aims to indicate additional dimensions of physical reality, expanding it with metaphysical and semantic dimensions. Reality, and therefore also management, do not have to be one-dimensional and take place only in the physical sphere; adding extra dimensions gives meaning,

(H4) Aestheticisation can change the perception of the management process by permanently referring to universal values and, as a result, noticing a human being as a living and feeling being. It is not without reason that management in the spirit of efficiency and marketing is commonly associated with exploiting employees and the environment. A change of outlook – both in the case of managers but also in employees and, above all, in owners – should positively impact the change in the perception of management by society.

H5) Aestheticisation can be – apart from ethics and corporate social responsibility – an additional qualitative dimension drawing attention to the issues of universal values in management. It is due to two reasons. First, as mentioned in Section 1.4, ethics refers to morality, based on the value of good; whereas aesthetics is based on the values of truth and beauty and refers to the properties of phenomena that broaden the qualitative optics of reality. It is not enough for managers and organisations to focus on morality, that is, to act ethically. Morality is not objective, even though many efforts are made to make it so – for example, states imposing legal systems and trying to include the morality characteristic of their culture. Simultaneously extended to the issues of truth and beauty, ethical action becomes fuller and refers to an extensive range of arguments. Only truth, good, and beauty constitute the Platonic triad of universal values that complement each other. Secondly, one can see hypocrisy among many organisations implementing a specific business ethics policy (codes of ethics, codes of good practice) or conducting widely advertised activities related to their social responsibility. It is because these ethical and responsible programs are often utilitarian and ostensible (Saeidi et al., 2018; Secchi, 2007), acting as a kind of fig leaf or plaster for a bleeding wound. To help a patient with a bleeding wound, first, find the cause of the bleeding, stop it, clean the wound, and then dress it. On the one hand, carrying out activities that destroy the environment, and on the other hand, helping the environment means transferring resources from one pocket to another. The amount of resources will not change from these actions, and their quality will not improve. Also, in this case, the extension of the ethical dimension (the described sham morality) will be balanced only after considering the aesthetic dimension (truth and beauty).

(H6) Based on the theory of aesthetics and performance practice in art, it is believed that virtuosity, artistry, and creativity are the basic means of expression at the creator's disposal. Transposing these concepts and their application to the field of managerial and organisational activity, we can successfully conclude that they are also the essential competencies of a manager from the point of view of the aestheticisation of management. The concept of managerial virtuosity includes all the knowledge and all practical skills necessary for a manager to perform his work, but it does not exhaust the entire range of his influence and does not guarantee success in his activity. Managerial artistry is about how virtuosity is used to influence stakeholders: the manager and the organisation he manages can perform perfectly but contribute nothing of value to stakeholders, or contribute a great deal despite functioning imperfectly; the perfect combination will be a virtuosic manager and an organisation operating in a perfect way, which at the same time can influence stakeholders using universal values. In addition to virtuosity and artistry, there is also the competence of creativity, which is responsible for original and revealing activities. Not every manager and organisation must be creative; creativity is not synonymous with virtuosity or artistry. However, creativity should be based on virtuosity and artistry to be productive. Only then, constituting a crowning triad of competencies of the manager and the organisation, do virtuosity, artistry, and creativity mutually catalyse and complement each other.

(H7A) The role of an individual's identity is extremely important in any activity undertaken. Hence, it plays a vital role in the success of the creative activities of an artist, manager, and entrepreneur. It is since creative individuals, to influence the environment (in the spirit of the organisation as a work of art metaphor), must face many adversities, often exceeding the scale of difficulties of everyday problems. A strong identity regarding the role is necessary for such a creative activity to be initiated, carried out, and completed – especially in the constantly changing reality. An artist unsure of his mission or self-worth will not be able to create a valuable and robust work of art, and if he manages to do so, often, his self-criticism and dissatisfaction will force him to destroy the result. Therefore, working on identity, understanding one's own changing identity, "becoming" over "being", and the ability to think paradoxically are activities that should be constantly processed by a conscious creator in artistic, managerial, and entrepreneurial activity.

(H7B) Although art has been present in human life since the beginning of humanity, the majority of members of society, unfortunately, are not conscious participants of art, and thus they do not see the differences between the basic concepts of art. The same applies to the concepts of creativity and artistry. The conducted empirical studies confirm this state of affairs.

(H7C) The social perception of the creator (understood as a creative individual) and the social perception of the manager have much in common. It is commonly believed that a manager must be creative, forgetting that there are different faces of managers and not everyone is expected to have the same competencies. The complete classification of managers can be obtained by juxtaposing different scales of creativity with different scales of organisational effectiveness. On this basis, the following results are obtained: (1) a visionary manager – a person with high creativity but with low organisational efficiency; (2) a manager-re-creator (administrator) – a person with low creativity and low organisational efficiency; (3) a manager-craftsman – with low creativity, but with high organisational efficiency; and (4) a manager-creator – with high creativity and high organisational efficiency,

(H8A) Ubiquitous changes also affect the art world, the essence of which seems to be unchanged. Forced virtualisation and digitisation (similar to what recently occurred due to the COVID-19 pandemic) significantly affect the quality of the creative process in the aesthetic situation, depending on the form of participation in art. The creator, managing the creative process within the aesthetic situation, must consider the aforementioned factors because otherwise, his work will be incomprehensible – not due to the low quality of the work, but because the work in new, virtualised circumstances may change its properties. The presented results of the empirical study show which components of the aesthetic situation are modified due to the form of participation in art.

(H8B) The impact of forced virtualisation and digitisation on the quality of the creative process is different for each art discipline, because each art discipline, using different senses, reacts differently to digitisation and virtualisation. The presented study shows how individual arts react to the processes of digitisation and virtualisation. Based on these results, artists – consciously managing the creative process within the aesthetic situation within individual art disciplines – should appropriately modify the scale of virtuosity, artistry, and creativity so that their message is consistent with their assumption, taking into account the form of participation in art.

(H8C) Forced virtualisation and digitisation significantly affect the quality of the reception process because each art discipline, using different senses, reacts differently to digitisation and virtualisation. Therefore, the knowledge of this phenomenon should accompany the creators – consciously managing the creative process within the aesthetic situation taking place within individual art disciplines – so that they modify the scale of virtuosity, artistry, and creativity accordingly so that the perception of their message is consistent with the creative assumptions for the work, taking into account the form of participation in art.

(H8D) The impact of forced virtualisation and digitisation on the quality of the reception process is different for each art discipline, because each art discipline, using different senses, reacts differently to digitisation and virtualisation. The presented study shows how recipients of individual art disciplines react to digitisation and virtualisation processes. This knowledge should accompany the creators so that they modify the scale of virtuosity, artistry, and creativity accordingly and that the perception of their message is consistent with the creative assumptions for the work, considering the form of participation in art.

(H8E) Forced virtualisation and digitisation determine the need for changes in the process of managing the aesthetic situation (in terms of the creative process and the process of reception) for each art discipline in a different way because each art discipline, using different senses, reacts differently to digitisation and virtualisation. Therefore, the artist – as a conscious manager of the aesthetic situation, equipped with theoretical knowledge in the field of components and mutual relations between the components of the aesthetic situation, as well as with the results of research showing how individual art disciplines react to digitisation and virtualisation – will be able to manage more effectively the parameters of virtuosity, artistry, and creativity as part of one's work, depending on how one participates (live or virtually).

(H9A) Art and management have common denominators; their analysis and cross-reference add value to these areas. The following issues can be considered as common denominators connecting art and management:

1. universal values – without their presence, both art and management become sham activities: art becomes kitsch, and management becomes a soulless organisation in the spirit of the organisation metaphor as a machine;
2. efficiency – the creator of artworks efficiently; thousands of hours spent on practising and perfecting his competencies (virtuosity, artistry, and creativity) within the discipline of art allows him to manage time, resources, and skills effectively; does not waste resources on projects that will not add value; in turn, the manager strives to improve the efficiency of the organisation, otherwise his work will not be considered valuable, and he will lose his raison d'être in the organisation; efficiency in art and management contributes to building social capital;
3. a servant role – the work of art, not the artist, is at the centre of the aesthetic situation, therefore putting the artist and the manager in the first place (overuse of "I", "for me") is a distraction from the essence of the creative or management process and transferring it to a replacement area; a "good" work (organisation) does not need promotional activities[2]– a good novel or symphony will not get better because of the scale of promotion (although of course promotion affects perception); on the other hand, the average work

(malfunctioning organisation) requires active PR and promotional activities to focus the eyes of the recipients on "safe" areas; both artistic creativity and managerial activity are subservient to the goals set for them;

4. "becoming" over "being" – the identity of the artist and manager is not given immediately, nor is it permanent ("being"); its construction is a process ("becoming"); the process is more important than the result; the time of identity building brings psychological comfort to the individual;
5. adaptability – the artist and manager must act adaptively because their roles are menial; they should first internalise the goals, then observe, then act; adaptation can take into account many levels: from setting goals, through strategy building, to implementation, and to assessing the level of achievement of goals;
6. kitsch traps – when undertaking artistic or managerial activities, one must be aware of the narrow border between truth and falsehood (kitsch); this boundary is determined by references to the value of truth in work (organisation); crossing the border of the truth – both in art and management – pushes the creator and manager towards artistic and organisational kitsch; kitsch is popular and sells well, but lacks good taste;[3]
7. exposure to ignorance – ignorance can apply to any phenomenon because a multitude of factors determines it; both art and management (predominantly humanistic management and the aestheticisation of management) are especially exposed to ignorance because they touch on metaphysical, intangible issues, the recognition of which requires above-average sensitivity and effort, and it is not associated with an increase in income.

(H9B) Motives for undertaking creative activity may broaden the perspective of motives for undertaking managerial activity by components related to creative activity and the dimension of universal values. Creative human activity has been the subject of aesthetic analysis for centuries, thanks to which several theories have been developed to look at this intangible problem from new perspectives. The aestheticisation of management also applies to the motives for undertaking managerial and organisational activities, which can be successfully developed based on analogies to creative artistic activity in the spirit of the organisation metaphor as a work of art.

(H10) Artistic improvisation brings a number of essential issues to management because it is a particular form of creative activity. It requires being adept at navigating the aspects of virtuosity, artistry, and creativity while permanently keeping the focus on a specific purpose and context and monitoring these issues in real time, by one person.

(H11A) The theory of aesthetic kitsch can be successfully applied in management because it refers to the value of truth. Aesthetic kitsch theory can help organisational actors better perceive inappropriate organisational behaviour.

(H11B) Ignorance and kitsch in management can, based on dialectics, help in understanding the essence and meaning of aestheticisation of management. It is because phenomena that are difficult to explain directly are sometimes easier to explain by describing opposites.

(H11C) Understanding the essence of ignorance is crucial in eliminating ignorance concerning the aestheticisation of management, because in order to be able to fight a phenomenon effectively, one must understand its cause and not act on its effects. Ignorance is not always the result of deliberate action by the ignorant.

(H12) Counteracting ignorance regarding the aestheticisation of management requires knowledge of the field and examples of its practical application to be effective. Due to the complex nature of ignorance and its various faces, it is advisable to get to know this phenomenon from the theoretical side as fully as possible. Moreover, the aestheticisation of management is a topic that has been present in the literature for a relatively short time and even less in practice. Therefore, a particular need is to describe this phenomenon and show its practical applications to inspire others to follow this beautiful path with real examples.

It seems that the holistic model created and analysed in detail, ordering the issues of management aesthetics together with the presentation of the systemic dependencies of the elements of this model, allows the main objective of the monograph to be considered achieved. This model can successfully perform a central function concerning the complete and systemic understanding of the phenomenon of the aestheticisation of management. Placing individual issues in management aesthetics within this model will allow us to see these analytical issues as part of a synthetic whole, which should be the phenomenon of management aesthetics. The analysis presented in the preceding six chapters made it possible to achieve the specific objectives set for this work, which concerned:

1. application of the aesthetic situation theory based on management theory as a meta-model for management aesthetics; this meta-model organises the previously analytically presented problems of management aesthetics, constituting the backbone of all considerations in the field of management aesthetics;
2. filling the gap in the literature in the field of management in terms of the lack of publications addressing the problem of management aesthetics holistically and systemically;
3. terminological arrangement in the field of concepts (including virtuosity, artistry, and creativity) in the spirit of aesthetics in the field of management so that the correct use of concepts related to abstraction and metaphysics organises and facilitates the perception of the phenomena of management aesthetics;
4. application of the theory of aesthetics in terms of sources of creative activity, types of creative personalities, the role of motives for creative activity, and the role of inspiration in creative activity based on management theory;

5. application of issues related to artistic performance practice, e.g., in the field of improvisation and creativity based on management theory and practice;
6. developing the issue of the role of the manager's identity – as one of many creative personalities – in management activity;
7. defining undesirable phenomena in management practice relating to the lack of universal values as organisational kitsch and their analysis with the use of aesthetic tools;
8. developing the phenomenon of ignorance towards the aestheticisation of management so that the understanding and analysis of the phenomenon of ignorance support the process of removing barriers to the dissemination of aestheticisation of management;
9. development of methodology and implementation of research analysing the quality of the aesthetic situation and differences in the quality of the aesthetic situation from the perspective of the artist understood as the manager of the aesthetic situation;
10. developing a methodology and conducting research analysing the quality of the aesthetic situation and the differences in that quality from the perspective of the recipient of art, whose reception process is shaped by the artist – understood as the manager of the aesthetic situation – through a work of art;
11. development of methodology and implementation of comparative research in the field of simple creative identities (artist, creator, manager, leader, and entrepreneur) and the mutual impact of the identity of the manager and the identity of the artist;
12. development of methodology and implementation of research analysing the complex creative identities of artists-managers and artists-entrepreneurs, and the implications of the results for the theory and practice of management;
13. application of the conceptual and cognitive apparatus from the discipline of management in the theory of artistic creativity and aesthetics, thus filling the gap in the management literature in the field of publications devoted to the essence of holistic art management.

Implications for the theory and practice of management resulting from the undertaken analyses and empirical research in the field of the application of aesthetic theory in the field of management are as follows:

1. management can be perceived not only as an activity focused on economic efficiency, but also as a process constituting the area of influence of the manager on the environment through the managed organisation;
2. treating individuals participating in the management process in a way that takes into account their dignity and the right to implement universal values allows to give depth to management in the spirit of humanism; it should be emphasised that humanistic management is not against economic efficiency;

humanism should be perceived as an additional aspect of organisational activity focused on economic efficiency;

3. recognition of the role of identity (and work on identity) in managerial activity, especially managerial activity understood as a synthesis of the science of management and the art of management, allows to draw attention to the manager's self-awareness and self-organisation even before he starts to influence the environment through the entrusted organisation;
4. the development of management theory based on theories about art, roles, and characteristics of artistic creators can be revealing; since – according to the theory of aesthetics – there are different types of creative personalities, it is worth examining whether the development of managers' creativity should take into account this typology and whether methods of developing managers' creativity should be differentiated following this typology;
5. the presented models based on the theory of aesthetics regarding the development of creativity can bring benefits when used in managerial activities – both at the level of self-management and at the level of the organisation;
6. the results of empirical research confirm that some managerial skills can be learned and taught, but not everyone, despite undertaking the same managerial education, will become an effective manager; each individual has a unique set of personal characteristics, and it is their compilation that determines predispositions to act in both the world of art and the world of management;
7. understanding the contexts, components, and relationships between components, in terms of the metaphor of the organisation as a work of art, can help in a fuller understanding of the manager's role as a management artist; just like the aesthetic situation, management should holistically take into account all entities and elements of the management process with particular emphasis on universal values that are introduced into the real world through the organisation; applying the theory of aesthetics in the process of management, artistry can be considered as a kind of higher level of management; the highest degree in the gradation – administrator, manager, management artist;
8. looking at the creativity of the manager and managed teams from the perspective of artistic creativity can help to understand and stimulate individual and group creativity;
9. awareness of the aesthetic dimension of managerial activities and organisational behaviours, seen through the prism of kitsch as anti-actions and anti-behaviours, can broaden the perception of both the manager's behaviour and the behaviour of other actors in the world of the organisation;
10. awareness of the phenomenon of ignorance regarding the aestheticisation of management and the complex structure of this phenomenon can help managers counteract this ignorance and, consequently, expand the use of humanistic management to benefit themselves, the organisation, and the entire society.

Limitations of the conducted analyses and empirical research are as follows:

1. the application of aesthetic theory in the field of management should be moderate and careful; because an organisation, compared to a work of art, is usually a more complex and dynamic organism, so even minor changes within it may result in far-reaching and even irreversible consequences for stakeholders;
2. the metaphor of the organisation as a work of art applies primarily to senior managers (those whose decisions affect the entire organisation) and not to operational managers; however, in the case of possibly autonomous actions of lower-level managers – taking into account a fragment of the organisation as a work of art in a specific time perspective (determined by the time of this manager's activity) – this metaphor can also be successfully applied here, e.g., an organisation department as a work of art of this manager department;
3. the considerations presented in this work should not be treated as a call for the uncritical introduction of art creators (even those who are experts in their artistic fields) to managerial positions; while art creators can add value in terms of raising the level of creativity in the organisation, there is no guarantee of synergy between the artistry in the field of art and the artistry in the field of management; the transfer of creativity in the field of art to the organisation will undoubtedly be revealing, however, the lack of knowledge of the realities of a specific organisation and industry, and managerial virtuosity, may result in far-reaching problems, causing more harm than good;
4. samples of primary quantitative research may not be representative of the common problems analysed; for example, the majority of the sample (88.3%) in "Research methodology 2" were people with bachelor's, master's, doctorate, and professor qualifications, who by definition are more aware of their behaviour and better prepared to present their perception of intangible properties compared to the rest of the society; therefore, it is difficult to transfer the obtained results to the less educated part of society;
5. synthetic conclusions may not be representative for the whole society due to the abstractness, complexity, and vagueness of the analysed research problems;
6. the research was conducted during various phases of the COVID-19 pandemic, which – due to the deep repercussions of the effects of the pandemic and the resulting restrictions – could affect the views and opinions of the respondents.

The most important *recommendations for future research* include seeking answers to the following questions:

1. What are the differences in the effectiveness of traditional management based solely on economic efficiency as opposed to humanistic management?

2. What is the perception of humanistic management by managers and stakeholders of the same organisations?
3. At what stages of the organisation's development does humanistic management work best in terms of effectiveness?
4. In which sectors of the economy does humanistic management work best in terms of effectiveness?
5. How do art creators who manage the aesthetic situation perceive the change (loss/gain) in artistry and creativity concerning different forms of art distribution?
6. What are the differences in the level of artistry and creativity perceived by art recipients concerning various forms of the reception process in individual social groups (cultures, communities), considering various sociological criteria (age, gender, wealth, education)?
7. What are the differences in the perception of one's own creative identity concerning the perception of this identity by individual social groups, considering various sociological criteria?
8. What are the differences in the perception of one's identity concerning the perception of this identity by individual social groups depending on the level of wealth and age structure?
9. How is the perception of organisational kitsch shaped in different cultures, communities, and types of organisations?
10. What is the perception of the management aestheticisation phenomenon among managers and stakeholders of the same organisations?
11. What is the perception of the aestheticisation of management among managers and stakeholders of different cultures?
12. How do different value systems determine management aesthetics?
13. How do individual religious denominations influence the perception of management aesthetics?

The aestheticisation of management and the metaphor of an organisation as a work of art allow us to look at management and organisation from a new perspective, which is no longer a revolution. Instead, this is an evolutionary change towards expanding the perception of reality in the art of management by additional dimensions. The overriding goals of this change should be the pursuit of improving the quality of life and noticing the unobvious beauty in the world around us.

Notes

1 Of course, this is by no means about forgetting about financial efficiency when applying aesthetic theories in management processes.
2 Of course, apart from the marketing approach necessary for promotion.
3 In no way should any artistic and managerial activity that has a high rate of return be considered kitsch by definition.

References

Saeidi, S. P., Othman, M. S. H., Štreimikienė, D., Saeidi, S. P., Mardani, A., & Stasiulis, N. (2018). The utilitarian aspect of the philosophy of ecology: The case of corporate social responsibility. *Filosofija, Sociologija*, *29*(1), 39–51. https://doi.org/10.6001/fil-soc.v29i1.3630

Secchi, D. (2007). Utilitarian, managerial and relational theories of corporate social responsibility. *International Journal of Management Reviews*, *9*(4), 347–373. https://doi.org/10.1111/j.1468-2370.2007.00215.x

Appendix

Interview questionnaire for the study "Managing the Aesthetic Situation from the Creator's Perspective"

This questionnaire was used in the study, the methodology of which is described in the Introduction of the monograph (see "Research methodology 1"), while the conclusions are described in Section 2.3.2, "Management of the aesthetic situation".

1. Which art discipline do you represent (choose/mark/describe the right answers)?

   i. MUSICAL ARTS (instrumental/vocal concerts, oratorios):

      1. composer
      2. performer (instrumentalist, vocalist, conductor)
      3. other (sound director, etc.)

   ii. PERFORMING ARTS (theatre, opera, ballet, dance, mime, performance):

      1. actor
      2. director
      3. screenwriter
      4. other . . .

   iii. LITERARY ARTS (prose, fiction/non-fiction, drama, poetry):

      1. editor
      2. translator
      3. writer
      4. other . . .

   iv. AUDIO-VISUAL ARTS (movie, clip, video game):

      1. actor
      2. director
      3. editor
      4. screenwriter
      5. other . . .

v. VISUAL ARTS (painting, drawing, photography, sculpture, ceramics, architecture, comics, design, fashion)

   1. creator (painter, photographer, sculptor, architect, fashion designer, etc.)
   2. other . . .

2. Your gender:
3. Your birth year:
4. How long (from which year) have you been involved in the artistic activity?
5. Is artistic activity for you the basic or additional (one of many) forms of professional activity?
6. Your artistic education:
7. Your beyond-artistic education:
8. Your nationality (national identification – What nationality do you belong to?):

A. **How do you assess the impact of the pandemic ESPECIALLY ON YOU as an art creator in the following areas?** (5-point Likert scale: −2 = very negative impact, −1 = somewhat negative impact, 0 = neutral impact, 1 = somewhat positive impact, 2 = very positive impact):

9. No live public performances of your play;
10. Transferring your artistic performances to virtual reality;
11. Opportunity to participate in your art in accordance with the personal preferences of the recipients (shaping the time and length of participation, adjusting the parameters of the work, etc.);
12. Limiting your real contacts with your team/group members;
13. Limiting your real contacts with artists of YOUR artistic profession;
14. Limiting your real contacts with artists/creators of OTHER artistic professions;
15. Limiting your real contacts with people (generally);
16. More time to relax;
17. More time to develop artistic knowledge (reading, watching, etc.);
18. More time to develop/practise artistic skills;
19. Your level of creativity;
20. Your mood/humour;
21. Your mental state;
22. Setting your life goals;
23. Realisation of your life goals;
24. Setting your artistic goals;
25. Realisation of your artistic goals;

26. A better understanding of human nature manifested by operating in limited circumstances.

B. How do you assess the impact of the pandemic on YOUR DISCIPLINE OF ART IN GENERAL (i.e., you together with creators, recipients, institutions, sponsors, etc.) in the following areas? (5-point Likert scale: −2 = very negative impact, −1 = somewhat negative impact, 0 = neutral impact, 1 = somewhat positive impact, 2 = very positive impact):

27. No live public performances of his own art;
28. Transferring your own artistic creation to virtual reality;
29. Opportunity to participate in your own field of art according to the personal preferences of the audience regarding the duration of participation, length of participation, volume control, etc.;
30. Limiting real contacts with members of your own team/group;
31. Limiting real contacts with artists of the same profession;
32. Limiting real contacts with artists (creators) of other professions.

C. Evaluate the level of YOUR APPROACH to individual features/properties of YOUR ART by comparing traditional/live and digital/virtual methods of artistic activities/participation (5-point Likert scale: −2 = very negative impact, −1 = somewhat negative impact, 0 = neutral impact, 1 = somewhat positive impact, 2 = very positive impact):

33. Your intrinsic motivation to start creative activity – LIVE;
34. Your intrinsic motivation to start creative activity – VIRTUALLY;
35. Your intrinsic motivation to continue and finish your creative activity – LIVE;
36. Your internal motivation to continue and finish your creative activity – VIRTUALLY;
37. External motivation to start creative activity – LIVE;
38. External motivation to start creative activity – VIRTUALLY;
39. External motivation to continue and finish creative activity – LIVE;
40. External motivation to continue and finish creative activity – VIRTUALLY;
41. Your creativity – LIVE;
42. Your creativity – VIRTUAL;
43. Your inspiration to create – LIVE;
44. Your inspiration to create – VIRTUALLY;
45. Your contact with the audience – LIVE;
46. Your contact with the audience – VIRTUALLY;
47. Your opportunities to delve into topics that concern society (or your audience) – LIVE;
48. Your opportunities to delve into topics that concern society (or your audience) – VIRTUALLY.

D. How do you anticipate the situation in YOUR FIELD OF ART after lifting the restrictions of the pandemic? (5-point Likert scale: −2 = absolutely not, −1 = rather not, 0 = hard to say, 1 = rather yes, 2 = definitely yes):

49. Sooner or later everything will return to the way it was before the pandemic;
50. Real-time public performances will be streamed virtually in parallel;
51. My field of art will be divided into two subcategories: live/traditional and virtual/digital.

E. Answer the following questions (5-point Likert scale: −2 = definitely LIVE, −1 = rather LIVE, 0 = hard to say, 1 = somewhat VIRTUAL, 2 = definitely VIRTUAL):

52. Which form of participation in your art is conducive to attracting more audiences to your art?
53. Which form of participation in your art gives greater satisfaction to the recipients of your art?
54. Which form of participation in your art helps to better please the audience of your art?
55. What form of participation in your art helps to better engage the audience in your art?
56. Which form of participation in your art allows the recipients of your art to experience catharsis better?
57. What form of participation in your art allows for better contact between the recipients and the work itself?
58. What form of participation in your art allows for better contact between the audience and the creator/performer of art?

F. Answer the following questions:

59. What reasons/motives/inspirations are most important to you when creating your art, when the aesthetic situation takes place LIVE, and what when the aesthetic situation takes place VIRTUALLY? Are there any differences?
60. Do you see any differences in your creative process knowing that your work will be (is) presented LIVE and VIRTUAL?
61. Has the COVID-19 pandemic started or only intensified the process of digitisation/virtualisation of your artistic discipline?

Index

Note: Page numbers in *italics* indicate a figure and page numbers in **bold** indicate a table on the corresponding page.

FSC
www.fsc.org
MIX
Papier | Fördert
gute Waldnutzung
FSC® C083411

Kolibri 360 GmbH
Ferdinand-Jühlke-Straße 7
99095 Erfurt, Deutschland
produktsicherheit@kolibri360.de